From those who have read this book:

*Most visionaries don't share their secrets,
but once again Joe Sugarman proves that he
is not "most" people. Secrets reads like a
novel but is filled with business-building ideas
that prove how important it is to seek out the
breakthroughs and learn from your mistakes.*

> Jerry Reitman, Executive VP (retired)
> The Leo Burnett Company
> Author of *Beyond 2000*: *The Future of
> Direct Marketing*

*Your book can help thousands of people get
started and then do well with mail order,
helping them get free of the rat race. You are
a subversive influence to the status quo.*

> Wayne Green, Ph.D., Publisher
> 73 Magazine W2NSD/1
> Peterborough, New Hampshire

*Imagine reading a Joe Sugarman ad that
runs 400 pages. You're captured in the
beginning, intrigued throughout the copy and
can't stop until you've finished. That's this
book! I cried (the cancer story). I laughed (the
Alan Glans story). I wore out three highlighters
underlining passages. Enjoy and learn the
secrets of direct marketing from the man who's
been there, done that.*

> Murray Raphel
> Raphel Marketing, Inc.
> Atlantic City, New Jersey

Joe is well known throughout Europe as one of America's most innovative creative geniuses. His book is intelligent, witty, easy to grasp and a good read. If I were a professor I would make his book compulsory reading for my students (and colleagues). Read it and profit from his outstanding ideas.

Walter Schmid, Founder
Montreux Direct Marketing Symposium
Kuesnacht, Switzerland

Who totally changed mail order marketing by pioneering the inbound 800 number? Who was the only man with the immense knowledge and chutzpah to pioneer hugely successful direct marketing seminars costing attendees thousands of dollars—long before others like Jay Abraham and Ted Nicholas caught on? Who created the first mail order catalog where copy was king and one product per page was offered—long before Comtrad, Herrington or The Sharper Image? Whose very readable and often outrageous marketing war stories are filled with spectacular insights? It's the legendary Joe Sugarman of BluBlocker fame. I read Marketing Secrets of a Mail Order Maverick *in one sitting; I expect to go back to the well often.*

Denny Hatch, Editor
Target Marketing

Joe Sugarman has always been my hero! He is a marketing genius, the world's greatest copywriter and one of the most brilliant innovative thinkers I've ever come across. You'll enjoy this book for the great war stories and the brilliant case histories, but Joe also provides vital lessons for anyone in advertising and direct marketing. I highly recommend it.

> Alan Rosenspan
> Sharon, Massachusetts

First from his early direct marketing career to his recent infomercials Joe Sugarman has become a legend here in Australia. But as good as he is at mastering all forms of direct response advertising, he is just as good at teaching it. This book is an excellent course in how to find the right product and turn it into a big success. His stories alone are worth the price of the book but his marketing "secrets" are even more valuable. Don't miss the fun, entertainment and information this book offers.

> Eddy Boas, Former Chairman
> Pan Pacific Direct Marketing Conference
> Sydney, Australia

Joe's book is Joe to the core. A constant stream of wit, wisdom, stories and case histories. It leaves you with a deep respect for his incredible experience and knowledge. However long you've been in mail order, take my advice, read it.

> John Frazer-Robinson
> The Frazer-Robinson Partnership
> Ferndown, Dorset, England

I found what you had to say not only interesting but easy to follow. What struck me was that this book is so different from almost all the others on direct marketing and mail order. It tells what actually happens and why it happens without the many theories of what should happen. I would certainly recommend it for anyone in the direct marketing business as a super refresher course.

Charles M. Cavanagh, President and CEO
Direct Marketing Days in New York, Inc.

From the participants who attended my seminar and learned what you are about to:

It gave me a valuable insight into the real and actual workings of a mail order company. I learned from JS&A's failures and successes. I learned how to buy space, how to know which magazines to advertise in, and I received valuable insights into the ways you break the rules to succeed. It was one of the most enlightening experiences of my life.

> Frank Schultz
> Alamo, Texas

Enough time has elapsed since your seminar for me to have realized substantial results. As an added measure of value, I have found your education applicable to other areas of business as well as to the areas you addressed.

> Diana L. Dawson
> Namco Industries

I would highly recommend to anyone in our field that they take the time to attend your seminar. I am sure they would find it most beneficial and well worth the time as I did.

> Richard A. Viguerie
> Richard A. Viguerie Company

I have attended many seminars during my thirty years in the advertising, direct mail and promotion business, but never have I come away from any seminar with the degree of enthusiasm and the feeling of having gained as much as I did from yours.

> A. Harvey Cinamon
> Cinamon Associates

Thanks for an excellent seminar. It was great, more than worthwhile. You are great!

Wallace M. Bradley
Digital Equipment Corporation

I traveled 9,000 miles to attend your seminar, and can state it was worth all the time and effort. I came away with a full understanding of ad creation, media selection, product selection and order implementation. I understand many of the pitfalls and rewards of the mail order business. Now it remains for me to implement what I have learned.

Archie W. Mason
Monarch Trading Company
New Zealand

I attend a lot of symposiums, congresses and seminars, and I must confess that they have only polished up the know-how I already possessed. One must look for winning twists that separate marginal profit from big profits. What is unique about your seminar? It is the only seminar with a twist for big profits. Returning to Europe, I immediately worked with my new mail order secrets which I have learned at your seminar. I am sure that within a very short time, they will pay out for me.

Gert Mandelartz
Dusseldorf, Germany

As I reflect on the experience, its value continues to increase. Even if Lane Research does not initiate direct response marketing, I will have benefited far beyond my pre-seminar expectations.

Stephen Kurtin
Lane Research

Marketing Secrets

At his exclusive marketing seminar,
Joseph Sugarman taught copywriting, marketing and
creativity to a group of mail order enthusiasts who
went on to achieve incredible success. This book
reveals many of the same marketing secrets that he
shared with his students, each of whom paid
thousands of dollars to attend.

Books by Joseph Sugarman

Advertising Secrets of the Written Word
Marketing Secrets of a Mail Order Maverick
Television Secrets for Marketing Success
Success Forces
Triggers

Marketing Secrets

of a

Mail Order

Maverick

②

Joseph Sugarman

*Stories and
Lessons on the Power
of Direct Marketing
to Start a Successful
Business, Create a
Famous Brand Name
and Sell Any
Product or Service*

Printed in the United States of America

Publisher's Cataloging-in-Publication Data
(Provided by Quality Books, Inc.)

Sugarman, Joseph
    Marketing secrets of a mail order maverick : stories and lessons on the power of direct marketing to start a successful business, create a famous brand name and sell any product or service / Joseph Sugarman—1st ed.
    Includes bibliographical references and index.
    ISBN: 1-891686-06-2 CL
    ISBN: 1-891686-07-0 PB
    1. Direct marketing. 2. Advertising, direct-mail. I. Title.
HF5861.S84 1998   659.13'3
                                     QBI98-126

Attention: Schools, Ad Agencies and Corporations. DelStar books are available at quantity discounts with bulk purchases for educational or business use. For more information, please contact DelStar Books at the address below.

06 05 04 03 02 01 00 99 98   10 9 8 7 6 5 4 3 2 1

Cover design: Ron Hughes
Cartoonist: Dick Hafer

DelStar Books
3350 Palms Center Drive
Las Vegas, NV 89103
Phone: (702) 798-9000
Fax: (702) 597-2002

To Mary Stanke
with gratitude for your
dedication and devotion

Whatever you can do or dream you can, begin it. Boldness has genius, power and magic in it.

—Goethe

Contents

Marketing Secrets of a Mail Order Maverick

Foreword

A Valuable Document to Study and Learn From

By Henry Hoke, Publisher, *Direct Marketing* magazine

I've known Joe Sugarman for almost as long as he's had his company, JS&A. I remember when he started running those big ads in *The Wall Street Journal* and I remember the innovation he brought to direct marketing through his unique copy approach and marketing concepts.

Marketing Secrets of a Mail Order Maverick is a splendid opportunity for you to learn some of the really powerful concepts Joe has developed through his illustrious career as one of our country's top mail order practitioners.

In this book you will get to know Joe and his unique thought process, some of his great creative ideas and how he implemented them, and finally, how he started several companies from the power of his pen and a big idea—of which Joe has had many.

But what I particularly like about this book is Joe's candor. You get to know him—his personality and his brilliant mind. He's not afraid to face his mistakes and share the wisdom he learned from them. And that's what makes this book so unlike any I've ever read.

There are many painfully candid moments that he shares with us. Like the time he fell in love with his copy and ended up losing money on a laser beam mousetrap. Or the time he tried a bold new marketing technique that drew such a successful response it caused him to lose a fortune.

I like the structure of this book. Joe gives us a marketing lesson and then a marketing story and does this throughout the book. This technique is like having a main course of meaty information and then following it with a nice dose of ice cream. His insights into marketing come from being in the trenches, so his advice is practical and well presented. His marketing stories are so intriguing that you'll read them like a well-written novel—learning every moment you journey with him on his exciting path.

The research he has done for you and the mistakes you can avoid by following his advice make this a very valuable book indeed. I encourage you to read it from cover to cover, and if you feel as I do, this will become a classic mail order reference book for many generations to come.

Acknowledgments

To Those Who Made It Possible

I wish to acknowledge the many people whose support, advice or guidance has made this book and my experiences in direct marketing possible. First and foremost is Mary Stanke, the president of both JS&A Group, Inc. and BluBlocker Corporation—for 26 years you were always the one to pick up the pieces, disaster after disaster. I would create the mess and you would clean it up. Never complaining, always supportive and encouraging—the wind beneath my wings. To Mary's husband, Bob Stanke, who handled all of our printing needs as general manager of his printing company—we could always count on you.

To my family for the love and support we shared during our close times together. You are all on unique paths of your own now and I'm proud of you all.

To Pete Hoke of *Direct Marketing* magazine, who stood by me during my FTC crisis when most of my peers turned the other way—your loyalty and support will always be remembered. To Richard Thalheimer of The Sharper Image, a great competitor and a class act.

To Bernard Gittelson, author, entrepreneur and public relations man extraordinaire—thanks for your advice, guidance and great humor. To George Gerstman, my attorney and friend for most of my business career—I've learned so much from you. To Dan R. Iannotti, a former client turned partner who played a role in a few of my companies—thank you, Dan. To Peter Vizel— your friendship knows no limit.

To Vito Simanis, who designed many of the beautiful logos and brochures for us. To Steve Sugar, who designed many of our catalogs, and to Ron Hughes, who has designed the great packaging we've used as well as the cover design for this book. To Rod Stemo and Jim Zorn, who shared with me their photographic skills. To Dick Hafer, whose cartoons were specially drawn for this book and who has been a great supporter.

To Jon Spoelstra, a seminar student who went on in life to

distinguish himself as one of the great sports marketing persons of all time. To Gene Clark, healer, carpenter, car mechanic and good friend—you are the hidden treasure of the great island of Maui. To Harvey Wagley, an early mentor, without whose encouragement and financial support there would never have been a JS&A—thanks for your faith during the very early stages of my career.

And to the many friends I've met in direct marketing. To Murray Raphel, one of the world's premiere public speakers and the person who, along with his son Neil, first encouraged me to write this book. To Jerry Reitman, whose public service and devotion to the industry has been an inspiration to me. To Gary Halbert, the Prince of Print and one of the best copywriters I know. To Joe Cossman, one of the early pioneers in this business.

To the many people who have given me the opportunity to speak all over the world. To Walter Schmid, who gave me the opportunity to speak several times at the Montreux Direct Marketing Symposium in Switzerland and who organized my first Swiss seminar in St. Moritz. To Eddy Boas, the founder of the Pan Pacific Direct Marketing Symposium in Australia, for the opportunities to speak in your wonderful country. To Kay Eguchi, who brought me to Japan as a speaker on numerous occasions.

A special thank-you to the people who played a role in the production of this book: Lyn Chaffee, Doug Easton, Ron Hughes, Virginia Iorio and Nancy Kleban.

I wish to acknowledge all my wonderful seminar participants who learned from me and went on to create or build successful businesses—all through the power of their pens and the direct marketing skills that they learned at my seminars. I learned a great deal from them too. Finally, I wish to thank, with humility and gratitude, all those who have exchanged their hard-earned money for this book. May you too learn and prosper.

Introduction

The True Path to the World of Abundance and Opportunity is Through Marketing

Marketing is a constant battle for your hard-earned money.

This book is based on the direct marketing lessons I taught for 12 years at a very exclusive seminar. Only 20 participants were invited to attend each one and they paid from $2,000 for the first seminar in 1977 to more than $3,000 by the time I ran my last one in 1988.

Phase one of my seminar focused on how to write effective and powerful advertising copy. This book focuses on phase two of my seminar—direct marketing techniques and the marketing lessons that I taught. It is certainly not the bible on marketing nor will it cover many topics that other marketing books cover, but it does cover some important aspects of using direct marketing to start a business and promote a product or service.

This book assumes that you already have the skills to create or recognize a great direct response ad. What I will now show you is everything from how to pick a product or service to how to sell it through direct marketing. And finally, we can all learn by example. So a good part of this book covers several of my actual marketing experiences, the strategies I used, the results of those strategies and what they taught me. Some of them were not successful. But I explain why and reveal the lessons I learned from them.

Marketing's function is not necessarily to entertain, inform or communicate. Marketing has a very serious and direct purpose. It is to cause an exchange of one form of wealth for another.

Marketing involves movement, motion and action. Marketing is not just a mental exercise but also includes emotional and physical factors—all combined to accomplish one major goal—the exchange of your prospects' hard-earned money for your product or service. And because emotion is so important and unpredictable in this process, it requires experimentation, testing, experience and wisdom to know what works and what doesn't. That's where this book comes in.

I have done the experimentation for you and experienced the consequences. I have fought in the direct marketing trenches for over 25 years. I have risked millions to build a business while covering a payroll and feeding a family. I have seen what really works and what doesn't and I have taught these principles for years in an intensive seminar that inspired some of the finest students of direct marketing.

In Section Two of this book, I cover some concepts I've never shared even in my seminars because I only discovered them after I stopped giving the course in 1988. I discuss why response rates may vary and the forces that determine that variance. This information may surprise you. I even cover complaints and how I've responded to them, what I've learned from them and why they are so valuable. And finally, I explain the effect the operations end of your business has on sales and discuss some of the considerations you should make while you run your business.

There are two types of chapters in this book—one that features a marketing lesson and the other that tells a marketing story. I start out the book with a marketing story and then follow it with a marketing lesson and then repeat this process throughout the entire book.

The stories may have nothing to do with the lessons that are sandwiched in between. They are simply to give you a sense and flavor of what it is like to be a direct marketer in the mail order business. There are also valuable lessons in the stories and you will learn a great deal from them. But the true nuts and bolts of what you need to learn to be a mail order practitioner will be found in the marketing lessons.

So relax in your easy chair with your yellow marking pen and really put this book to good use. Learn what people from all parts of the world learned at my seminar—from young entrepreneurs just starting out to experienced practitioners at major corporations.

It's time to share these secrets and my experiences so that you too can tap into the world of abundance and opportunity that is just waiting for you.

Section One

Preview

Copy and Mail Order Sales

Now you are ready to learn some of the important lessons I've learned on what it takes to convince a person to exchange his or her hard-earned money for your product or service.

In this first section of the book, I show you how and where to find a product, how to negotiate a deal and how to protect your product if it happens to be your own invention. There are some aspects of this process that may surprise you.

Next I share some facts about layout and typography that I didn't learn until late in my career but which had a major impact on my advertising—things that I wished I had learned much earlier. You'll be amazed at the difference a typeface makes.

I discuss photography and describe many of my experiences preparing pictures for an ad layout. Then I cover the part of my seminar course that will save you a fortune—the buying of media. This alone is worth the entire price of this book.

Finally, I discuss testing: where to test your ad, how to go about conducting a test and how to interpret your test results.

And it's all done in a progression that will guide you into the world of mail order as if you had attended my very expensive seminar.

And like my first book on copywriting called *Advertising Secrets of the Written Word,* there are plenty of stories and humorous experiences that will keep you entertained and will help reinforce your learning process.

So prepare to embark on some very exciting adventures— like the story of the first time I experienced a Super Bowl.

A Marketing Story

The Super Bowl Promotion

This warning appeared as a large ad in the Chicago Tribune attacking my team—only, I wrote it.

Computers Etc. was a small computer store in an outdoor shopping center in Deerfield, Illinois, near Chicago. The owner worked very hard to sell his computers. If he was lucky, he'd sell maybe five computers a day. On a weekend, he might be lucky enough to sell ten.

Imagine what the owner must have thought one day when he arrived at his store only to find a line of people circling the entire shopping center waiting for our JS&A store to open—customers standing in line to buy a computer. And we weren't really even in the computer business.

We sold over 1,000 of these computers in one day in one of the most incredible sales in the shopping center's history. Here's how it happened.

Visual Technology was a company near Boston that started making computers during the very early stages of the computer industry—well before IBM introduced their first personal computer. At the time, the CP/M operating system was the system of choice for most computers, but when the IBM PCs first appeared in 1983, the older CP/M models quickly lost their value.

Software companies stopped developing CP/M software and started making software for the IBM, and pretty soon CP/M computers had dropped in value and were becoming obsolete. Visual Technology had approximately 600 of the units left in their inventory and asked me if I would be interested in them. They previously sold at retail for $2,500 but Visual Technology was having cash flow problems and needed to move all their obsolete or potentially obsolete merchandise. Their offer to me was, "We'll give you $1,000 worth of software, the complete system including the monitor, keyboard and computer—all for only $250 per unit if you'll take the whole lot off our hands for $150,000."

I said I'd think about it and get back to them.

At about this time in late 1985, the NFL playoffs were taking place and both the Chicago Bears and the New England Patriots were advancing to the Super Bowl. I talked to the sales executives at Visual who were located in Boston and we teased each other at every opportunity. "Your Bears aren't worth a damn," they'd say. And I'd come back with, "But you guys don't have a refrigerator in your lineup."

The Bears had just finished an almost undefeated season losing only to the Miami Dolphins. The Bears' controversial quarterback, Jim McMahon, was so outrageous that he was becoming a media celebrity. And finally, one of the linemen, William Perry, was so big and heavy (well over 300 pounds), he was nicknamed the Refrigerator. It was a team made up of wacky personalities that seemed to all come together into one incredible force in time to play football each Sunday.

The Super Bowl was creating tremendous hype in Chicago. The Bears had just beaten the Giants and they were Super Bowl bound. New England had upset all predictions and were headed to New Orleans to meet the Bears. The stage was also set for a JS&A sale of Super Bowl proportions.

I agreed to buy the remaining inventory if Visual would do two things: 1) Let me write an ad on their behalf to run in the *Chicago Tribune,* and 2) allow me to pay them for the computers after I had a chance to sell them following the Super Bowl. They agreed to both terms, shipped me the computers and I created the ad shown at the start of this chapter.

Taking full advantage of all the hype was a lot of fun. The ad for Visual basically said that if the Chicago Bears won, all those who mailed us the coupon in the ad would get a chance to win a free computer—a $2,500 value. They would have to buy the $1,000 software package for the low price of only $400. On the other hand, if the New England Patriots won, then all of those participating would have to write Visual and congratulate them.

The promotion was really a fabulous opportunity to get an outstanding value. It cost well over $400 to make the computers, and keeping my profit to only $150 per unit, I could make money, Visual could liquidate their inventory, and the consumer would get one heck of a value.

After running the ad in the *Chicago Tribune,* we received over 12,000 responses and were deluged at our store with people wanting to see what the unit looked like. In the meantime, when Visual found out about our strong response, they advised me that they found an additional thousand computers in their warehouse and would we be interested in taking them under the same terms?

We agreed. We now had 1,600 computers.

To make sure the Bears would win, I flew down to New Orleans and stood in the stands to root them on. And they won. Big time. And we were now ready to make our own promotional touchdown.

We sent out notices to everybody who entered. This would be a first-come, first-served offer and if they showed up at our door on Sunday one week after the Super Bowl, they would be eligible to get a computer for just the discounted price of the software.

When I arrived very early in the morning, the line was already forming. In fact, five people camped out in the January cold to get one of five computers with software that we agreed to give away free to the first five people who showed up. And within a few hours, 1,600 computers were sold. We had to rent a large truck to keep in front of our store in order to feed the demand of those waiting in line.

It was dark at 6 AM when I arrived at the store, only to find a few hundred people already waiting in line to claim their "prize."

After picking up a computer and paying $400, one customer said, "I've never won anything. Thank you. This is a real thrill." Another said, "Boy, when I got that notice in the mail that said I was eligible to pick up the computer, I couldn't believe my good luck."

Owner in Shock

The owner of the other computer store walked over to see what we were doing and saw us selling a computer every few seconds. There was no time-consuming sales pitch, no demonstration necessary. The computers were just being sold as fast as the truck could bring them over from our warehouse.

In taking advantage of a number of events and circumstances and tying them into a unique promotion, I was able to liquidate an incredible number of computers on a local level and earn almost $250,000 on practically no investment. But think about all the coincidences that had to be in place for this promotion to be successful. We needed a successful Chicago football team, we had a product that was manufactured in the opposing team's city, and we had an outstanding value. We also felt very confident that the Bears would win.

But what if they hadn't won? What if the Patriots had indeed upset the Bears? No problem. We had captured everybody's name in our computer. We could easily have written the entrants and given them the same offer to show that "the guys at Visual were good sports anyway."

Visual Technology was so impressed with the results of our promotion that we ended up with several of their new products to place in our catalog. And the owner of that computer store in the mall?

The computers just flew out the door.

He'll never forget that single day when JS&A sold more computers in two hours than he did in an entire year.

The Super Bowl promotion is what happens when you have an exciting product presented to you and you develop a strategy. But how do you find a product in the first place? That's what Marketing Lesson 1 will teach you. And you might be surprised. It's actually a lot of common sense and a few important secrets.

Marketing Lesson 1

How to Pick the Perfect Product

Having the ability to create a great mail order ad is only a small part of the entire process of creating a marketing success. First you need something to sell.

This chapter is devoted to the selection process—namely, how to select the perfect product that will harmonize with your customers and cause them to reach into their pockets and exchange their hard-earned money for your product or service. The closeness of this harmony dictates your success. For if you can appeal to a large market with a product that relates to that market and if you can write great copy, your chances of success are greatly enhanced.

A Point in Time and Space

Reaching a state of harmony in marketing a product involves forces over which you have little control. It is truly the wild card in the game of marketing. Having a product resonate with your customer represents a point in time and space where a variety of forces coincide, transcending your ability to control them. You can have the worst copy and a miserable presentation, but if the product you have chosen is the right product at the right time with the right price and in the right medium, your chances of success are extremely good. Great copy and that perfect concept—both will tremendously enhance your success. But in reality, after years of selecting products and then testing to determine their success, I have learned that I can never predict where in the time and space continuum a product lies.

Try selling a thousand different products and you might end up with just a hundred that could be considered a modest success—enough of a success to present in a catalog. Twenty of those hundred might be considered extremely successful—the type of products that would be strong enough to run as print ads. and earn you handsome profits. And out of the twenty products that are potentially successful print ads, one will be a blockbuster—so big that it will dwarf all of the others by a significant margin. Maybe another BluBlocker sunglass or an Apple computer or a Microsoft operating system.

Product Life Cycle

One of the difficulties in picking that right product is what is called the "product life cycle." A product typically will languish around in the marketplace in various configurations for a period of time, doing very little. Then it will be presented in a configuration that meets the needs of the marketplace, and sales will start to really take off. Competition recognizes the potential and jumps in to get their share, thus expanding the market. To accomplish this, the competition either lowers their price, provides a few unique features or improves on their quality. Finally, sales reach their peak and start to drop as in a bell curve.

1. Period of Languish

The first phase of a product life cycle is called the "period of languish." It's not where you want to be. You want to be at the point in the life cycle where the new configuration of that product—its price and its concept—is ready for rapid growth.

2. Period of Discovery

I call this rapid-growth period the "period of discovery"— the point in time and space when the product is discovered by the public as being harmonious with their needs and desires, when they are anxious to exchange their hard-earned money for the product and when nobody else but you, the first person to market the product, realizes this.

3. Period of Competition

The next phase I call the "period of competition." It is when everybody else realizes you're onto a good thing and that you've found a dynamic new product or product category. Everybody jumps in to fill this little niche you've discovered or to compete against you. You can control the product category and become the leading company in that product if you know how to utilize all the tools necessary to expand the market. This isn't easy,

NO... I DON'T BELIEVE THAT THIS PRODUCT IS IN THE "DISCOVERY" STAGE YET.

but it can be done, and later in this book we will talk about doing just that. Being the first, being the quickest and knowing what to do will give you the edge you need to fully exploit that potential big winner.

4. Period of Decay

And then there is what I call the "period of decay"—that point in time when the product has already peaked and yet few realize it. Sales can only go down. Unfortunately, this period actually starts just before the product itself peaks. It is the sucker period when people are sucked into the product or product category just in time to see competition reach its peak and product demand drop precipitously.

Many people who participate during the "period of languish" fail because they were just too early. They had a good hunch about a product but didn't have the right timing, price or product configuration to achieve success. And many people who try to jump into a hot product during the "period of decay" eventually fail too because the demand is sinking rapidly while the competition is expanding rapidly. Only the really big players survive.

Thomas Watson Jr., former head of IBM, once said, "There's a fine line between eccentrics and geniuses. If you're a little ahead of your time, you're an eccentric, and if you're too late, you're a failure, but if you hit it right on the head, you're a genius." The object in the marketing game is to be perceived as a genius and not as a failure or an eccentric. And having been all three, believe me, it's more fun being a genius.

A Good Example: The Ion Generator

Let me give you one example of this concept from actual experience. The product is the ion generator. An ion generator is an electronic product which emits negative ions. Negative ions were proven to cleanse the air by attaching themselves to pollutants in the air and causing those pollutants to precipitate to a grounded surface—either to a filter or the closest grounded object.

I was marketing consumer electronics during the '70s and I started noticing articles in magazines about ion generators. Then ion generators were being offered to me for marketing that were quite costly. Some sold for over $1,000 and were professional models used in "clean rooms" and in hospitals. Then came the less expensive versions that cost around $300 and had various industrial applications.

Product literature from companies selling ion generators came across my desk and I started getting a sense of an emerging market for this product that required direct marketing to properly exploit the item. Sitting on a retail shelf, the product would draw little interest. I also felt that the ion generator had very good mass market appeal if the price point could be held to under $100. In fact, here is a good time to give you my first product principle.

Product Principle 1: The product must appeal to everybody in a category.

You want your product to appeal to all women or all men or all men and women or all tennis players or all handymen or all computer owners or all computer owners who own CD-ROM drives. In short, you want the product to appeal to all people in a specific category.

In my business, I was targeting the mass market—all men and women. And the only thing restricting me was the price. Although everybody wanted clean air, the price point had to be low enough to attract the largest number of people in that category. This brings us to the next product principle.

Product Principle 2: The product must be priced to appeal to the largest segment of a category.

Sure you can pick a product that appeals to the mass market, price the product so that only the top 5% of your prospects are willing to buy it, and you will still have a very successful business. But you won't dominate the category. Let's get back to my story.

Here I was, getting articles on ion generators, reading about them in magazines and looking at a few products that were offered to me but were too costly for the mass market—the market in which I was specializing. If I had a tennis product, my ads could appear in category-specific publications such as tennis magazines where all the readers are tennis players, but the ads might do poorly in *Popular Science* where only 12% play tennis. I wanted to appeal to everybody in hundreds of magazines and I always looked at my product selection in this light.

One day in 1978 I received a call from Josh Reynolds, who claimed that he was the inventor of the mood ring—a fad during the '70s. The mood ring used liquid crystal technology and as your body heat changed, the color of the liquid crystals changed and thus your mood was reflected by the color of your ring. There was even a color chart to tell you what the colors meant. He told me, "Joe, I had great success with the mood ring but I couldn't get them out fast enough. Others copied me and I was knocked off so fast, I never really made a lot of money." This brings me to my next principle.

Product Principle 3: Unless you dominate your category, the demand you create is quickly filled by others.

Josh then proceeded to tell me that he had developed a new product called the Energaire ion generator and that it could sell for $69.95 and provide all the benefits of other, more costly ion generator products. Instinctively I knew that this might be the magic price point. First, it was considerably lower than any of the other models that were available, and second, at $69.95 it was priced within reach of the majority of my market. It had mass market appeal. Josh seemed like an interesting guy and his product was exactly what I was waiting for, so I invited him to my office where I promptly agreed to conduct a test in the Southwestern edition of *The Wall Street Journal*—that's where I ran all my test ads at the time. (I discuss more about testing in Marketing Lesson 8.)

In determining the best way to market this product, I realized that the mass market would be attracted to its air-cleaning properties but I needed something dramatic to get them into the copy. The product looked strange. It was a cylinder with the top slanting down and a small ball of steel wool at the very top center of the product, the ion-emitting portion of the unit.

To get my potential customers to read the copy after looking

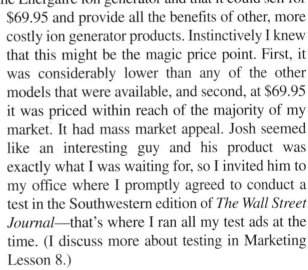

I called attention to the ugliest part of the product.

at a picture of this strange-looking machine would require an unusual headline. The part of the unit I did not like from an esthetic product design standpoint was the small ball of steel wool at the top center of the unit. It really took away from the beautiful design. So like some approaches I've used before, I took the worst aspect of the product and made it the most attention getting. The headline read: "Miracle Fuzz"—a play on the steel wool and the fact that this fuzz was the magic component that distributed the negative ions. The ad copy was as follows:

Headline: Miracle Fuzz

Subheadline: A new space-age invention and the same effect as lightning combine to create the world's first home oxygen regeneration system.

Copy: You need oxygen to live. You can live without food for 60 days, without water for seven days, but without oxygen, you won't make it past two minutes.

That small piece of fuzz located on top of the cylinder shown above emits negatively charged electrons which attach themselves to molecules of oxygen thus creating ionized oxygen.

The ad went on to explain the effect of creating ionized oxygen without ever mentioning ion generator or negative ions. I was subtly distancing myself from the other companies who had ion generators and I was coining my own terms.

I can remember my anxiety when I prepared the ad. I wasn't sure it would work. Was the headline too trite? Was the concept too unusual to be accepted by the mass market? It wasn't a matter of being concerned about being too early in the product life cycle because in the very early stages of the cycle, you don't know if you have a salable product.

Josh looked over the ad copy that I sent him and approved it. "If this doesn't sell it, nothing will," he commented.

New Product/New Category

Josh's job was to supply the product. And finally when we received our first shipment, we placed the ad in the Southwestern edition of *The Wall Street Journal* and waited for the response. The response was heavy—one of the biggest reactions to an ad that I can remember for any product that I ran in this edition of the *Journal*. It was a big hit and we knew that we had a major product on our hands. We knew, but nobody else did. Our ad in the *Journal* was first seen by a very small percentage of the total *Journal* readers and the public in general. And even if somebody did see the ad, they had no idea of how heavy the response had been.

We had discovered not only a major new product, but a product category as well. We were at the "period of discovery"—discovering a product whose point in time and space was harmonizing perfectly with the consumer. People obviously read the ad and responded. They reached into their pockets and exchanged their hard-earned money for our product. And after the flush of excitement and the realization that we were about to launch a major new product category, I also realized that this single product would earn millions of dollars for my company. The only question was, how long would this product's life cycle last? When would the competition enter the business? And my biggest worry—could the company making the product supply enough of them?

The life cycle lasted longer than I thought possible. Despite competition and despite the flood of imitation products, we managed to sell hundreds of thousands of these units over a period of eight years. The "period of competition" lasted until the product reached a peak over the following three years and surprisingly dropped little from its introductory period. Today it has developed into a product category with a variety of product configurations offered by a number of companies. It is one of the best-selling products on QVC as well as the Home Shopping Network—both TV shopping channels. And you will frequently see it in consumer electronic or lifestyle catalogs.

A Classic Example

The ion generator story above is a classic example of bringing a product to public awareness to determine if it is in harmony with the public. First I read about the product, then saw versions that either were too expensive, didn't quite fit the needs of the consumer or were so strange that the consumer didn't quite relate to the product. Then I found a product that had the right price point, the right configuration and seemed to fit the market scope that we established for ourselves, the mass market.

I then learned everything I could about the product, positioned the product by coming up with the best concept for selling it, photographed it to bring out its drama, wrote the ad, set the type and designed the layout to create a pleasing environment. And then of course, we tested it. I remember my feelings just before I ran the ion generator ad. "Who is going to buy this product?" I thought. And the only reason I really felt compelled to run it was that it fit my parameters—the rules I had established for myself when evaluating other products.

Clean air had a mass appeal. A product that could filter out even the most microscopic particles was new and different. The price point was a popular price point. And finally, the product required direct marketing and in particular my copy-laden style of presenting a product.

There were other product categories we discovered in the same way as the ion generator. Some did not last as long, but others lasted a long time. The pocket calculator, the cordless telephone, the digital watch, BluBlocker sunglasses—all are products I introduced during their "period of discovery," and all went on to become major new products on retail shelves.

But the story above really doesn't tell you how to find that great new product. I've only shown you how a product came to me. This brings me to my next product principle.

Product Principle 4: Successfully offer your first product in a category and others will offer you similar products in that category.

After I first offered a pocket calculator and did a major job with it, I had other companies coming to me with their pocket calculators for me to market. Then came other consumer electronic products and before I knew it, I had more products than I knew what to do with.

When I was looking for a publisher to publish my book, I first went to a bookstore and looked at every book that covered my subject. I was searching for the name of a publisher who published most of the books I selected. From this activity, I was able to select two publishers. Once you establish expertise in a specific area, others will tend to come to you with similar products. It's simply common sense.

But how do you find that first big product? How do you find that pocket calculator, the ion generator or even the digital watch?

Emotional Understanding

My first suggestion is to stick with the type of product that you have an emotional understanding of. This comes from being intimately involved with the category yourself. For example, I am a gadget person and like electronic gadgets. I am an amateur (ham) radio operator (W9IQO). I love photography and did much of the photography for my catalogs. I am a commercial, instrument-rated, multi-engine pilot. (What better gadget is there than an airplane!) In short, I really understood my product category with a passion that emotionally involved me. And so when it came to judging whether a product was suited for my customer, I first asked if it was suited for me.

Don't select a category because that's where the money is. You can see the disadvantage right away. You won't have the emotional understanding of your customer and you need that. In fact, you really are selling to yourself when you offer a product. I sell all the Joe Sugarmans of the world each time I run my ads.

A good story to highlight this was a promotion I did in one of our catalogs. I created a doctorate degree in Gizmology as a spoof and announced that I would award a graduation certificate to any customer who had all of the following credentials: "an electrical engineering degree, was an accomplished photographer, Amateur General Class radio operator, commercial instrument-rated, multi-engine pilot and a collector of gadgets."

Actually, I also had a second class of customer entitled to the degree, namely: "Any customer who bought anything from our catalog."

The first set of criteria actually represented me except for the electrical engineering degree. I had spent three and a half years studying for that degree but was drafted into the U.S. Army and spent the next three and a half years in Germany with Army Intelligence and eventually with the CIA. I never went back to get my degree.

Nevertheless, I received, to my amazement, responses from hundreds of people who fitted the first set of criteria and who requested their free certificate, sending me proof of their eligibility.

You Already Get the Magazines

Let's assume that you are passionate about a product category. You probably already get the consumer magazines that cover that particular category. Now that you are looking for products in that category, a good source might be the trade publications that go to people who sell products in that category. For example, if you are an avid skier, you might already be a subscriber to *Skiing* and *Ski* magazines. But now you should request a subscription to *Ski Business* or any of the other trade publications in that category.

Usually in these magazines will be a listing of trade shows where you can go to see the latest developments in ski products such as ski lifts, boots, clothing or bindings. You should read these publications, visit ski shops, go to the trade shows—in short, really become an expert in the industry. You already have the passion, but now it's time to complement it with knowledge.

Industry Trade Shows

Often at these trade shows, the industry leaders are featured speakers at seminars and conferences. Attend all the sessions you can. You can meet with product inventors or manufacturers who have unusual products at the prototype stage and are still in the process of determining their marketing plans. Cram all the knowledge you can about the industry, the products that are currently best sellers, the products that have sold well in the past, the cycles in the industry (all industries have them) and even some of the big industry miscalculations. Everything helps and all this new knowledge will give you not only the emotional understanding of the products in this category but the nuts and bolts as well. In short, become an expert.

Approach Manufacturers

My very first product was one of the first pocket calculators, the Craig 4501. I read about the development of the product in *Business Week* and persistently searched for the manufacturer until I found him. And when I did find him, I asked to see his representative, who just happened to be in my area. Craig Corporation, the company distributing the calculator, was not the manufacturer. They simply purchased the electronic circuitry from Texas Instruments and had a company called Bowmar assemble it in Boston. They had no idea how to market it. After all, this was not a car stereo—a product they were currently selling. It was not something that would go screaming off the retail shelves. And at $240, who would buy it?

So when I proposed that I sell it through direct marketing, they jumped at the chance to work with me to see if I could. They only made an initial run of 5,000 pieces. After all, this was a real gamble.

Direct marketing is an exciting alternative for many companies and there are manufacturers with very little experience in this area who would love to work with somebody who has the experience.

My success with the pocket calculator gave me the credibility to approach other manufacturers and get exclusive rights to introduce their products. This often allowed my company to be the only company to sell a product for a period of time.

Negotiating the Best Price

Let us assume that you have found a very exciting product and the manufacturer is willing to give you the opportunity to sell it. What next?

First, you want to negotiate the best possible price. You want to explain that you are going to put on a direct marketing advertising campaign on behalf of the manufacturer and for that campaign you need the best possible profit margins. The better the margins, the more advertising dollars you can spend, the more advertising exposure the manufacturer's product will get and the more product you'll be able to sell. And indeed you are telling the truth.

Let's take an example. If a manufacturer gave me a very hefty profit margin vs. a manufacturer that didn't, I would spend and therefore risk more money to sell the higher margin product. For the low margin product I would advertise cautiously, being careful not to spend my dollars on media that might not work. As a result, I would not sell as much.

Ironically, at the very end of one of my typical advertising campaigns when I examined the profits earned from products with large and small margins, the percentage of profit in both instances was close to the same. I made the same percentage of profit with a product with good margins as I did with a product with smaller margins, even though I sold more of the high-margin product and made more total profit.

The profit percentage is directly related to the risk factor. The bigger the margins, the more of a gamble I would take, and consequently I would even risk losing money in some magazines just to get the widest possible exposure. I would always make sure that the ad I placed for products with smaller margins would produce a profit, so I never took the risks that I would with high-margin products nor did I get the exposure. So, give me hefty margins, and I'm going to take bigger risks and spend more money and consequently sell much more product than if I proceeded cautiously with a low-margin product.

I would tell this to manufacturers. And when they worked with me and provided me with good margins, we did very well. You have to explain this to a manufacturer when you're negotiating prices.

Another tactic is to become an expert on the product you are negotiating for by finding out what the costs of all the components are and then adding them up. Using this knowledge and showing the manufacturer that you know what a product actually costs provides a logical basis for asking for as low a price as possible. But there are other factors that have to be negotiated as well.

The Returned Products

The manufacturer wants to know what happens to the product that comes back as a result of your customer guarantee or return privilege. Remember, you're going to get back as much as 10% of your products on average and maybe even more. Who absorbs the products that are returned? Do you send them to the manufacturer and is it built into the price? Or do you keep it and figure out later what to do? This is something that has to be worked out in advance.

My preference was always to have the manufacturer take the product back at no cost to us. After all, they have the facilities to inspect and repackage, thereby saving you a chore that you might not be able to handle. And besides, if the product is not acceptable to the consumer, it may have a lot to do with the manufacturing of the product. For these reasons you, as the direct marketer, should let the manufacturer handle the returns.

Sometimes this is impossible, as the product is being imported from outside the country and the deal you have made with the manufacturer does not cover any returns. You then have to order a certain amount of extra packaging and break the returns into two piles. One, from those who are returning the product unopened. Much of that can be returned to stock.

The second pile is for product that has been used and returned. It has to be checked out, repackaged and then not returned to inventory but sold through your store or factory outlet as refurbished merchandise at a lower price, even though it is practically new. Never sell refurbished products as new. Not only is it illegal, but it isn't fair to your customer who is expecting a new product. It's also very simple to open up a little factory or warehouse outlet store and sell the returned merchandise to customers in your immediate area. JS&A always had a store in our warehouse where customers could pick up some good bargains.

Three Additional Points

This chapter is not meant to cover all the issues involved in finding the right product. Many times it is pure serendipity. I discovered BluBlocker sunglasses on the way to see another product. A manufacturer's representative handed me a pair to try on while we were driving one sunny day in Los Angeles.

But there are still three points I would like to make before I conclude the subject of how to find the perfect product, and they are all significant lessons. The first point involves a story that was told to me by a direct marketing executive.

The Public Is Boss

I was talking to a highly regarded owner of a catalog house that was a publicly listed company on one of the major exchanges. I had accepted an assignment from his company to propose ideas and some names for a series of new catalogs they were planning to launch. During our many discussions, the executive confided in me and told me a story of a mistake he made and the lesson he learned.

His company offered a set of pots and pans in their catalog for only $19.95. For years this set sold very well, often in the millions of units. But the executive (let's call him Fred) was embarrassed over the quality of the pots and pans. "They were as thin as could be," he said, "and probably only lasted a few months before they warped so badly they had to be thrown out. They were junk but they sold year after year after year.

"So when Revere Copper and Brass came out with their set of copper-bottom pots and pans, I discovered that I could practically duplicate their set and sell mine for $69.95 and they would compare very closely with the $269.95 set from Revere. I could upgrade my best-selling pair and really provide one hell of a value as well as a product that would not warp.

"But to be able to offer this value, I had to order over a million sets of these pots and pans. A million sets—a major investment. I was convinced that the consumer would realize the value we were providing and we would have a huge success.

"When we offered the set in our catalog, it bombed. And it bombed so badly that it took us several years to liquidate the entire inventory. Meanwhile, our $19.95 set kept selling and selling. And I was really disgusted with the consumer. Here I was offering them such a great bargain and look what they did to me."

Fred had fallen for the biggest fallacy in marketing. It is not the marketer who decides the best product for the marketplace but the public. The public is boss. They, and only they, decide which product will sell, and they vote with their hard-earned dollars to back up that vote. And if you think you can outguess them, think again. It's almost impossible. That is the major point I want to make here. With all the experience I have had in marketing, with all the successful products I've launched, I cannot tell which product will be the next discovery without testing the product and having the consumers' votes tell me.

The Free Market

My second point is an observation and it is simply this. When a new product is discovered and the response that it generates is substantial, it is a very strong sign that this product is of great benefit to the public. The marketplace will then generate, in the most efficient way, in a free market society, the product required to fill the greater need of the public.

A good example of this principle is with BluBlocker sunglasses. We discovered that sunglasses that blocked all the UV and blue-spectrum light provided protection needed by the public and they "voted" for our product in great numbers. But our price and quality were high. We encouraged a number of companies, by our absence in the lower-priced category, to produce products that were nowhere near the quality of our sunglasses yet filled a gap in the market. I could have entered the low end of the market but I didn't. But the public benefited in the end. Those that wanted high-quality sunglasses bought mine, and those that wanted cheaper sunglasses bought my competitors'. Later I produced and successfully marketed sunglasses at the lower end of the price range but it took me a while to realize the share of the market I had relegated to those who copied me.

The point to be made from both of these examples once again relates to the dynamics of the marketplace and the importance of the public in the product selection process. They are the smartest and most efficient voters in the world. They dictate who is on target and who is off target. They make sure there is enough competition by demanding a variety of product options. And it is this diversity of selection that eventually fills the best needs and requirements of the public. If you keep these facts in mind, you've learned a great lesson which can be summed up in the final product principle.

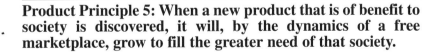

Product Principle 5: When a new product that is of benefit to society is discovered, it will, by the dynamics of a free marketplace, grow to fill the greater need of that society.

The issues discussed here are from my experience. Many times I've been asked by people how I found a product and many of the ways I've found them are given in this chapter. There are other issues concerning product. What if you invent your own product? You have to make a prototype and arrange for manufacturing. I'm not covering these issues in this book as an entire book can be written about that subject. But the issue of protecting your product from somebody else copying you is a subject that you may find important and which I cover shortly.

The third point I want to make about products can best be described in Marketing Lesson 2, in which I relate the very important lesson I learned from Bobby Darin, the late pop singer. But first it's time for another marketing story.

What happens when an entrepreneur finds himself in a position where he is unable to do anything to solve a problem? He simply does *something*. And that is the basis for the marketing story that follows.

A Marketing Story

The World's Highest Paid Copywriter

This is the story of an ad I wrote about a personal tragedy. The story has such unusual twists that it definitely makes for one interesting experience as you will soon discover.

In 1972 my mom was diagnosed as having colon cancer and despite all the treatments available at the time, she was slowly becoming sicker and sicker. She was operated on but it was too late. The cancer had spread throughout her entire body.

I was this take-charge successful entrepreneur who recognized a problem and then did something about it. And yet I was helpless in trying to get my mom back to health. Finally in 1975 she passed away. It was a slow, torturous death.

Despite the success of my company, I had always kept a low profile. I never used my name in any of my advertising and avoided any publicity. But after my mom's death, I wanted to do something—anything—a tribute to my mom that she would have been proud of, and I wanted to do something that would help others avoid what she went through.

The story started out innocently enough. I was raising money for the American Cancer Society. But what happened became an adventure that lasted 12 years.

My Services Free of Charge

My idea was to raise money for the American Cancer Society. I would run an ad in *Advertising Age* magazine—the advertising agency trade publication—offering my services as a copywriter, free of charge, for one week to someone randomly selected from everybody who entered my contest. All those who participated had to send me a check payable to the American Cancer Society. I would record the contributor's name and then I would select the winner at random from among all the entrants.

I would then go to the winner's place of business and write copy for one solid week, paying all my own travel expenses.

Bragging about being the world's highest paid copywriter was not my typical style. And this was the first time my picture had appeared in any of my ads in print. But I knew that I had to do something very bold, imaginative and definitely positive.

The ad ran in *Advertising Age* in March 1976 and the response was immediate and strong. One company had each one of their 100 employees send me $5. Another company pooled all their money and sent me one check for $1,000. And thousands of others simply sent me their checks with words of encouragement and condolences for my mom. One of the entrants, Carla Laufer, was so moved she cried when she read the ad and sent in a small contribution.

Drawing Time Came

Then came the time for the drawing. If I were writing a movie script, it might sound something like this:

Cut to a commuter train speeding toward Chicago from Indiana. Carla Laufer, the assistant marketing director of a small sports marketing firm in downtown Chicago, is sitting on the train reading the morning newspaper.

Suddenly there is a screeching sound, a huge thunderous crash and Carla is thrown across the train. She gets up, very shaken, and tries to help the other passengers. The train is off the tracks. Injured passengers are all over the compartment and as she is helping a number of other passengers, the paramedics arrive. Carla pulls herself together, calls her boss, Jon Spoelstra, from the scene of the accident and tells him that she was in a train wreck and that she'll be late. Jon actually thought Carla was joking.

Cut back to the cancer promotion drawing. I'm standing by my computer along with somebody from my accounting firm who is witnessing the drawing. All of the contributors have been entered into the computer and their checks have already been submitted to the American Cancer Society. Jerry White, our computer consultant, is standing by the computer ready to randomly select the winner.

Cut back to Carla. The train accident happened fairly close to downtown Chicago. It would be easier for her to go straight to her office and tell her boss what had just happened than to go home to an empty apartment. Her clothes have blood stains on them from some of the other passengers, but fortunately Carla is OK. As Carla enters her company's office Jon Spoelstra stands up at his desk and sees that indeed something is wrong. "Are you OK, Carla?"

"I'm OK, I'm OK—just a little shook up but I'll be fine."

Carla walks to her desk, throws her purse onto it and sighs. "But some of the other passengers were in pretty bad shape. There were tons of ambulances at the scene. But as for me, nothing was broken so I just wanted to leave."

Carla then puts her head down on her desk and sobs. "I'll be OK in a little while. I just haven't had time to digest what just happened. Go ahead, do what you were doing and I'll be fine in a few minutes."

Jon notices the blood on Carla's white blouse. "This must have been quite a day for her," he thinks. "I'll just leave her alone for a while."

A few minutes later, Carla's phone rings. She picks it up and answers, "This is who? Joseph Sugarman? Yes, this is Carla Laufer. I won your contest? This is some kind of joke, right? Sure. Do you mind if I call you back? What's your number?"

Carla then walks into Jon's office. "OK, Jon, who's playing the practical joke. If you're trying to cheer me up, don't go pulling a practical joke. Who did you put up to calling me?"

Jon looked puzzled. "What are you talking about?"

Carla continued, "I just got a call from somebody who says he's Joe Sugarman telling me that I won his contest. I wasn't born yesterday. Who did you put up to this?"

"Carla, I didn't put anybody up to anything. Chances are that it *was* Joe Sugarman. Maybe you *did* win his contest."

Jon Spoelstra was a big fan. He followed my career from the early JS&A days and when he saw I was running this contest, he showed the ad in *Advertising Age* to Carla, who was so moved by it that she sent in a contribution.

Carla immediately went back to her phone and called the number I had given her. I answered the call.

"Carla, I really am Joe Sugarman, president of JS&A, and you are indeed the winner of my cancer promotion. Congratulations."

She Finally Believes Me

After a number of assurances Carla finally believed me. She had thought that I was one of her friends playing a practical joke because they all knew she had entered my contest.

"You let me know where and when you want me to show up at your office and I'll spend a week writing all the copy you want," I told her.

It was a totally random selection process, but to end up with somebody from nearby Chicago as the winner made it really easy for me. "From all the responses I got from all over the U.S., to get one right in Chicago when I'm here in Northbrook (a Chicago suburb) makes it really convenient, so you pick any week or spread it out over a month and I'll be there."

Then Carla confided in me, "I was so impressed with what you did that I just wanted to enter for the sake of helping you reach your goal. I didn't expect to win and besides, my boss Jon Spoelstra is having a difficult time and we are probably going to close down his company anyway. But I've got an idea. Why not get together for lunch next week. I know Jon would appreciate meeting you and that's all we really want to do." We set the time and place and Carla hung up. This was truly a day she wouldn't forget.

We Meet for Lunch

I met Carla and Jon for lunch. Jon was a tall, lanky former basketball player and Carla was his assistant—an attractive young girl in her mid 20s. Carla was very bright and had a heart of gold. She told me about the train wreck and how she really didn't believe it was me on the phone and how that day was so traumatic—to be involved in a train wreck and then to receive the good news about winning the contest. But to her it was simply enough to tell me how much my ad had moved her and to express her appreciation for all that I had done.

We said good-bye after lunch and that was the last I saw of Carla for many years. But I did see Jon again.

About five years later, in 1981, Jon Spoelstra attended my seminar. He was now the general manager of the Portland Trail Blazers basketball team and had been in that position for the past few years. "When I told my boss about coming to your seminar and that it cost $2,000, he thought it was outrageous. But I convinced him to let me come and assured him that it was a great investment."

Jon Learns a Lot

Jon absorbed the material like a sponge. He learned a lot. And I shared with the other seminar participants the story of how Carla had won my cancer promotion and the role Jon had played in that story.

Jon told me that he had followed my advertising for years and that he tried to emulate what I had done but really was unsure of himself. He needed the seminar and, as he told me later, "It was like I was walking around in a dark room and suddenly somebody turned on the light. It was probably one of the most influential experiences of my entire life."

Cut to January 27, 1987. I'm in Portland, Oregon, at a large downtown hotel. I'm giving a speech to a large group of marketers. I finish my speech and then step off the podium to meet the guests who had questions for me or simply wanted to meet and talk to me.

"Joe, remember me?"

I looked up and recognized Jon Spoelstra. "What a surprise. How are you?"

Jon explained that he was doing just great. He was still the general manager of the Portland Trail Blazers and doing an excellent job of building attendance as well as assuring the team's marketing success. He finally had made it and made it really big. And the Trail Blazers were known for having the most successful front office in sports. "Your training has really paid off," he said. But then he dropped a bombshell. "Did you hear about Carla?"

"Jon, I haven't spoken to Carla since the time we first went out to lunch. How's she doing?" I asked.

"Joe, she's got terminal cancer and the doctors have given her only a few months to live."

Fighting for Her Life

"What?" I said. "You're kidding me?" Jon then explained that Carla had discovered lumps in her breast and went to the hospital. They ran some X-rays and didn't find any cancer. Later it was learned that the lumps were cancerous and that the doctors in the hospital had totally misdiagnosed the X-rays. Carla was in the process of suing the hospital while fighting for her life.

What a shock. Here the winner of my cancer contest had gotten cancer herself. She was young, vivacious, and had a bright future only to be stricken with this horrible disease.

But something clicked. I had just come back from Maui, Hawaii, where I had met Gene Clark, a Hawaiian healer. He was highly recommended to me for a sore back I had and he turned out to be very effective. He used Hawaiian lomilomi massage techniques along with reflexology and even acupressure to treat many of the problems of his clients. I had three treatments from him and he really made me feel great.

He Worked on the Immune System

During one of the discussions we had while I lay on his treatment table, he explained how the immune system played a major role in many diseases. He told me that he worked on the immune system when he worked on the body and that by boosting the immune system, you can get rid of even the most horrible diseases. "Even cancer?" I asked.

"Oh, yes. Even cancer," was Gene's reply. "I've done it before."

I didn't think much about his comment although I did somehow believe him. He had an all-knowingness about him, a magic touch and a great deal of confidence in his own ability.

I asked Jon, "I met this Hawaiian healer while I was on Maui and he claimed that he could cure cancer—or at least could boost the immune system, which in turn could possibly cure cancer. Do you think Carla would be willing to go to Maui, at my expense, and get treated by this guy?"

Jon said, "Why not call her and give it a try?" And so Jon gave me Carla's number. First I called the healer. He told me it would take about ten days but that he was confident he could effect a cure. Then I called Carla.

I Could Finally Award Her

I told Carla how I felt strongly that I could help her rid herself of the cancer. She never took advantage of the prize anyway and this was a way I could finally award it to her. Would she go along with this wild, crazy idea? I would pay all her expenses including the cost for the treatments which would take about ten days. After all, she was given just a few months to live. What did she have to lose?

I remembered my mom and how helpless I felt. But now I no longer felt helpless. I was able to at least do something. I was in control, and in my own way I had maybe found a rather small but personal means to conquer cancer.

Carla accepted and within a few days she was in Maui being treated. By coincidence, I had planned a trip to Maui with my family around the last day of Carla's treatments. I called her and arranged to meet with her at my hotel to find out about the results and her impressions of Gene, my healer friend.

The moment Carla saw me she ran up to me and wrapped her arms around me and gave me a big hug. "I'm free of cancer, Joe. He did it. I no longer have cancer."

"Are you sure?" I asked.

"I haven't taken any tests yet, but I know it's gone. This guy you introduced me to is incredible."

Cancer Disappears

Carla returned to Chicago. Her doctors ran numerous tests and could not find any cancer. She came back a week later for more tests as the doctors thought that maybe the previous tests were not done right. Finally the doctors admitted that the cancer was gone. If anything, there was just a small trace of it in one part of her body. But they would monitor it and if she required any treatment, they would give it to her.

She never explained to her doctors how she got rid of most of the cancer. They wouldn't have believed her anyway. But she was alive—free of this horrible disease that took the life of my mother and almost took Carla's life. The winner of my cancer contest had indeed won. She beat the disease. "The universe works in strange ways," I thought.

On May 1, 1987, Carla wrote me a nice letter shortly after she had returned to the mainland. It read:

> Dear Joe, I tried to figure out a real clever way to start this note, but I couldn't.

Then I thought about baring my soul for you, so you might better understand who was on the receiving end of your generosity, but that probably isn't necessary. Any woman who, without hesitation, would fly 4,219 miles to get worked over by a total stranger needs no explanation.

Let me say this. I'm glad I have you to thank for being my angel of mercy because most people couldn't begin to appreciate what you've done for me. My doctors think I went to Maui for some un-American, mumbo-jumbo cure. What they don't understand is for the first time in 14 months, I started taking responsibility for this mess. My idea of being a good patient was not flinching when someone stuck me with a needle or not crying when I had to do things I didn't particularly want to do. You gave me the opportunity to start making choices, and that is something that I forgot I had the right to do. If Gene didn't know beans about healing, he still was able to make me feel as though I was leaving no stones unturned in a battle which requires every last piece of artillery.

I'm not a Holy Roller or a foxhole convert. I fall somewhere in between. I've been asking the Big Guy for help, and I know He gets a ton of requests, but I really feel like you were the answer to my prayers.

Thank you, Joe. I'll keep in touch. If there is anything I can do for you, don't hesitate to ask.

Cut to 1988—one year later. On October 24th of the previous year, I had been involved in a head-on collision with a drunk driver. My Volvo was demolished and I ended up in the hospital with broken ribs and bones, broken ankles and shoulder—a mess. Carla came to visit me at my home during my long recovery. We talked about her recovery and what it meant to her. How she was now working for The Disney Channel and was really enjoying herself. Then she presented me with a Mickey Mouse Disney Channel jacket. "Here's a small gift," she said. "I don't see you walking around town in a Mickey Mouse jacket, but then again, the only other thing I could bring you was a Mickey Mouse hat and I didn't think that was your image either."

We laughed and then she asked me, "Why don't you go see Gene yourself? He'll get you well in no time."

After a few months, I did just that. I flew to Maui and spent about a month in rehabilitation, then returned to Chicago.

Several months passed. I was getting stronger and although

I was still experiencing pain in my right ankle, the accident had left no other scars. It was time for another trip to Maui to visit my friend Gene and get a few more treatments.

Carla Calls with News

While I was in Gene's studio, the phone rang. It was Carla. "Joe, I've got good news and bad news for you. First the good news. I've just been awarded $1.5 million as a settlement in my lawsuit. I'm now a millionaire."

"Wonderful," I said. But I knew there was something else I was about to hear that I wasn't going to like. "Now what's the bad news?"

"I've got the cancer again," answered Carla. "This time it's in the liver. But the doctors are very optimistic and I'm doing just fine."

"Fine?" I said in disbelief. "You're not doing fine. You get yourself over here to Maui and get some treatments right away."

She told me that she would and said she would call me in two days with the flight information.

Two days later she called but not with the information I wanted to hear. "Joe, my doctors tell me that I'm too weak to travel. But they have assured me that I'm doing fine, and will do fine under their care. Please don't be upset, but I'll be fine."

I tried once more to convince her to come to Maui for her treatments. But it was to no avail. I then told her that I understood her decision, and after some small talk I wished her a speedy recovery. One week later her mom called. Carla had passed away.

Almost a Full Year of Life

Her mom told Gene that our combined efforts had been responsible for almost a full year of life in which she seemed to blossom and grow and appreciate the really meaningful things that many of us never learn to appreciate. I miss Carla. I still have her Mickey Mouse jacket and the very thoughtful letter she wrote me. I'm sure she's met my mom by now too. They certainly have something in common.

Jon Spoelstra went on to lead the Portland Trail Blazers for 11 incredible seasons before becoming president of the New

Jersey Nets. In New Jersey he built up the Nets' attendance and was responsible for their acknowledged success as well. He recently resigned after four and a half years and has written an excellent book on marketing called *Ice to the Eskimos*, his third marketing book.

Eventually I recovered completely from my October 1987 car accident. I set aside a certain percentage of the proceeds from my catalog to support many of the drunk driving campaigns throughout the country.

And the healer? Gene is doing just fine. He's still helping people on the island and he plays another interesting role in my life as you'll soon read in the next marketing story, "The Miracle Oil of Hawaii."

But before we move on to our next lesson, there is actually a little more to this story. In 1990, I read about a car dealer, Carson Pettit, in Devon, Pennsylvania who was holding his own cancer contest. The dealer was going to give away a brand-new 1990 Mercedes 500SL sports car to the highest bidder with the proceeds going to the American Cancer Society. The car was in such demand that the 500SL was selling for well above its sticker price and I really wanted to get one.

The Volvo I bought to replace the one that got smashed up was great transportation but it was time to upgrade. "What a great way to raise money for a cause that I believe in," I thought. I wrote for the details and the bidding form and then filled it out. When I arrived at the local Federal Express office to mail the form and meet the deadline, I stayed in my car for a few moments as a realization suddenly hit me. What if I won the contest? The winner of my contest died of cancer. I returned home and never mailed the form.

Sometimes we pick up important pieces to a puzzle when we least expect it. And that is how I came across the next marketing lesson. I was listening to an "oldies but goodies" radio station when I heard the story of Bobby Darin and how he made it big. It struck such a responsive chord that I have used the story at practically each one of my seminars. See why in the next marketing lesson.

Marketing Lesson 2

The Bobby Darin Approach

A very important lesson I taught at the seminar was one that I learned from the late Bobby Darin, a popular singer of the 1950s. It was the story of how Bobby Darin became famous.

Darin was a young singer in New York who for a long time tried unsuccessfully to break into the music business. He would go to record company after record company trying to convince them to make an album of him singing popular but old songs.

He was rejected. First, nobody believed that the music industry would accept old pop tunes from an unknown young singer. And second, the hot music at the time was good old rock and roll sung by black artists and called the Motown sound.

He Harmonized with the Public

Darin was quite frustrated and took things into his own hands. Did he cut his own album by himself? No. Did he convince a record company to record him? Yes, but not in the way you would think. He simply sat down and wrote a tune that fitted or harmonized with what the public was buying at the time. It was called "Splish Splash" and the words started out, "Splish splash, I was takin' a bath 'round about a Saturday night," and went on to tell a story about what happened when he took that bath. The single became a smash hit and sold millions of copies. In the recording, he even sounded like a Motown recording artist.

Darin recognized what the market wanted and he created something that harmonized perfectly with that market even though his song was far from the music that was in his heart. He made the practical choice to put aside his desires, put aside his ego and goals and just cut a record that would sell and earn him the recognition he needed to record the type of music he wanted to record.

Despite the hit record, which became a million-seller, he still couldn't interest any record company in recording him for a pop album. So he took his earnings and made an album himself. One of the hits he recorded was an old song called "Mack the Knife." Not only was his album a smash hit, but "Mack the

Knife" became a multi-million-selling single throughout the world and Bobby Darin went on to be known not for "Splish Splash" but for the music he loved best—popular jazz oldies.

Power to Follow Your Dream

There are many lessons to be learned from this one example. First, realize that often you must go with the established way of doing things in order to accomplish your goals. You've got to harmonize with the marketplace first and then, once you have an established reputation, it's easier to try something different that you yourself want to try. So you first meet the needs of the market to raise the capital *you* need and then go for your dreams. Once you've raised your own funds, you can do anything you want. You can pursue a course of action that nobody else would believe possible. Take my BluBlocker sunglasses as an example.

If I had walked into a sunglass company's office and said that I had an idea, "Offer a single pair of sunglasses, a single style with an unusual lens, through direct marketing," I would have been kicked out of their office or at best I would have been humored and escorted out. First, sunglasses were never sold this way. They had always been sold at retail. Second, nobody ever offered just one style. And finally, didn't everybody have to try on a pair and see how they looked before they bought? But I had the dream and I went for it because I had the money to back my idea. I ran one of the most successful print campaigns of my career.

Imagine what that same company might have said if I brought them the idea of presenting a single pair of sunglasses on a half-hour TV commercial back when infomercials were still in their infancy. "Spend a half hour selling what?" might have been their response.

Very often we as direct marketers have a dream but not the resources to go out and pursue it, nor do we have the people who believe in us. Then the course of action should not be to keep pushing your idea but to figure out how to sell something that will harmonize with the marketplace and earn you the money to allow you to go for your dream.

A Different Twist

I also use the Bobby Darin example to convince people who come to me with a concept or idea that seems really too far out of the mainstream to harmonize with the marketplace. In some cases, their product needs a slightly different twist to work even though that is not what they envisioned for their product. The new change usually involves removing a component or making the product cheaper or presenting it in a totally new way.

Inventors of products or even manufacturers are often not willing to make a sacrifice to harmonize with the marketplace. In fact, inventors are probably the worst of the group. It is their invention—an extension of their ego—and to think that you, a stranger, want to change something to make it more acceptable to the public? How dare you! It's like you are telling them that their child is ugly and needs plastic surgery. If you are an inventor, don't be afraid to accept criticism and change to fit the vibration of the marketplace.

And manufacturers are no better. They have invested thousands, even millions, to develop something and nobody really wants to admit that a mistake was made and the product should be changed. Let me give you a perfect example of this.

The Clock Calculator Example

It was 1973 and a calculator company, APF, came to me with their new product. They were all excited about it and felt that they had the greatest and most exciting breakthrough in electronics since the calculator was invented.

So confident were they that they were willing to pay for the cost of my test ad. "Joe, this product is so hot that you'll sell millions," said the president of the company.

At the time, a good desk calculator with a large display sold for around $69.95. Prices in 1973 were still quite high for calculators, so $69.95 was a very attractive price back then. APF had sold their calculators successfully at $69.95 but felt that with their latest innovation, they had the ultimate product for my company—truly a revolution in electronics (or so they thought).

"What's the innovation?" I asked. The company president and his national sales manager had come to visit me personally to present the product. He unwrapped a special box to show me his prototype.

The calculator was the same calculator he had been selling for the past year but with a new feature—a clock that ran in the calculator display when the calculator wasn't being used. "What do you think?" they beamed. "We plan on selling this for $99.95." He unveiled the product as if he were unveiling a newborn child.

Not in Harmony with Consumers

I didn't like the idea. I explained that the consumer felt that a calculator was a serious business tool, turned on when it was needed and turned off when it was not. I had been selling them for almost two years and had a pretty good sense of the product and its emotional appeal. Putting a clock into the display and keeping the calculator on all the time was not in harmony with the consumer and therefore would not be successful. Increasing the price was a mistake and if I had a choice I would have offered the product for less, about $39.95, in order to get rid of their inventory. I just felt that it wouldn't sell.

The company president didn't believe me. "What?" he blurted out. "It costs much more than the standard model and it's so revolutionary—why should we even consider selling it for less?"

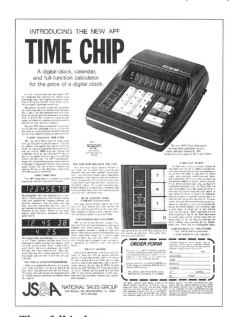

They fell in love with my ad copy and were ready to sell me thousands of their stupid calculators.

I agreed to write an ad to prove my point. "I will write a great ad and let you approve it. I will then run the ad in *The Wall Street Journal.* We'll measure the response and if it's successful, we'll create a nice advertising campaign for you."

I sent APF the ad and they loved it. "If this doesn't work, I'm getting out of the calculator business," said the president. And so I ran the ad.

It bombed. And the product was eventually closed out at $39.95 a year later. When you are not in harmony with the market, the marketplace doesn't respond. Taking a product and making it harmonize with the prospect is simply a matter of good listening and observation. It doesn't take genius. It takes a good eye and ear, and a little intuition helps.

The Ruler Evaluation Technique

There is also a logical way of looking at how I came up with my evaluation of the product. In order to understand it, visualize a 12-inch ruler as representative of the full marketplace potential for this product. The 12 inches could represent 12 million people who were prime prospects for a desk calculator at $69.95.

Simply by raising the price of this basic product, you'll likely eliminate two-thirds of the market. You end up with just 4 inches on the ruler as prime prospects for this product. Remember, the product was perceived at a $69.95 price point and you have raised it $30. The higher price will eliminate the majority of the market especially when people have a price point of a desk calculator already imprinted on their minds.

Now, of the 4 inches left, how many of those people are willing to pay extra for a clock in their calculator? My guess: maybe a fourth of the remaining prospects, and I feel that I'm probably generous on this guess. That leaves 1 inch, or only one-twelfth of the potential market.

Of all the prospects left, how many of them have watches or clocks in their offices and really don't need a clock in their calculator? Probably most of them, thereby leaving a tiny fraction of an inch left.

So here you have a product which sold for $69.95 and had a full 12 inches of prospective purchasers—all reduced down to a fraction of an inch because the manufacturer raised the price and added a component that the consumer really didn't need or want. It doesn't therefore take a genius to figure out that this product was doomed from the very beginning.

The final product principle I would like to leave you with is simply this:

Product Principle 6: Your product must harmonize with your prospect. If it doesn't, make sure that you change it so it does.

Remember Gene Clark, the Hawaiian healer? He was involved in another interesting episode in my life after my car accident in 1987. In the next marketing story, I explain the interesting set of circumstances that fell into place at that time and the product that evolved.

A Marketing Story

The Miracle Oil of Hawaii

Miracle Oil of Hawaii

I discovered the oil by mistake. But what it did was no mistake. I was experiencing a miracle.

Gene Clark tries to block this shot of himself in front of the beauty shop.
"I don't want to be famous," he insists.

By Joseph Sugarman

You are about to read something that you might find hard to believe. I know that I did. But if you read this, you'll be in for a pleasant surprise.

Gene Clark is a carpenter in the village of Kihei on the island of Maui in Hawaii. When the local people get sick, they call on Gene and he would give them a "treatment." They would quickly recover and soon Gene would be back at work pounding nails.

I discovered Gene by accident. I sprained a leg muscle and the little old lady at the cottage told me to see Gene. "He's not a doctor," she said, "but he's performed miracles around here."

BACK OF BEAUTY SHOP

So I looked up Gene, met him in back of the local beauty shop and for a few dollars he gave me a treatment. He spread an oil-like substance over my leg and massaged the sore muscles. Within a few hours after he finished the pain seemed to disappear.

The next day I was back in perfect shape, jogging and swimming as if nothing was ever wrong. Before I left Hawaii, I bought a sample of the oil from Gene. Then the miracles started.

For the next year, whenever I had a stiff muscle or joint I would apply the oil and in a few hours the pain seemed to go away. I even ran out. Whenever I exercised and got a few stiff muscles, I would apply the oil on one side of my body and nothing on the other. Sure enough, the one side without the oil would remain stiff while the side with the oil would be fine in a few short hours.

Soon, I started using the oil before I exercised and discovered that both my strength and endurance increased. Then I used the oil on just one arm and noticed my strength in that arm increased.

CLINICAL TESTS

After all my experiments, I felt that I had discovered some mysterious Hawaiian secret and maybe a revolutionary product idea. I flew to Maui once again to find out the secret to this mysterious oil.

I met Gene for lunch and told him that his oil should not just be limited to his patients. If the oil could be sold nationally, he could give up pounding nails for a liv-

ing and create his own health spa, Gene listened. And, as we talked, he finally unveiled the secret to his miracle oil.

The oils are made from plants. It seems that every plant has what is called "essential oils" and the essential oils to a plant is what our blood is to us humans. For example, when a plant is attacked by a fungus, the essential oils change quickly to combat the fungus by producing an ultimql properties just like our blood carries antibodies to fight disease.

There are some essential oils produced by plants that testing has proven can penetrate through layers of human skin. These oils then go straight to the muscle tissue to soothe those muscles and relieve pain by helping to eliminate the by-products of muscle strain such as lactic acid. Circulation in the area is also improved.

Only a few people in the world know how to grow plants to cause them to produce the essential oils that can help humans. The oils have to be extracted in an age-old method passed down from one family to the next. And it takes thousands of pounds of plants to produce just a few ounces of the essential oils.

TOO EXPENSIVE

Gene described the many steps required to create the oil and one conclusion was clear. Because of the thousands of pounds of plants required to make just a few ounces of the essential oil, the oil was too expensive to market as a replacement for the common over-the-counter preparations. A small 12 ounce bottle would cost $240.

Then it hit me. I realized that my treatment with Gene only required a few drops of the oil. The other products on the market required the application of much more oil and were a lot less effective. They left an oily residue and often had a strong odor where Gene's oil did not.

So I convinced Gene to supply me with small containers of the substance to market to my customers in two small one ounce bottles which I promised to name after him. "Clark's Rubbing Oil." With the small sized bottles, there's enough oil to supply any serious athlete, anybody with muscle problems or anybody who wants to excel in their sport. With

average use the oils should last a few months depending on the amount applied. Then came the breakthrough.

Before I sold a single bottle I conducted clinical tests. I was no longer going to be the only judge of my new product's efficacy. Sure enough, weight lifters using the oil saw as much as a 20% increase in their strength compared to those athletes who did not use the oil prior to exercise. That was all I needed.

EXPERIMENT WITH HALF

Let me send you two one ounce bottles of Clark's Rubbing Oil. Rub the oil from one of the bottles on your body before you exercise or where you have pain. Experiment with half your body using the oil on one side and nothing on the other. Experience for yourself the effect of this outstanding new product.

If, for some reason, you do not notice a dramatic difference—one so noticeable that you know within the first few applications, then keep the oil from the bottle you've used and return the unused bottle for a refund of your full purchase price. No questions asked.

But if my hunches are correct, you'll find as many uses for it, that you'll become one of our steady customers.

Gene Clark has just opened his new health spa. He has some of the finest equipment on the entire island and will be selling hundreds of bottles of his new oil. And hopefully, so will we.

Why not discover what Gene, a small group of athletes and I have already discovered? Try Clark's Rubbing Oil at no obligation, today.

To order, credit card holders call toll free and ask for product by number shown in parentheses or send a check plus $3.00 for delivery to the address below.

Trial Order (1600CC2) $29.95

Dr. Gene's spa is located at 851 Kihei Road in the Kamaʻole Beach Plaza Shopping Center in Maui.

JS&A

One JS&A Plaza, Northbrook, Illinois 60062
CALL TOLL FREE 800 228-5000

Gene blocked the camera to avoid appearing in the ad, but we got him anyway.

Truth is sometimes stranger than fiction. And so it is with finding products. But sometimes products have a funny way of finding you, as you will soon discover.

Gene Clark is a Hawaiian healer, described in my cancer promotion case history in the previous marketing story. I met him pretty much the way I described in my ad shown here. But it was how a product was discovered, how a small business started and how the product was eventually brought to the public that makes for an interesting case history.

I had been receiving treatments from Gene for a while when I realized what a wonderful talent he possessed. But despite his talent, he had to practice his trade in a small room in the back of a beauty shop. He had no private studio himself, no facility that he could call his own, and he relied on the beauty operators to make his appointments.

I offered Gene an observation as I was lying on the table getting one of his treatments. "Gene, you can only treat one client at a time. But if you were to duplicate yourself and treat thousands at the same time, then you'd be able to afford your own spa."

"I don't understand," he said.

"Gene, in my business, I write an ad, place it with a magazine and then the magazine prints my ad and duplicates my message to thousands of people. I then sell my products which are duplicated by my manufacturer. In short, I've figured out a way to duplicate my selling skills and the products I offer. Now, if you have a product and I can help you by writing an ad and getting that product manufactured, you can earn extra income and open your very own place."

Gene smiled. "I have just the product."

After the treatment, Gene took me behind the beauty shop and walked over to some herbs growing behind the parking area. He bent over, pulled out one of the herbs and said, "If you have a health problem with your lungs, you chew on this and it will help."

Not Broad-Based Enough

Somehow, the idea of a weed that you chewed on and that was for a specific condition was not the broad-based idea I was looking for.

"Gene, what I'm looking for is something that really helps a lot of people—like a Hawaiian weight-loss program or a program to give you more energy. Converting your herb into a product is difficult to do. You've got to be concerned about medical claims that the FDA doesn't like. Even if your product did work, you'd have to spend a fortune in testing to prove that it is what you say it is. And something as common as an herb gives us little protection over any competitor who may want to copy it." I told him that I would think about something he could sell and I left for the mainland.

Package on My Desk

When I arrived in my office, there was already a package on my desk from Chris Hahn, who represented a company called Spa Health Consultants. Chris was presenting a new product—a massage oil—but in an unusual way.

He sent me an ad that he had written in the typical style I use. The headline read: "The Dallas Cowboys and the Houston Oilers were moving too slowly so we decided to go to Joseph Sugarman for help." The copy went on to explain how this magic massage oil developed from plants relieved pain and increased strength and was indeed used by the Dallas Cowboys and the Houston Oilers. The products that accompanied the ad were a few bottles of massage oil using, as its basic ingredients, essential oils from plants.

The ad that Chris wrote used many of my copy techniques to explain his product as well as his frustration in marketing it. A plea near the end of the ad asked me to help the company manufacturing the product. The ad was written for only one person—me.

Not only was the product well presented, but here I had been racking my brain trying to think of a product for Gene when I realized I was now holding it in my hand. "Incredible," I thought. "What a coincidence. This is just the right product for Gene."

Gene Likes the Product

So I sent the oil to Gene for him to try on a few of his clients. He called me with his report. "The oil is good. I can see where this is really a good product."

That's all I needed. I returned to Maui and visited Gene. I told him about the oil and suggested calling it "Clark's Rubbing Oil." I thought it was a good idea to use him in the ad as the person who helped develop the oil.

But Gene had not developed the oil and I needed to add some authenticity to the ad. So I had Gene work with the manufacturer to blend various oils into what was called Oil A and Oil B. Oil B soothed the aches and pains caused by sore muscles, and Oil A was put on before exercise to prevent any tightening of the muscles. It was really Gene's product now, and it was so good that I began to use it myself.

Conducted Double-Blind Studies

To make sure we could make certain claims about the product, I conducted a scientific, double-blind study using a large group of athletes. The results were positive.

On my next trip to Maui, I had my camera with me when I visited Gene. "Gene, let's take some pictures to add a personal touch to the ad for your oils." I then went out in front of the beauty shop and told Gene to hold up his hand as if he were blocking me from taking his picture. I'm sure he thought this was strange, but I knew that an unusual photo tied into an unusual story would make for a really interesting mail order ad.

The photo turned out great and the ad ran in numerous publications—mostly health and fitness magazines, but also science and airline in-flight magazines. The ad was a success. The oils started to sell and Gene was making a nice royalty. He moved out of the beauty shop and into his own studio.

Gene Becomes Famous

Gene was also becoming famous. People were reading the ad for Clark's Rubbing Oil and going out of their way to find Gene. There were some who flew into the local airport, took a taxi to Gene's new studio and received treatments using the new oil. One of his visitors was Jimmy Bowen, the former singer and manager of such famous country acts as Garth Brooks and the Judds. He later had Gene fly to Nashville to work on his star clients as well.

Eventually the oil stopped selling and things returned back to normal for Gene. However, he had increased his client base, had his 15 minutes of fame and ended up with a studio of his own.

This is an example of how, with a little bit of serendipity, I was able to help a friend help others by finding a good product and promoting it. Gene still has his famous clientele and he is still hard at work helping others.

Let's say you've created your own product or you have the opportunity to offer somebody else's product in a mail order ad. What are some of the things you must know to protect yourself in the event you have a very big winner? I cover this in the next marketing lesson along with ways you can inexpensively protect your product and your creative efforts from being copied.

Marketing Lesson 3

Protecting Your Own Product

What if you invent a product yourself and want to market it? First, you'll want to protect it from anybody else stealing it. Contact a patent attorney, present the concept and have your attorney do a patent search to see if somebody else has already invented it. Your attorney will also check for what is called "prior art"—an invention that was patented before and either is currently valid or has expired. If there was prior art and the patent expired, then you can still make and sell a product that uses this patent but you won't be able to get protection. That's OK. A patent, in many instances, doesn't give you that much protection anyway.

Patents

There often seems to be a way to go around a patent. Even if somebody copied you exactly and you sued them, the litigation expense and the time it takes to litigate could cost you a fortune and may not be worth it in the long run. When the company that steals your idea is very big, you might think that it makes sense to pursue them with a lawsuit. Get ready for a surprise. A big company can tie you and your lawyers up in court for so long that it will drain your entire life savings. In fact, that is the common weapon of a litigious big company. They can afford the wait and the costs that you can't.

There are some attorneys who are willing to take a patent case on what is called a contingency basis. This is an arrangement made between a lawyer and client in which the lawyer's fee is based upon how much the lawyer collects from the infringer, but this arrangement is not very common in patent suits. Again, many patents don't afford the individual as much protection as you might think.

If you are a big company, on the other hand, it does pay to have a patent. First, you are big enough to protect it without going down the drain in the process, and second, if you're fighting somebody who has fewer resources or is less litigious, chances are they will capitulate and pay you for the opportunity to have you disappear from their lives.

But it is always nice to have the words "Patent Pending" or even the patent number on a product, as it gives the competition a reason to think twice before copying your product.

Non-Disclosure Agreements

If you want to present a product to a potential marketing partner or manufacturer, you should have them sign a non-disclosure agreement, whether you can get a patent or not. A typical form is included in the back of this book in Appendix B. A non-disclosure agreement basically says, "I'm going to let you in on a little secret if you promise not to copy my idea or tell anybody else about it." It's not a foolproof way to prevent somebody from stealing your idea or product, but it will make the marketer think twice about doing it. Many marketers won't sign one for fear of unwarranted litigation, so it's either show them the product and take your chances or know who you're dealing with from the start. This is good advice for doing business anyway.

I have listed other ways you can protect yourself through the U.S. government in Appendix B. Some are relatively inexpensive and definitely worthwhile, since you never know the potential value of your invention. The protection you can give it once you start in business may prove to be quite valuable in the future.

Trademarks

One of the strongest protections you can get is a trademark. Name your product, reserve the name with the Patent and Trademark Office and if you're the first out with this type of product and the name is a good one, people will identify the entire category with the name of your product. A good example is the name we gave our sunglasses—BluBlocker.

When I discovered the benefits of filtering out blue light, I came out with the BluBlocker product name. Now when people refer to the sunglasses with the orange lenses they think of us. Our name is now famous. It was the same for Kleenex, Jell-O, Xerox and dozens of other leading brand names. But there is another advantage to having a trademark registered with the U.S. government. Protection.

In my case, any company that uses the name Blue Blockers,

Blue Block or anything confusingly similar to BluBlocker is violating the trademark law, and I can take that company to court and litigate rather quickly. In some cases, the government will even seize the merchandise, brand it as counterfeit and put the counterfeiters in jail. We had one instance where goods bearing the name Blue Block were seized at the U.S. port of entry by customs officials and destroyed.

Even if we had the strongest of patents, it might take years for us to defend a patent in court. But with a trademark, you can have the weight of the entire U.S. government, customs officials and law enforcement officers on your side if somebody rips off your name. Often the offender is simply sued in a civil proceeding, but you have a lot more going for you than if you just had a patent. So give your product a great name and then blast out into the marketplace and establish that name.

We are very serious about protecting our trademark.

International Registration

Once you do have a great name for your product and see its potential as an international product, start registering the name in foreign countries as quickly as possible. We are living in a global economy and unless you protect a strong trademark throughout the free world, I can guarantee you that it will be taken by somebody else trying to copy your success.

I saw the potential with the BluBlocker brand name. I registered it in all the major countries throughout the world. I was asked by my attorney if I wanted it registered in South Africa and I declined. At the time, South Africa was going through a lot of turmoil and I didn't think I would ever market the product there. Then about three years later, an infomercial company with a South African partner wanted to run our infomerical there and was unable to because a company had stolen the exact same name and was blocking our entry into that market. You never know.

Patents vs. Trademarks

Do I own any patents? Yes. In fact, I own a number of them. Do I bother to enforce them? On only a few occasions. I often have to weigh the advantages against the disadvantages, the costs against the time required to pursue the matter and the importance of the product to my bottom line. I often pass on taking any action. On the other hand, we guard our trademarks with a vengeance. We spend thousands of dollars a year to prevent rip-off artists from stealing the goodwill created by our name. And not only must you actively protect your trademark, but to legally keep a trademark, you must defend it or the courts sometimes will not grant you continued protection.

Patents are now granted for a period of 20 years from the date the patent application is filed. When patents expire, the patents are available to everybody to copy or use. Trademarks can be first reserved and then they have to be used on a product shipped across state lines to qualify for a federal registration.

The Patent and Trademark Office publishes your trademark to see if there is any opposition to you receiving it. Maybe somebody else has been using the name you want to use but hasn't registered it yet. That's the purpose of publishing your name—to flush out any possible conflicts. If there are none, and your product has been shipped over state lines with your trademark on it, then you will receive a registration and you may start using the ® symbol along with the mark you have registered. Until then, the trademark must carry only a "TM" symbol. Even after the mark is registered, it can still carry the TM mark. And finally, once you actively use the trademark, it can be renewed every ten years for as long as you actively use it.

It costs about $1,500 for a thorough patent search, and the final patent application can cost at least $3,000 to file depending on the complexity of your invention. A trademark can be registered for about $600.

Protecting Your Trademark

There are some precautions you can take when you use a name. First, you register the primary name you want. Then you think up names that might be confused with your name but could also be registered by other companies, and you register or reserve those. This is called "name blocking." For example, I registered the name BluBlocker and used it on my infomercials to sell my sunglasses. When 50% of my friends would walk up to me and say that they saw me on TV selling "SunBlockers," instead of

BluBlocker, I realized there would be confusion if somebody registered SunBlockers and started to compete with me. So I found out that somebody had indeed registered the name Sun-Blocker after I came out with my BluBlocker name, but the person who obtained the registration had suddenly died. I bought the name from his estate.

Another good example of name blocking is the use of a phone number that spells a word, or what is commonly called a vanity phone number. AT&T was able to use the phone number 1-800 OPERATOR and urged the nation through national advertising to call that number to make collect calls. MCI realized that many of those calling AT&T would spell 'operator' wrong and reserved the number 1-800 OPERATER. Sure enough, MCI was siphoning off millions of dollars in business that AT&T was generating simply because of AT&T's failure to use the technique of name blocking.

You also make sure that your organization uses the name properly. Misuse could cause a company to lose its registration. For example, I once did consulting work for Xerox Corporation. They made it very clear that if I used the name Xerox as a verb, as in "I need to xerox a sheet of paper," this would be improper use. Companies have lost their trademark rights when the public no longer perceives the trademark as a trademark. Good examples are the words 'vitamin', 'aspirin' and 'linoleum'. These were once trademarks but the companies that owned them lost their rights.

I once did a promotion with Coca-Cola in which I was required to use their trademark in a promotional piece. Once they signed the agreement, they handed me a sheet of paper with the restrictions I was under in using their mark. This was a two-page document with very strict rules. But at the end, they summarized the document and simply said:

"'Coca-Cola' and 'Coke' must be used only as the brand names for the product of the Coca-Cola Company. Never can their use be condoned to convey any other idea and never can they

When you use "Xerox" the way you use "aspirin," we get a headache.

X Boy, what a headache! And all because some of you may be using our name in a generic manner. Which could cause it to lose its trademark status the way the name "aspirin" did years ago. So when you do use our name, please use it as an adjective to identify our products and services, e.g., Xerox copiers. Never as a verb: "to Xerox" in place of "to copy", or as a noun: "Xeroxes" in place of "copies". Thank you. Now, could you excuse us, we've got to lie down for a few minutes.

THE DOCUMENT COMPANY
XEROX

XEROX,® The Document Company,® and the stylized X are trademarks of XEROX CORPORATION. 56 USC 580.

Some corporations are very serious about their trademarks. Here's a full-page ad from Writer's Digest.

be displayed in a way which would permit the public to read into them any other meaning."

All major corporations are very serious about their trademarks and protect them vigorously. You should too if you own one.

My Patent Story

I mentioned earlier that I had several patents. The first patent I owned was for a grounding system for the ion generator which I referred to in Marketing Lesson 1. The story is worth telling because it is both entertaining and a really interesting lesson proving the point that anything can go wrong.

There is a classic movie called *The Producers* with Zero Mostel that was popular some years ago. It was about a con artist who figured out that if he produced a Broadway play, promising 50% of the profits to each of a dozen investors (giving away more than 100%) and the play failed, his investors would be out their money and he could pocket the extra investments and nobody would be the wiser. All Zero Mostel's character had to do was to make sure he put on a play that would fail.

So he did everything he could to make sure it would bomb. He called it "Springtime for Hitler," hired the worst actors and, in short, produced the worst play in the history of Broadway. But something went wrong. The play was so different that it opened to rave reviews, became a huge success and Mostel's character was in serious trouble because now he had to pay many times his profits with dozens of people who each expected to receive half of the profits. In short, Mostel's character was hoping for a failure to accomplish a goal and ended up with a huge success.

A Parallel Experience

The Producers comes to mind when I think about the time when I once hoped for failure. My good friend and patent attorney, George Gerstman, was taking a bike ride with me one Sunday afternoon. We'd often ride out into the woods and discuss various legal issues or even some of the unusual cases in which I was involved.

But this one day, George was particularly excited. "Joe, I've just heard of a tax loophole that might benefit you. You simply invent a product, sell it to your company and the proceeds that you receive from your company are taxed as capital gains."

"Hmm," I said. "What's the catch?"

George replied, "There is no catch. Well, maybe one small one. But it's not one you'll have to worry about. Your patent claims cannot be approved for at least a year."

But I had questions. "What if the claims are allowed within a year?"

"Don't worry," said George, who himself was a former U.S. patent examiner. "First, the patents I deal with sometimes take over a year just to get a response. And then when we do get a response, there are typically at least some claims that are rejected."

I indeed had invented something recently. It was a filter system for the ion generator. The first models generated negatively charged ions which attached themselves to pollutants and then the pollutants would attach themselves to the closest solid surface that was grounded—sometimes a wall or desk lamp or some nearby object—leaving black stains. My invention created a grounded filter system that attracted the particles, thereby avoiding damage to walls or nearby objects.

Patent Submitted

George worked on the patent and submitted it to the U.S. Patent Office. It was all-encompassing and had such broad claims that it prompted George to say to me, "Joe, if this is eventually approved by the Patent Office, you'll own the entire ion generator market. I've made this broad as hell."

Normally patents take almost a year before the patent examiner sends a "first action," which ordinarily requires modifications or corrections. But only nine months later, George was sitting in his office when his secretary walked up to him and said, "Mr. Gerstman, congratulations. You've got a 'first-action notice of allowance' made of all the claims."

George smiled and turned to his secretary. "You're kidding? That's incredible. A 'first-action notice of allowance'! This is wonderful. Whose patent is it?"

"Mr. Sugarman's," was the reply.

"What? Sugarman's patent? Oh no. That's terrible." George had switched from the happiest and most amazed patent attorney on Chicago's LaSalle Street to the most disappointed. You should have seen the confused look on his secretary's face.

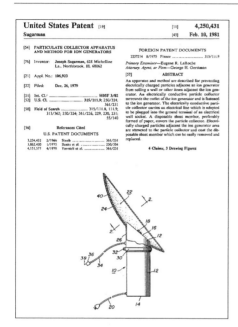

This is the patent I received for my invention. I now controlled the category.

I Now Had a Monopoly

But I now had a monopoly on the entire ion generator filtration market. I owned such a broad patent that nobody could compete with me. I was king of the ion generators. And I was out the cost of the patent and any hope of saving taxes on my invention. The IRS has since eliminated the loophole. And within about five years, I had several infringers—smaller competitors who were adding filters to their ion generators. Was I upset? Not really. Look at all the help my patent was providing others, and besides, for me to fight these infringers would be a total waste of my time and money. It was my first invention and there were more to come after that. But it was the one I remember the best.

Copyright Protection

There is another protection you can get and that is from the copyright laws. Simply putting a copyright notice at the end of your ad will afford you some protection against anybody copying the ad copy.

I've had several instances where competitors used my copy with some slight modifications to sell their products. Simply by having a copyright notice on my ad gave me a very solid case when I needed to file a lawsuit. All you need to do is put a small ©, the year, and your name or the name of your company at the very bottom right portion of your ad. For example: © 1998, by Joseph Sugarman. You don't need to file anything with the Copyright Office as you can do that later, or never for that matter. But if somebody copies you, you file the papers with the Copyright Office and then have legal protection for a period of 75 years from the date of the copyright.

In Marketing Lessons 1-3 we've discussed some valuable knowledge on products. In Marketing Lesson 1, you learned that so many factors are involved in finding just the right product that even the most successful people who select products cannot predict a product's popularity. You only know for sure after it's presented to the public when the public responds by exchanging their hard-earned dollars for the product you are offering. And you've examined the product life cycle from the "period of languish" to the "period of decay." You looked at the life cycle of the ion generator and saw how it was discovered and launched. You read of different ways products are found. In Marketing Lesson 3, you got a good perspective on patents and trademarks as we discussed how to protect your product.

Now let us say you have found a great product, come up with a great name, protected the name by registering it with the U.S. Patent and Trademark Office and have even written a great ad and plan to protect it by placing a copyright notice at the bottom of the ad when you make your final layout. The next step is to make a layout to best showcase your product and provide the best environment for its sale.

In Marketing Lesson 4 we cover just that. I will show you how simple changes will enhance comprehension and response, how your layout should flow and what type font you should select for your ad. I wish I knew early in my career what I'm going to teach you in that lesson.

But first it is time for a marketing story. The story is about something I did that started a major direct marketing trend that has made shopping by mail very convenient. And it all happened quite innocently as you will soon read.

A Marketing Story

The Origins of Toll-Free Order Taking

This was the first mail order ad to use the phone company's new toll-free number.

This is the story of a defining moment in the history of my company—a moment of time that also changed the course of history in the whole direct response industry. Before I get into the story itself, a little background.

When I first started selling pocket calculators in 1971, occasionally I would get a call from a business executive or consumer giving me a sob story about how he or she needed a pocket calculator either in time for Christmas or for an important meeting or some other upcoming event.

They would explain that they didn't have time to send in the order form with their credit card number and signature to meet the deadline. This was before the popularity of the toll-free number and before credit card order taking by telephone even existed. There was no way you could order by phone without first sending in a check or mailing in your credit card information on a coupon with your signature.

The stories I would get on the phone were either intimidating or, on occasion, genuinely moving and I would frequently make an exception and accept the order on the phone and simply mark "Mail Order" in the signature panel of the credit card voucher when I submitted it to the credit card processing bank.

Our credit card processing bank never minded or even noticed and the customers all paid their credit card bills on time. There was never a problem. Not even one.

As the months went by, I started accepting more of these orders. In fact, one customer made a practice of it. I would frequently get a call from him and he would simply say, "I need another calculator, so charge it to my Visa card." It was a quick and easy way to handle an order and the customer one day told me that using the telephone was actually a lot easier than going shopping.

Advent of the Toll-Free Order-Taking Number

In the fall of 1973, after almost two years of accepting phone orders, I heard about the advent of the toll-free number. AT&T was running an advertising campaign about the advantages of having a number that people could call for free. Free customer service was their big push.

I saw a little more in the concept. Why not make a toll-free number available to the public to order calculators with their credit card? I had never had problems before accepting credit card orders over our regular line. Why not offer customers an easier way to order?

It was September of 1973 to be exact. I was operating out of the basement in my home in Northbrook, Illinois. My business was flourishing—the same business I had started in order to offer the first pocket calculator. My basement already held three employees and, on occasion, temporary help whenever I received a huge response.

Toll-Free Line Installed

The telephone company came and installed the toll-free line. I was all set and ready to advertise. But I didn't want to make a big deal out of the toll-free order line in my advertising because I was concerned, quite frankly, that people would recognize this as an easy way to rip me off. Dishonest consumers could give me fraudulent credit card numbers and I could be left holding the bag for a lot of bad orders. I was indeed exploring new ground. By blatantly advertising toll-free order taking, there were also questions. Would the credit card companies object? Would the customers rip me off, leaving me with a major loss? I didn't know.

And then there was the matter of how much response I would get. Would the enhanced response be sufficient to justify the cost of the toll-free line and the possible loss I might sustain from customers trying to rip me off? These were my concerns back then just before I ran my first ad.

I decided to run a new ad for a new version of the pocket calculator as a test in the Southwestern edition of *The Wall Street*

Journal and test both the calculator I was offering and my new toll-free concept.

Prior to this time, I would place a test ad, wait a week, start counting the mail-in responses and if everything worked out well, a few weeks later place the ad in the other editions of *The Wall Street Journal*, the only publication I was advertising in at the time. This entire process took over a month by the time I eventually advertised in the other editions of the *Journal* and received the response.

One full month was a long time. Calculator prices were continually dropping and a product that was hot one week could be cold the following as a result of the introduction of a new model. It was critical to get an ad into a publication, get the response and then either sell out or stop selling that model before it became obsolete.

That first ad with a toll-free number was placed and the next day we would find out if my idea worked.

Our small staff arrived early that morning. Mary Stanke and Mary Ann Haire—both having been with me for two years—came into the office prepared with order forms and pens to take the phone orders if they came in.

The Orders Pour In

From the moment they walked into the basement until late that day, the orders poured in. One right after another. Lunch had to be brought down to the basement as there was literally no time for a break. Whereas it normally took over a week to break even from an average print ad, we had broken even and were earning a wonderful profit by that afternoon.

The toll-free number had so enhanced response that it had taken what traditionally would have been just an average product and made it a major hit. And the speed of the response gave me my answers right away. After my test ad, instead of waiting a few weeks to get the final results and then waiting a few weeks before I could roll out in all the editions of the *Journal*, I could reduce my time from first test ad to final rollout to only ten days.

All day long that first day, I kept shaking my head in disbelief. Was this really happening? Could I have discovered a major breakthrough in direct response advertising? And finally, would

The response was quick and heavy.

I get ripped off like crazy? It didn't matter.

I figured that the response was so great that even if I was ripped off, the success of the promotion would more than cover the losses. But I still didn't want to make too big a deal out of my use of the toll-free number, so I kept it rather small at the bottom of the ad near the coupon. More like the "P.S." in a letter.

The next time I ran that same ad was in the Midwestern edition of *The Wall Street Journal*. I didn't want to go into the full run as I would be too swamped and couldn't handle the response. Besides, maybe the response was a fluke. I expanded cautiously. The concept indeed worked again and we were literally buried with phone calls and orders. I also noticed that our mail-in response dropped but it was still strong. In short, there were many people who were accustomed to mailing in a coupon and so they continued to do just that.

No Problems Experienced

By the end of the promotion, we waited to see how many rip-offs we would get and we got none. We waited to see if our bank would complain and we got no complaints. We measured the response against anything we had done before, and this promotion was one of our most successful—far exceeding anything earlier except for our first pocket calculator. We had indeed discovered a major breakthrough. But how long would it take before one of my many competitors caught on?

I tried the toll-free number in later ads and all of them worked. Our business, because of the toll-free number, was now expanding rapidly. No longer could Mary Stanke and Mary Ann Haire handle the response. We needed more phone lines, which meant more people, which also meant more cars parked in front of the house and possibly complaints from the neighbors. I don't blame them. My neighborhood wasn't zoned for business and the front of my house was already looking much like a parking lot.

So I expanded by renting retail space only a few blocks from my home at a busy intersection. Not only would I have more space but I could handle any retail traffic that might come from the advertising response. And there was always a lot of response—a steady flow of cars pulling up. People couldn't believe that the business they had envisioned as a very large one was operating out of a suburban home in the middle of Northbrook, Illinois, and later out of a small 1,000-square-foot store.

None of My Fears Materialized

After about six months of running ads with toll-free numbers I made several observations. The number of people who tried to rip us off was practically zero. The increase in sales was incredible and none of my fears of what might or might not happen with the banks handling the credit card transactions materialized.

Your sales budget too small to reach across the U.S.?

WATS changed all that for JS&A National Sales Group

Joe Sugarman's company was selling mini-calculators. Then Joe wrote some hard-sell ads and got an 800 number customers could call for more information or to place an instant order. Things began to happen fast and soon Joe was running his ads in the *Wall Street Journal, Playboy* and *Time,* always including the 800 number. Sales quadrupled! Joe got so many calls, he had to add 15 operators to handle the business. WATS can change things for you, too. But first, you need to tell our WATS expert what needs changing. For more information and literature, call toll free 800-821-2980. In Missouri, call 800-892-2217.

WIDE AREA TELECOMMUNICATIONS SERVICE

WATS can change all that.

The Bell system ran this national ad promoting its toll-free service and JS&A's success.

In fact, we started to get positive recognition for what we were doing. AT&T used our company as one of its success stories and featured us in *The Wall Street Journal* and other national publications as an example of how business could boom with their new service.

But I also noticed something very interesting. Nobody was copying me. Not yet. Nobody else was using a toll-free number in any of their ads.

My Competitor Calls

One day I got a call from Mervin (not his real name), one of my knockoff competitors who always seemed to be copying my latest approach or my last copy line. But I was on friendly terms with him and I would, on occasion, take his calls and discuss the state of the industry, making sure that I didn't divulge any trade secrets. I'm sure finding out information from me was always one of his goals in our conversations, although I never gave him anything of value (nor did I ever lie to him).

The call I got from him that day was typical. He was hinting at the fact that he had been seeing our ads with toll-free numbers and was wondering if we were being successful with them. He commented, "I bet you get ripped off a lot?"

I paused for a moment and said, "Mervin, I've never lied to you, right?"

Mervin paused for a moment and said, "No, you haven't." And indeed, I never had, even though he was one of those competitors whose copying I had to put up with. And I wasn't going to lie to him this day either. But I certainly didn't want him to copy the most successful idea I had ever used in any of my direct response advertising.

"Well, Mervin, let me give you some advice—from competitor to competitor. Don't use a toll-free number in any of your ads. I'm serious. Don't use a toll-free number in any of your ads."

Mervin thanked me. "Joe, that's what I thought. I appreciate your openness and candor."

And with that Mervin quickly hung up. He had gotten my truthful answer, which he interpreted exactly the way he wanted to interpret it. He didn't have the smarts or enough guts to give a toll-free number a test and I confirmed his anxiety. Incidentally, he finally caught on after six more months of our advertising the toll-free number, which launched an entire revolution in the direct response industry, making catalogs easier to buy from and print ads more responsive.

A New Industry Is Created

In fact, the impact of the toll-free number went beyond just its use in advertising. As more and more catalogs jumped on the bandwagon and as more and more print ads were carrying these toll-free numbers, companies were formed whose primary business was to do nothing but take these phone orders.

Pretty soon a major new industry of toll-free order taking was started in Omaha, Nebraska, and it remains a major industry there today. In the early stages of the toll-free number, you couldn't have one toll-free number that worked nationally. In your home state, you needed a separate toll-free number. And since this was really confusing in an ad, many companies appreciated the fact that they could have an order-taking service in a less populous state like Nebraska taking their orders. Also, Omaha operators had a pleasant and neutral midwestern speech pattern.

Eventually the separate numbers for states were eliminated and only one number was needed. And finally the phone companies allowed the use of vanity 800 numbers which had not been allowed before. In fact, JS&A owned the number 1-800-GADGETS.

Catalog Industry Takes Off

Soon TV offers carried toll-free numbers and both the catalog and the TV direct response industries took off like a rocket. The convenience of shopping by phone and the ease of buying by mail were indeed the wave of the future. Order-taking services soon became very sophisticated by entering orders directly on computer and then transferring those orders by modem to computers located at their clients' offices, allowing clients to have instant access to these orders. Everything became paperless.

The industry grew and continues to grow with order-taking services that now specialize in TV offers, catalogs and miscellaneous direct response programs. And it all started from a simple gamble that even my closest competitors were at first reluctant to try for almost a year.

This was the origin of toll-free order taking. You will see in a later marketing story in Section Two how the toll-free number grew from being my little secret to permitting me to expand my business dramatically through the sale of one single product— a pocket calculator called the DataKing 800.

It would seem logical that if you publish an advertisement —any advertisement—you want it to be read and comprehended by as many people as possible. And if there were rules you could follow that would allow you to produce advertising that received high comprehension scores, you certainly would follow those rules. But what are those rules? And what happens when you don't follow them? Find out in Marketing Lesson 4.

Marketing Lesson 4

The Role of Typography and Layout

Type can come in thousands of different faces, but there is one face you'll want to use after reading this chapter.

Let us say you now have an incredible product and you are ready to advertise it. I am assuming that you are already skilled in copywriting and can write a great ad. Your next step is creating a layout and selecting a typeface for your ad. So let's start with a short discussion about typography.

Thousands of Typefaces, Thousands of Personalities

There are thousands of typefaces that exist to express the written word. And just as we all have different personalities, so does type. Type can be very bold and heavy or very light and airy. Type can be very graceful, complex and even dull. But regardless of the typeface's personality, the type has to be read and comprehended.

We all know how important it is to have what you've written read by your prospect. It's the most important purpose of any written communication that you create. But even if your prospect reads all your copy, there is one more factor that has to be taken into account and that's comprehension.

Let's use a little logic and a good example to illustrate what I've just pointed out. If you attract 1 million people who start reading your ad and you end up with only 320,000 people who comprehend it because you used the wrong typeface, then you're making a big mistake—something that would be easy to correct if you knew the right typeface to use. I'm therefore going to show you the best typeface and best layout to use and then I'll discuss what happens when you vary from these proven parameters.

A research scientist in the mid '80s had looked for published studies on the comprehension of typography and the effect various layout elements had on a reader. He searched in vain as there was nothing available.

So he conducted his own research over two years using scientific research principles. The first test examined the difference between serif and sans serif type. A serif typeface has thick-and-thin lettering with small curlicues on the tips of many letters and is the most commonly used typeface in books and written text. This book for example is set in a serif typeface. A sans serif typeface has letters of uniform thickness without the small curlicues ('sans' meaning 'without' in French) and is often used for headlines. An example of both typefaces is shown below:

This is a serif typeface.

This is a sans serif typeface.

The research results showed that if 1 million people saw ad copy set in a serif typeface, the message would be comprehended by approximately 670,000 readers. If the ad copy was set in a sans serif typeface, the comprehension dropped to 120,000 readers—a dramatic difference caused only by a change of typeface.

This research was given to me by one of my former seminar participants from Australia. At my seminar we had people from all over the world and many times they would give me reports and research from faraway sources to present to my students. The irony is that for years I had been using sans serif type for all of my body typeface. The reason was to give my ads a little different look than the typical advertising message. The minute I found out the difference in comprehension levels, I switched to a serif type, although I've got to admit that I've never tested this myself to see how sales are affected. But the comprehension scores were enough to convince me to switch. That was in 1987 and I've never gone back to using my old typeface.

The Best Layout for Comprehension

Now let's talk about layout. If we take a typical layout format with the picture at the top and a headline in the middle and the copy below it (Ad A) and then we compare comprehension scores with an ad having the headline in the middle of the copy (Ad B), the comprehension scores for 1 million readers show a dramatic drop from Ad A to Ad B, even if both ads use serif type. The difference is that 670,000 readers will comprehend Ad A and only 320,000 people will comprehend Ad B.

*The conventional
layout (Ad A)*

*A nonstandard
layout (Ad B)*

Which ad will be easier to comprehend?

The explanation for this dramatic drop in comprehension is as follows: We're taught to read from left to right, starting at the top left corner of the material and continuing until we reach the bottom right corner. The eyes gravitate naturally to the top left corner, which is called the "primary optical area." Then the eyes move across and down the page obeying "reading gravity."

The eye does not willingly go against reading gravity, with one exception—reading a line of type to the right and returning to the left again to begin the next line. Any variation from this pattern causes an interruption to reading rhythm. The point to which the eye returns is called the "axis of orientation." If this axis is altered by typographic means, the eye is likely to rebel and cause the reader to stop reading.

Reading Theory 1: Any layout design which forces the reader to work against reading gravity or fails to return the reader to a logical axis of orientation tends to destroy reading rhythm and should be avoided.

Now let us take this a step further and add a new element to the ad—a hot red color. The introduction of color attracts the eye and increases our readership from 1 million to 1.6 million, but the use of color works against comprehension to such a degree that the potential army of readers who receive the message clearly is reduced to only 272,000—a dramatic drop from the 670,000 who comprehended the ad without the color. This brings me to my next theory:

Reading Theory 2: Certain typographic elements impede readability by throwing unnecessary distractions into the reader's path, thereby interrupting the reading rhythm.

Very often legibility is not as important to an ad agency as an exciting layout and a dynamic product illustration. However, a layout design that is exciting but incomprehensible is nothing

69

more than a beautifully painted square peg trying to fit into a round hole.

Reading Theory 3: Typography fails if it allows the reader's interest to decline; it fails absolutely if it contributes to the destruction of the reader's interest.

Any design that comes between the copywriter and reader is wrong, but the trick is to discover what elements come between the two. Reading is a skill which is slowly losing out to television and the Internet. Even skilled readers have a limited time each day for reading, so it is essential that typography waste none of this valuable time and none of the energy and concentration required for the reading process.

The Final Conclusions of the Research

So what are some of the conclusions of all this research? The following are the very basic conclusions regarding typography and layout as they relate to reading comprehension:

1. Use serif type for copy. Serif type beats sans serif type by a factor of 5 to 1. Need more be said?

2. Always use a black headline. Solid black headlines are five times more powerful than headlines using a very bright color.

3. Justify your lines of type. A totally justified column of type is twice as effective as a column with a ragged-right setting and seven times more effective than a ragged-left setting.

4. Use serif type for long headlines and sans serif type for short headlines. For headlines, plain serif type is more effective than sans serif type, but not by that much.

5. Use a roman typeface over italic. The singular use of italic type has about the same comprehension scores as the singular use of standard (or what is commonly called roman) type. It doesn't much matter whether you use italics or roman, but if there is a choice, I would go for the more common roman type.

6. Use a standard layout. Layouts that comply with the principles of reading gravity are at least twice as effective as layouts that interfere with reading gravity. So keep to that standard layout even if it seems boring.

> JS&A also saved on the processing of orders. With all orders accumulated, processed, and shipped in one batch, the processing costs were reduced. By insisting on checks with orders, we also saved on credit card charges. We were literally able to sell calculators with a one dollar mark-up and make a profit.
>
> So it all added up to tremendous savings, lots of fun, and another example of the creative marketing approach that has made JS&A America's largest single source of electronic calculators and other space-age products.

The widow is the only word in the last line of a paragraph. Your goal is to get rid of it. The edited version is shown below.

> JS&A also saved on order processing. With all orders accumulated, processed, and shipped in one batch, the processing costs were reduced. By insisting on checks, we also saved on credit card charges. We were literally able to sell calculators with a one dollar mark-up and make a profit.
>
> So it all added up to great savings, lots of fun, and another example of the creative marketing approach that has made JS&A America's largest single source of electronic calculators and space-age products.

The Lonely Widow

There is one last point to make about type. Very often space is at a premium when you set type for an ad. Each word is important and the more words you can fit into a column, the better.

Very often at the end of a paragraph there is a single word left over, the only word on that line. That word in typographic parlance is called a "widow." Very often by changing or dropping a word or two earlier in the paragraph, you can eliminate the widow and thereby have more space for other lines of type in your ad. Getting rid of just four widows will gain you four more lines and give you room for an additional paragraph.

There is one aspect of typography and layout that has really changed thanks to today's powerful computers. When I started setting type, I used a phototypesetter and then later graduated to a computerized typesetting system that cost over $30,000. But I still had to paste up the typeset copy that the computer generated. Today, even the average personal computer has the capacity to not only set type but do entire layouts. No art boards are required and often all you need to do is hand a computer disk to a printer.

If you do not have experience with type and layout, go to a graphic designer who does. But insist on a layout and the typeface that you know works most effectively as described in this chapter.

So now you have a great layout that follows reading gravity. You have selected a beautifully clear and easy-to-read serif typeface for your body copy and you have eliminated any widows you had left over after you set the type. Our next marketing lesson will examine the subject of photography.

But before we get to that, let me pose an interesting premise. I create a great ad. I am going to use that ad to effect tremendous political awareness throughout the world. I have a supplier ready to supply me with a product around which I can advertise and bring this awareness to the country. But something goes awry. Read about it in the next marketing story called "The Ad That Never Happened."

A Marketing Story

The Ad That Never Happened

RUSSIA STINKS

I was really sick to my stomach over the Korean 747 massacre. But here's what I'm doing about it.

By Joseph Sugarman, President JS&A Group, Inc.

I was damn mad. Like many Americans I wanted our government to take swift positive action to punish the Soviets for the slaughter of 269 innocent people. Instead, all I heard were words.

What you are about to read may seem incredible but it will give you a very positive way to punish Russia directly without going through our government.

The story starts out a few years ago when a well-known American publisher released a book on Russia written by an American. CBS was so impressed with the book that they bought the rights and produced a movie which was aired nationally in May of 1982.

When the book was released, it became a best seller, it got rave reviews and had the potential of reaching the top of the *New York Times* Best Seller List. In fact, the *Cleveland Press* called it "The fastest selling book ever." Then something strange happened. Books were mysteriously disappearing from bookstore shelves and in place of the book appeared a collection of public statements by Brezhnev—a book from the same publisher. Then the plot gets even thicker.

The author started getting strange calls from Russians—veiled threats against his family.

A reporter investigating the case has been unable to get a response from the publisher.

The KGB and the Russian government, it seems, were so strong in the United States that they were able to suppress a best selling book, get their propaganda distributed in place of the book and weave a strange web of circumstance that to this day still remains a mystery.

The book they tried to suppress was the incredible story of an American trapped in Russia for 45 years and his eventual escape. It reveals the brutality of the Russians, their thinking and as the *American Book Review* stated, "It's the story of cultural mutation of the weirdest kind and most frightening order. An unbelievable true story."

The *Wall Street Journal* stated, "Americans must read this remarkable book." The *Chicago Tribune* called it, "More powerful than Solzhenitsyn." And the *Houston Post* exclaimed, "Chilling and revealing. It happened to an American."

The story behind this book came to me the very day the Korean Airliner was shot down. The author had managed to get his book released from his former publisher and wanted to offer it again to the public.

If this book can indeed become a best seller, it will do more damage to the Soviets than those weak threats made by Washington. It will do more to anger the Soviets, and at the same time, awaken Americans to what is the real Russian menace.

Our company will offer this book for sale nationally. All proceeds will go towards additional advertising until it becomes a best seller despite the Russians and regardless of the cost. Every penny made on this book will go back into more advertising so this ad will appear in more newspapers and magazines so we can distribute more books. And, if there are any profits left, they will all go towards a worthwhile cause—the families of the victims.

If this "Russia Stinks" ad reaches over 100 million people and we sell a million books, we will have done more to punish the Russians than anything our government has said and done. Plus, Americans will discover the incredible facts about a foreign power which can censor a book right here in America.

Join me in this cause. Send $14.95 plus $2.00 for delivery or credit card holders call our toll free number 800 323-6400 and I'll send this book by return mail.

The book is entitled "Coming Out Of The Ice," by Victor Herman. I guarantee you'll quickly realize why the Soviets want this book suppressed and why it got such rave reviews or I'll refund your money in full. Help us strike back. Order a copy today.

JS&A

One JS&A Plaza, Dept 123
Northbrook, Illinois 60062
Il. residents add 6% sales tax. ©JS&A Group, Inc. 1982

It was a bold and brazen move by a small American mail order company to attack the Soviet Union. But the publications didn't cooperate.

Some ads are so powerful that they cause a major shift in consciousness. And it is with this idea in mind that I created this ad. I was hoping, through the power of my pen, to make America aware of the atrocities that had been perpetrated by the Russians not only against an indefensible airliner but against a major American author.

In 1983 the Russians shot down a Korean Airlines 747 jet over the ocean on a flight to Korea, claiming self-defense. America expressed outrage. All 240 passengers and a crew of 29 on board Flight 007 were killed including a U.S. congressman. But America wasn't doing anything about it.

This story starts out on the very same day as the plane was shot down. I was approached by the author of a book entitled *Coming Out of the Ice*. The book was apparently at one time about to become a national best-seller. CBS bought the rights to the book and did a documentary on it and rave reviews were written in hundreds of newspapers throughout the country including *The Wall Street Journal,* the *Chicago Tribune* and the *Cleveland Press*.

The book was written by an American, Victor Herman, who was arrested and sent to Russian prisons to experience the greatest humiliation any American has ever had to endure, and he lived to tell about it. Victor Herman's book told the story of how he was captured, his experience in Russian prisons and how he escaped—a tale of endurance and adventure.

But suddenly something strange happened. The publisher pulled this best-selling book from the bookshelves and replaced it with a book of public statements by Leonid Brezhnev, the former Russian premier. And Herman started getting phone calls threatening him with death if he dared do anything more with his book.

In my ad copy describing the book and the action taken by the publisher, I wrote:

> The KGB and the Russian government, it seems, were so strong in the United States that they were able to suppress a best-selling book, get their propaganda distributed in place of the book and weave a strange web of circumstance that to this day still remains a mystery.

I decided to use the downing of the 747 as the news event to trigger American awareness of what was going on right here in the United States with this repressed book that the Russians did not want distributed. And I offered to take every penny of profit generated by the sale of the book and turn it back into the advertising of the book until at least 100 million people read my ad about what Russia did to this American author.

Wrote Powerful Headline

I wrote the ad and used a very powerful headline. Anyone leafing through a magazine with this ad couldn't miss the headline, "Russia Stinks." And the ad captured the feelings of many Americans. They had had it with the Russians and this would be a well-received poke at the Soviets.

I decided to take a major gamble and send the ad without testing it to *Time* magazine to run for immediate national exposure. I had a proof made of the ad and sent it to *Time* for their approval.

The ad was rejected. *Time* magazine refused to run it. It was too controversial and did not fit the format of their magazine.

I was shocked. I sent the ad to a few other periodicals including *The Wall Street Journal*. It was refused by all these publications too.

By this time, the publicity surrounding the 747 airliner disaster had cooled down. I was also told that there might be a hang-up in getting books to fill the orders. "Hmm," I thought, "could it be the KGB interfering?"

And finally, I was told rather clearly that I could not use that headline. Maybe something a little less bold and definitely not as controversial.

I decided to scrap the project. I no longer had the desire to fight the publishers of these magazines, nor was I willing to change the headline to something bland. And besides, the heat of the controversy had pretty well subsided. And then what about my family and the KGB? I didn't mind sticking my neck out, but I didn't even have the support of my book suppliers in this venture.

It Never Ran in Any Magazine

The ad never ran in any magazine or newspaper, and as far as I know the book never again was sold in a bookstore. The lesson learned here is that there are times when indeed things don't work out and events happen that you least expect. I least expected to be rejected by *Time* magazine and all the rest of the publications. And I certainly didn't expect the book to suddenly be in short supply when I had been told there were tons of them available.

But maybe it was the KGB at work. And maybe they would have gone after me had I run my ad. I really don't know as this is all speculation. I tied into a current event to get my marketing angle and I created a tremendous amount of curiosity in the ad with a very bold headline and compelling copy. But it never ran and I'll never know if it would have worked.

It's now time to delve into the next step in the creative process, which is either drawing sketches for your layout or employing what most products require—photography. In the next marketing lesson, I provide you with an in-depth discussion about photography, its inherent drama and its value.

Marketing Lesson 5

The Value of Photography

The saying that a picture is worth a thousand words is often true. And you might think that in a print ad a good photograph is a critical element in selling your product or service. It is, to some extent. But in this lesson, I want to put into perspective the relative value of a photograph in the entire scheme of your ad campaign.

You must look at whatever it takes to tell the full story of your product. When you need a photograph to help tell the full story, you use one; if not, you don't. But you still must keep in mind the *main* purpose of any photograph—to get your prospect to read the copy, and in particular, the first sentence. "What?" you might be thinking. "This guy Sugarman must have gone off the deep end. Without a picture, how can you sell a product?" Let me answer that.

A Picture in Perspective

Let me explain my theory of the importance of pictures relative to other elements in an ad by using an analogy of test scores where 100% is a perfect success.

With selling in print, you don't get a passing score with an 80% or even a 90% score. You've got to have a 99% score or you won't be very successful. And let us say that the product itself represents about 80% of that score. The copy probably represents anywhere from 15% to 19%, so you can see how important copy is relative to any other element.

But let us say that the copy represents only 15%. What elements constitute the remaining 5%? They are the visual elements such as the layout, headline, typeface, order vehicle, logo and of course photography. If you divide all these elements into the remaining 5%, you can then see, based on my approach, that photography is not as critical as you might have thought.

I've proven this throughout my own career. It all started when I ran my very first ad. It was on the world's first pocket calculator and appeared on the back page of *The Wall Street Journal*.

The truth about pocket calculators.

The ad contained 3,000 words, had no order form or toll-free number and didn't offer a single product for sale.

SUPER SALE!

This was the smaller mail order ad buried inside the Journal. *The response overwhelmed us.*

I deduced that the back page was probably one of the most read and that if my ad appeared there, I might get pretty good response.

The ad did very well. But I got a call from my sales rep at the *Journal* who told me that I couldn't run the ad again on the back page because the *Journal* did not want to run mail order ads on that page. Their rule was, "no ads with mail order coupons on the back page."

Sounded pretty silly to me, but I'm not one to challenge their rules. So in the next ad that I ran on the back page, called "The truth about pocket calculators," I used only type. It was a whopping 3,000-word ad. There was no photo, no coupon, no order vehicle and not even a hint of readers being able to order anything through the mail. I simply put one line at the very end of the ad that said, "See our calculator ad in today's issue."

Of course the ad inside the paper was our standard mail order ad complete with photos and everything else you normally put in an ad. And it drew such a strong response that it buried us. It was probably the first ad I ran where the mail came in sacks.

Once again, I got a call from my *Journal* sales rep. "I'm sorry, Joe, but you won't be able to run that ad again. The *Journal*'s policy now is, 'no ads on the back page that aren't mail order ads but that refer to other ads on the inside of the paper that are mail order ads.'"

Yep, you read it correctly. Later that same year I ran another ad on the back of the *Journal* with only type called "The Future of the Pocket Calculator." There was no coupon, no reference to any ad on the inside of the *Journal,* just a mention at the bottom of the ad that to order the calculator I was describing, you had to simply send a check to our address. Somehow the ad squeaked through.

My prospects had to read the copy, trust me and order my calculator without knowing the brand name or even what it looked like. The ads without photos in *The Wall Street Journal* brought some of the most successful responses I've ever had. And I've run other successful ads without photos as well.

Important but Not That Important

I proved very early in my career that while a photograph can be important, it is but a very small part of the overall reason for the success of an ad. There are some cases where the photograph is critical in telling the story, but other cases where it is not. And when I was pushed to become innovative to get an ad on the back page of the *Journal*, I broke a few advertising rules and proved that you don't need a photograph under certain circumstances.

Now that I've minimized the value of a photograph relative to other elements, let me do the opposite and focus on how a photograph can sometimes be one of the most important elements in an ad. Let's take the example of the jogging computer ad.

The Jogging Computer Episode

This story is about a product called the JS&A Jogging Computer. One of my contacts in Japan was a Japanese gentleman called Kay Eguchi. When he was adopting his American name, somebody forgot to tell him that Kay was a woman's name. But it was too late and he kept the name for his entire career. Kay was a fan of mine. He loved to tell his friends in Japan how successful our promotions were and how we just ran one ad and if it worked, we ran it throughout the U.S. in hundreds of publications.

One of his contacts was a very high-level executive at the parent company of Panasonic in Japan called Matsushita. Panasonic had developed a computerized jogging system that was very unusual. It consisted of a platform on which you ran in place. In front of the platform, in a separate unit, was a long thin device that had a digital readout. As you ran in place on the platform, the computer sensed each step and the step registered on the digital display. It also had a pacing mode so that the unit clicked off a cadence allowing you to jog at a particular speed.

A Fad in Japan

It seemed like a pretty dumb product to me. But in Japan it was the current fad and selling like crazy. Kay had recommended

JS&A as the premiere company to introduce the product in the U.S. Panasonic in the U.S. had turned it down as they felt it was really out of their typical line of product categories, so I had a wonderful opportunity to run it on my own as an exclusive product for JS&A.

I looked at the product and realized that it would seem rather dumb showing somebody running in place on this stupid platform. First, the size of the unit was relatively small, and second, the product really looked very stylish on its own. Showing somebody on it would only diminish the effect of the sexy part of the unit, which was its good looks.

So I had a photograph taken of only the unit itself, making the product the star of the ad. The jogging computer looked very impressive, so my approach seemed the right way to go. I then described the product and its use in the ad, letting my prospects use their imaginations to understand how it worked and even how it would look in their homes or offices. I accurately gave the dimensions of the product and described it very clearly and dramatized it through the use of a very exciting and striking photograph that filled up the remaining space of the ad.

The ad ran and was a moderate success. We placed it in a number of publications throughout the United States, sold our inventory and had to reorder the item several times. But our Japanese partners were restless. They wondered why we had not sold much more. They called for a meeting.

Panasonic Not Happy

At the meeting in my offices in Northbrook, Illinois, the head of the division responsible for the product, two of his representatives and Kay sat around the conference table. After ten minutes of small talk, Kay started wringing his hands and moaned as he explained the reason for the meeting.

"Joe, Panasonic in Japan really appreciates the exposure you have given the product. We really appreciate the orders you have placed and we enjoy very much doing business with our American partner. However, we feel that the product is not selling to its full potential in the American market."

I knew this was going to come up. But my experience told me that this product, for the American market, was not going to

This picture in full color displayed the product in its most dramatic angle.

be a big winner. In Japan where space is at a premium, where it is difficult to jog outdoors and where homes and apartments are very small, the jogging computer made sense. But this was America and this product was not going to be as successful as it was in Japan. Kay continued.

"We think we know why the product is not successful. We think we can understand why you are not selling enough. We think that if you follow our suggestion, you will find that the product will sell so much more that you will have a difficult time keeping the product in stock if you make some of the changes that we are suggesting." In short, Kay was telling me, "Change your ad and do it our way."

Kay went on to explain that we were not showing how the product was actually used. Why not show somebody actually running on the unit?

I explained my strategy. The product looked a lot more exciting with the drama that I conveyed in my photograph. Putting a real person in the photo would destroy the real drama that the product conveyed. It would destroy a little of the curiosity that I needed in order to sell the product. And finally I explained that it looked rather silly to an American to be running in place on a stationary board.

They all wrung their hands, moaned and made facial expressions like they were suffering various kinds of internal or intestinal distress. Finally Kay spoke. "Joe, we are willing to pay to have you rewrite your ad and test the concept we are proposing."

Second-Guessed and Flustered

If I appeared flustered, I was. Here I had a successful product which was mine exclusively. I felt that my strategy was indeed working and yet I was having my partner second-guess me.

I reluctantly agreed. I told them that they didn't have to pay for a thing but that I would test the new version against the old version and see if it made any difference. I didn't even have to have a headline in the ad, they said—just the new photograph

The picture lost a lot of its drama with somebody running on the product.

They tried to knock us off, but with the wrong picture.

would work to increase sales—that's how confident they were of their suggestion.

The first thing I did was contact my photographer and we reshot the unit with a beautiful model jogging in place exactly as Kay wanted. The photo turned out great and would certainly attract attention to the ad. And when I ran the ad, I ran it in full color instead of black and white as it had been before. The new ad not only had everything Kay wanted, but it was in color (which he didn't expect) and this should have increased the response.

I ran the new ad in a few publications and it bombed completely. Response was cut to about a quarter of the previous response. True, it wasn't a really good test. A good test would have been to have both ads run alternately in the same magazine—something I discuss in Marketing Lesson 8 on testing.

It was clearly a good example, however, of the excitement and drama of a product being lost with the wrong photograph and of the photograph being the critical element in the ad. Because of the photo, the ad succeeded at first and failed later.

In copy, it is dangerous to tell too much, and in a photograph it is dangerous to show too much.

As a small side note, one of my rivals got hold of a competitive product from Hong Kong that was very similar to mine and thought he would knock off my "success." He used a very similar copy approach and copied my ad format exactly. But he copied the wrong ad approach—the one recommended by the Japanese. Naturally, his campaign was a disaster.

By now you're probably wondering to yourself, "OK, Sugarman, you've got me really confused. What is the real answer then? Is photography totally unimportant or is it critical to the success of an ad?"

If you recall, I assigned certain values to the various elements of an ad, pointing out that the product is responsible for as much as 80% of an ad's success and that the remaining elements, including copy, comprise the remaining 20%. I also said that you can't get a passing score with anything less than 99%. Yes, even 98% is failing. What I didn't say is that some of these elements will vary in value depending on the nature of the product and the marketing approach. So in some ads, product will represent 70% and maybe the copy 28%. Or maybe photography will represent 30% instead of less than 5%. There is no hard-and-fast rule. If anything, the rule is simply that there is no rule—just approximate values that various elements may have which should be kept in mind in creating the ad.

A good example of the power of a photograph to get you to read the copy and buy the product is an ad that I wrote for

MDR vitamins. First I used a photo of a guy cringing as he held a vitamin pill. Then I tested the same ad, but this time using a photo of two beautiful models. The increase in response was 30%. This was a valid test as both ads ran alternately in the same magazine.

In my copywriting philosophy, the primary purpose of a photograph is to get you

There was a 30% increase in response when we used the beautiful models.

to read the copy—that's how important I feel the copy of an ad is. But there are other purposes as well. The next important purpose is to tell the full story. And finally, now that you understand there is no hard-and-fast rule on the importance of photography in your advertisement, let me review what I have tried to accomplish in photography during my career and some of the lessons that I have learned.

If I were to pick out times in my career where there were breakthroughs in my use and understanding of photographs as a graphic element in an advertisement, I would have to look at two major points in time—both involving economics.

The Professional Hand Model

The first was a photo session for my very first pocket calculator. Besides a normal product shot of the calculator, I wanted a photo of a hand holding the calculator to show size.

I found out the name of a highly recommended photographer who had a photo studio in downtown Chicago, about a 40-

minute drive from my home in the suburb of Northbrook. When I arrived, the hand model was already there waiting for me. I had never hired a hand model, so when this six-foot-tall guy approached me and asked what kind of shirt he should wear and whether he should wear

He had a complete wardrobe stolen from the best shops in Chicago.

cuff links or just a plain buttoned cuff, I looked rather puzzled. "I don't know," I said. "What did you bring with you?"

With that the model opened up his large briefcase to show an array of suit jacket sleeves and shirt sleeves. That's all—nothing was attached to the sleeves—just the sleeves themselves. Each sleeve was meticulously cut from some expensive suit or shirt. He had a rainbow of shirt colors, dozens of suit fabrics and even a section of cuff links and other hand jewelry. Of course. Why didn't I think of this? That's all he really needed for his job. Why carry an entire wardrobe full of jackets and shirts when all he needed could fit into a briefcase?

I wondered how he got so many of his sleeves. "Easy," he said. "I go into various department stores and when nobody is looking, I snip off the sleeves. I'm careful not to go back to the same store twice and I only do about two suits per store."

"What a rotten thing to do," I thought. Stores throughout the city must be asking how and why a few of their suits had their sleeves cut off, and here I was face-to-face with the culprit.

We got down to business and I selected the suit jacket sleeve, shirt and cuff links for the photo. And when it was all

On the other hand, my hand was just as good—I'm seen here holding a disc from the Kodak disc camera—and my modeling fee was reasonable, too.

completed and I got the results, the photographs looked great. But when I got the bill for the hand model, I couldn't believe the cost. It was as costly as a professional female model in a full body shot. So it got me thinking.

I looked at my own hand. Not bad. It wasn't gnarly or bad-looking at all. Quite the contrary. In college, I had one girl tell me that my hands looked like those of a surgeon—a classic shape of authority and stature. I had the kind of hand that could easily command the top end of the pay scale of any hand model. And besides, I was cheap.

So from then on I used my own hand to model all my products to show size and a human relationship with the product I was holding. My hand appeared in magazines all over the country and Canada for more than 15 years while I was running mail order ads. It was one of the most photographed hands in the world. My hand was famous. I even had a photograph made of just my hand and passed them out with my autograph to anybody requesting one at some of the speeches I gave. And it wasn't easy living with a famous hand. I had to be careful and not injure it. I couldn't expose it to the sun to any degree. And as my wife found out, I couldn't use it to do any hard manual labor around the house.

Careful What You Show

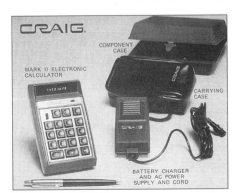

Many of our customers expected the pen, too.

One of the other lessons I learned in that very first photo session with the hand model was to be careful about what I included in a photo as a size reference. I showed in one scene a calculator, the power supply, the carrying case and enclosure for all the elements and then a beautiful Parker pen to show the size relationship of the calculator to the pen.

Although there was nothing mentioned about the pen in the ad or the literature that came with it, there were a number of people who called or wrote and were upset that they didn't receive the pen with their purchase. The point: Be careful what you put in your photograph, as consumers may expect it with their purchase.

85

Becoming a Photographer

The second major event that changed my relationship with photography occurred around 1980. Instead of going to downtown Chicago to have the photography done for my ads, I used a photographic studio in Northbrook, my local community. I had used this local company for the previous eight years.

My latest project was a full-color brochure I was putting together about an artist. I was buying his paintings of outer-space scenes, making prints of them and then selling the prints to my customers. I needed around ten photographs of the paintings for my brochure and was given a price of $200 per photograph. I questioned the price. I could see where there would be setup costs for the first painting, but then each subsequent painting could be placed on the same stand and quickly shot. And spending $2,000 for something that would only take a few hours seemed very high to me.

Despite my reasoning with them, the studio stuck to their price. I just needed something simple, quick and inexpensive and we couldn't agree on the price for it.

I looked at the setup that was required and reasoned that for $2,000 I could buy the equipment myself, shoot my paintings, and end up with the same results and the equipment as well. And what if I ever needed any more photographs? I'd already have the equipment to shoot my next session of paintings for just the cost of the film.

I had a lot of experience with photography throughout my life. I started taking pictures when I was just eight years old, was a photographer in high school, and had my own photo lab in college. I had experience in color photography and processing as well as many of the other techniques involved in photography. So it was not something foreign to me.

I set up my own studio and bought the equipment necessary to shoot the paintings. I bought a 4" x 5" view camera, lighting and tripods to hold the painting while I photographed it for the brochure. The results were excellent. And from then on I was hooked.

My next step was to expand the studio to do some minor tabletop photography. It soon escalated into a larger studio and then more equipment and before long I probably had one of the best-equipped studios in the entire Chicagoland area. I had three Hasselblad cameras, several 35mm cameras and I did all of the photographic work for my catalog. My lighting equipment was state-of-the-art and there wasn't a photography-related gadget or gizmo that I didn't own and use.

At the time, I was also doing my own typesetting, layout and paste-up, so every catalog that I produced was really a complete reflection of my own personal efforts in everything from copy-writing to typography and, of course, now photography as well.

During this period, which lasted for about five years, I took thousands of photographs. It gave me an appreciation for some of the drama you can bring out with the proper photograph. I traveled to Hungary where I took pictures of Erno Rubik (of Rubik's Cube fame). His designers had created a new electronic game. I photographed a doctor in Germany and his new invention.

Hundreds of uncut $1 bills. The Treasury agent was ready to confiscate all of our catalogs when this picture was snapped of Bernard Gittelson and published in our catalog.

After I photographed somebody with a sheet of $1 bills and ran the picture in my catalog, I received a call from the Secret Service asking me to burn the remaining catalogs. I didn't know that you were not allowed to photograph money in color regardless of the reproduction size. Fortunately, there weren't any catalogs to burn as they had already been distributed, but the call surprised me.

I lugged my photo equipment and lighting all over the country and to many other continents. It was one of the most creative periods of my life.

Photographing my subjects in different settings and creating stories from those photographs also gave me a unique perspective. I was accomplished in all phases of catalog and ad production including writing the copy, setting the type, creating the layout, doing the photography, and doing the final paste-up. But it was this flexibility of being able to determine the drama in a product through either copy or photography and then photographing the product and controlling the outcome of that photo session that really gave me an edge in my work.

I took photos all over the world. Shown from left to right: A doctor in Germany who invented a new diagnostic device, a banker in Louisiana who invented a jogging watch and three Hungarians from Budapest who created an electronic game.

I could not only edit and craft the copy but also control the graphic aspect of my work. Of course I could have hired a photographer and only directed the photography but having the experience of doing photography myself gave me an even better understanding of what really works in a photo.

I stopped doing the photography in 1985 and turned over the creative elements except copywriting to a design firm in San Francisco called Sugar/Acheson. They still do much of my work. As my company grew, I had less time to do the actual production.

Using Photography Well

Another consideration that is very important when determining what kind of photograph to shoot is that photography has to help tell the full story of your product. A photograph should assist the copy in telling the full story, and not the reverse. To capsulize the value of photography:

Photo Theory 1: Photography offers you the opportunity to complete the story, express the visual drama in your product and enhance the likelihood of prospects reading your copy.

There are still some bits of advice that I can pass on to you about photography. The first is to become acquainted with photography yourself. You don't have to be a photographer, but when directing a photographer, it is ultimately you who makes all the critical decisions regarding the shot.

If you have experience, you'll know which lens to use to create the most dramatic shot. Should it be a wide-angle lens which might distort the perspective or a telephoto lens which might blur the background? These are decisions you make to prepare the photographer for the photo session so he or she can release the drama that you know is in your product.

Direction Is Critical

If you give a product to a photographer without giving specific directions, he will shoot the product as a product. He will

Always direct your photographer

The final responsibility rests on your shoulder.

show as much about the product as possible in the best possible lighting and, in short, produce a very technically correct picture, missing all the drama. Your direction is very critical.

Sometimes you don't want to reveal too much in your photograph. Sometimes you don't want to take the logical course and shoot with a model as was the case with my jogging computer. And sometimes you want to take an unusual camera angle that conveys the emotion of a product. This can't be done by simply delegating the project to the photographer. It requires your participation as a director just as surely as a movie requires a director.

Selecting Models

If you are taking shots of a model with your product, I have a few words of advice. Select a professional model—not your next-door neighbor or the attractive lady at the coffee store whom you want to "discover." Chances are whoever you get won't really compare to a professional model who has made it through the ranks and whose photogenic image has already been proven. This goes for your kids as well. It's tempting and quite an ego boost to use Junior in a shot—not to mention the savings—but be careful. Often the end result does not justify the savings. Of course, if you were born with a surgeon's hand . . . well, then you go for it.

Selecting Photographers

When selecting a photographer, consider the particular shoot that you are arranging. For example, if I need to photograph a sexy model displaying my product, I'll call a friend of mine who has shot several sessions for *Playboy* magazine. He knows how to work with models and make them feel relaxed and get "into the shoot." If I was doing product photography or what is called tabletop photography, I'd select somebody who had a pretty good reputation in that area.

You don't have to go for the most expensive photographer you can find. There are many who do an excellent job and are reasonable. The crucial difference is in the direction. Get an average

Out of the thousands of shots, we captured this pensive look. She had to look beautiful and appear to be listening to the sound.

photographer and direct him or her properly and you'll end up with some great photography. Get a great photographer and don't give any direction and you'll end up with average results.

Finally, I have an unusual theory about photographers that you can use to judge if they are any good:

Photo Theory 2: The difference between a good photographer and a bad photographer is that a good photographer doesn't show his or her bad pictures.

If you are shooting a model, shoot as many shots as possible. Film and processing are cheap compared to what you will spend on the photographer and the model, and what you can eventually lose in not having that ideal shot. I'll end up with thousands of model shots at the end of the shoot. You never know which shot will have just that right angle, smile and product drama.

When you select your final photograph, keep in mind that you are telling a story. Does the photograph tell the story you need to tell about the product? Does it bring out its drama? Does it grab the reader and get him or her to read your copy? These are the really important points in your selection process.

Model Releases Are Important

Another experience I had with a model taught me a good lesson. I once had a model photographed in a rather neutral shot and several years later discovered the shot and decided to use it again as part of the package design for some vitamins. After the product was marketed, I was threatened by the photographer that the release signed by the model was a one-time-use release and I wasn't entitled to use the picture again without paying an additional payment. From then on, I always made sure that the models I photographed gave me a full release. Which brings out another point.

Make sure you have releases for all the photographs you take of people. This will avoid legal action in the future. We have extensive release files for every person we photograph regardless of whether we're shooting for TV or print ads.

Size of Film

I have also discovered that there's a lot of flexibility in what size film you can use to take your pictures. You can often get outstanding results from a simple 35mm slide. Today's film allows you to bypass the large-format cameras and shoot with the convenience of 35mm, although when shooting tabletop shots or even models, many photographers like the 2-1/4" format, and when trying to correct perspective in an unusual shot, many prefer a 4 x 5 or even an 8 x 10 format. The best advice I can give you in this area is to let your photographer decide. You tell the photographer what you want and let him or her pick out the best and most flexible format for the job.

The Use of Color in Photos

When should you use color in a mail order ad? I believe there are three reasons for using color. You can apply these reasons as criteria to determine whether it pays for you to use color or not. The three reasons for using color are as follows:

1. To Tell the Full Story

You may need color to tell the full story of your product or service. For example, if you are showing an expensive piece of jewelry and want it to look its best, color adds to the value of the jewelry and helps tell the full story of its beauty. If you have a colorful object whose strong appeal is its color, then color will be needed in the ad to tell the full story about your product.

2. To Create an Environment

When you sell in an expensive retail store, the environment often is elegant and upscale. In print, color will do this for an expensive item to create the environment of an upscale offering. If you were selling a closeout or a tremendous value, then color would be the wrong environment. You wouldn't expect to buy cheap things in a very elegant store.

3. To Increase Sales

If you're planning a national advertising campaign and have no reason to use color to either tell the full story or create the environment for your ad, then you must first test the ad in both color and black and white to determine the percentage increase (or decrease) of response when color is used. In my experience, color often does not justify the higher media costs charged by magazines for the use of color.

If media costs were consistent and each time you used color you paid a small percentage premium to do so, then color could be a good option. But color can add from 10 to 100% to the cost of your advertising. And since the extra cost of a color ad reduces your potential profits, then color should be looked at from a very practical point of view. And that means testing and common sense. Can you afford to pay up to double for the cost of an ad? Are you better off just running your ad in black and white even though you know color will increase sales of your product?

The answer is "yes and no." You have to look at each magazine and determine whether its cost for printing your ad in color is above or below a certain benchmark. For example, if you establish the fact, through testing, that using color in an ad brings in at least 20% more response, then you can justify paying up to 20% more for the use of color.

The One Big Drawback to Color

The only truly difficult problem in using color is the time it takes to test your ad. (I discuss testing later in Marketing Lesson 8.) Often you have to allow a few months for any magazine to run the ad and then wait a month to determine the difference in response. You may not have time to wait for the results.

To sum up, you've got to use common sense. See if adding color to your ad will enhance its sale by telling the full story and creating the proper environment. If it doesn't, then you don't need color. I have often been able to run my ads twice in black and white for the same cost as once in color, and with much better results.

In the above discussion, I talked about color as it relates to photographs only. As you learned in Marketing Lesson 4, color has to be used very cautiously in a layout. Later, in the chapters on media and testing (Marketing Lessons 6 and 8), you will learn more details on how to determine whether color is a good option for your mail order ad.

Final Suggestions

Finally, I have a few suggestions for anybody remotely responsible for using photography in a mail order ad. The first is to take a photo course or read a book on photography. Learn about the purpose of each type of lens and the differences and advantages of various types of cameras. There are some very good nontechnical books at your local library.

My second suggestion is to cut out pictures of product shots you like from various magazines. This collection will help you when you're communicating your needs to your photographer. It's a lot easier to say, "Look at this picture—that's the kind of effect I'm looking for," than trying to verbally describe a visual effect.

These suggestions will prepare you to use photography to enhance the value of the advertising you create and maybe, as in the case of my jogging computer, it will be the critical factor in your ad's success.

There is a remarkable ad I ran only in my catalog that worked incredibly well—so well that a new business was built around it and many people benefited. The following is the marketing story of a stock-market genius and his computer program.

A Marketing Story

Dial-An-Option

PRODUCTS THAT **THINK**®

Million Dollar Telephone, page 21.

16

The cover of our catalog introduced this new and exciting service.

The most difficult products to sell are miracle products—the ones that seem too good to believe. The miracle product either is so advanced, has such unbelievable features or represents such a major price breakthrough that the consumer doesn't believe you. Your offer therefore needs a tremendous amount of credibility to succeed. And very often great products will die because there isn't enough credibility in the advertising to overcome the consumer's natural skepticism.

What I am about to relate to you is a story about a service that seemed too good to be true. If you're skeptical when I tell you about it, that's OK. I felt the same way when I first found out about it. But let's escape from reality for a moment and imagine you're able to predict the future.

Let us say that you have a computer program that can predict the movement of the Dow Jones Industrial Average a week in advance of any major market move. It can tell you what direction the Dow is going to move, when it will make its move and how volatile a move it will be.

You are able therefore to invest in certain stock options with the information your computer gives you, and you can often double or triple your money in a few short days.

The sister program in your computer tells you something else of value. It will predict the general direction of the market over a six-month period and actually select those stocks for you that have an excellent chance of increasing in value.

You have discovered a powerful program—a program that can make you wealthy beyond your wildest imagination. You can run rings around Warren Buffett or George Soros or any of the major fund managers and stock experts. But you have this desire to help other people—especially the little guy.

And with this background, let me introduce Jerry. I have changed his name as he values his privacy and you'll soon discover why.

The Law Starts to Wear on Him

Jerry is a former New York City lawyer who worked for several years as corporate counsel for many major New York companies. He has a brilliant mind and came to the attention of many of his elder law firm partners who mentored him throughout his career.

But the law was starting to wear on Jerry. He was tired of the law scene, tired of what he saw around him and he wanted to contribute to society through a profession other than the one for which he had lost respect.

During his law days, he came up with an idea that he felt could lead to determining the direction of the Dow Jones Industrial Average in advance of any major move. But it required a computer and at the time he had little computer knowledge.

So in his spare time he learned not only how to operate a computer, but how to program one as well. It didn't take long before he was programming complex algorithms into his computer and developing one of the most powerful programs of the '80s. He then quit his law practice and with his new wife moved into a modest home on Long Island, New York.

Jerry further refined his program. He tried it out himself. It worked. And worked spectacularly. Now what to do?

Jerry figured that if he could market his program, he could generate a nice income for his family. He didn't want to just use the programs himself. If he could provide the power of his program to a small group of people—small investors who didn't have a chance against the major institutions—he could help them to prosper. Then he could achieve the goal he wanted to achieve—to help others and do what he enjoyed. "The money will flow to me, I know," Jerry said to his wife. "I'd rather provide a service that can really help a lot of people than to keep it for just myself."

Program a Major Breakthrough

Jerry had followed my career through catalogs and print advertisements in many of the leading magazines he read. He felt that his program was a major breakthrough and he liked the way I had of presenting products that explained them in a very clear and concise way. He knew that I would probably enjoy the challenge of selling something that actually predicted the future.

Jerry called my office and spoke to Mary Stanke, who at the time was my assistant (now she is the president of JS&A). Mary suggested that Jerry simply send in a description of his product or service and we would respond to him in a timely fashion.

When Jerry's letter arrived, I was fascinated by what he claimed. Could such a program exist? Could anybody wield such power? And why isn't he the richest man in the world by now?

I flew out to visit Jerry personally. You can get a pretty good idea of what somebody is like by meeting him or her in person and since I was going to be in New York, it was a simple matter to visit Jerry in his home on Long Island.

A Remarkable Presentation

I sat at Jerry's desk as he plugged in a number of figures and showed me how the market was going to react over the next six months. He showed me some of the written reports that outlined the predictions he had made and their accuracy. It was truly a remarkable presentation.

But why didn't Jerry use this information himself? Jerry explained that he really wanted to help the small investor and my immediate thought was that this guy had to be one of the most principled individuals I had ever met.

If his computer program worked, I suggested a plan that would allow him to help the greatest number of people. "Set up a service with a unique name. Something like 'Dial-An-Option' would be a great name. Have a membership program receive bulletins from you advising them of an impending rise or fall in the stock market and then recommend what options they should buy to capitalize on the market move. We could then sell the information and make daily updates available on the phone once the information is disseminated."

Proof That It Works

Jerry liked my idea but before we would even offer this service, Jerry wanted to prove to me that the program worked. "I want you to experience the program in real time," he said.

Then one day in late summer, Jerry called me and said that the stock market would be making a dramatic move up during the next seven business days. Then he told me what options he would recommend buying to profit from this information.

I watched the market make a major unexpected spurt to the upside, and the options that Jerry had picked all doubled in value.

I waited for a few months to test the program again and the same thing happened, but this time I was able to make several thousand dollars.

"This program works," I thought. "But the problem will be convincing people that it really does work. It's too good to be true."

I chose my catalog as the vehicle. I felt that the program wasn't quite ready for widely distributed business publications because I sensed that there might be quite a bit of skepticism. I made the first introduction as a front cover announcement in my catalog. My customers trusted me. They knew that if I said a program worked, it worked and it was worth trying. This came from years of selling quality products, providing good customer service and developing the trust of my customers—a trust I never violated.

Software Program Also Offered

In the catalog I also offered a software program Jerry had created that allowed people to pick out the stocks best suited for their portfolios. I named the program "Halographix" and offered it in a totally separate ad.

The announcement in my catalog drew a large response resulting in 2,600 members, which meant we had created a very powerful mailing list. And all were waiting for that first Dial-An-Option signal. The first signal was generated from Jerry's computer about a month after we reached the 2,600 member mark. We sent everybody the signal via Federal Express and

This ad touting Jerry's new software program appeared in the stock publication Barron's.

initiated our telephone hot line to keep our members informed of our thoughts on a daily basis. And the stock market responded perfectly as thousands of members who invested in the program made a profit.

I Had to Register as Advisor

I then received a letter from the Illinois Attorney General's office. What I was doing was acting as an investment advisor and I had to register as such and even take a test. If I flunked the test, it meant that I could not sell the service that I had already set up.

So I studied quite hard over a period of a month, took a very extensive test and became an official and authenticated investment advisor authorized by the State of Illinois.

When the next signal came out, it too was successful. By this time, I was putting a great deal of my own money into the program. I had invested $20,000 and made $40,000. I made it quickly—within a week—and I made it honestly even though it seemed like this indeed was too good to be true.

I then shut off the enrollment ranks at Jerry's suggestion. We were getting too many members. And if everybody was betting that the market would be going one way, it could possibly affect the course of the market.

Jerry had always warned me about the possibility that the program was not perfect. "We might get a bad signal and then our customers might lose all their money and that is something that we cannot be liable for."

Fine Print Was Extensive

Jerry, using his legal background, made sure we had all this information stated on each report we sent. In fact, the legal fine print at the bottom of the report was quite lengthy and very clear. We weren't responsible if the signal did not perform as predicted.

But the signals did work. Flawlessly. Month after month, whenever we issued a signal, the market responded and we made money ourselves and for our members. During our first year in 1985, there were about five signals.

We had reached a point in the program when everybody started to put their money into the program in major amounts. Enthusiasm and confidence were quite strong and I was getting personal calls from members who were now mesmerized by the reports and their results.

Everybody Seemed Happy

"Joe, I just wanted you to know that I made $50,000 in one week by following your advice." Another caller told me, "Joe, the money I've just earned will pay for my child's education."

Everything was great. Then in 1986 a signal was generated by Jerry's computer and we disseminated it to all our members. We all waited. And waited. And waited. Something was wrong. The program was not calling the market correctly. The signal called for the market to go up in a few days, but it was starting to go down.

Jerry was feeling the pressure. "If this signal doesn't work," he said, "then we'll lose many of our members. But on the other hand, if we don't advise them that the signal isn't working this time, we are also doing them a disservice. Joe, I suggest you leave a message on the Dial-An-Option telephone hot line that the signal was a failure and that people should liquidate their positions."

I did just that. The investors lost money and cancellations in the program started to roll in. Three days later after I had everybody liquidate their position, the market made a major move in the direction we had predicted. The program had indeed worked, but Jerry had gotten nervous because the market move didn't happen when he expected it. Indeed, the program should allow a certain amount of time for the market to react. Sometimes the market works quickly and other times it works slowly, but it always works within a certain time frame. This was part of our learning curve.

Cancellations Pour In

After the market made its move, we received more cancellations, this time from people who were upset that we told them to liquidate their positions when all along we shouldn't have said a thing. I then started to get lawsuit threats. One member threatened to sue me for the $100,000 he lost even though all our literature clearly pointed out the risks.

In subsequent weeks, after everything settled down, we ended up with less than 1,000 members from our original 2,600. During the next signal, we recommended a safer position. If the market went up, investors would make money, and if it went down they would also make some money to hedge against the possibility that the signal was wrong. But the signal was right. And again, everybody did well.

Several more signals were sent out over the course of a few years and they all worked well. The market was relatively volatile—sometimes moving up and sometimes going down—but in each case the Dial-An-Option program worked amazingly well along with the other program, Halographix, which predicted the long-range direction of the market.

The Crash of 1987

Then came September of 1987. Jerry mentioned that the market seemed to be heading for a major move down but that his system still had not confirmed any move. But finally it did. Jerry's computer generated a major signal indicating that the market was going to make a dramatic move down. An alert was sent to all members. But the market continued up during the next few days, and members, very confident after a string of several winning signals, took even greater positions. They were all convinced that the market would soon sink.

And then came October 19, 1987. The market took a 500-point drop and continued dropping the next day in one of the most dramatic moves in U.S. stock market history. Dial-An-Option members made a small fortune—some earning ten times what they invested in the Dial-An-Option signal. And Jerry's future was assured.

During my activities with Dial-An-Option, I got involved in a vitamin program and BluBlocker sunglasses and was devoting most of my time to these activities. I also realized that I had made more money trading stock options than I had running the Dial-An-Option club. But I must admit it was a lot of fun working with Jerry and helping others make a lot of money even though there were a few problems with disgruntled investors because of one bad signal that really wasn't bad. In fact, the program has never been wrong during the twelve years it has been running. That has got to be a record in itself.

Jerry Capable of Handling It

I decided that the Dial-An-Option club and the Halographix program were not programs that I could devote my full efforts to and still effectively run my business. I also felt that Jerry was capable of handling the membership program. His integrity brought him the respect of all his members. I handed over the entire membership program to him, at absolutely no charge or future royalty and even assisted him in the transition. I had complete confidence in Jerry. He still believed in helping others earn money and enjoyed the entire marketing process—a far cry from his old law practice. "I'm happy with what I'm doing—helping others— and I'm earning a nice income so I have no complaints," he confided in me.

So I worked with Jerry over the next year by helping him edit some of his mailings. He picked up many writing and marketing pointers from our previous interactions and wrote excellent copy.

Jerry Becomes a Great Marketer

Jerry did beautifully. And within a year, he was able to run the club himself and build up the membership. In fact, in the nine years since I turned the reins over to Jerry, he has managed to develop a very loyal group of members who swear that he is a rare individual indeed. And talk about becoming a great marketer. One of Jerry's mailing pieces earned him $400,000 from a $4,000 investment. I don't know of any other direct marketer who has ever had a 10,000% return on a mailing.

Jerry has become a close personal friend. In fact, I visited him, his wife and their two young children in Florida where he moved four years ago from New York. His business has done quite nicely over the past several years and Jerry enjoys a very loyal and dedicated following.

"The only time any one of my members drops out is when he or she dies," Jerry says. I helped get Jerry the members initially, but Jerry, through his principled way of running a business, demonstrated how to keep a loyal clientele and how to achieve some of the highest response rates of any direct marketer.

Jerry prefers to keep a low profile. Respecting that, I have not used his real name. But his story is so unusual that I had to relate it here as an example of a service that was too good to believe and an example of how to market it.

Having read Marketing Lessons 1-5, you're now at a point in the direct marketing process where you found the perfect product and protected it, then took your written copy and presented it with the most effective type you could find and created great photography—pictures that really captured the drama of your product. The ad is finished. The world is now waiting to learn about your new product. What's next? If you're like most direct marketers, you'll need to advertise and you'll need to buy media. Marketing Lesson 6 is a very valuable chapter on this process. It outlines the things you'll need to do to make sure you obtain the best value for your media buy. I would say that of all the chapters in this book, this one is the most valuable as it may make the difference between your success and failure in this business. Read it and see why.

Marketing Lesson 6

The Media Challenge

I FIRST THOUGHT THAT I WOULD MAKE MY CAREER IN ADVERTISING... BUT LATER SWITCHED TO "MASS" MEDIA.

The main lesson that I hope you learn from the media concepts presented in this chapter might surprise you.

> **Media Theory: The single most important factor in earning a profit from any mail order campaign in print or on TV is how cheaply you buy your media.**

When you select a product, you should already know what the product costs you. You also have the opportunity to choose the retail price point at which you will be offering your product or service. Let's say you want to conduct a print campaign and you have a 55% margin on a $100 item. This means that you will make a gross profit of $55 on each product you sell before you factor in other costs.

You know that you have fixed costs as well as the cost of the product—fulfillment costs, for example. But you know those costs exactly, so the only variable is the cost of media.

Now let us say that you have the opportunity of advertising in *Time* magazine. And let us say that the cost of a full page in one of *Time*'s regional issues is $10,000.

You run your ad. The response rolls in and you end up earning a gross profit of $8,000—$2,000 short of the break-even point. You have a failure. But what if you were able to buy that same space in *Time* magazine for $5,000 instead of $10,000? If you bought the space at this lower price, you would have actually earned a $3,000 profit—and consequently had a success.

In this example, the only difference between success and failure is the cost of the media.

"Ah," you say. "I understand that different publications charge different prices, but aren't they pretty much fixed prices?"

The answer is no. There are many ways you can obtain lower prices for media if you know what to do. And if you are a good buyer of media, you will soon realize that where you really earn your profits is in buying your media as cheaply as possible and not in the margins you have for your product.

This rule also applies to TV, radio and any other negotiable medium with the exception of direct mail and catalogs where there are no media costs—just printing and fixed postage rates. Every dollar you save on media goes right to the bottom line.

Saving Money on Media

This chapter will cover the ways you can save money when buying space in print media. With this knowledge you can really add to your profits, and in some cases, this is the only approach that will even earn you profits.

Later, in Marketing Lesson 8, I cover the subject of testing and I show you how testing will dramatically sharpen your direct marketing skills, limit your downside risk and put you in a position to earn really good profits on your product. Good media buying will ensure even greater profits.

Let us assume that you accept the fact that media buying is very important. I will cover how to buy at very good prices a little later in this chapter. Let's now cover the basics and then we will get into the skills and knowledge you will need to buy media effectively.

Preparing Your Ad

Let us say you have written an ad. You have a great new product, the right kind of margins and you are ready to place your ad in a publication for a test. (Later, in Marketing Lesson 8 on testing, I describe *The Wall Street Journal* and my testing procedure, so I won't go into that here.) Now let's look at what you have to do to prepare that ad for the publication.

The first thing you should request from any publication is their rate card, their audited publisher's statement and, of course, a copy of their publication. The rate card will not only tell you the rates but give you the mechanical requirements for your ad.

Magazines are printed on different presses and with different methods. It is your responsibility to provide an image of your ad in a format that they can incorporate into their printing system. The rate card will list the maximum dimensions your ad should be to fit into the magazine's page format.

This information is usually on the rate card but it may be in a publication called *Standard Rate and Data Service (SRDS)* available at most libraries. There are different *SRDS* books for different publication categories. For example, there's one for trade publications and there's one for consumer magazines. In some cases the publication might require a film negative. In some cases it might be a film negative with "right reading emulsion side down." Or finally, it might be a computer format. It is your responsibility to provide the publication with the exact format they require.

To provide the correct format, you simply call one of the pre-press services located in your city. This type of company specializes in converting the original artwork or computer-generated image you have prepared into the form required by the publication. They probably have the *Standard Rate and Data Service* book required and can look up the publication and determine the specifications without having to see the rate card.

You give the pre-press company either your original paste-up or, as is now very common today, a computer disk with your ad already in place. The company then takes it from there and sends the required format to the printer and the proofs to you and to the publication's main office. This procedure is specified on the rate card or in the specifications that you can find in the *SRDS* book.

Keying Your Response

Now let us say you have finished with your test in the first publication. Your ad is very successful. You now want to "roll out" or extend your test into several other magazines. How do you determine which magazine draws which response? It was easy to know the amount of response from your first test because there was only one magazine in which you advertised. But now you have several.

The trick here is to key each of your ads with a code. Since most of your response may be received over the phone, if you use a toll-free number you should put something in your ad so that the person ordering from it will also reveal where he or she saw it.

Before the advent of the toll-free number, this was real easy as all you had to do was put a small number in the coupon so you could easily sort the responses when they came in to determine their source. But with the toll-free number, I have found it easiest to simply make the key code part of the product's order number. So if somebody calls up and orders Product Nr. WS1234, I know instantly that the order came from *The Wall Street Journal* without asking the customer where he or she saw the ad. In *Popular Science,* the product code might read, "PS1234." Some companies say, "Ask for extension 35." But this often encourages extra conversation.

Selecting a Publication

When your ads are ready to run in several publications, you must select the ones to advertise in. How do you choose them?

The first thing I would do is decide on the category of publication that your prospect might be reading. When I say category, let me list a few: news (*Time, Newsweek, U.S. News and World Report*), shelter (home-type magazines such as *Better Homes and Gardens*, *Home and Garden*), airline in-flight, fraternal, religious, fashion and glamour, automotive, health, special interest (*Skiing, Flying,* etc.), men's magazines (*Playboy* and *Penthouse*), travel and leisure, science, computer, state, city and even suburban magazines. There are also many other special-interest or trade publications. Newspapers that primarily cover news in specialized fields may target specific reader groups too. All of these publications can be found in *SRDS* books, or simply go to a big newsstand and look at the publications.

Within each category of publication, there are often many magazines. For example, if I wanted to reach a scientific audience, I might advertise in *Scientific American, Popular Science, Popular Electronics*, maybe a few computer magazines. If my product had broader appeal than just the scientific community, I might try the in-flight airline magazines. There are as many in-flight magazines as there are airlines. So, in general, if an ad works very nicely in one airline magazine, chances are it will work in the rest of them too. In short, the publication has what is described as good "rollout potential."

And finally, if my product has mass market appeal, I could advertise in practically any magazine and have a pretty good chance of success if my test ad was successful enough.

Determining a Responsive Publication

Let's say that you've picked a few prospective publications. Now what do you do to limit your chances of losing money in any of them? First, look for other mail order offers in the same publication. Then look to see if those mail order offers are offering similar price points or a similar product. Some magazines are very effective at selling products under $19.95 and others are more effective selling products over $50. Simply by scanning the publication, you can get a really good sense of what will work in that publication.

If there are no mail order ads, be careful. This doesn't mean that a mail order ad won't work. I've discovered some great publications that had hardly any mail order ads in them until I started advertising. But if you are just starting out, it's not worth the risk. Stay with the proven mail order-oriented publications.

Getting the Best Value

The next thing I would check is what is called the "cost per thousand." You determine this by taking the cost of your ad and dividing it by the circulation of the publication. This single figure will be very revealing to you as you compare publications. For example, if one of your selections had a cost per thousand of $20 and a very similar publication had a cost per thousand of $15, with all things being equal, the less expensive publication would be the one to advertise in. Cost per thousand can also give a hint as to what type of offer will work in a publication.

If the cost per thousand is very low and there are a lot of mail order ads in the magazine, chances are the products' price points are low. On the other hand, higher cost per thousand figures usually mean that the magazine reaches a higher demographic group, purchasers of higher-priced goods.

Let us say I ran the same ad in *Elks Magazine* as I did in *Forbes*. If *Elks* costs $7 per thousand and *Forbes* costs $40 per thousand, what might be my response? This is an unfair question. If my product sold for $19.95, chances are it would have made money in *Elks* and lost money in *Forbes*. The *Forbes* reader is quite upscale and that is what advertisers are paying for. But you pay a premium in *Forbes* for that upscale reader. The $19.95 ad is more likely to produce a profit in a $7 per thousand publication like *Elks Magazine* than in *Forbes*. You might sell the same number of products per thousand to the *Forbes* readers, but you are paying so much more for the privilege.

Now let us say you've decided on the magazine categories you want, examined all the publications available within those categories and selected the ones that appear to have the most mail order advertising. You've checked that the price points for those mail order products are similar to that of your product, and you have closely examined the cost per thousand of each of the publications and selected the lower-priced publications, assuming all else is equal. Now you are ready to call the publication and buy the space, right? Wrong!

Getting Media for Less

If you are one of the unfortunate people who started in the mail order business by calling up your friendly magazine representative to order a page in their magazine based on their rate card, you are probably not now in the mail order business. Let me list the following steps to obtaining media at a lot less than the costs printed on the rate card:

1. Form Your Own Ad Agency

First, I would recommend forming your own advertising agency as part of your company. Ad agencies typically request and receive a 15% discount from the publishers on the ads that they place. Simply print up some stationery with your agency's new name and you are now an ad agency. If you have questions about this, many publications are available at your local library that can give you tips on forming your own agency. It can simply be an in-house agency, a sister company or a company within your own company, but you definitely need one and the savings of 15% can be substantial. You'll also need to make up an "Insertion Order" form. That is simply a purchase order for advertising space and I have included a sample in Appendix C.

2. Contact a Space Broker

Next, contact one of the many space brokers who handle media either as barter or as representatives of the publications. I use Stephen Geller Associates in New York. Geller has a list of magazines that actually owe him space. Let's take a hypothetical example: The XYZ Hotel in New York needs advertising in *New Yorker* magazine and offers Geller rooms in exchange. *Fortune* magazine needs hotel rooms in New York and offers Geller space in their magazine in exchange for rooms. *New Yorker* magazine needs airline tickets, which Geller just got as part of a swap with a travel agency, and offers Geller space in the *New Yorker* in exchange.

Meanwhile, Geller is ending up with a lot of space and a lot of hotels and a lot of airline tickets and, coincidentally, companies who can use all these things. He is also able to offer me some space in *Fortune* magazine for an incredible discount after all this swapping is finished. I pay cash and Geller actually makes a profit himself from these transactions. And he deserves it. Anybody who can keep track of all that confusion deserves to earn a profit.

This type of broker can earn credit applicable toward magazine space and TV time in many other ways, including everything from exchanging merchandise for space to buying large blocks of space at a time. Now here's the key. If you contact the magazine's sales representative before you contact the broker, you're out of luck. Once you are listed as a direct customer of that publication, you no longer can deal through a broker. You're stuck paying full price for the ad minus, if you've formed your own ad agency, a 15% discount.

And how big can the savings be with a broker? Anywhere from 25 to 50% off the rate card price. That's right, up to half off. In addition, you can still get your 15% agency discount and an additional 2% off for paying your bills on time.

3. Last-Minute Closing Opportunities

Your broker may call you and say, "Joe, I've got this ad space in *Playboy* and there's a closing coming up in two days. I'm willing to sell you the ad space at a steal if you can decide to accept my offer before anybody else calls me." This is what is called a "last-minute closing" and can happen for a number of reasons. Maybe one of the advertisers dropped out after making a commitment. Maybe at the last minute the publication added four more pages to accommodate a few new advertisers and had one of the four pages available to either a public service account or a cash-paying customer at a discount. In their case they are giving the space away at a discount and in your case you are getting it for a bargain, and they still come out with enough money to cover the cost of the paper.

Now, there are publications that don't barter their space. And the best you can do is get the 15% agency discount and maybe 2% off for prompt payment. But your broker can advise you which ones do and which ones don't. Sometimes you can even negotiate a deal whereby your broker makes a little less and you run your ads a little more. Hey, anything is possible.

4. The Mail Order Discount

You can also find out from reading *SRDS* if the publication offers a mail order discount. Very often they do and it can be as high as 20%. Why? They know that in the mail order business, money is often made on how cheaply the mail order company can buy the media, so the publication cooperates and encourages mail order advertising by allowing the mail order advertiser to get a slightly better rate.

Brokered space, special mail order discounts, and last-minute closing deals are generally not available to the mainstream advertising community—only to mail order advertisers. The publications need an outlet for their remnants just like a factory outlet store for brand-name products does and they let the bargain hunters (the mail order companies) shop there. This brings up another way to save money.

5. Remnant Advertising

Very often a national publication has regional editions. For example, *The Wall Street Journal* has a Southwestern edition and a Midwestern edition as well as four others. There are even smaller editions within the larger editions. In some publications, you can pick the region or the state or even the city you want to advertise in without having to invest in the complete run of the publication. For example, a Ford dealer in Memphis need only advertise in the Memphis edition of *Time* magazine where his prospects are located.

But let's take a case where the magazine has page 45 sold to a big advertiser who, for whatever reason, doesn't want to advertise in Illinois. The magazine ends up with what is called a remnant. It must sell the Illinois space to somebody. Sometimes this is very difficult. So the magazine will offer their remnant space at a considerable discount. They've already made a nice profit and sold the space to the big spender from the ad agency, and the space they are selling you is being offered as a convenience to them. I've often gotten offers to run my ads in remnants that covered half the circulation of a magazine but in almost a checkerboard pattern across the U.S. And sometimes my ads run in one big block covering one big chunk of the U.S. But they often pay off because I am paying far less for the space.

Remember, you make your profits not from the wonderful margins you are making on your product and not from the wonderful ad you have written, but from the money you save when buying media.

6. Per Inquiry Deals

Per inquiry placements, or PI deals, are another way you can not only save money but also have no risk. In this arrangement the magazine carries your advertising at no cost but it shares in your profits. Orders can be sent either to your order fulfillment service or to the publication directly and then forwarded on to you for processing.

It may seem like a great idea for the mail order operator, but in the long run it is not the best way to go. First, there are very few publications that will do this. Second, if a publication does it, they may be doing so badly that they can't get advertisers to buy space so they're giving it away. If a magazine did well, the response would encourage more advertisers, and the magazine wouldn't need to offer a deal like this.

Third, you must keep accurate records of each order. Often you do this by having the order go straight to the magazine and then they forward the orders to you. Or you use a neutral order-taking service who also sends reports to the magazine.

Finally, you are at the whim of the publication. If they don't want to run your ad one month, they push it to the next. In short, you lose a lot of control. I have never found any PI deal worth doing. Many writers of "how to" mail order books refer to the PI deal as a risk-free way of getting into the mail order business. Don't believe it.

Analyzing Responsiveness

Now you've created that great ad, you've tested it, it has tested quite well and you've selected the best publications to advertise in. You've saved a small fortune by purchasing your media through a broker and by using only the types of publications that offer you good cost per thousand and mail order discounts. The response comes pouring in and you wonder why one magazine does better than the next. Why? What are some of the possible reasons? Why do some of the magazines turn out to be more responsive than others? The following are some of my thoughts on that subject.

1. Editorial Content of Publication

First, the publication's editorial content and vitality must be appealing and relate very strongly to the readers' interests. A responsive reader will be interested in the editorial content of the entire magazine or newspaper. The greater the interest, the more responsive the reader. The reader must look forward to receiving the magazine each week or month, and must read it soon after it arrives or after it is picked up on the newsstand. The reader must list it as one of the two or three publications he or she most enjoys reading and typically will save back issues. Such a publication represents to me the environment for a good responsive reader.

Think of the publications you personally like and the magazines you look forward to receiving. It will tell me a lot about your interests and passions. If you really understand the product or service you are offering and you have a passion for it, chances are you already receive several of the magazines you should advertise in.

2. Integrity of a Publication

Second, a good responsive publication is one whose editorial integrity is so highly protected that its readers sense this and trust that publication implicitly and thus trust the claims made by its advertisers.

We once tried to place an advertisement for a biorhythm calculator in *Scientific American* magazine. It was refused. The publisher felt that the science of biorhythms was not a proven science and if the magazine were to carry the advertisement, it would be endorsing the concept. *SA* also refused to run cigarette ads as they felt that it would be an endorsement of the ads' tar and nicotine claims.

Because *SA* is so highly concerned about its editorial content, it also is very concerned about the advertising messages it carries, for it realizes that if the editorial content is to have integrity, so must each advertisement. I respected *SA*'s decision not to run my biorhythm calculator even though I was very disappointed.

The Wall Street Journal is trusted. The *Journal* monitors the ads it runs and anything they question, they won't run. They don't allow the sale of health products or vitamins with unsubstantiated health claims. They stay away from anything too controversial (as I discovered when I tried to run my Russia Stinks ad), and they make sure their advertisers are established and responsible companies. The reader senses this and responds. Contrast this with a publication that runs an outlandish misleading story and contains ads that are too hard to believe, and you've got the perfect environment for a lack of trust.

3. The Cost per Thousand

Finally, one of the ways to judge a publication is by its cost per thousand. The really high-priced publications that don't have mail order discounts get very few of my ads because too often they don't work. On the other hand, the publications that have a reasonable cost per thousand are the ones where I can advertise and consistently earn a profit.

Position of an Ad

Another topic that you need to become familiar with is an ad's position. Where should an ad go in a magazine to produce the best possible return?

The first choice and one you should insist on, is that your ad appear on a right-hand page. Think about it. Your coupon normally will be in the lower right-hand corner of your ad. If prospects need to cut out the coupon, they should be able to do it easily. If your ad is on the left-hand page, it becomes a lot more difficult to cut out the coupon because it is on the part of the page that is attached to the spine of the magazine. You can insist that your ad appear on a right-hand page in your instructions to the publication. In addition, the right-hand side is the side that is consistently looked at first when leafing through the pages. Having an ad there increases the chance that your prospect will see your ad.

After getting a commitment from the magazine to get a right-hand page, I have always tried to get a position towards the front of the magazine. It is my theory that the closer to the front you are, the more likely you are going to be read. Another factor is prestige. If a magazine gives you an up-front position, it is as if the magazine is showcasing your ad and saying in essence that they are proud to place your ad in their publication. In *The Wall Street Journal*, I tried first for the back page of the paper and, as a second choice, a right-hand page in the first section. In some publications, there are editorial and advertising policies that require your ad to go in the back of the publication where they gather all their other mail order advertisers. You then have no choice.

The Word "Advertisement"

If your ad looks very editorial and in fact is very close to the editorial format of the publication in which you are advertising, the publication will often place the word "Advertisement" at the top of your ad. So I always specifically state on our insertion order that the publication not use the word "Advertisement" above my ad. My mail order ads always have the JS&A logo at the end and although they are very editorial looking, it is obvious that they are being run by my company. Putting "Advertisement" at the top of one of my ads feels to me like the publication is saying, "We want to warn you that this is not part of our editorial material," and thus would raise a little doubt in the minds of my prospects. On the other hand, there are many ads without a corporate logo that indeed look like part of the publication's editorial content and should have the word "Advertisement."

Very often, people who have read my ads and later commented to me about them referred to them as articles instead of ads. "I read your article in *Popular Science*," they'd say, or maybe, "your article in *The Wall Street Journal*." So even if they had seen the JS&A logo and "Advertisement" above the ad, most people thought they were articles anyway. I've never tested the difference in response with or without the word "Advertisement," so this is one area that needs to be explored further.

Most of my promotions succeeded. But there were plenty that failed. And from the ones that failed you always learn a lesson. Sometimes the lesson is painful and sometimes it is costly—but it is from the losers that you learn the most. And especially the biggest losers, which I tell you about in my next marketing story.

A Marketing Story

The Biggest Losers

We had an exclusive arrangement, our test was successful, but something turned sour.

At the height of my career in direct marketing I had the reputation of being a real winner. It seemed that people thought that everything I touched turned to gold. The trade press was referring to me as a marketing guru and companies large and small were coming to me with their products.

In reality, I was not the big success that everybody held me up to be. I had probably failed more times than most people could imagine. In fact for every ten ads that I wrote, there was a time when only a few of them became successful. But their success more than made up for the losers—except in a few instances, and these were really costly mistakes.

You often learn from your mistakes. And if they cost you a bundle, you learn big-time. So I've decided to share with you my biggest losers and explain why I miscalculated so badly. There is a consistent theme to all of these stories. See if you can pick it out.

The Checkbook with a Brain

It was 1975 and our company had done very well over the past several months. We were well entrenched in our new corporate offices, everything was flowing beautifully and a wonderful opportunity came our way.

A company in Texas, Corvus Corporation, called to tell us that they had a revolutionary new calculator product called the CheckMaster that did something no other calculator had done before: It remembered what your previous balance was. It had the shape of a checkbook holder, which meant that you could keep your checkbook inside the calculator holder. Instead of having to use a separate calculator and write your check transaction in your checkbook, you could enter your transactions directly into the memory of the unit.

I know that many of you might feel that this is very common and no big deal with all the neat gadgets we now have today. But back then, the CheckMaster was truly revolutionary.

The president of the company, Charles Sevren, suggested that I come down to Texas as they were willing to give me an exclusive for the product if I was willing to spend a certain amount of advertising dollars promoting it.

So I flew down to Dallas, met with Sevren and his staff and they worked out a great deal for me. I would, upon my return to Chicago, sit down and write an ad for this product. I would then test the ad in the Southwestern edition of *The Wall Street Journal* as I did my other products. Then, if the results were good, I would agree to spend $400,000 in national advertising to sell the CheckMaster.

I created an ad called "Checkbook with a Brain" and tested it in the Southwestern edition of *The Wall Street Journal*. The ad broke even—just squeaking by with a slight profit.

"Hmm," I thought. "If it just broke even, and I roll out in all of the magazines that I've advertised in before, I could possibly do quite well." First, I had an exclusive on the product. No competition. Second, the effect of running the same ad in many different magazines gave a message to the consumer that this was a successful product and that they should join the bandwagon and buy the thing. I realized this from previous experience. And finally, I had this great-looking ad with great copy and quite frankly wanted to get the JS&A name out there again. Big mistake.

I ran the ad nationally. And a few weeks later as the response was starting to pour in I realized, based on previous sales and my current projections, I was about to lose $250,000. The ad was not doing well at all. What I didn't anticipate was that we were entering one of the worst recessions in a long time and consumers were retrenching. They weren't as anxious to buy on impulse as they were when I tested the product, which had only a break-even response then anyway.

It gave me a sinking feeling. I had worked for one year to earn $250,000 and now I was watching all that money go down the drain. I had been wrong. First, I hadn't realized that the market conditions could change this dramatically. And like any campaign you run in mail order, you can't bet the house on it. Second, your test is an indicator of how much confidence you should have in risking money for a national campaign. And my test told me that I should have proceeded very cautiously and forgotten about the exclusive arrangement that the manufacturer had promised me.

Finally, I was right about one thing. Everybody thought I had a huge success and was making a killing. Even my competitors. In fact, in a common display of curiosity, one of my competitors, Mervin (who you may remember from the marketing story on toll-free order taking), called and asked me, "Joe, I've been seeing tons of ads for the Checkbook with a Brain and I was kind of, you know, wondering how you were, like, doing."

I didn't want to lie so I answered, "You wouldn't believe how I'm doing!"

To which Mervin responded, "No, I believe it. I see your ads all over the place. You seem to get all the neatest products. You really are lucky."

"You should have my luck," was my response.

The Mickey Math Calculator

Another big loser I had was the time I came up with a very humorous idea for a calculator ad. I was visiting the Consumer Electronics Show in January of 1975 when I came across the most ridiculous calculator I had ever seen. It was designed for children and it was the size of a large writing tablet. The company managed to get the rights to use the Mickey Mouse image and they called the calculator "Mickey Math."

What was unusual about the product was the price. Mickey Math sold for only $19.95, well below the price of most other calculators on the market, which normally sold for $39.95. In fact, one of the most popular scientific calculators was the Hewlett-Packard HP-80, which sold for $400 if you could even find one. The low price of the Mickey Math reflected the manufacturer's desire to hit the children's market.

As I talked to the president of the company, I came up with a brilliant idea. Why not offer these calculators to executives as conversation pieces? They were so cheap and it was such a wild

Presenting
Mickey Math™

$19⁹⁵

The newest executive calculator will do more than just give answers.

©WALT DISNEY PRODUCTIONS

Impress your friends, figure little deals, close sales and feel smarter with the world's most powerful calculator.

Alco, one of America's largest manufacturers of paper clips and rubber bands, has developed a space-age computer miracle.

HERE'S WHAT IT CAN DO

You're a salesman. You're at lunch with a prospective customer. While discussing prices, your customer pulls out his $400 Hewlett Packard HP-80. You pull out your $19.95 Mickey Math. Two minutes later you walk out with the sale.

You're the financial vice president of a major U.S. corporation. You're at the board of directors meeting. The chairman of the board poses an important financial question and points to you for the answer. You open your briefcase and pull out your Mickey Math. The next day you're promoted to president.

Success stories like the above are real possibilities when you own a Mickey Math calculator. In fact our guarantee of satisfaction clearly states, "If the Mickey Math calculator does not make you rich, famous, more interesting and smarter, return it any time within two weeks for a prompt and courteous refund." And no other calculator company could dare make that guarantee.

FOR LITTLE DEALS ONLY

Mickey Math has six large, yet powerful digits. That's why we recommend it for little deals only. Its full-floating decimal, four-function constant and algebraic logic (you perform the functions as you think) make working complex problems a breeze.

You can do chain calculations, derive negative balances and figure all kinds of answers automatically, all by pressing little round buttons. It's truly the ultimate calculator.

Mickey Math is only 1" x 7½" x 7½" and fits conveniently in your briefcase, suitcase or the trunk of your car. It weighs only 14 ounces and its built-in, space-age handle makes it fun to lug around.

THEY'LL NEVER FORGET YOU

Give Mickey Math to somebody you want to impress: your boss, banker, State Farm insurance salesman or favorite General Motors executive. They'll not only be getting the latest in space-age technology, but they'll never forget you.

It is true that the Mickey Math calculator was designed for children. The instruction booklet with its colorful pictures and clear examples is designed to stimulate math interest and create little geniuses.

But as America's largest single source of electronic calculators and other space-age products, we feel Mickey Math's place is with the executive—as a business tool and as a major element in his day-to-day, decision-making process.

If you're looking for the perfect gift or a great business tool, we urge you to act quickly and order your Mickey Math electronic calculator at no obligation today!

EXECUTIVE ORDER FORM

☐ Yes, please rush me Mickey Math electronic calculator(s) @ $27.45 each ($19.95 plus $2.50 postage and handling complete with one year warranty and explicit Mickey Mouse instructions. I understand that if I do not become rich, famous, more interesting or smarter, I may return Mickey Math within two weeks for a prompt and courteous refund.

☐ Please add the $4.95 AC adapter which will allow me to conserve battery power while using the calculator at my desk or during lengthy executive conferences.

☐ Please add the $5.00 padded carrying case.

Clip out Executive Order Form and mail with your check to the address shown below.

JS&A NATIONAL SALES GROUP

DEPT XXX 4200 DUNDEE RD
NORTHBROOK, ILL. 60062 (312) 564-9000
©JS&A GROUP, INC. 1975

We came up with a brilliant idea and ordered every piece we could get our hands on.

idea, it just might work. In fact, I was so confident it would that I bought out the supplier's entire inventory—5,000 pieces. I now had a total exclusive and the supplier wasn't going to be importing any large quantities unless I totally sold out.

I went back to my office and within a few hours I had one of the most incredible ads I had ever written. It was funny, it was well written and it had the most unbelievable guarantee I had ever come up with. The following is an excerpt:

"You're a salesman. You're at lunch with a prospective customer. While discussing prices, your customer pulls out his $400 Hewlett-Packard HP-80. You pull out your $19.95 Mickey Math. Two minutes later you walk out with the sale.

"You're the financial vice president of a major U.S. corporation. You're at the board of directors meeting. The chairman of the board poses an important financial question and points to you for the answer. You open your briefcase and pull out your Mickey Math. The next day you're promoted to president.

"Success stories like the above are real possibilities when you own a Mickey Math calculator. In fact our guarantee of satisfaction clearly states, 'If the Mickey Math calculator does not make you rich, famous, more interesting and smarter, return it anytime within two weeks for a prompt and courteous refund.'"

The copy went on to describe the product in more detail. But I was so convinced that I would sell out quickly (remember, I only had 5,000 of these things and I normally sold over 20,000 of most products), I decided to do something that I had not done for a long time. I removed the credit card option from my offer. You had to pay by check. I also eliminated my toll-free number. After all, there was no need for it since this was a mail-in-only offer.

I tested the ad in the Southwestern edition of *The Wall Street Journal,* where I tested all my ads, and waited for the response. I waited and waited. Something was wrong. Did the *Journal* forget

The response did not meet our expectations.

to run the ad? I called. No, they didn't forget. The *Journal* representative assured me that it had run, and followed up with, "I'm sorry."

We received a grand total of 12 orders. This was one of the worst disasters I had ever had. But I knew why. In trying to hold down my response to 5,000 orders I eliminated the convenient credit card option. There was no toll-free number for ordering, and finally, there was the headline. The advertising experts always say to put a benefit in the headline, and my headline simply read, "Presenting Mickey Math."

So I changed the ad completely. I added the credit card option, I added the toll-free number and I changed the headline to add a real benefit. It now read, "Get Rich Quick."

I ran the ad again in the Southwestern edition of the *Journal*. This time it pulled only 8 orders. It was a complete bomb. And I ended up with 4,980 unsold Mickey Mouse calculators.

The moral here: Don't get so wrapped up in your incredible ad copy that you lose sight of the fact that you've got a product to sell. And don't buy 5,000 of anything until you are confident that you can sell them. I got caught in the ego trap and fell in love with my own copy.

The Laser Beam Mousetrap

Ralph Waldo Emerson is often quoted as saying that if you build a better mousetrap the world will beat a path to your door. Actually, his exact words were: "If a man write a better book, preach a better sermon or make a better mousetrap than his neighbor, though he build his house in the woods, the world will make a beaten path to his door."

I had never, previous to this time in 1977, invented anything on my own. I was in the business of selling the most novel and newest of electronic products—the better calculator, the better computer, the better telephone answering unit—but I had never sold anything that was mine. I had not yet invented the better mousetrap.

That was all about to end. Somebody had approached me with a new laser beam device that focused a powerful beam of

*"Build a better mousetrap,"
Emerson said,
so we did.
And then what?*

light to a fine point with a half million watts of power. I racked my brain to come up with something that really made sense for the consumer market. I thought to myself, "You know, Joe, you've never invented anything yourself. You've never come up with that better mousetrap. That's it! Why not invent a better mousetrap?"

I remembered what Emerson had said and I decided to build, without question and without compromise, the finest mousetrap the world had ever known.

The Laser Beam Mousetrap sold for $1,500 and all I needed to do was sell one to break even in the Southwestern edition of *The Wall Street Journal*. Just one.

The company that brought me the laser beam device also used their laser technology to create holographic pendants—1-3/4-inch diameter holographic images surrounded by a gold-tone rim and supplied with a chain. Perfect for Mother's Day.

My concept was to offer the Laser Beam Mousetrap as an attention-getting device with the hopes of selling a few to cover the ad cost and then to also offer the $20 pendants in time for Mother's Day to earn my profit from the program.

But Mother's Day was fast approaching. And I once again had an ego attack and fell in love with my copy. So I simply decided to spend $20,000 on a small national campaign figuring for sure I'll sell enough mousetraps to break even.

The campaign ran in *The Wall Street Journal* and a few other publications in which we always did well, and guess what? It was a total bomb. I didn't sell a single Laser Beam Mousetrap and I didn't sell enough pendants.

But the copy was incredible. My favorite passage is: "The entire system is mounted on a polished walnut base which can be handsomely displayed in any office, board room, or rodent-infested area."

The Laser Beam Mousetrap ad was another good lesson.

YES, I AGREE, YOU **HAVE** INDEED BUILT A BETTER MOUSETRAP. BUT COULD ANYONE **AFFORD** IT ?

First, I should have tested. The urgency with Mother's Day approaching was no excuse. If, for some reason, I couldn't have quickly tested, then I shouldn't have taken the chance. Second, a good product shouldn't be dependent on a specific holiday to sell. It should be something that could sell at any time of the year. And finally, Emerson may have had some great ideas, but I wonder how he would have made it as a marketing person.

The Importance of Testing

The theme that weaves itself throughout these examples, as you may already have realized, is the importance of testing before committing to run a major campaign and of listening to what the tests tell you. In the case of the CheckMaster, I ignored the message that the test gave me, namely to be cautious, and in the case of the other products, either I plain committed to buying too much of the product (as I did with Mickey Math) or I didn't test the ad but justified running it quickly in time for a holiday (as with the Laser Beam Mousetrap). In all cases, falling in love with my ad copy affected my decision as well.

I had many other experiences with products that bombed. At the time they were painful experiences. I spent the time to first select the product, photograph it, write the ad copy, enter the ad copy into a typesetting computer and then paste up all the elements into an ad. Then I had to test the ad. If I lost money on the test, no big deal. All I lost was a few hundred dollars, and a lot of time and effort. I learned something new, but it was still painful to know I had wasted not only my time but the time of those around me and the hopes and dreams of the supplier.

But the rewards of winning far surpassed the pain of losing. And it wasn't whether I won or lost that was important. Was I playing the game? Was I really contributing my talents, my creativity and my drive to bringing new and exciting products to the consumer? I really worked at it. And in the process I was rewarded with a few really lucky breaks.

In the many years that I had losses, none was more significant than the two that follow: my protracted battle with the Federal Trade Commission (we'll save that for the next marketing story) and a promotion that we did with National Car Rental. First the National Car Rental promotion.

The Car Rental Premium Wars

The year was 1982 and Budget Car Rental had announced a car rental program with incentives. Rent a car from Budget and you received, free with your car rental, a tote bag.

The promotion worked so well for Budget that they increased the prizes and started offering a few more pieces of luggage. Market share was dropping at the other car rental companies and everybody blamed the business that was being taken away by Budget.

National Car Rental, Hertz, Avis and a few smaller agencies decided to take action to protect their market share, so they offered premiums of their own. National called JS&A and asked us for a few suggestions. About this time, I was going to the Far East and I informed National that I would search the trading companies out there and if I found something, I would let them know.

Free gifts and our catalog too. It was a dream made in heaven. Or was it?

While in Taiwan I discovered a small, spherical-shaped alarm clock about 4 inches in diameter with an LCD display and alarm clock function buttons. It was really a clever idea because it made a great travel alarm and it was something that you could collect and give as gifts. The premiums from the other car rental companies weren't as imaginative.

National liked the clock, which I named the "TimeBall," and suggested that we put our well-recognized JS&A brand name on the product to add value. National would then offer it in their ads and at their car rental outlets.

The car rental war was on. We procured the product in the Far East and imported them as quickly as possible. It wasn't easy doing this program as the quantities were enormous, there were problems with our supplier and we ended up having to switch suppliers right in the middle of the program. But we did well and although profit on the program was not that great, it was profitable and it did give us good national exposure.

Then the war escalated. National was starting to pull ahead of the other car rental agencies as their premium, the TimeBall, was recognized as the leading premium in the market. The others had to do something so they added a few more premiums, and JS&A was again called on by National to add a few more premiums to its program. We found a portable travel iron and a hair dryer, slapped our JS&A brand name on them and they were added to the program. I would guess we brought in about a million TimeBalls, 200,000 hair dryers and 100,000 travel irons—all premiums for just renting a car one time.

Premium War Escalates

Then World War III broke out. All the car rental agencies were determined to bury their competitors. They began releasing complete catalogs with hundreds of products, and car renters were now urged to save coupons and redeem them for higher-priced products that cost hundreds of dollars. Practically no advertising was devoted to why a consumer should rent a car from Hertz or why Avis was a better company to deal with. It was a war of premiums.

National again approached JS&A and told us that they wanted to expand their program. They wanted us to offer them a complete catalog of products to tie in with their promotion. The price they were willing to pay for the more expensive premiums was very tight, however. Could we come up with a plan to keep the price of the products very low and have the program benefit us by virtue of their wide distribution?

The battle heated up as everybody in the car rental industry started giving away free premiums.

At National's hundreds of locations, we would have the opportunity of distributing our catalog with National's premium program inserted right inside it. Car renters would see our catalog and buy our other products as well as redeem their coupons for the premiums. It seemed like a program that made good sense. National would win because not only did they have our beautiful catalog to distribute, but the premiums they would offer would cost them only slightly more than they cost us. We were happy to have our catalog distributed free of charge by National and therefore could make a profit on the products we would sell from our catalog—some of which had good margins.

It made sense but it was a fatal error of judgment. It turned out that after we shipped the million or so catalogs to be distributed by National their customers ignored our catalog and just redeemed the coupons they had for the free premiums. Very few products were sold from the catalog itself, which resulted in a major loss for JS&A as well as for the entire National program.

So Much Effort in Vain

All the energy to process orders and procure product was in vain. All the hours of work, the travel to the Far East, the visits to National Car Rental in Minneapolis—all of this was for naught.

In retrospect we made two mistakes in judgment. First, when you are redeeming points in an incentive program, and something you have to buy is mixed with something you might get free, the tendency is to focus on the product you get for free and ignore the one you have to pay for.

The second error in judgment was to assume that the mass market (which we were addressing) would be interested in buying via mail order. Typically you send your catalog to proven mail order buyers—prospects who have bought via mail order before. If the buyers should match the demographics of your typical customer, chances are the catalog will be successful. Here we were distributing our catalog to non-mail order buyers who had no proven interest in our electronic products and who didn't fit the upscale demographics of our basic customer. It was indeed a costly error of judgment.

In the next marketing lesson, I relate some of the experiences I've had in a few media battles. These are not the kind in the press but with the publications themselves and the advertising they sell. The stories are interesting and will also give you some insight into the process of buying media.

Marketing Lesson 7

Media Experiences

My experiences with media are many. But the most unusual experience came from a magazine published by the Carte Blanche credit card company in 1978.

Not Exactly Carte Blanche

The magazine was called *Carte Blanche* and was represented in Chicago by Sydney Lightstone—an older, stately gentleman who was thrilled to work with me. Why? Because we consistently increased the number of our ads in his magazine year after year. And for good reason. The cost per thousand was reasonable, the upscale audience was perfect for our products, and the response was always among the strongest of any of the magazines we advertised in.

So responsive was this publication, I could place almost all my ads in the magazine with some assurance that they would work even if they didn't work anywhere else.

In one issue we ran 10 full-page ads. Sydney really appreciated the order and, as a result of JS&A's ads, he was the top salesperson working on the *Carte Blanche* account.

One day I received a strange call from Sydney. "Joe, you're not going to believe this. In all my days as a magazine rep, I have never seen anything like what you are about to receive in the mail. It's a letter from the head of advertising for the magazine and you're going to be quite shocked when you receive it. Please call me when you get the letter and please don't ask me to read it to you before you receive it."

The Letter Arrived

The next day I got the letter. It was from Doris Kitchen, the vice president of marketing for *Carte Blanche* magazine, and indeed I understood what Sydney was talking about. In the letter, Ms. Kitchen acknowledged our increased volume of advertising and explained that while she welcomed our ads because of the "quality and character of the format," she was concerned that there was too much mail order advertising in her publication, which could generate an effect that was not "wholly in keeping with the overall image we are trying to build for the magazine."

Her next paragraph, however, really made me laugh: "We are further concerned that when an advertiser has a dominant number of pages in the book (such as your January/February 10 pages in a 76-page magazine), this may imply some type of involvement on the part of *Carte Blanche*. Presently, subscribers (who are actually members), when writing or talking to us, will refer to 'your advertisement' rather than recognizing they are those of a paid advertiser."

She went on to tell me that she was limiting the number of pages we could run to only four and then asked that I understand her desire to increase the impact of all advertisers through this restriction.

A Groundbreaking First

Think about it. Most magazines would die to have 10 ads in a single issue. And I had never heard of any advertiser being restricted because of placing too many ads. This was a first—a groundbreaking concept on the part of *Carte Blanche*.

I called Sydney on the phone and told him I received the letter. "What do you think?" he asked.

"Sydney, you call Ms. Kitchen and tell her that I received her letter and that I understand perfectly. In fact, tell her that I'm going to do my part to help her get more advertisers."

Sydney thanked me for my understanding and we hung up. The following month I placed an ad in a national trade publication, *Advertising Age*, in which I duplicated Doris Kitchen's letter with a strong warning written across the bottom of the ad. The copy read as follows:

> WARNING: This letter from *Carte Blanche* should be a warning to all other national magazines and newspapers, especially the ones in which we advertise. If we're successful in your magazine, watch out. Issue by issue our ad volume will increase. Then without notice, you'll find yourself dominated by one advertiser. People will talk. Management will grumble. And you'll be forced to take the very same measures *Carte Blanche* took. PS: If you are a national advertiser with pretty ads, please help *Carte Blanche* out. Run some advertising with them. They need your help.

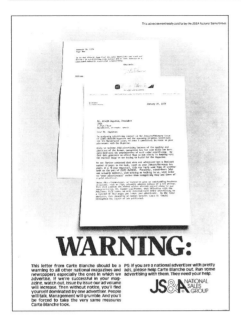

WARNING:

This letter from Carte Blanche should be a warning to all other national magazines and newspapers especially the ones in which we advertise. If we're successful in your magazine, watch out. Issue by issue our ad volume will increase. Then without notice, you'll find yourself dominated by one advertiser. People will talk. Management will grumble. And you'll be forced to take the very same measures Carte Blanche took.

PS: If you are a national advertiser with pretty ads, please help Carte Blanche out. Run some advertising with them. They need your help.

JS&A NATIONAL SALES GROUP

The ad ran in
Advertising Age
and warned all the
other publications
to be very careful
when they dealt
with us.

The ad ran. Sydney called me and we had a good laugh. But then the telegrams and letters started to pour in. All basically said the same thing: "Joe, dominate us." I must have gotten letters from dozens of magazines offering me all kinds of deals to run just a few of my ads. And from *Carte Blanche* I heard nothing. They never sent me another letter. We eventually reduced the number of ads we were running to only four. But many of the advertising deals we got from other magazines as a result of running the *Advertising Age* ad more than paid for the advertising costs.

Sharper Than I Anticipated

In the early '80s I had a battle with another advertiser over media. A competitor was challenging our firmly entrenched position in the front of most magazines in which we advertised.

We had always gotten page 1, for example, in all the airline magazines. This not only set the tone and prestige for our company but also gave air travelers a consistent place to look each month for the latest in electronics and the latest advertising approach from JS&A. We received many fan letters that would simply say, "I just wanted you to know that the only reason I look in the airline magazines is to read your ads." And the in-flight magazines weren't the only magazines where we were running our ads very close to the beginning of the publication.

One day, I got a call from our in-flight magazine rep—the guy who represented advertising placed in about half of all the airline magazines. "Joe, I've got bad news for you. It seems that our San Francisco rep has muscled in on our first-page position and we're going to have to give it to another advertiser."

"What!" I shouted. "You find out who this advertiser is and let me talk to the publisher."

No sooner did I hang up but I got another call from another one of the magazines we advertised in regularly. "Joe, we've got to push you out of your page-one position for another advertiser on the West Coast."

He too wouldn't tell me the name of the advertiser because apparently this was one of the stipulations the advertiser made.

A New Company

This was a revolt. Not only were we the leading advertiser in many of the magazines in which we advertised, but we were one of the largest of the mail order companies in the U.S. Who was behind this incursion into our turf?

It didn't take too long to find out. Some upstart company out of San Francisco called "The Sharper Image" was advertising a watch. Not only did their advertising find its way into many of the far-forward positions we had previously held for years in the magazines, but they were creating an exciting new look—a different look from my approach. There were very dramatic photographs, good copy and a slightly different layout—novel since most of the other mail order companies tried to copy our format.

At my seminar, I would present my competitors' ads. They copied everything I did. The layouts looked very similar and the copy approaches were similar to mine. At the seminar, I would show some of The Sharper Image ads and comment: "Watch this company. Not only are they aggressive in beating us out for page positions in magazines, but they are the first company that isn't directly copying me. They've innovated with their own style and if anybody will be successful, watch, it will be them. They're a class act."

Then about six months later, I got a call while I was planning my next seminar. It was from the president of The Sharper Image, Richard Thalheimer. "I'd like to attend your seminar for free. Right now I don't have much money, but that's OK because someday I'm going to be hugely successful and you'll be happy that I did attend."

I thanked Thalheimer and told him that everybody had to pay to attend and that when he could afford it, he should give me a call.

Prediction Proves True

Of course the rest is history. The Sharper Image became a very successful company and Richard Thalheimer, its president, became a very successful merchant—just as he had predicted, and as I had predicted for his company.

In later years, a few of his former employees attended my seminar. But Thalheimer never did. Today, I'm proud to count Richard as one of my friends and somebody I've always respected in this business.

There are many more "war" stories I could relate about my experiences with the media and the characters with whom I've had to deal. But the two above are among the most interesting and ones which I felt you would also enjoy.

In the previous marketing story, "The Biggest Losers," I discussed many of my failures and the lessons that I learned. They were often painful and expensive but they did teach me a great deal. But probably the most painful lesson I learned was when I took on the Federal Trade Commission in a protracted battle that lasted six years. But there is always a silver lining or a benefit that sometimes isn't apparent when you go through one of these horrible experiences. And that is what happened many years after the experience I am about to relate to you. See if you can guess what benefit I realized almost 17 years later.

A Marketing Story

The FTC Battle

The Monster That Eats Business

In which the most dangerous monster in America tries to eat one small business and gets indigestion.

It was a fight to the very end. And indeed they got indigestion. But I almost got eaten alive in the process.

Every now and then there comes a defining moment in your life when events take a unique twist and you end up going in a totally different direction. That is what this story is about. From the twists that I experienced, I entered a new phase of my life in which all my skills of marketing were pressed into action only to bring me to the realization that indeed there was one marketing challenge I wasn't going to win. First, some background.

The year was 1978—a peak year in my career. Our advertising was appearing in hundreds of magazines, and new product innovations were being introduced to the public through our company. Major corporations were coming to me with their products. And our sales were escalating rapidly as if all my efforts were finally bearing fruit. It felt great.

All that success was earned through hard work and a genuine concern for the consumer. I really cared about my customers. And this care was reflected in the way we conducted every aspect of our business.

Then came two minor events that changed the course of my life. The first was three major snowstorms that hit the Chicago area and the second was simply the delivery of one of my catalogs to a customer in Chicago.

Each week for three weeks, starting late in December of 1978 and continuing on into January of 1979, Chicago was hit by a major snowstorm. So much snow had accumulated that many of our staff couldn't make it to work. In addition, our computer broke down and we couldn't get service people out to our offices to repair it. Finally after weeks of struggle, we managed to get our computer repaired and all our orders filled.

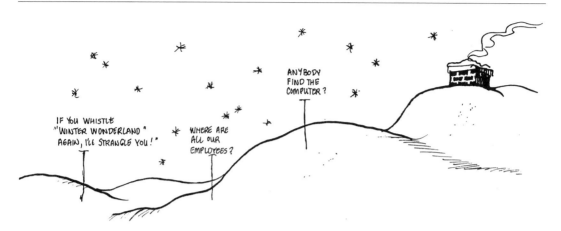

In the illustration: "IF YOU WHISTLE 'WINTER WONDERLAND' AGAIN, I'LL STRANGLE YOU!" — "WHERE ARE ALL OUR EMPLOYEES?" — "ANYBODY FIND THE COMPUTER?"

Three major blizzards buried us.

The second event was the delivery of a catalog. Walter Baron was a JS&A customer. He enjoyed our catalogs and occasionally bought from us. Walter coincidentally worked for the FTC.

The FTC (Federal Trade Commission) is the government agency in charge of regulating advertising and business practices in general. They had just promulgated a new mail order rule that required companies to print in their catalogs the simple phrase, "Warranties available upon request." This new rule was designed for those consumers who wanted to inspect the warranties of the products being offered before they purchased them. We would have been happy to comply with this new FTC rule, but we didn't know about it.

Walter Baron observed that we had not published the notice. He could have picked up the phone and told us that we omitted it and we would have corrected it in our next issue, but instead he turned the catalog over to a young FTC investigator, Thomas Westhoff, in January of '79. Westhoff visited JS&A, had conversations with our staff and called a week later.

"Mr. Sugarman, this is Mr. Westhoff from the FTC. We have decided to fine your company $100,000 for not shipping your products on time and for not notifying your customers during the time your computer broke down."

I explained the circumstances of our computer breakdown and that everything was finally fixed and only a few complaints had been received.

"It doesn't make any difference. You broke the mail order rule and the rule does not allow for any mitigating circumstances. Not one."

I sat down with members of the FTC and tried to work out a settlement.

My attorneys advised me to pay the penalty. "It doesn't matter if you're right or wrong. They're out to get publicity and build their careers and you should pay their penalty and get on with your life."

This was indeed a nightmare for me. I had worked hard to establish a good reputation with my customers. And then I thought, "What is our government coming to? If I allow this to happen, what will the government do to the next guy? And what about the other agencies in government? If they could arbitrarily go around fining companies just for the sake of getting publicity to build their careers, what kind of government would we have?"

I tried to negotiate a dismissal. But the FTC wasn't at all interested. They wanted their $100,000. Then in February of '79 I got a phone call from Pete Hoke, publisher of *Direct Marketing* magazine, calling to give me some good news.

"Joe, you have been selected by the New York Direct Marketing Day staff to be the recipient of the "1979 Direct Marketing Man of the Year" award. I am asking that you come to New York in March to accept the award before the 3,000 people who will be in attendance."

I couldn't believe the call. I never expected to be picked from all the eligible people in our industry. I was only 40 years old and there were certainly many more people who had been in the business longer and were better qualified. But as Pete told me, "You were the unanimous choice of the committee and we are looking forward to giving you that award."

My lawyer pleaded with me not to do it.

After I hung up I realized something. It was a wonderful award to receive, but I was about to be fined by the FTC for $100,000 for violating the rules of the same industry that was about to award me their highest honor.

This was a dilemma for me. I felt trapped. But instinctively I felt that there was something terribly wrong if a good, decent businessman could be singled out and attacked by the government.

In an effort to resolve my conflict with the FTC, I created a print ad to run in all of the magazines in which we ran our advertising asking for support—not financial support but the moral support of businesspeople and consumers all over the country. (Incidentally, the cost for this ad campaign was not tax deductible as a business expense since it was considered political advertising.)

Just before the ad was completed I was told that a Customs official was requesting $200,000 in penalties from our company. If we didn't pay it, we would not receive any of the other shipments we were expecting which had to be cleared by Customs. The official wouldn't tell us why the penalty was being levied, for "security reasons." "What?" I thought. "Now we can't even find out why we are being penalized."

In this case, I had no choice. I had to pay the $200,000 or not get any more product through Customs. I'd be practically out of business. Or I could pay the fine and then give the case to what is called a customs lawyer—somebody who specializes in customs cases. Indeed, I called the attorney who was recommended and who knew the Customs official who fined us. "Yes," he said, "they do this all the time and recently there has been a lot of it. Don't expect to get relief for at least three years, even if you prevail."

The war started with this ad that ran in November of 1979.

About the time of my encounter with the Customs Service, my ad broke, first in *The Wall Street Journal*, then *The New York Times* and then in dozens of magazines we advertised in nationally. The ad copy is as follows:

Headline: FTC Revolt

Subheadline: You've heard of the tax revolt. It's about time for an FTC revolt. Here's my story and why we've got to stop federal bureaucratic regulation.

Copy: I'm pretty lucky. When I started my business in my basement eight years ago, I had little more than an idea and a product.

The product was the pocket calculator. The idea was to sell it through advertisements in national magazines and newspapers.

Those first years in the basement weren't easy. But we worked hard and through imaginative advertising and a dedicated staff, JS&A grew rapidly to become well recognized as an innovator in electronics and marketing.

THREE BLIZZARDS

In January of 1979, three major blizzards struck the Chicago area. The heaviest snowfall hit Northbrook, our village—just 20 miles north of Chicago.

Many of our employees were stranded—unable to get to our office where huge drifts made travel impossible. Not only were we unable to reach our office, but our computer totally broke down leaving us in even deeper trouble.

But we fought back. Our staff worked around the clock and on weekends. First, we processed orders manually. We also hired a group of computer specialists, rented outside computer time, employed a computer service bureau, and hired temporary help to feed this new computer network. We never gave up. Our totally dedicated staff and the patience of many of our customers helped us through the worst few months in our history. Although there were many customers who had to wait over 30 days for their parcels, every package was eventually shipped.

WE OPENED OUR DOORS

During this period, some of our customers called the FTC (Federal Trade Commission) to complain. We couldn't blame them. Despite our efforts to manually notify our customers of our delays, our computer was not functioning making the task extremely difficult.

The FTC advised JS&A of these complaints. To assure the FTC that we were a responsible company, we invited them to visit us. During their visit we showed them our computerized microfilm system which we use to back up every transaction. We showed them our new dual computer system (our main system and a backup system in case our main system ever failed again). And, we demonstrated how we were able to locate and trace every order. We were very cooperative, allowing them to look at every document they requested.

The FTC left. About one week later, they called and told us that they wanted us to pay a $100,000 penalty for not shipping our products within their 30-day rule. (The FTC rule states that anyone paying by check is entitled to have their purchase shipped within 30 days or they must be notified and given the option to cancel.)

NOT BY CONGRESS

The FTC rule is not a law nor a statute passed by Congress, but rather a rule created by the FTC to strengthen their enforcement powers. I always felt that the rule was intended to be used against companies that purposely took advantage of the consumer. Instead, it appears that the real violators, who often are too difficult to prosecute, get away while JS&A, a visible and highly respected company that pays taxes and has contributed to our free enterprise system, is singled out. I don't think that was the intent of the rule.

And when the FTC goes to court, they have the full resources of the US Government. Small, legitimate businesses haven't got a chance.

We're not perfect. We do make mistakes. But if we do make a mistake, we admit it, accept the responsibility, and then take whatever measures necessary to correct it. That's how we've built our reputation.

BLOW YOUR KNEE CAPS OFF

Our attorneys advised us to settle. As one attorney said, "It's like a bully pulling out a gun and saying, 'If you don't give me a nickel, I'll blow your knee caps off.'" They advised us that the government will subpoena thousands of documents to harass us and cause us great inconvenience. They warned us that even if we went to court and won, we would end up spending more in legal fees than if we settled.

To settle would mean to negotiate a fine and sign a consent decree. The FTC would then issue a press release publicizing their victory.

At first we tried to settle. We met with two young FTC attorneys and agreed in principle to pay consumers for any damages caused them. But there were practically no damages, just a temporary computer problem, some late shipments, and some bad weather. The FTC then issued a massive subpoena requesting documents that will take us months to gather and which we feel was designed to harass or force us to accept their original $100,000 settlement request.

Remember, the FTC publicizes their actions. And the higher the fine, the more the publicity and the more stature these two attorneys will have at the FTC.

If this all sounds like blackmail—that's just what it appeared to be to us.

We did ship our products late—something we've admitted to them and which we publicly admit here, but we refuse to be blackmailed into paying a huge fine at the expense of our company's reputation—something we've worked hard eight years to build.

We're not a big company and we realize it would be easier to settle now at any cost. But we're not. If this advertisement can attract the attention of Congressmen and Senators who have the power to stop the harassment of Americans by the FTC, then our efforts will be well spent.

ALL AMERICANS AFFECTED

Federal regulation and the whims of a few career-building bureaucrats is costing taxpayers millions, destroying our free enterprise system, affecting our productivity as a nation and as a result is lowering everybody's standard of living.

I urge Congressmen, Senators, businessmen and above all, the consumer to support legislation to take the powers of the FTC from the hands of a few unelected officials and bring them back to Congress and the people.

I will be running this advertisement in hundreds of magazines and newspapers during the coming months. I'm not asking for contributions to support my effort as this is my battle, but I do urge you to send this advertisement to your Congressmen and Senators. That's how you can help.

America was built on the free enterprise system. Today, the FTC is undermining this system. Freedom is not something that can be taken for granted and you often must fight for what you believe. I'm prepared to lead that fight. Please help me.

Note: To find out the complete story and for a guide on what action you can take, write me personally for my free booklet, "Blow your knee caps off."

The response was quick and heavy. First the FTC issued a

Against the law, they issued a press release smearing my reputation.

press release which announced that the case was pending and there was a basis for the charges which they couldn't disclose quite yet.

Then the response started to flood in. Even though I specifically refused to accept contributions, people were sending me checks—$50, $100, even $1,000 checks with strong letters of support. I returned all the checks.

The letters were very heartwarming. I had made a move that could literally force me out of business. These people realized it and expressed unconditional support for what I was doing.

I even got letters from people who were victims of other bureaucratic agencies that made my case seem almost mild by comparison. There were people who were put out of business, who quit their own business and retired rather than battle the government, and finally there were citizens who were just plain appalled by what the FTC could arbitrarily do.

Many of the writers took time out to send a very lengthy letter to their senators and congressmen with copies to me. Others wrote the FTC directly.

Many of the letters were beautifully crafted by people who wrote from their heart. Common themes were love of country and a deep concern for the abuses of power at all levels of government. I would often read the letters and experience the full spectrum of emotions—some letters brought tears to my eyes while others even made me laugh.

One of the letters that lightened my day was from a Mr. Harold Miller who had read my FTC Revolt ad in *Popular Science* magazine. He was obviously outraged and so much so that he had to grab a piece of paper and jot me a handwritten note of support and request the free booklet I offered in my ad. His letter read, "Please send me your free booklet as referred to in your ad in the Feb., 1980 issue of *Popular Science*. Thank you and I hope you beat the bastards."

Mr. Miller put a large asterisk next to the word "bastards," then signed his name, gave his address and then put another asterisk below referring to the terrible word he had just called the FTC. His next comment began almost as an apology for being so vulgar—as if he wanted to apologize for using the word. It read, "that might be a strong word to use but I think the sons-of-bitches deserve it."

The free booklet called "Blow your knee caps off" with the subtitle "The story of the FTC attack against JS&A Group, Inc.," contained the story of the FTC battle and included letters from those who had already responded to my ad along with examples of how the U.S. government handled its own mail orders paid by check. They handled them terribly. U.S. government customers had to wait months to get a reply for their back-ordered products.

I then created an FTC "Battle Report"—a monthly summary of the activities that were taking place in my case to keep my supporters apprised of my activities. By May of '80, the FTC was throwing charges at us in the press. NBC was doing a story on the battle when Mike

JS&A/FTC Battle Report

We issued regular reports to our supporters on the bizarre events of my case.

Wallace of *60 Minutes* called me and requested a story too. I thanked him for his interest but said I was already doing the story on NBC and felt that he would not want to duplicate what NBC was doing. He agreed and appreciated my disclosure.

Publicity about the battle was running in magazines and newspapers throughout the country. I was asked to speak at several major political events including the Libertarian Party convention where one of the officials suggested I run as their candidate for president.

The FTC was throwing charges against me that were totally false and misleading. And the press was following the line of the FTC, publishing the FTC side of the story. Often the press would print whatever the FTC gave them without calling me first.

Then in the fall of '80 the harassment from the FDA (U.S. Food and Drug Administration) started. The FDA wanted to investigate our warehouse to see if we were violating any of their rules. Then the IRS announced they were doing a full audit. Both agencies admitted that they worked together. "There's nothing unusual or secret about it. We all try to help each other out," was one bureaucrat's comment. But one good thing did develop.

I also got a call from my customs attorney. He advised us that the U.S. Customs Service had dropped their charges against us completely and were returning our deposit. It would take about two months to get us the refund.

I questioned my attorney on how often charges were dropped against a company. "Never," was his answer. "In all my years in this office, I've never had the Customs people simply call me and drop a case."

Agencies such as the FTC were almost totally independent and accountable to nobody. The Congress of the United States had jurisdiction over the FTC and oversight responsibilities were handled by the House of Representatives' Sub-Committee on Oversight and Investigations of the Committee on Energy and Commerce headed by John Dingell, a congressman from the Detroit area.

If I could bring this case to the attention of the oversight committee, maybe I could effect change in our government. I needed my supporters to rally again to my side and write the committee to request a hearing.

In order to explain the complicated set of circumstances to the public and win support, I employed Dick Hafer, a political cartoonist in Washington who called himself "The Comics

THE COMICS COMMANDO

Dick Hafer saw what was going on and helped put what was happening into perspective.

Commando." Dick took on cases such as mine after fully investigating them. If he believed in my cause, he would take on the responsibility of explaining my battle through a comic book. His comic books were simply written, humorous and easy to read. Hafer used humor to entertain and keep the interest of the reader as he slowly explained the circumstances of my case. It was a perfect vehicle to get my story across.

Hafer first investigated our case thoroughly. He found out that there were practically no complaints against our company in any of the Better Business Bureaus throughout the country and that our reputation was excellent. He studied the law, the case itself and interviewed people who could substantiate what I had been claiming. Like many others familiar with the case, he came away with the sense that this was a good example of bureaucratic harassment.

Even the executive committee of the Direct Mail Marketing Association sent a delegation to JS&A offices to inspect our operation and they too walked away impressed with our efficiency.

Cartoon Book Is Mailed

Dick drew up a 24-page cartoon book entitled "The Monster That Eats Business—the story of how a bureaucratic agency tried to eat one small businessman and got indigestion."

I mailed the comic book to all my supporters throughout the U.S. The response again was quick and powerful. Chairman Dingell's committee received thousands of letters—some pleading with his agency to set up an oversight hearing for a fair airing of my complaint.

I finally received a call in the spring of 1981. Chairman Dingell would hear my case. He would hold a special oversight hearing in Washington.

Finally I would be able to present my case and my facts to a group of elected representatives of our government and get a fair hearing. Finally I could expose the lies they were making to discredit me. Finally I could expose the weakness of their case and show that they still couldn't find anything despite the extensive search of our records.

My company was now at a very low point. Our staff was reduced considerably, the company was losing money and I was unable to focus or concentrate on running let alone building the company. All of the suppliers who previously were coming to me were now taking their products to The Sharper Image—once a smaller competitor.

I also owed a lot of people. I couldn't afford to pay my attorneys and my overhead. I had to sell equipment, my office building, everything I owned to stay afloat. I even announced in one of my newsletters that I was now accepting "contributions" and I received a lot of them. I kept track of each one and eventually paid them all back.

I also met Jere Glover, an attorney from Tennessee who was a good friend of Albert Gore Jr., then a congressman from Tennessee who happened to be on the committee. "It wouldn't hurt before the oversight hearing for you to meet with Gore in his office and tell him a little bit of your side of the story," Glover told me. "If he sees that you're not the crooked businessperson the FTC and the media have made you out to be, it might be worth it."

I agreed and that is exactly what I did. Glover and I made an appointment with Gore's secretary, and on September 17, 1981, the day before the oversight hearing, I met with Gore.

I Meet with Gore

As I was ushered into Gore's richly paneled office, he was seated in a leather chair behind his desk. Gore stood up, shook my lawyer's hand and then walked around his desk and shook my hand saying, "Nice to meet you, Mr. Sugarman."

In front of his desk were three leather chairs and a couch. He motioned for us to sit down. The room was dark as a result of the dark paneling. It reminded me of a very conservative lawyer's office.

Gore crossed his legs in a very relaxed fashion and after some small talk, I started to explain my position in the case and gave Gore a brief overview of what had happened during the past year.

I explained to him that I was a small businessman who tried to run his business in an honest and ethical way. I then explained the sequence of events as concisely as possible and ended with the statement, "Look, I don't expect you to stand up and say this guy Sugarman has been unfairly attacked and this case should be dropped. All I am asking for is a fair and impartial hearing so that the actions of the FTC in their attack against me can be looked at very closely. And I just wanted you to meet me personally and see that I'm not the crooked businessman that the FTC has portrayed through their publicity. I really care about my customer, about running an ethical business and providing a service to my country."

Gore listened intently throughout my explanation. He seemed to sympathize with me, often nodding his head as if in agreement with what I was saying.

Good Feelings from Meeting

After I finished, Gore kept nodding his head, paused for a moment and then said, "I think I understand your position and appreciate the opportunity to meet you, Mr. Sugarman. There are excesses in government. We all know that. And that is why we hold these hearings in the first place. I'm really glad I had the opportunity to meet you and hear your side of the story. I know when the facts are presented, the committee will make fair and just recommendations. Thank you for taking the time and coming to see me."

Glover, sensing that the meeting was coming to an end, rose and said, "Thanks, Congressman Gore, I appreciate the time you've taken. I'll look forward to seeing you at the hearing."

I stood and shook his hand as we departed from his office. As I left the Sam Rayburn Building in Washington where Gore was headquartered, I looked at my attorney and said, "That was a great idea meeting with Gore ahead of time. He seemed like he would be fair and impartial."

Glover agreed. "He's not going to act like he's on your side, but we've certainly given him second thoughts about the FTC's actions. And that was really the purpose of the meeting."

It was indeed a relief for me to know that Gore would not be hostile towards me during the hearing. And I could now see why having a lawyer from Tennessee, the same home state as Gore, made sense.

The hearing was scheduled for the next day—a day I had been looking forward to for a long time. I had worked very hard to have "my day in court." I had fought the good fight and now was the payoff I had been working so hard to achieve. I had done something very few businesspeople had ever done. I had fought a government agency and then had the opportunity to bring them to task for the abuses that they had inflicted upon me. To some I was a hero; to others I was a fool. But now was my opportunity to prove just who I really was. What my company stood for. I slept well that night.

Dark Clouds over Washington

Glover arranged to have a limousine pick up my staff and me the next morning. It was Friday, September 18, 1981, the date of the hearing. Mary Stanke, at the time my assistant, and three of our customer service people who might be asked to testify accompanied me to the hearing. They were very knowledgeable about our customer service procedures and would honestly answer any questions about the computer breakdown.

I can remember that morning as if it were yesterday. Dark clouds hung low over Washington. When the limousine picked us up, Mary commented to me that she felt she was going to a funeral. Little did I realize at that moment how right she was.

I sat in the audience and looked around the room. In the audience was the future head of the Direct Mail Marketing Association, Jonah Gitlitz. Dozens of my supporters filled the room. There were supportive congressmen, businesspeople and the media. Several TV cameras were positioned in the TV area of the room. Dingell, Gore, and a few of the other congressmen were seated in their chairs and the proceedings started.

It might as well have been my lynching. Everything that I had worked toward was systematically destroyed during the proceedings, which took almost three hours.

To my surprise, the FTC had flown in three people from Chicago—former JS&A employees who had been fired for not taking care of our customers properly. One employee was a customer service supervisor who spent his time on the phone selling Shaklee vitamins and not supervising his staff.

The FTC staff sat at the table and put up a convincing smoke screen for the press and the public.

The oversight hearing was called to order and the TV cameras started to run. As the meeting progressed I realized that I was being ambushed by the committee, not only by the ex-JS&A employees who were called on. Even Gore himself was on the well-rehearsed attack.

Then one of the congressmen on the committee held up a stack of papers and said, "Mr. Sugarman, you say that you had very few complaints from customers who did not receive your product, but I have a dozen letters here that say that you did not deliver products at all." The TV cameras were whirring away. (Later, after the hearing, when we had the opportunity to look over the 12 complaints, we saw they had nothing to do with the supposed FTC rule violation and were not even complaints but simply correspondence from customers who had requests.)

They even pulled out a letter from a crippled child who was waiting for his chess computer and didn't get it. The TV cameras continued whirring away. (Later when we checked, we found that we indeed had sent it and it got lost in the mail. We had actually mailed a second brand-new one even though we hadn't yet gotten the results of the trace that we initiated.)

Every one of the congressmen slammed us—all prepped by the FTC staff, who of course paraded their own set of witnesses. Their witnesses (my ex-employees) were not very credible, but nevertheless they were part of the barrage of missiles being thrown at me. Gore joined in the lynching as the most aggressive and seemed to relish questioning me and presenting bogus or slanted evidence supplied by the FTC. All while the TV cameras whirred away.

151

I have lost millions of dollars in ventures that didn't work, I have had people disappoint me with their dealings, but this had to be the most embarrassing and disappointing moment of my life. I felt ripped apart by both the congressional oversight committee and the FTC in a cleverly planned public lynching. And when it came time to chastise the FTC, the committee made only mild admonitions like, "Now the next time, you should not issue press releases on a company when you have not checked the facts." There were several other stronger recommendations made but in a very smooth and matter-of-fact way at the very end of the proceedings when most of the reporters were long gone and most of the gallery had emptied.

The hearing ended. The congressmen left the room, the remaining observers left the room and I was left alone with just my staff and my attorney, Jere Glover.

Glover kept shaking his head in disbelief. He told me that he would call me in a few days but that he was shocked and disappointed. He left the room. Dick Hafer, the political cartoonist, walked up to me as he was leaving and said, "I'm sorry," and left the room. We then all left the room ourselves and walked into the hallway.

In the hallway, there were no reporters to get any final statement from me, no supporters were there to congratulate me for standing up to the FTC—just an empty area with people rushing to go home at the end of the day.

We walked towards the area where the limo was waiting for the short ride to Washington National airport where I had my plane hangared—a twin-engine Beechcraft Duke.

It was dusk by the time we arrived. My staff took their respective seats in the six-passenger Beechcraft Duke and I climbed into the cockpit. Mary Stanke sat in the co-pilot's seat. I noticed Mary crying. "What's wrong?" I asked her.

She simply knew how much work and effort we had all put into this fight and saw how the oversight committee had ganged up on me. "I feel really bad for you and all that you sacrificed. I know how disappointed you must feel."

When I got home, I couldn't work, I had a rough time eating and I spent the entire week with my family. During the week, I reflected on the experience and the realization that this wasn't really a fair fight at all. The FTC could use the taxpayers' money to go after anybody and then force that person to settle instead of facing what I went through. The FTC lied, cheated and distorted the truth. They ganged up on me with their own oversight committee. It wasn't a fair fight at all. I realized that eventually I would have to settle.

Dick Hafer, himself a reporter, wrote the following editorial which summarized the hearing from his viewpoint. This is a slightly condensed version which appeared in my "Battle Report" following the hearing.

Headline: Reactions of a Witness

Byline: by Dick Hafer

Copy: I had never actually witnessed a real, live mugging before. I had always sort of imagined that the site of an experience like this would be a dimly lit, sleazy alley, somewhere in the bowels of a great city.

Well, it was in a great city, but it wasn't in an alley and it wasn't dimly lit. Was it sleazy? Draw your own conclusions.

This particular mugging took place in Room 2123 of the Rayburn House Office Building, in Washington, D.C. on September 18, 1981.

Normally one would be grateful if the assault were recorded on videotape by no less than eight cameras and if fifteen or twenty reporters were present to gather all of the facts, including the names of each one of the gang that committed the ghastly act.

The press joined in on the mayhem. By the end of the day, the savage perpetrators left an honest businessman for dead. His reputation had been smeared, his ethics challenged and his honesty questioned. Probably few businessmen could survive publicity of this ugliness . . . but I believe that Joe Sugarman is one of those who can.

MAJORED ON MINORS

Throughout the day, the few members of the Sub-Committee on Oversight and Investigations (House Committee on Energy and Commerce) that bothered to attend the hearings majored on minors. They consistently avoided the important issues of bureaucratic arrogance and misuse of power and zeroed in on individual letters, semantics, etc. This reporter came away with the clear impression that the committee and the agency (the FTC) were working hand-in-hand to cast JS&A in the worst possible light. It seemed to be the typical government tactic of "circling

153

the wagons" whenever another member of the federal gravy-train gets in the way of a few arrows.

For example: The committee counsels repeatedly grilled Joe on whether or not the FTC threatened him with a twenty million dollar penalty. Joe kept telling them that the FTC boys kept warning him that they could fine him $10,000 for each of the 2,000 violations. He admitted that the actual, literal words "twenty million dollars" were not used, but that it had been not a difficult thing to multiply the oft-mentioned 2,000 times $10,000. Not difficult for Joe. Not difficult for the audience. Not difficult for a fourth-grader. Not difficult for the wino behind the loading dock of the Rayburn Building.

Very difficult for the congressmen and their counsels. (Well, look . . . they have to study law, but maybe arithmetic isn't required.)

THE KNIGHTS OF THE VIDEO TUBE

And guess what the knights of the video tube featured. You guessed it. They showed the fearless committee wrapping itself in their collective flags and asking Joe if the FTC really said "twenty million dollars" and when Joe answered, "Well no. Those were my figures . . .", the cameras snapped to a halt, while Joe was finishing the fact that he simply used normal arithmetic to total up the segmented threat. And all over video-land people were yelling, "Look Harriet . . . they got the crook!!" This precise method of telling the story was used on not only the NBC station in Washington, but also on the ABC affiliate. They both seem to have a finely honed flair for the dramatic, if not for the accurate.

All day long, the committee and their comrades from the FTC were throwing around one charge. Over and over and over. Joe had told the story of how they were accusing him of poor service during the great storm and computer failure of the winter of 1979. But they, fair little devils that they are, were not even discussing the winter of 1979 . . . they were going back into Joe's own files and spotlighting the fact that from August of 1977 to December of 1978, JS&A had shipped 22,000 orders late! This was pointed out over and over. What was not pointed out, sad to say, was that this is not necessarily a violation of the FTC Mail Order Rule. It would be a violation only if the company failed to notify customers of the delay and gave them the opportunity to cancel. The cumulative effect of this barrage over an entire day was devastating.

LITTLE TIME TO VENT ON FTC

It was a little disheartening that the fearless inquisitors seemed to vent all of their anger on Joe and had precious little left by the time the FTC took the stand. They seemed to smell out a good lead on the reason that the FTC originally sought out JS&A and how the investigator handled himself, but then they lost interest and moved on.

Three ex-employees of JS&A were wheeled out onto the center stage and with great distress listed the sins of the mail-order firm as they observed during their long tenure (a few months) before they were terminated, for cause. This was maybe the best part of the show. It was truly inspired comic relief in the dreary proceedings.

Late in the day when all the media types had left or fallen asleep, several interesting things happened. Joe finally began to recover from his shock and began to fight back effectively. For most of the day, he reminded me of that crazy coyote on the Road Runner cartoons. You know, that special look, where he peers into the camera just after having a locomotive smash him head-on, or after the umpteenth boom goes off in his undies . . . and all his fur is either burned off or mashed? Remember? That was Joe. Understandably.

GORE'S LINE OF QUESTIONING

Probably the most blatant example of the lynch-mob mentality (aside from the unreal character I'll mention at the end of this article) was the line of questioning from Congressman Gore, when he held up a magazine advertisement by Joe, publicizing his seminar in which he explores the route to success. Congressman Gore, nearly salivating with delight, pointed out that Joe was telling how he teaches his students how to "break the rules."

To any person really searching for the truth, it could not be more obvious that Joe is referring to the "rules" of promotion. He's telling the world that he doesn't advertise in the same old way, but rather blazes new trails for others to follow. In fact, the ad quotes *Forbes* magazine as saying, "Joe has some unorthodox marketing approaches, but they work." It couldn't be more clear that the ad is speaking strictly of breaking the marketing rules. But to the congressional mentality, Joe was far more sinister . . . he was obviously referring to breaking government rules.

DISAPPOINTED IN OUR SYSTEM

All in all, I was totally disappointed in our system. I suppose that everyone sees any action with their own peculiar perspective, but I left believing that the committee and the FTC had blatantly overplayed their hand. I suppose that they feel that they put Joe in his place, and, in fact, that's the way the media saw it.

I'm only sure of one thing. Joe seems to me to be honest to the point of hurting himself and I couldn't find anyone in the industry that doesn't hold his integrity in the highest respect. But perhaps the most telling comment I've heard in all my interviews

155

was a statement made by an industry leader. He said, "I really respect Joe. He runs as honest an operation as there is in the mail order business, but I don't dare get in his corner. He's picking on somebody too big. The government is gonna chew him up and spit him out!"

Then again, they may choke.

The Aftermath

By the time settlement negotiations with the FTC were over, it was six years after my battle began. I had lost in the eyes of my peers and all the bad publicity had almost destroyed the reputation I had worked so hard to build. My company was in ruins. I was broke and owed over a million dollars.

I had no choice but to settle with the FTC. Even though I was right, it would cost me at least another $250,000 and two years to defend myself and I didn't see any advantage to spending any more of the taxpayers' money either. It was over. The FTC, who by this time was asking for $250,000, settled for $115,000 payable over a three-year period because they knew I couldn't pay the full amount.

Minor Role in Politics

As time went on, I took a minor role in politics. I testified in Washington to help pass the Equal Access to Justice Act in 1981 which compensates small business people for legal fees whenever they are unfairly attacked by a government agency. I gave many speeches to business groups and inspired others to stand up for what they believed in too.

But I had to start focusing now on what was left of my business and how I was going to pay everybody I owed. Slowly, over the following few years, I dug myself out of the cellar, paid back all of my debts and returned everyone's contribution to my FTC campaign.

During the years of my fight (from 1979 through 1984) I had literally lost my business and almost had to start over. I have often thought, "What would have happened if Walter Baron had not received our catalog while he worked at the FTC? What if there had been only one snowstorm and our computer never broke down?" And of course, the big question many people ask me, "Joe, would you have done it again knowing what you know

now?" I've never regretted what I did. I stood up for what I believed in. Sure, if I would have known what was going to happen at the oversight hearing, I might have handled things differently, but that's all speculation. I lost a costly battle but I eventually won the war—rebuilding my business even bigger than it was before.

The Silver Lining

There is one final anecdote I would like to share which shows that even the most horrible experiences have their silver lining or their unrealized future benefit. As I finished my previous book on copywriting and started looking through my records for possible quotes and endorsements for it, I realized that the then Congressman Gore had, at one point in the oversight proceedings, said something nice about me before launching into one of his vicious attacks.

I checked the congressional records and found that statement made by Gore, which was: "You have a real talent for promotion and writing advertisements." I am now using that quote to promote my book.

You now know how to buy media, place your advertisement and wait for the orders. There is one more step before you run your ad and that is the critical function of testing. And it is critical. In fact, it's what makes direct marketing one of the most efficient advertising methods—far superior to any other method—as you'll discover in the next marketing lesson.

Marketing Lesson 8

The Critical Function of Testing

This is one of the most important lessons in this book as it is the real key to successful direct marketing. If you can master the lessons in this chapter you will be able to:

1. Save yourself a great deal of money.

2. Improve the results of what you've done.

3. Discover the most reliable research method in marketing.

In my previous book, *Advertising Secrets of the Written Word*, I talked about the big advantage retail has over mail order, namely immediate gratification. A purchaser can pick up the product, examine it and bring it home right after purchasing it. The big advantage that mail order has over retail is curiosity. A customer's curiosity often compels him or her to buy the product. Taking this to the next level, the big advantage direct marketing has over every other form of advertising is testing.

Let's first discuss the concept behind testing as it relates to marketing. In my above-mentioned book on copywriting, I taught my readers that we buy on emotion and justify our purchases with logic. I used buying a Mercedes-Benz automobile as an example.

Reason for Purchase

If you ask John Deep Pockets, a new Mercedes-Benz purchaser, why he bought a Mercedes, he might mention the technology, the safety features and the handling of the car. But that is only the logic he uses to justify the purchase. The real reason has an emotional basis—something that the purchaser might not even realize.

Maybe he purchased the car because he just wanted to satisfy a deep desire to own an automobile he has dreamed of owning for a long time. Or it might be to show the world that he can afford such a luxury. Or it simply might be a deep desire to belong to the group of people who own a Mercedes. Maybe his father told him that he was a nobody and would never amount to anything and the Mercedes is his way of proving his father wrong. It is difficult to pinpoint the emotional reasons compelling a purchase because even the purchaser often doesn't fully realize those reasons either.

When you create a direct response ad, you hope that you have presented all the logically important justifications for the prospect to purchase your product. But you must determine the emotional reasons why people buy that particular product too. And since every product has its own nature—its own dramatic way of releasing that emotional desire in the prospect—sometimes you have to experiment or, in the case of direct response, test.

A Point in Space and Time

In addition, you have to be at that point in time and space when the product you are offering is in harmony with the market. It must have the right price point, be presented in the right media and be promoted at just the right time.

That is why, with all my experience and with all the success I've had in direct marketing, I cannot predict in advance if a product is going to be a success. I can guess but I can never predict with certainty. And that is why testing is so critical in the direct marketing process. You can never predict what emotional response the consumer is going to have toward your product, your advertising and your placement in the time and space continuum.

Changes to Increase Response

Testing also gives you the opportunity to determine what slight changes in an advertisement will cause the greatest increase in response. Almost every one of the elements of an ad can be changed, modified or enhanced in order to boost response. But it usually is the copy that makes the most dramatic difference. Testing can tell you what approach works the best. And most of the time, the one approach you think will work is not the one that works. And finally, testing can clearly tell you at what price point a product should be sold to maximize profits or to increase sales.

The Testing Process

First, let's discuss the testing process involved when you've completed a mail order ad and you are ready to run it in some publication. You've already given it your best shot. You're pleased with the photography, the layout, the price point and the copy. Your headline grabs the attention of the reader and that subheadline gets the reader right to the first sentence. And your first sentence is a beauty. And so is the second sentence and the third and the fourth. You've created the perfect environment for your product or service and you've used many effective copywriting techniques. You've done all you can do short of running the ad and determining if the product will sell.

The next step is obviously to run the ad. But here is where caution comes into the picture. As effective and as good as your ad might be, it still could be a total disaster and not sell anything. Believe me, some ads I've run that I thought were going to make me a fortune cost me a fortune because I never tested. Or if I did test, I spent too much money on the first insertion.

The key therefore is to spend as little as possible on the cost of your test ad. Typically I used the Southwestern edition of *The Wall Street Journal*. It was the smallest and cheapest edition of the *Journal* and gave me the opportunity to test my ad in a good sample of my customer base. Another big advantage was the short lead time I needed to get my ad into the *Journal*—usually about a week. The quicker I got my test results, the sooner I could advertise in other magazines.

The *Journal* also allowed me to use another testing technique that made using the *Journal* even more of a value. I could do what is called an "A/B split." I would submit two different versions of the same ad to the *Journal* and they would run each version in every other paper. This meant that I could test two different versions of the same ad on the same sample of their subscriber base and at the same time.

Let's say I didn't need to test anything except the ad. My price was pretty well locked in and my approach was the best I could do. Once you've written your ad, if it works, chances are there will be no immediate need to test a different price or copy approach. And I've found that typically I will rarely need to test anything else (such as the headline, the offer, etc.) until I know whether the product will sell.

Running the Test Ad

I would prepare the ad for the *Journal*, the ad would run and the response would come in. To determine the success or failure of the ad, I would first figure out the total cost of the product. I would add up the cost of fulfillment, the cost of the product, the shipping and handling costs, the costs for handling any return of product under the trial period, the credit card charges and everything else except for the actual cost of advertising.

If you receive 100 orders for a $100 product and you can earn $50 per product, then obviously you made $5,000. Let us say the cost of the ad is $1,000. You take the $1,000 and divide it into the $5,000 profit and you end up with a 5 to 1 ratio of profit to ad cost. In short, for every dollar you spent on advertising, you received back $5 in profit. This would be a good response and would prompt me to say that the product is successful, the ad is good and that I should experiment and continue testing by running the ad in several other magazines which I have determined from previous experience to be about as good as the *Journal*.

I therefore used the *Journal* as my benchmark. At the time, I knew that *Popular Science* would give me a 6 to 1 ratio based on previous ad campaigns. I knew that *Scientific American* might give me a 7 to 1 ratio and *Business Week* a 4 to 1 ratio. I also knew that I could now advertise in all the other editions of the *Journal* and expect very similar response to my test ad. In fact, by advertising in the remaining regional issues of the *Journal*, I could reach ten times the audience and consequently pull ten times the response. If I earned $4,000 from my test ad, the full run in the *Journal* would net me $36,000 more in profit.

For years I always used the Southwestern edition of *The Wall Street Journal* as a test vehicle. Many of my seminar participants also used this testing approach. And soon others who had heard of my approach were also running their test ads in that edition. There were so many test ads running in this edition of the *Journal* that pretty soon the Southwestern readers became the most responsive mail order customers of all *Journal* readers. They were so accustomed to seeing mail order ads and became such frequent purchasers of mail order products that they became some of our best customers. In short, they saw so many more ads than any other *Journal* edition readers, they became conditioned to buy via mail order.

Of course, the *Journal* is not the only publication in which you can test. Several publications have many regional editions with short lead times that give you pretty good response for mail order offers. It really depends on your target audience.

Using the benchmark of the *Journal* to gauge response and then running ads in several other magazines which I knew would do well is the first step in what is referred to as a "rollout." A roll-out is simply the act of rolling your successful ad out into other publications. But what if you have no benchmark and it's your first ad? You cautiously select another group of publications that you believe will work for the ad. I gave you some pretty good hints of what publications to choose in Marketing Lesson 6 on media.

What if your test ad is a total disaster and you end up with very little response? Chances are you've got a product that won't work or a concept that is far off the mark or a price point that is too high. There could be a dozen other reasons but these three will play the biggest role. Should you change certain elements of the ad and retest? From my experience, the ads that don't work rarely can be saved. I've had experience with many ads that didn't work even after I tried very hard to get them to work. Product represents about 80% of the reason an ad works or doesn't work. Of course the product that doesn't work might be your only product and you may be working for a company responsible for selling it. In that case, you continue to try to make the ad work. In a minute, I'll explain how.

A Passing Grade

You can produce a terrible ad, but if you have a good product it is still possible to get a decent response. But the response will be marginal. Remember our analogy in Marketing Lesson 5 about needing a 99% score to have a successful ad? In mail order advertising, if your goal is a big success you can't get 80%. You've got to score no lower than 99% to really make it. A good product and a poor ad is not the combination that will bring you blockbuster results. Getting 99% means presenting the proper concept, the right price and optimizing the other relationships that go along with a good product in a good ad.

Now let's cover what you need to do if your ad barely breaks even. Let's also make the assumption that you have a good ad. You've run the ad at a cost of $1,000 and let us say your response is 20 orders and you make a profit of $50 per sale. You end up with a net profit of zero, but you didn't lose anything and the ad did show promise. What do you do?

The chances of your having a huge success are rather limited. Again, from experience, an ad that breaks even usually will mean that it could be improved but that its chances of being a block-buster are remote. If it can be improved, there's a good chance that it will be both profitable and successful. So why not look at the ad again and see if maybe there is a new approach you can use, a newer concept, a lower price point, a more exciting photograph or even a new headline? This is where component testing comes into play—the art of determining which of the many elements of the ad can be changed to enhance the response.

By improving the ad, you stand an excellent chance of having a successful promotion that can run for several months—even years—and produce a nice profit. There is nothing wrong with this kind of response. In fact, a few correct changes could even double response. A good headline and picture could add another 30% to the response rate and the graphics treatment could add another 20%. Add all these subtle but important changes to that ad that had a 1 to 1 ratio and produced no profit and you could conceivably receive revenue at three to four times the cost of advertising and thus make a nice profit.

The Control Ad

The ad that you first created is called the "control ad." You want to run the control ad in an A/B split with your new version to determine if the changes you made will make any difference. For example, I wanted to test the price point of a subscription to a newsletter in my Consumers Hero program. One ad featured a price of $10 and a second version had a price point of $5. The test would tell me which price point produced the best return for my investment. The test results showed that the $5 price point pulled double the number of members as the $10 price point. I ended up with the exact same dollar return and twice the number of new members with the lower price. Since it costs money to handle the orders of each new member, the bottom line results showed me

164

that the $10 offer was the more profitable by a very small margin. But the concept of the ad was to increase the size of my mailing list as well as to produce a profit. Each new name was valued at more than the membership fee, and I could count on at least a few orders from each new member.

With that in mind, it was obvious that the lower price point was the answer. In a subsequent ad I tested some new copy at the end of the ad and found that the response rate doubled. This result clearly taught me how critical changing certain elements was to ad response.

It is through testing methods and experiments such as these that a direct marketer begins to learn the secrets of what really works and what doesn't and even how effective various elements are—secrets that few in a conventional ad agency will ever learn. And for this reason, mail order copywriters and entrepreneurs are among the most effective writers and marketers in the world. They have learned from experience and from their failures through a process of testing. They know what works and it often is not what logic dictates.

There are a few more lessons I've learned about testing that I'd like to share with you.

Every Ad a Test

First, every ad you run is a test and each time you run your ad it's a test. And that holds true, even in a national campaign where you have the same ad running in dozens of different magazines. Some magazines will produce a big response, others will produce poor results and some will fluctuate over time. In a print campaign, this data becomes critical, especially when you run that next ad campaign.

Testing Theory 1: Each and every ad you run is a test.

When we ran our infomercial on hundreds of TV stations throughout the county, we examined the response from each station to determine the results. If we saw a drop-off in response from one of our selected stations, we carefully noted it and followed the next exposure on the same station to see if it dropped off even more.

I've seen a few companies go bankrupt by running their

infomercials without any real understanding of this concept. They just take the total number of orders they receive from all the stations and multiply that by the profit they receive for each order to get their bottom line figure. Then when the program response starts to tail off, they don't know which station is working and which station isn't. In reality, they could still be running their program quite successfully if they had dropped the stations that didn't test well and focused on the winners. This strategy kept us on TV for six consecutive years until we went into the retail market with our BluBlocker sunglasses.

Every Element a Test

The second lesson that I would like to share with you is that over time you should always test every element in your advertising—especially if every ad that you run contains that element. A good example of this is a test campaign I ran in the various airline publications. I was printing an eight-page flyer that was being inserted into all the airline magazines. At the time we were undoubtedly the largest advertiser in the airlines' in-flight magazines, often having eight full pages in each issue.

By printing the insert ourselves, we were able to break the printing run into four different groups (you could call it an A/B/C/D split). We could therefore test four different printed versions of the same ad. For years, I had been running just our toll-free number in our ads. People would easily see it, so I felt that I didn't need to have a coupon. (Almost all of our response came in on the phone as opposed to the mail anyway.) Besides, without a coupon the ad would look more editorial, in keeping with the environment of the publication.

But now was my chance to test this concept and see if I was right. Keep in mind that I had been running these ads for over ten years and spending millions of dollars to place them in hundreds of large-circulation magazines.

The four different versions of the full-page ad were as follows:

1. The format I had been running for over ten years (no coupon, just our toll-free number). That was my control.

2. A vertical dotted line running up the entire left side of the page near the spine of the magazine. The ad asked readers to tear

Which ad pulled the best? We were shocked and embarrassed by the results.

out the page along the dotted line and take it with them to order on our toll-free number when they arrived at their destination. (This was in the days before the air telephone service became so widely used.)

3. Just a dotted box around the ordering information, making the ad look more like a typical mail order ad with an arrow pointing to the box advising prospects to tear out the coupon.

4. A combination of (2) and (3) above: a dotted line at the spine and a dotted box around the ordering information with an arrow pointing to the coupon.

The standard JS&A control ad looked elegant. The ad with the dotted line at the spine looked pretty much the same because the line didn't affect the elegant look of the layout. The dotted box bothered me a little bit, but the combination of the dotted line and dotted box made the ad really look messy. And at first I was wondering if I should even run it like that. But I did. And the results made me feel like the stupidest guy in mail order.

Did you guess the winning ad? It was the last version—the worst-looking of all the approaches. It won by a wide margin over the standard JS&A control ad with 30% more response. The ad with the dotted box around the ordering information did very well too. I realized that I had been using the least productive approach for over ten years without ever testing and I realized how much profit I didn't make, simply because I did not test these formats. From then on, all of our ads became uglier and more profitable.

I also learned later how important typefaces were to the success of an ad. I then immediately changed the typeface I had been using. (I discussed this earlier in Marketing Lesson 4.) If you use the wrong typeface—one that will hinder comprehension instead of enhance it—you are making a tragic mistake. Once again, testing will reveal the best choice.

Another example of the importance of testing involved the time I determined that 80% of the viewers watching our infomercial watched the show and waited until the end before they called in and bought my product. This meant that at the end of the show it was critical to motivate the viewers to order. That bit of testing and the information we obtained from our research was very important for my future infomercial productions.

Try Everything

There is a lot more that could be said about testing, but the purpose of this chapter was to introduce you to the concept and its importance. There is no reason why a prudent direct marketer who tests should experience terrible losses. In the beginning of my career, I would have nine failures for every success. But the single success was more than enough to make up for every one of my failures—all because I tested. Regardless of your feelings about a product or an ad that you've created, test it. If you have a wild idea about a headline or the position of a picture or a caption or anything—go for it. Some of the really breakthrough concepts have come from some of the most off-the-wall inspirations.

I have often been asked by my students about focus groups. Can't a focus group be used to determine the possible success of an ad? The answer is no. People in a focus group realize that they are being used to judge a product, concept or ad campaign. They will give you what they think you want to hear. Because they don't actually have to make the tough decision to exchange their hard-earned money for that product or service, the results won't tell you the true potential of your ad.

In the mid '70s, I would run my ads in *The Wall Street Journal* and commission a group called The Daniel Starch Company to let us know the impact of the ads. In the "Starch Readership Report," information showed that often our most successful ads had poor reader recollection and readership and our worst ads showed strong recollection and readership—there was no consistency or relationship to actual response rates. Once again, this is an example of how research can't be relied upon to determine the true response to an ad that requires the exchanging of somebody's hard-earned money for a product or service.

John Wanamaker, the famous New York merchant, once said

that 50 cents of each dollar was wasted in advertising but he didn't know which 50 cents. In direct marketing, we know exactly what is wasted. And most of the time there is nothing wasted at all. In fact there is a gain.

If you're interested in learning more about mistakes that you can avoid, I would suggest reading several of the really great direct marketing books available at your local library. Often they contain techniques that will help you avoid some of the mistakes that I made. For example, there was enough information about printing dotted lines around a direct response coupon to encourage me to eventually test the concept. But I didn't pay much attention to those books; I felt that my approach was unique and would set the image I wanted for my company. I have listed some of the great direct marketing books in the back of this book in Appendix E.

If I were to summarize my philosophy on testing various elements in an ad, I would say the following:

Testing Theory 2: Testing each element of an ad and the entire ad provides a valuable tool in 1) determining what really works in an advertisement and 2) avoiding the magnification of a costly mistake.

A seasoned direct marketer is often a far better marketing person than anybody you'll find at an ad agency. The seasoned pro has been through the trenches. He or she has experienced the successes and failures and has seen what has worked incredibly well and what has totally failed. He or she has learned from all this experience. Somebody without this experience can only guess. And by now you have learned that guessing can be very dangerous.

Testing your ad before you make a major commitment to the product or to a national campaign is critical for the future success of your company. It is the rule by which you must always view everything you attempt.

Testing Theory 3: A successful test should accomplish three things: 1) Tell you if your ad is profitable, 2) Give you a level of confidence to determine what your next media expenditure should be, 3) Earn a profit.

Even if your ad is successful, you should continue testing various elements in the ad to improve the response. Also, the telephone operators who take the orders can be briefed and given various scripts to improve sales. Often, just a change in phrasing will increase response.

The greatest tool a direct marketer has is the ability to test and to learn from that test. And it is a very costly education. But master the techniques and learn from your failures and mistakes, and you'll have the most valuable tool you'll ever use in your marketing career.

To summarize, the following are the eight benefits of running a test:

1. You'll get an indication of the profitability of your ad.

2. You'll develop a degree of confidence in the success of your product. For example, if it was very successful, you can then plan on risking more for advertising than if the ad was marginally successful.

3. You'll learn if the product was accepted by the consumer.

4. You'll learn something about the typical buyer's demographics—young, old, male, female, etc.

5. You'll get feedback from the buyer. It might be about your ad, your product, his or her reason for buying the product—a lot of clues are available to you from a test.

6. You'll earn a profit or at least minimize your losses.

7. You'll get an idea of response patterns. Do the orders take a long time to arrive? How long does it take to receive all your orders? Some ads are saved and reviewed before any action is taken to buy a product.

8. And finally, you'll see how your ad looks in print, how it fits in with the other competing messages in your magazine or newspaper.

Another way to learn without the costly expense of experiencing failures of your own is to learn from others. So in Section Two, I relate case histories of mail order promotions that I have personally conducted and the lessons that I learned. If you can learn from my mistakes, your education will be a lot less costly.

So far in this book you've learned many of the concepts that took me years to understand and then implement. You've learned how to pick the perfect product, how to protect your product and then how to determine the best format in which to present it. You've learned concepts that I didn't discover until well into my career, such as the most effective typefaces to use, the best layout and the use of color. Then we talked about testing and the very critical role it plays in direct marketing.

In the next section, I introduce you to some of the very subtle relationships you need to learn to be a good direct marketer. Once again, I feature a marketing story in between each marketing lesson. And once again, you will learn a great deal from the stories as well as from the lessons. So get ready for some more good advice and some adventures in the exciting world of direct marketing.

Section Two

Preview

Direct Marketing Relationships

You've learned some of the really important basics in direct marketing from the advice I've given you in Section One. And indeed there were many lessons to learn.

You are now ready to refine your knowledge and learn some of the more subtle lessons I've taught in my seminars—lessons that will enhance what you've already learned from this book.

Many of these lessons you will not find anywhere else. Some have come from years of observation, some from unusual circumstances and some from many mistakes and personal discoveries.

The materials that follow will enhance and even supercharge your understanding with subtle insights that I often had to learn the hard way.

Marketing Lessons Are Quite Powerful

First, in Marketing Lesson 9, I take you through a series of comparisons between print or mail order advertising and direct mail marketing. Understanding the relationships between these two powerful direct marketing tools will help you understand the importance of certain elements in both a mailing and a mail order ad.

Then, in Marketing Lessons 10 and 11, I cover the effects that publicity and price have on sales and explain how to overcome price resistance in your offer. In Marketing Lesson 12, I cover the return rate and why there is a balance between what you sell and what you get back from customer dissatisfaction. Sometimes, under certain circumstances, you want to have more dissatisfied customers than you would believe.

In Marketing Lesson 13 and 14, I show you what you should avoid using in mail order ads and what causes poor response (it's not what you think). In Marketing Lesson 15, called "Complaints," I explain the wealth of information you can get from listening to unhappy customers. They often tell you more than how unhappy they are. And finally, in Marketing Lesson 16, I show you how you can enhance sales through the way you set up your organization and I describe the options that are available to you. But there's even more.

It is in this section where the marketing stories I relate take on even more significance. I now take you into the major JS&A promotions—the marketing stories of ventures that resulted in something big. For example, the successful launch of six new companies, a dramatic increase in business as a result of two promotions, and the launch of a major brand name, BluBlocker.

I start out with the story of the *GADGETS* catalog and how we created thousands of Ph.D.'s. I then skip back in time to the very first major JS&A promotion, for the Craig 4501 calculator—the one that launched my company and my exciting career in direct marketing. I then describe the dramatic increase in business I experienced when I took our toll-free number and a successful new ad for the DataKing 800 and advertised in dozens of national publications.

You'll then see how I started several companies—from my membership company, Consumers Hero, to the companies I set up to market Picasso tiles, the Pocket CB, and the Bone Fone.

There is one underlying theme that ties all of these stories together—each was created through the use of direct marketing know-how and the power of my pen.

And you too can harness that power. Whether you're old or young, male or female, black or white, the opportunities are here and the abundance awaits you.

Section Two will fill in many of the missing pieces you need to complete your knowledge as a direct marketer and will provide you with a number of concepts I've never revealed before—any one of which could result in a huge success. So study the lessons, enjoy the wealth of information you'll find in the stories and learn from them. The fun continues.

A Marketing Story

The *GADGETS* Catalog

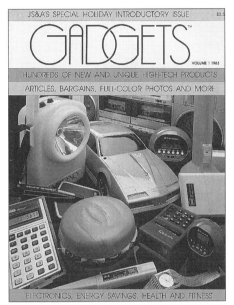

A well-executed catalog with a theme that ran throughout its pages.

In 1984 I had a great idea for a catalog. I realized that there were a great many people who were very much like me—they just plain loved gadgets. I also realized that the JS&A catalog, *Products That Think,* was primarily targeted toward new technology or the very serious products that resulted from the integrated circuit and its many spin-offs.

The JS&A catalog required lengthy explanations, many pictures and a very serious tone. Products were costly and were so unusual that if I didn't explain them thoroughly, nobody would buy them.

I also reasoned that there was room for a catalog totally devoted to gadgets—products that were less expensive, didn't require long descriptions and would take up much less space in a catalog.

I came up with the name *GADGETS* for the title of the catalog and even secured the toll-free number 1-800-GADGETS. I then devoted the catalog to many products—an average of three per page as opposed to the typical JS&A products that required up to two or even three pages each.

The catalog looked very much like a magazine with an introductory article that kicked off the entire issue. The article was a tongue-in-cheek approach to the gadget fanatic or the person who loved gizmos—another name for gadgets. The copy introduced the concept very nicely and is worthwhile reading if you want a sense of the catalog and my frame of mind at the time.

Headline: Gizmology Doctorate

Subheadline: JS&A is awarding a limited number of doctorates to qualified gizmologists. You may qualify.

Copy: To be called a doctor in American society is a most cherished honor. It takes hard work, talent, persistence and total dedication.

But there's no reason why an average American who holds a full-time job can't strive for a doctorate in Gizmology which is the study of gizmos and gadgets.

If you love gadgets, then becoming a gizmologist can be one of the most rewarding experiences of your life. The prestige, respect and the standing in your community, coupled with the personal satisfaction of practicing gizmology is incentive enough to take the plunge. And qualifying is not too difficult.

To qualify for a degree you must fall into one of two categories— one very restricted, the other much less restrictive. Here they are:

Category 1: You must be a graduate engineer in electrical engineering as well as a certified multi-engine, instrument-rated pilot, plus an active amateur radio operator along with being a serious amateur photographer. Now we realize that not everyone qualifies, especially for all of these skills. So we've made our second category somewhat easier.

Category 2: You qualify if you purchase any product from this JS&A catalog. No matter what you buy, even if you can't read— just ordering something makes you so qualified you wouldn't believe it.

We created a new and exciting profession.

Pass the qualifications in either of these two categories and we will send you a beautiful certificate. You can proudly display the certificate on your wall announcing to the world that you have passed the rigorous qualifications necessary to earn the title of Doctor of Gizmology, and consequently have become a registered Gizmologist.

Let me depart from the copy for a moment. There were almost a hundred people who sent me their qualifications which matched exactly the very strict qualifications listed in Category 1.

What I had listed in Category 1 were practically my qualifications. Although I didn't graduate as an electrical engineer, I did study electrical engineering for three and a half years in college until I was drafted into the Army. Other than this one fact, I met all of the other qualifications. I was an instrument-rated, multi-engine pilot, an active amateur radio operator and a serious amateur photographer. In short, I was looking for all of those fools out there who not only had the same tastes in gadgets that I had but who experienced many of the same things that I experienced in the pursuit of my love of gadgets.

I was also making fun of myself. I was poking fun at those people who really love their gadgets, and my copy was giving them a chance to laugh at themselves. The copy continued:

I even got license plates from three states to further the theme.

> Think of how impressed your friends will be when they discover that you've earned this coveted degree. Think of how impressed your business associates will be when you sign your letters with your new title. Think of how embarrassed people will be when they don't even know what a Gizmologist is. And what about those old school chums of yours who must now refer to you as Doctor?
>
> If you pass either one of the two qualifications, you may claim your official-looking certificate free when you purchase a product from this issue. Or you may submit your engineering degree, pilot's license, amateur radio license and a sworn statement that you are also an awfully serious photographer.
>
> As a registered Gizmologist, you will want to open an office and set up your office hours. Remember, this need not be a full-time job, but it's silly to let your degree go to waste without at least a little practice.
>
> People will come to you asking your advice. They'll ask you what gizmo to get for a special gift, what home computer to invest in, what chess computer to buy, and what calculator works the best.
>
> Your primary reference will be the JS&A publication *GADGETS*. Here within these pages you'll find some of the most exciting new gizmos and gadgets ever assembled under one cover. Each product is fully explained and available for purchase.
>
> Personally owning many of the products featured in this issue will also help to make you a good Gizmologist. This way, you can talk from experience and we can move lots of inventory.

Note here the disarming approach I used above. It's humorous and extremely frank. Later in Marketing Lesson 13 I talk about the use of humor to sell products. I tell you to avoid using it as the purchase of a product is a very serious matter not to be taken lightly. Then how, you might ask, can I use humor in this very important introduction when later I tell you that you shouldn't use humor at all? Let me explain.

First, I am not selling any product but welcoming you into my "store" (my catalog). You're about to experience a fun time. In the process of going through my store, you are going to find a few products that you will want to buy, and at that time I become very serious with my sales pitch. There is no humor. But when I welcome you into my store, you are greeted with a certain degree of fun and anticipation. The humor gets you curious. You want to go deeper into the store to experience the nice feelings you are getting from the introduction. And that is the purpose of the humor at the very start of the catalog. I now continue:

> How much to charge your patients is a personal matter between you and them. A Gizmologist in Beverly Hills, for example, can charge lots more than one from Cleveland. After a few years in practice, you may want to open up a local museum in your community and contribute your gadget collection. Check with your accountant to see if you can get away with a nice tax write-off.

> Doctors are notorious for their investments in tax shelters—investments designed to reduce their high tax bite. As a registered Gizmologist, JS&A will recommend investing in gizmos. There are several attractive space-age investments right in this issue.

> Imagine investing in the neat Tasco Zoom binoculars on page 19? Or how about the clever Sound Switches on page 35? Remember, these gizmos could be depreciable if their purchase is for business purposes. Of course, always consult with your accountant and never buy a gizmo just to get a tax write-off.

> Finally, as alumni from the JS&A school of Gizmology, you'll want to receive refresher courses which we will send you each time we issue a new catalog.

> In the meantime, we urge you to apply yourself today. Study this issue of *GADGETS*. Experience the thrill of discovering the latest in gizmos. Fill out the order form and order a whole bunch of things and don't forget to ask for a Doctor of Gizmology certificate.

> We will send you an 8-1/2" x 11" beautifully printed certificate on thick parchment paper that you'll be proud to frame and hang on your wall. You can imprint your name on the certificate with ink or with a typewriter. If you order more than one product and would like two certificates—one for a gift and one for you, please feel free to order two. Sorry, only two to a family. But please act fast. We can only award about a million of these degrees this year.

There was also a picture of the certificate with the following caption:

The beautiful Doctorate of Gizmology Certificate. The great JS&A Seal of Gizmology features the American Eagle, a shield with a stylized circuit board and the Latin phrase, "Primus Amor Meus Machina," which means, "My First Love is Gadgets."

We only had a million of them to award.

The *GADGETS* catalog did very well, selling many of the gadgets we displayed in it. We also included a few of our copy-intensive JS&A catalog items, which also did well.

Finally, I was amazed at how many people had the same qualifications that I did. As I mentioned earlier in Marketing Lesson 1, very often the best products to market are the ones that you yourself relate to very strongly. And certainly, the products I offered had drawn those people who appreciated what I appreciated and had similar hobbies and tastes.

But the *GADGETS* catalog had only one issue which lasted almost a year. Within a few years, I was heavily involved with the sale of BluBlocker sunglasses and my future catalogs reflected less of a line of gadgets and more and more sunglasses. But the introduction was part of a well-executed catalog that set an exciting and fun tone for the entire presentation and was a good complement at the time for our JS&A catalog, *Products That Think*.

Marketing Lesson 9

The Direct Marketing Comparisons

The students in my seminars studied how to relate what they knew about print advertising to other forms of advertising and direct marketing, among them direct mail, catalogs, and TV advertising including infomercials. If they could learn the relationships, they would also realize the critical importance of certain elements in any medium of advertising.

Elements Compared in Various Media

Let us take a typical direct mail package with an envelope, letter, brochure, order form and return envelope. What would be the equivalent of the headline of a print ad in a direct mail package? In short, what is the element that actually first draws your attention?

The answer is the envelope. It's the element that attracts and compels you to open it and read the contents of your mailing just as the headline compels you to read an ad.

What then compares to the photo in a print ad? The answer is the brochure in a direct mailing. And finally, what compares to the all-important text of a print ad? The answer is the personal letter in a direct mail package.

Letter Most Critical Element in Direct Mail

What this says about the direct mail package is that the letter is probably the most critical part of the package. And many direct marketers could tell you of experiences where they changed the wording of their letter and doubled response, yet by changing parts of their brochure, not much happened. The direct mail letter is therefore very important to your mailing.

In a catalog, the cover functions like the headline of a print ad. The basic catalog copy and photography are equivalent to the brochure of a direct mail package, and the single most important part of the catalog copy is the letter usually located in the front of the catalog, from the owner of the catalog to his or her customers. This means that if you don't have a letter to your customers, you are missing a very powerful element in your advertising.

The TV Comparison

There is also a very powerful element in the effective use of TV. In the case of an infomercial, the first few minutes of the show can be compared to the headline of a print ad. If you don't get the viewers to stop and "open the time envelope" so they can watch your show, you've lost them to some other show. The comparison to the copy of a print ad is a little more complex. It is the combination of the personal message by the owner made during the show and the contribution of the show's host or hostess. The rest of the show can simply be compared to the power of the photos of a print ad or the brochure of a mailing.

In a catalog, you can test the difference in response when you place a personal letter setting the tone for your catalog and introducing some of your favorite merchandise. When you are running an infomercial, make sure that if you are the owner of the company you appear in the commercial to introduce your product. Your passion for the product will come through to your audience.

Understanding the relationships of a print ad to other forms of direct marketing allows you to see the impact of various elements so you can then give them the proper focus when you prepare your catalog or mailings. For example, if you've learned that the letter is critical to a direct mailing, then you will give a great deal of attention to that letter and what it says.

I have received many mailings where there wasn't even a letter enclosed. Obviously, the marketer didn't realize what you now know—the importance of including a letter in each mailing.

Finally, there are two big differences between direct mail and print mail order advertising: the sorting process and media costs. First, media costs. In direct mail there are none. You simply pay Uncle Sam for your postage, pay for the printing and rent that mailing list. The second big difference involves the sorting process.

The Sorting Process

When you receive your mail, what is the first thing you do? If you're like most people who receive a lot of mail, you sort it into two piles. The first pile is for the mail you definitely want to open. I call it the "keen interest" pile. It may contain personal letters, bills, statements and notices from your bank or credit card company—communications you would classify as important and which you are keenly interested in opening. Also in this pile are the catalogs you are interested in reading.

The second pile consists of the advertising mail you aren't interested in opening and the catalogs that don't cover any topic of interest. This pile is called the "circular file" pile. Very often, the circular file pile goes right into the garbage. It's not even opened.

Now which pile would you want your mailing to be in? The keen interest pile, of course. Then how do you get your envelope or your catalog into that pile? I'm glad you asked.

If you send a catalog, you have chosen your mailing list very carefully and therefore the person to whom you've sent it is either already a customer and therefore the best prospect for your product or service, or else somebody with a tremendous proclivity to purchase from you based on his or her past mail order purchasing patterns. I'll discuss mailing lists shortly.

The main means for getting your catalog into the keen interest pile should be your mailing list. Sure, you want an attractive cover. That goes without saying. But even more important than the graphics on the cover or the beautiful picture or the product shot, you want to select the right list—the real key to getting your catalog into the keen interest pile.

Keen Interest Strategies

What can you do to get your envelope placed in that keen interest pile and get it opened and then read? If you're a bank and it's your credit card bill that is being received, you can feel quite assured that it will be opened every time. That's why credit card and oil company syndicators who put offers on return envelope flaps have done quite well. First, their solicitation is opened. Second, their customer is already a bank customer—a prime prospect and already familiar with the company soliciting them. Finally, the person receiving the offer is pre-qualified. He or she already has a credit card and therefore has the credit history and the means to pay for the merchandise.

A credit card or oil company syndicator contracts with a credit card company or oil company and puts solicitations in with the billing statement. The bank or oil company receives a

BluBlocker sunglasses became a very successful syndication piece for the banks and oil companies.

commission based on what is sold and the syndicator has one of the most qualified lists possible. The bank makes enough money to cover the cost of its mailing and the syndicator earns a nice profit. Each side wins.

There are major syndicators who specialize in this business, as there are advertising agencies who specialize in making the mailing pieces that are included with each mailing. The agency who did our flyers operated out of Chicago and is called J&R Advertising. They're the experts in knowing how to create a small flyer or envelope flap to attract the largest possible audience for a product or service.

The syndicator we worked with for many years is a company called Roy Thomas in Schaumburg, Illinois, who syndicated our BluBlocker sunglasses mailing piece through their clients quite successfully. It's a great way to sell our product. We've also created small mailing pieces, commonly called "package inserts" that we offer other direct marketers to stuff in with their mailings. It's an economical way to deliver your message so it gets opened and read.

Getting Your Own Envelope Opened

But what can you do to get your own envelope opened, if you're not a bank or financial institution? I have a suggestion. The next time you get your mail, sort it into the two piles I suggested. See what prompts you to open an envelope in the keen interest pile. I would guess that it is something that either looks official and requires you to open it or resembles one of the categories of envelopes that normally, and without question, would go into that pile.

The most effective way to get your envelope into the customer's keen interest pile is to make it look like it's a letter or a personal solicitation and not just bulk mail. You can use a postage stamp, have the letter hand-addressed or at least make it look like it has been personally addressed on a computer or typewriter. It should look like it comes from a single individual and is being sent specifically to the customer.

Another way to make sure your envelope is opened is to send it to the person most qualified to receive it as in my catalog example earlier. This time, indicate somehow on the envelope that the mailing is an offer that this particular person might be interested in reviewing.

For example, I subscribe to *Writer's Digest*—a publication for aspiring writers. I own an Apple computer. I'm inclined to open many of the solicitations that come to me about writing, as this is my focus right now. I'm also interested to open what is mailed to me relating to computers, and in particular word processing and desktop publishing programs. On the other hand, I wouldn't be interested in an envelope offering me a chance to "earn more income than you ever thought possible." That goes into the circular file pile. Even if the envelope got me to open it, chances are I wouldn't respond. On the other hand, that mailing from the tape club looked inviting, as I was interested in buying a few movies I've always wanted.

A Personal Letter

In print advertising you want to match your ad as closely as possible to the article format of the medium in which you are advertising. This is also true in direct mail. In direct mail, you want to make your message appear like a letter. A letter is a very personal form of communication from the sender to the recipient—from one human being to another. Your mailing should look like a personal letter or an important-looking piece of correspondence. It is therefore imperative that your envelope not look like an advertising mailing—it should have a postage stamp and no loud slogans on the envelope itself. It should look like an envelope you would send to a friend.

I once received a mailing from *Popular Photography* magazine soliciting me to advertise in their magazine. When I got the hand-addressed envelope I thought the letter was actually a personal message for me. When I opened it, inside was a personal hand-written letter and a picture of a family—husband, wife and children. I started reading the letter, thinking that it might be from somebody I knew. The letter started out in a rather casual tone and didn't get into the sales message until much later. The copy tied into the picture and the magazine, talking about the average family and what they spend on photography and the demographics of the average family. It was very powerful in that it was personal, got me to open the envelope right away and then compelled me to read the entire message. We did respond and bought a page from the magazine.

Used Same Technique

In fact, I once did some consulting work for Allstate Insurance Company and used the same technique I mentioned above in the *Popular Photography* example to solicit insurance business for them. It was a very novel approach and got incredible readership.

There are many ways to personalize your message, and you can choose or create based on what you observe from the mail you yourself receive. Just be more sensitive to your reaction to the different types of approaches companies use to address their mail to you, and pick out the approach that you feel worked best on you.

There are two general aspects of direct mail that require your attention. The first is the mailing list and the second is the role of human nature. First let's talk about the role of human nature.

Human Nature and Your Mail

Typically, when you do a mailing, the mail is assembled by your mailing house, put into mail sacks or trays, taken to the post office and then delivered to your prospect. During the time your mail is sent from your mailing house there are two places that are potential black holes for your mail—the first is the mailing house itself and the second is the post office.

Mail can be held at a post office for a long time while other, more important tasks are done. Sloppy postal employees could lose a few trays here and there or at best not care when your mailing gets out. One of the techniques used by some of the most savvy mailers is to go to a nearby small town and mail letters from there. A small town really appreciates the business and will give your mail the attention it deserves. Some mailers even truck their mail miles away to do this.

The other black hole is the mailing house. They get paid in advance for the postage, so it stands to reason that for each letter they don't mail you'd get refunded that amount because the total dollar amount of mail sent is noted on the postal receipt from the post office. But not always. There are some postal employees who can easily put the wrong figure on a postal document and earn a few extra bucks from the mailing house who then goes on to pocket the rest of the money. A portion of your mail doesn't get delivered, the postal employee and the mailing house share a little of your booty and nobody knows the difference.

It's important that I mention that this situation is rare. Most mailing houses and postal employees are totally honest. But which ones? And is your mail being handled properly? Of course you can seed your mailing with the names and addresses of all your relatives and friends or use a service that provides names and addresses throughout the country for auditing purposes to see which ones don't get your mail, but by then it might be too late. And then who would be at fault—the mailing house or the post office?

Gary Halbert, a guy who has probably mailed millions of pieces of mail during his life in direct marketing, finds that vigilance and an appreciative small-town post office are your safest bet when it comes to making sure your mailing gets through.

Gary also publishes a newsletter that he's been mailing for ten years presenting his thoughts on some of the profit opportunities in direct marketing. I subscribe to it and highly recommend it. (See information on the Halbert newsletter in Appendix E.)

Lists Respond Differently

Mailing list costs vary to a certain degree, but certainly not as much as print advertising costs. For example, running a print ad might cost as little as $5 per thousand or as much as $50 per thousand subscribers—a ten-times spread. Mailing lists do not have this spread. A good list may rent for $100 per thousand compared to $50 per thousand for a less popular list for only a two-times spread.

But even though lists may differ little in cost, there is a definite hierarchy of responsiveness among them, based on the nature of each list—this is a unique and very important aspect of direct mail.

Comparison Theory: In print advertising, the place you make your money is often in the media savings. In direct mail, the place you make your money is in the responsiveness of the mailing list that you rent.

To be a good student of direct mail it is important that you study mailing lists. Work with a list broker who is not only knowledgeable in this area but can advise you which lists might work well for your product or service. When I rented my mailing lists to send out my very first major mailing for a pocket calculator, I consulted with a list broker and coded my lists and response cards so I knew exactly from which lists my responses came. It was enlightening to realize the difference in response that I got from the various lists.

I told my list broker what I wanted—lists of accountants and engineers. These were the people who I thought would be perfect prospects for my mailing. He, however, selected high-income business executives working at large corporations and mail-order buyers of a product similar to my pocket calculator. Guess who won. My broker, hands down. His four list selections outpulled my six lists by such a large margin that I lost money on my first mailing. It was only because I listened to my list broker that I managed to find two lists that did work quite successfully. Good list brokers generally really know their stuff.

You can hedge your bet when picking a mailing list if you realize how the mailing list hierarchy is structured. For it is the one area of direct mail—the list—that will make or break a mailing. Pick the right list and the spread from the poorest list to the most effective might mean a ten-times greater response. In print advertising, media costs differ, whereas in direct mail marketing, it is the mailing list itself that makes the big difference.

The Ten Lists

In one of his newsletters, Gary Halbert described ten mailing lists, with each subsequent list being more responsive than the previous one. Let's take an example that Halbert gives of a mail order merchant who wants to market an expensive investment book to a mailing list. The criteria that the merchant uses to pick a mailing list and the responsiveness of that mailing will be determined in the following order:

1. You can get a mailing list out of the phone book. You will get the poorest response.

2. You can get a list out of a phone book from high-income areas. This will do better.

3. You can then target the names from the phone book of just those in the higher income groups who are professionals of a particular type. Now you're getting better, but you're not assured of a success. This is similar to the lists I selected—accountants and engineers—that didn't do well.

4. To get a better response, you buy a list of *mail order buyers who are wealthy*. Chances are you'll do a lot better than the first three lists and maybe even make a profit.

5. But let us say you refine your list to those wealthy mail order buyers who have a *history of buying an investment book by mail*. Your chances have now increased dramatically.

6. But you want to do even better. So you buy a list of mail order buyers who have a history of buying an investment book by mail and who have *purchased several times*. Bingo, you are now doing even better than the previous five lists. You've added frequency of purchase as a qualifier to make the list more effective. The buyer is in the habit of buying investment books by mail—and a lot of them.

7. Now you are really getting sophisticated and you buy a list of mail order buyers who are wealthy, who bought an investment book by mail, who have purchased several times and *paid big money each time they purchased*. Gadzooks—you'll do even better. These customers have the big bucks to buy on impulse.

8. By now you're coming to the attention of everybody in your company. How can you top your past results? Easy. Just locate mail order buyers who are wealthy, who bought an investment book by mail, who have purchased several times, paid big money each time they purchased and who *recently purchased*. That's right, recency of purchase is a vital factor and it makes your list that much more responsive. Remember my earlier example of my current interest in writing and computers and the related mailings I was getting? Right now, I'm inclined to open up those envelopes and read the solicitation and maybe make a purchase. I might not, however, be as inclined in the future once

I stop working on these books I am now writing. Recency of purchase indicates current interest and likelihood of another purchase.

9. Could you top that last mailing? What list would you select that is any different from the list you already selected? How about mail order buyers who are wealthy, who bought an investment book by mail, who have purchased several times, paid big money each time, recently purchased and *the list is working like crazy for other mail order companies.* In short, a list with a track record of strong response.

10. What's an incredibly successful mailer going to do to improve your response now? Don't despair, there is an even stronger list—so strong that it will dwarf the rest of your list selections and by a large margin. What is it? Your own customer list. Period.

It is in the proper selection of a mailing list where you make your money. Recency, frequency, high-ticket purchase, the right demographics and a proven track record—all add to the power of your mailing to produce a profit. Skimp on any of these categories and you pay more to make the same sale. Pay too much and eventually you will lose money. It's just that simple.

This holds true for catalogs as well. But a good catalog company should have a good customer list already—a list that they have serviced very nicely with great products and wonderful customer service. The catalog company generally rents outside lists to augment its own list, but its lifeblood is its very own customer list.

To Review

Let us review for a moment where we are in the marketing process. You have learned from Section One the parameters you need to select the best product and have selected a product. You have a sense of what stage of the product life cycle you are in and a pretty good idea of the size of the market to which your product appeals. You've also protected your product, and if required, selected the media and bought the media at the right price.

In the meantime, you have created the ad that you plan to run using the right typeface and the correct layout devoid of unnecessary distracting color or design elements. If you've used a photograph, it is one that accurately portrays the nature of your product and the emotion it evokes.

Finally, you have then tested the ad to determine its potential and you have planned for your national rollout. Congratulations. You're on the way to making your first million and building a wonderful company to back it.

But there are a number of things that you might like to know once you start to get your response. For example, how do you determine what an acceptable return rate might be? And what will publicity mean to your sales? Answering those and a number of other important questions is the purpose of the rest of the marketing lessons in Section Two that I'm about to present.

But before I do, it's story time. And the following marketing story is about how I started my first mail order company, JS&A, my first mail order product and introduced the first pocket calculator. It is also the full story of how I found my most responsive mailing lists as I briefly described in this chapter.

A Marketing Story

The Craig 4501 Calculator

Our very first mail order ad on the back page of **The Wall Street Journal.** *It made history for us in many ways.*

This is the story of how JS&A Group, Inc. was founded. JS&A is my direct marketing company which had the privilege of introducing some of the most innovative consumer electronic products of the '70s and early '80s. Its start was rather modest and small but it soon became the engine that powered many of this nation's most successful products and along the way created a number of companies to handle them.

First a little background. In 1971 I had a small advertising agency that serviced several accounts—mostly ski resorts, political candidates and a tape and record distributor in Chicago. I lived in a unpretentious but well-mortgaged home in Northbrook, Illinois, with my wife and new-born baby. I ran my business out of my home.

In that year, I read an article in *Business Week* about a new product that was just coming to the marketplace called the pocket calculator. The circuitry was developed by Texas Instruments and the product was going to be manufactured by Bowmar Corporation in the Boston area.

I was captivated by the idea. I had recently had the opportunity to play with a very large $700 electronic calculator and found it to be an impressively fast, labor-saving device. I thought the new pocket version that I had been reading about might even make a great mail order item, perfect for one of my accounts, Alltapes, Inc.—a record and tape distributor. They had a mail order division and I felt that the calculator would be a good item for them to sell.

In the meantime, I called every name I could find to locate the manufacturer or his representative—somebody who could sell me a sample to present to my clients. In fact, I still have the original article I read and all the notes on it from my early phone calls.

(handwritten notes in margins:) (617) 263-7711 Uncle Molnar (219) Toralto BOSTON ROAD (# 747-3121) ACTON, MAS Mr HANOVER

TECHNOLOGY
Calculators slim down in size and price

U. S. makers now have smaller chips to combat Japanese competition

As calculating machines have shrunk in size and price with each advance in integrated circuitry, Japanese electronics manufacturers have gradually taken over the industry. Japan today makes virtually all the calculators sold in the U. S., even those marketed under labels of American companies. But two new technological developments, which make possible a pocket-size calculator priced low enough for household use, should now bring a large share of the production back home:
- Texas Instruments, Inc., has introduced a metal-oxide semiconductor (MOS) chip that houses all the circuitry for a small calculator in a package half the size of a match book. The all-in-one chips, costing less than $20 apiece in large quantities, will trim calculator assembly-time to the bone.
- Ragen Precision Industries, Inc., a small diversified electronics company, plans to use two of its own complementary MOS chips to make a pocket calculator that will sell for around $100. This product could best the calculator business while open early next year.

Just three years ago it was unfeasible to make a battery-powered calculator designed to fit in the operator's hand. The first "pocket" calculator, which was made in Japan, did not appear until 1969. Requiring dozens of integrated circuits, it was bulky as a large paperback book and was priced at a hefty $400.

But late last month Bowmar Instrument Corp. of Ft. Wayne, Ind., began shipping the first of its new cigarette-pack-sized calculators. They are made entirely in the U. S. with the TI chip, and at $240 are the lowest-priced and smallest portables on the market. Yet they perform all four arithmetic functions, tallying up to 16 digits and displaying an eight-digit answer. The decimal point can be set anywhere, and floats freely to the proper location when the computation is made.

Made-to-order chips. TI has also lined up a second American customer, and three in Japan as well. Though the company makes its low-priced chip from a standardized design, each manufacturer can order customized variations—something new in MOS circuitry. By changing a single photomask used in the manufacturing process, TI can modify

the basic chip to produce, say, an automatic display cutoff to conserve battery power. Bowmar requested this feature, since the light-emitting diodes it uses for display can quickly drain the calculator's rechargeable battery. But TI says the chip will also interface directly with low-power liquid-crystal displays, which should be available to calculator manufacturers next year from RCA Corp. and others.

Advances in circuitry and displays are coming so fast that F. L. Krch,

Texas Instrument's MOS marketing manager, predicts: "In a year or so, you'll see the first electronic calculator priced below $100. That will open the huge home and student markets to calculator companies, and from there the volume can only drive the price further down."

Ira L. Lopata, president of Ragen Precision, agrees heartily. Says Lopata, with a devilish grin: "He's right, but he's off on his timing. We've got it right now." But the $10-million New Jersey company is not in production yet. It has signed a contract with Alexander's, Inc., the big New York-based department store chain, to deliver 20,000 calculators starting in mid-January. Alexander's will not reveal the retail price, but Ragen expects that initially it will be just over $100 and eventually below $80.

New ground. Ragen says that, with the exception of the batteries, it will make all the components, including its own liquid-crystal displays. Instead of a rechargeable calculator, these extremely compact calculators will use cheap throwaways. Explains Albert H. Medwin, mastermind behind the design and president of the Ragen semiconductor subsidiary responsible for production: "MOS circuitry requires that a reference voltage be on all the time. C/MOS doesn't. Our calculator [also an eight-digit model with floating decimal point] will draw so little power that the lifetime of the batteries will be equivalent to their shelf life." C/MOS circuits are widely used today by the National Aeronautics & Space Administration and by the military, but they have only been put into industrial and commercial products in the last year or two.

According to Lopata, his company will set up its calculator production line shortly. "Once we're sure all the details are right, we'll start looking to sign marketing arrangements with department stores in other metropolitan areas," he adds. "But right now we've got all we want to handle."

His caution is understandable. Last year a company called American Calculator Corp. sprang up overnight, boasting it would soon produce a very low-priced pocket calculator in this country. American Calculator is now defunct.

But Alexander's has complete confidence in Ragen. Says Vice-President Jerome Germain: "We've looked at the company, and they seem prepared to deliver. This product is going to start a whole new industry, just like the first home typewriter did."

50 BUSINESS WEEK: October 9, 1971 TECHNOLOGY

Ragen's Medwin engineered the design of his company's mini-calculator.

This was the page I cut out of **Business Week** *magazine and the notes I wrote in the margins in a desperate attempt to locate the manufacturer.*

After many, many phone calls I learned that Bowmar was making the product for a company called Craig Corporation—a car stereo manufacturer. The national sales manager, Lauren Davies, whom I talked to, was a little concerned about their commitment to this new product. Craig Corporation had agreed to accept 5,000 units for a first-production run and had plans to market the product nationwide. But at $240, who would pay for such a device that did simple math functions and how would they sell it? Their fear was that it would sit on the shelves of retailers and just gather dust.

Best Way to Market Product

My suggestion to Davies of using direct mail as a vehicle to test and eventually sell the item hit a responsive chord and he dispatched his sales representative in the Chicago area, Alex Molnar, with a sample to show me. I told Davies that Craig Corporation could, through my client Alltapes, discover the best way to market the product and maybe my client could become a good customer for them.

When Alex Molnar showed up at my home and presented the Craig 4501 calculator to me, I knew that this was going to be a hot product. My experience with the larger calculator I had played with and the miniaturization of this new version just told me that this was a winner.

Alex sold me that calculator for $141, which at the time was the wholesale price. I then presented the Craig 4501 to my Alltapes client for their mail order division and they rejected it. "Who would pay $240 to do simple math?" was their comment.

I had confidence in the product, however, and when I returned home, I thought to myself, "What if I sold it myself through a company I would set up?" The idea really appealed to me but there was the matter of money. I was strapped, having just moved into my new home in Northbrook and barely able to pay the mortgage. I had a child who was not even one year old, lots of bills and no working capital.

Would They Invest in My Idea?

All my life, I'd had people telling me that if I ever started a business they would invest in me. Maybe now was the time to find out if people would indeed invest in one of my ideas. I was 33 years old, had a small but profitable advertising agency and big dreams.

I did manage to raise $12,000 through a few friends. I promised them that I would not make a penny profit until they doubled their money. Once they doubled their money, then I would owe them nothing more.

The first test of the calculator took place on October 25, 1971—the day I've always considered as the start of my company. I had written the copy, done the photography and set the type for a flyer, letter, order card and envelope—a classic direct mail solicitation. I didn't realize at the time that this was the first time the pocket calculator was nationally advertised.

Purchased Ten Mailing Lists

I purchased ten mailing lists of 5,000 names each for a 50,000-piece mailing and keyed each one of the response cards so I would know which list drew which response. I was surprised with the results. I had selected accountants, engineers and other likely professions as possible targets for my offer but, at the advice of my list broker, I also selected the presidents of major U.S. corporations as one of my lists. To my amazement, one of only two lists that worked was the one I thought had the least chance of winning—the presidents of large corporations. It turned out to be the best list of them all.

Unfortunately, the other lists performed so poorly that the investors, instead of doubling their money, lost half. But all was not lost.

I called my investors in for a special meeting and explained what had happened. I told them about the ten lists I tested and that if I had just tested the two most successful lists, we would have made a profit. I also informed them that after Craig Corporation heard of the results of the test, they huddled and decided to drop the price to a retail of only $180. At that price point and with the right list, we should do considerably better and my investors would eventually double their money.

The investors stayed in the deal and I also managed to get my mailing house and its president, Harvey Wagley, to advance funds for the postage. Wagley, in his early 60s, also became somewhat of a mentor for me, giving advice, extending credit and being a real angel during the early stages of my career.

Mailing Is Sent

I sent the mailing to approximately 400,000 names and the results just blew me away. My investors received double their money back and I ended up with a $50,000 profit. I was on the way. By this time, I was using my home as a processing center and the garage as our shipping department. I had temporary help running all over the house helping out and my wife was handling the phone calls.

I called my company JS&A National Sales Group. I had been using the name JS&A (an abbreviation for Joseph Sugarman & Associates) as the name of my ad agency.

I was now firmly entrenched in my own mail order business. It was February of 1972 and there were a lot of rumors about the calculator industry and that prices were going to drop even further. I knew that by the time I could prepare another mailing and send it out and then wait to get the response, the entire calculator industry could change, have a big price drop and my mailing would fail—my price would be too high and I would be out of the market.

So I decided to take my direct mail mailing piece and transform it into a mail order ad for *The Wall Street Journal*. My strategy was simple. I could get into the *Journal* quickly and I could get my response within a few weeks—all before any major price drop.

My First Space Ad

So that's exactly what I did. I created the ad and did all the copywriting, used the picture I had already used for the mailing piece and did the layout and paste-up myself.

I then called *The Wall Street Journal* and arranged for an ad on the back page of the paper. Since my credit wasn't yet established in this new venture, I had to pay the $10,000 cost of the ad in advance as well as go through tremendous scrutiny by the *Journal*'s accounting and advertising quality assurance departments.

Also, before the ad could run, I had to hire more temporary help and a permanent employee to handle the response. That's when I wrote what was probably the most significant ad I have ever written. It was the little want ad that attracted a 32-year-old housewife who joined me to assume what started out as a part-time job and ended up as a full-time position. Mary Stanke joined me on February 28, 1972, and has been with me ever since. She is now the president of both my companies—JS&A and BluBlocker Corporation—and has been a major reason for my success. And she joined me the day my very first mail order ad ran in *The Wall Street Journal*.

The response to that mail order ad was incredible. Not only did we receive a strong response and make a profit of $10,000 within a very short time, but the ad woke up the entire retail industry and now everybody from Sears to the little office equipment retailer on the corner wanted to sell this hot new item.

Many Lessons Learned

We struggled to get enough product as we were now in direct competition with every major retailer in the country. It took until April before we had the Craig 4501 in stock, and finally able to fill our back orders. We did very well.

The lessons I learned from this experience were many. First, I would never have succeeded had I not keyed the order cards to determine the winning mailing lists. That one act permitted me to discover the most responsive lists and mail only to those names, thus creating the eventual success of my subsequent and very important mailing. As you learned from Marketing Lesson 8 on testing, every ad is a test. We can now add that every mailing is a test as well.

The second lesson I learned was how effective a mail order print ad could be in influencing the retail marketplace. I had to fight with Craig Corporation to get product once the retailers saw the success of my ad. I saw how I created such widespread demand for the product that major retailers now wanted to stock it.

I also learned how to process an order and handle customer service. I had never done this before but by simply using common sense and very basic materials, I developed the procedures and systems to handle whatever response we received.

The Many Coincidences That Made It Possible

One of the experiences I had was learning how important a person can be in your life and how many coincidences need to be in place for you to succeed. Had it not been for Mary Stanke responding to my simple want ad, I would have missed a great talent and the incredible loyalty and support she has provided for over 25 years. Had it not been for Harvey Wagley and his trust and confidence in me and the credit support he provided, I might not have had the funds or confidence to take the chance and launch my company in a big way. Had it not been for Craig Corporation and their national sales manager giving me the opportunity of introducing the first pocket calculator, I might have never had a product to sell.

There were probably a dozen or more coincidences that had to be in place for me to make the calculator promotion a success. Life often is like that.

But as a result, JS&A grew to eventually offer other calculators and then other consumer electronic products. And as JS&A grew, more and more opportunities came our way. We also knew that we would need to move out of the basement of my home and into something larger. We were running out of space.

And that is exactly what we did. We moved to a small corner storefront a few blocks from my home where I created JS&A's first retail store.

Before I tell the story of the opening days of our new store, it's time for another direct marketing lesson. And the next one is quite revealing. Publicity has always been viewed as a positive thing. "Get a lot of publicity and sell a lot of product," might be the conventional thinking. But it's not always so, as you'll learn in Marketing Lesson 10.

Marketing Lesson 10

The Publicity Factor

The one most important thing I've learned about media publicity is that it doesn't sell much product and it's better avoided.

Publicity may work under certain circumstances and I know of many public relations success stories, but what I'm referring to is generating media publicity for the sole purpose of selling a product or service. Let me relate a few examples to explain my position.

All the Rage Until . . .

The year is 1959. There is a trade show in New York City for the graphic arts industry and exhibitors from throughout the world are in attendance.

The excitement at the show focuses on a new product from Canon Corporation called the Synchroreader. A Japanese firm had developed a new electronic printing process that allowed for the high-speed printing of talking books. The concept was simple.

A printing press printed a magnetic film on the back of a sheet of paper as it was being fed through the press. The film was then magnetically charged as it left the press, leaving an audio imprint on the magnetic coating.

The Synchroreader, manufactured by Canon, was designed to scan the pages and play the audio. It was the advent of the "talking book," and it generated almost a euphoria at the show. The press loved it. The device was presented at a seminar to overflow crowds, and reporters called it the most exciting breakthrough in printing and electronics since the Gutenberg press.

"Talking books are on the way," was one reporter's comment, and the controversy followed. "The end of literature as we know it today," read some articles. Yes, this exciting new product was the sensation of the trade show and created more publicity than any other exhibit.

At the very same show, there was another new printing product being exhibited by a small company from Rochester, New

U.S. Will See 'Talking' Printing Process

A talking printing process which enables the reader to hear the message on a printed page is scheduled to be demonstrated in America this September. The unusual technique, developed in Japan, is to be shown to visitors at Spectra '59, an international printing equipment show, to be held at New York City's Trade Show Building, Sept. 6-12 (see page 59, this issue).

The process was invented by Dr. Hoshino, and further developed by Dai Nippon Printing Co., Ltd., and Canon Camera Company, Ltd., all of Japan. It incorporates the use of offset and rotogravure to print a conventional line and halftone image (black and white, or color) on one side of a sheet of paper and a magnetic recording film on the

Synchroreader machine which produces audible messages from a printed Synchrosheet will be demonstrated at Spectra show in New York in September.

other. Recording and audible message may be incorporated with the printing process for mass production, or on a personalized, recording basis. When this printed sheet, called the Synchrosheet, is placed in a small portable electronic device called the Synchroreader, a scanning head scans the sheet and produces a true quality voice or sound reproduction.

The developers speculate on possibilities for Synchroreader and the Synchrosheets. For example, they say the future newspaper might, conceivably, be one that will permit the reader to actually hear sounds of events, actual speeches (by the actual speakers), or news stories with personal interviews, etc., all directly from their newspaper.

The Synchroreader, they add, has other immediate, practical applications. It can be used in the study of languages. Synchrosheets can be bound in one book and the book placed in the Synchroreader, and act as a private tutor for students out of their classroom. Blind people will find Synchroreader as a complement to their seeing eye dogs.

Synchroreader can also be used as a tape recorder, and recording a voice of Synchrosheets so that two parties having Synchroreaders would be able to handle all correspondence with sound, and through the mails, as conveniently as written letters.

It was heralded as a major breakthrough in sound communication, but you probably never heard of it. Canon wishes they hadn't either.

York. But the press release for their new device was being ignored. The press simply wasn't interested. The small manufacturer tried creating interest among representatives of the trade publications that were also exhibiting at the show, but again nobody gave them more than a small mention.

Excitement Dies Down

After the trade show, the excitement died down and Canon tried unsuccessfully to market the Synchroreader. Within a year it was off the market. On the other hand, the small company from England went on to become an American Fortune 500 company. That small company was called Haloid Xerox and the product they were exhibiting was the world's first plain-paper copier.

I know this story firsthand. The Xerox copier was exhibited at Spectra '59 which I attended and the Synchroreader that was exhibited became mine after the show. I still have it.

Publicity Means Trouble

Since then it has been my experience that the products that get the most publicity often are the ones ignored by the consumer when they are available to the public for purchase, and the ones that often get ignored because they are not really newsworthy are gobbled up by the consumer. I'll explain why in a moment.

Flash forward now to 1975. I'm sitting in my office talking with four representatives from Canon who want me to sell their new electronic calculators in my national mail order ads. At some point I mentioned the old Canon Synchroreader and the Spectra '59 trade show in New York. They remembered the Synchroreader well.

The oldest of the Canon representatives told me that they had hired over 200 engineers to work on the Synchroreader project. It was their first departure from the camera business and when the product failed to sell, they felt compelled to use their engineers in some other capacity so they formed their office products division—a billion-dollar division today. Some disasters turn out pretty well, don't they?

Early-Warning Indicator of Failure

I have seen many of my products generate a great deal of media publicity when I first exposed them, but they did not sell. If a product got a lot of publicity, that was almost like an early-warning indicator of certain failure. Why is this?

It is my theory that products that generate a lot of publicity are so different that they have not yet harmonized with the public psyche. And it is because they are so different that they make news in the first place. As consumers we are a pretty dull lot. We are really very practical in our purchases. Remember, the act of exchanging our hard-earned money for a product or service is a pretty serious step—we are not likely to purchase something that is frivolous or make a purchase simply because of a well-designed attention-getting ad.

The Synchroreader may have gotten a lot of publicity because is was very different. But in reality, did consumers really want to have books or magazines read to them? And then with the growth of TV and the availability of radio for news and information, who required books or magazines to talk?

A Few More Examples

Ron Popeil is probably one of the great salesmen of our time. His food dehydrator has been running on infomercials for several years and he's sold millions of them on TV. But the product that got him the most publicity was his GLH hair formula—a cosmetic preparation that seemed to add hair when sprayed on a thinning bald spot. Parodies of the GLH product were made on *Saturday Night Live* and *The Tonight Show with Jay Leno* to name just a couple. But was GLH as big a seller as his food dehydrator—the product that didn't get much publicity at all? Nowhere near.

In selling over 10 million pairs of BluBlocker sunglasses over the past eleven years, we probably had one of the most successful infomercial products ever. Did we get a lot of publicity in the media? Hardly. Just a lot of sales.

When I offered my Laser Beam Mousetrap I got lots of

GIVE ME
A BREAK!

Ernie got lots of publicity but nobody would take his ad.

publicity but couldn't sell a single one of them. Ralph Waldo Emerson may have said that if you build a better mousetrap the world will beat a path to your door, but what he didn't say was that you should make sure it is not so different that it will generate publicity.

Ernie Hemple attended my seminar. His product was the Kitty Whiz Transfer System—a device that taught your cat how to jump up on your toilet and do its business directly into it. There were no messy litter boxes—nothing to do but flush your toilet. No, I'm not making this up. This was an actual product and it even worked.

He got plenty of publicity. He appeared on the TV show *That's Incredible* and dozens of news broadcasts throughout the country. He even had a video clip of one cat that jumped up on the toilet and after doing its business, flushed the toilet. Millions of people saw it on TV and read about it in newspapers and magazines. Did it sell? Not very well. In fact, some of the magazines that wrote about it refused to run his ad because of the sensitive nature of the product. The ad was in good taste but it was the product that offended the same editors who wrote about it as an oddity or a news item. The only sales he could generate were through publicity, but these exposures weren't enough to sustain his business.

You Want Control

And when you are selling a product, what can media publicity do for you in terms of sales? Very little. Although media publicity might get a lot of exposure for your product, when you run your own ad, you can control what is said about your product. Product sales can be ruined by bad publicity or an article written by somebody who doesn't really know or care about your product.

And don't be fooled by a lot of response to publicity generated by a product that you haven't even offered yet. I remember several products that we weren't sure about, but when they got a lot of media publicity and we received a number of unsolicited orders, we thought we had some real winners—only to find out otherwise.

So my basic rules of thumb are simply these:

Publicity Theory 1: Publicity will not tell you if you have a winning product. It can, in fact, be a sign that your product will not sell well.

Publicity Theory 2: Publicity often means that your product or service is not yet in the public mainstream and therefore will not appeal to your prospect.

As marketers we can create our own environment or our own way of positioning our product so that it harmonizes with the needs and desires of the consumer. If it sells, we know the product is a success. If it does not sell, we know we have to change, modify and retest our ad or accept the fact that the product will not sell. Its time has not yet come.

Media publicity for our product does not allow us to control our destiny. If anything, a product that generates publicity should be a sign that this product is not yet ready for a successful marketing campaign.

Publicity for your company, however, if done with the proper strategy, makes sense. I remember how I kept a very low profile when I ran my company until I discovered that I was encountering a great deal of competition. It then became my goal to make myself known to the press. Companies with new products would be attracted to our company and bring me the lifeblood of our existence—new products. After an article appeared in *Forbes* magazine about me, I got a call from the late Charles Tandy, chairman of the board of Tandy Corporation. He wanted to meet the guy behind those "successful and creative" JS&A ads. We developed a nice friendship and I had the opportunity to get to know some of the top people at Radio Shack.

Do not rely on media publicity as an indication that you have a winning product nor as part of your marketing program unless you have a well-defined corporate strategy and a proven product. In that case, publicity could simply be part of your corporate strategy—not to help maximize your mail order sales but to prepare the product for sale to the retail market.

As a rule, however, control your product's exposure in the media by limiting it to the ads which you select and pay for.

If you recall from the previous marketing story, after our success in selling the first pocket calculator we opened our first retail store. The next marketing story tells about that store and the events that then permitted a quantum jump in the success of my young company.

A Marketing Story

The DataKing 800 Calculator

I had no idea that the ad would pull at all. Until I ran it.

Our new store was rather unique. We outfitted it with a space-age theme, had a big mural of the surface of the moon and used some great-looking displays. And I gave it a great new name too: "The Brain Factory." I expanded the phone lines to three and had order stations set up in the corner. The store opened early in the morning and we were always busy taking orders as early as 7:30 AM.

It was a lot of fun setting up the store. I let my creativity run full blast and I created an environment that you couldn't find at any other place in the Chicago area or anywhere else for that matter. I dressed the clerks in white lab coats. I had attractive models acting as hostesses, wearing space bunny outfits for my grand opening and during busy weekends, and I set up a very unusual way to enter the store.

You stepped into a large cylinder, rotated the cylinder and then stepped out into a dimly lit room with a huge wall mural of the moon. To build curiosity in readers, I wrote the following ad which appeared in the *Chicago Tribune* and other local papers in the fall of 1973.

Headline: Introducing: The Brain Factory

Subheadline: The new JS&A space-age showroom will be hard to find, hard to get into, and impossible to predict.

Copy: Standing on the northwest corner of Sanders and Dundee in Northbrook, Illinois, is a small, one story white building. A sign on one of the windows indicates there is a State Farm Insurance office there. Off to the side is a brightly-painted purple door with the numbers "4200" to its left.

You enter the unmarked purple door and step into a small, dark, reception room. You press a large red button and you enter the

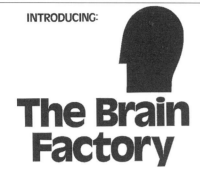

INTRODUCING:

The Brain Factory

The new JS&A space-age showroom will be hard to find, hard to get into, and impossible to predict.

Standing on the northwest corner of Sanders and Dundee in Northbrook, Illinois, is a small, one story white building. A sign on one of the windows indicates there is a State Farm Insurance office there. Off to the side is a brightly-painted purple door with the numbers "4200" to its left.

You enter the unmarked purple door and step into a small, dark, reception room. You press a large red button and you enter the Brain Cylinder. In a matter of seconds you find yourself staring into the Brain Factory—a showcase of the latest space-age, solid-state products. On display are digital clocks, watches, calculators, telephone devices and the latest in space-age technology.

Scientists in white robes and scar tissue drift around aimlessly groping at customers, removing their money, and passing out great bargains.

Space bunnies clad only in integrated circuits and space fuzz assist customers and add a delightful touch as they contrast against the scenic decor that surrounds the room.

Yes, the Brain Factory is a space-age experience—a place to see, touch, and buy the electronic products of the future. Will it succeed? Will a store next to a State Farm Insurance office, an entrance with no sign and a store with space bunnies and groping scientists endear itself in the hearts of Americans everywhere?

Quite frankly, we don't think so.

JS&A NATIONAL SALES GROUP
THE BRAIN FACTORY — SANDERS & DUNDEE ROAD
NORTHBROOK, ILLINOIS 60062 Phone: (312) 564-2900

The Brain Factory was my spin on how to attract a crowd at retail. They came and I learned a lot in the process.

Brain Cylinder. In a matter of seconds you find yourself staring into the Brain Factory—a showcase of the latest space-age, solid-state products. On display are digital clocks, watches, calculators, telephone devices and the latest in space-age technology.

Scientists in white robes and scar tissue drift around aimlessly groping at customers, removing their money, and passing out great bargains.

Space bunnies clad only in integrated circuits and space fuzz assist customers and add a delightful touch as they contrast against the scenic decor that surrounds the room.

Yes, the Brain Factory is a space-age experience—a place to see, touch, and buy the electronic products of the future. Will it succeed? Will a store next to a State Farm Insurance office, an entrance with no sign and a store with space bunnies and groping scientists endear itself in the hearts of Americans everywhere?

Quite frankly, we don't think so.

I was able to advertise in the local paper and even in *The Wall Street Journal* at their retail rate, which was a lot lower than the national rate I had been paying. The idea of opening a national chain of stores was foremost on my mind that winter of 1974. The store was doing quite well and our mail order business was growing.

In February of 1974 I was approached by a short, rotund gentleman by the name of Aaron. Aaron had a calculator for me to sell—a calculator that was the first in a series of steps that was about to change my business career and make a major impact on my company, for several reasons I was soon to discover.

Would I Undercut the Retailers?

The calculator was called the DataKing 878. Aaron wanted me to offer the product for $39.95 and showed me ads from other retailers who were charging $69.95. "What about the other retailers? Won't they be upset if I come out with the product at such a low price?" I asked him.

Aaron smiled. "I just saw one of your ads in *The Wall Street Journal* that I thought was ingenious," he replied. "It was an ad for a Craig calculator and you then later followed up with an ad rescinding the offer. But you gave the readers of the *Journal* a few days to purchase the calculator at the old price."

Aaron was talking about a mistake I had made. The manufacturer, Craig Corporation, wanted me to offer a calculator at $69.95 and through some lack of communication, I thought we could offer it at $49.95. The ad was small, so it didn't cost me that much to test. And the price was really the significant element in the ad since it represented a great value, so I didn't need much copy. The ad pulled well as I expected it to. But when the president of Craig Corporation saw it, he was livid. "How could you do this to me? My retailers—my good customers are screaming at me on the phone. Do you realize what you've done to me?"

I saw that I had hurt my supplier and apologized. I offered him a solution. "Why don't I run a retraction? It will prove to your retailers that I made a mistake and if I give my customers a few days to respond to the previous offer at the old price before the revised price goes into effect, I could possibly get enough orders to cover the cost of the retraction."

Retraction Response Stronger

Indeed, I ran the ad. And the response to the retraction was over four times stronger than the response to the original ad, which was a much larger-sized insertion. People were taking advantage of the opportunity before I raised the price to the correct one. Aaron had seen this as a pre-planned ploy to get more business, even though it wasn't.

"I can't do that," I protested. "First, the previous retraction was a true retraction. I was helping Craig Corporation by running it. And second, what about your current retail customers? Won't it hurt them? Is that what you really want to do?"

Aaron was insistent. "My customers are retailers who have treated me pretty rotten and I can't go back to them with the lower price point. But you can drop the price and by doing the retraction bit, you won't upset many of them who still have inventory. Besides, their customers probably won't see your small ad anyway."

I Felt Uncomfortable

Aaron seemed to make sense but I felt uncomfortable doing this. Imagine purposely going behind the backs of your customers to knowingly undercut them. If Aaron did that to them, what would he do to me if he saw a better opportunity?

I refused. "I can't do it, Aaron. I'd rather stay away from this deal."

But Aaron persisted, offering me an even lower price with no inventory commitment and even agreeing to pay for the cost of my ad if it didn't work. I finally agreed, justifying my decision by thinking about what retailers often did to me. They would wait until I ran an ad, stock up on the product I was selling and then undercut me in their ads in the *Journal*. This, in a sense, could be my form of getting even.

I agreed to run a test, which was successful, and then ran the smaller ad retracting the previous ad and sold more product with the retraction than with the original ad. And to my surprise, long after the ad ran and the deadline passed for the higher price, I would get orders for the higher price as well. (I sold it to my customers at the lower price anyway.)

Campaign Was Successful

The campaign was successful, Aaron ran out of product and appreciated my help in liquidating his inventory and we both went our different ways. Then about a few months later, I got a call from him offering me a brand-new calculator—one which he claimed was "so revolutionary, nobody would buy it."

The calculator was called the DataKing 800. It was manufactured by Rockwell International and made for Aaron's company, DataKing, Inc. But there was a hitch. The calculator was not selling. It was sitting on retail shelves and gathering dust. The display was a funny-looking liquid crystal display—a display technology that was being introduced for the first time. (Today, practically every calculator has a liquid crystal display.)

The keyboard was totally different. Instead of the typical square keys, the keys were narrow. The calculator was large and bulky and there was no AC adapter—something that other calculators all had. It was so different that Aaron could not sell them and no retailer wanted them.

Aaron reminded me of the success with the previous pocket calculator. The people at Rockwell International had suggested he stop by and visit with me to see if maybe I could find a way to move this product. Aaron met me at my home and we talked about the product and its features. I saw why it wouldn't sell. "This thing is so advanced, you need a direct response ad to really explain the features," I said. "Let me give it a try."

I Personally Like the Unit

Aaron and I worked out all the price details. I was to advertise the calculator for $59.95. I called Rockwell International to learn more about the display and some of the technology. I personally really liked the unit. When people would stop by the store, I would show them the DataKing 800 and ask for their opinion, but nobody wanted to buy one. Our customers usually came into the store to buy a calculator with traditional features and display and when they saw the DataKing, they just couldn't relate to it. Even with my best selling techniques, I couldn't persuade them. It was then that I wondered if my ad would even work.

But Aaron made me one promise. "If you can sell this product, I won't make it available to anybody else—just JS&A. You'll have a total exclusive." Big deal, I thought. Nobody could sell it anyway.

I tested the ad in March of 1974 in *The Wall Street Journal* and it sold thousands of units. It not only jammed our phone lines but kept them jammed for almost three days. It was the most responsive toll-free offer we had ever made and I looked at rolling it out and then repeating it again in the *Journal*—something I hardly ever did. Once I ran a product, it was often too late to run it again. It was either being sold at retail, which cut into our response, or being replaced by a newer and more advanced model. The technology and prices were changing so fast that there were very few ads that I would run twice in the *Journal*.

No Retail Competition

But the DataKing was different. Aaron promised me an exclusive arrangement whereby he wouldn't sell the product to anybody else as long as I sold it. And finally, there was nothing like it on the market—no new technology to take its place. So I ran it again in the *Journal*. And again, and again—seven times in all. And with each week and with each insertion and each edition, it produced a very nice profit.

Meanwhile, Aaron saw that we were selling a lot of calculators and saw this as his chance to move his inventory and even order more from Rockwell. He called and requested to see me in what he said was "an important meeting with significant consequences." We had already moved most of his 20,000 calculators and we had only about four national ads in the *Journal* at this point.

His message sounded important, but I was a little leery about what he had to say. "Joe, you've got the opportunity to really grow now. Why don't you take the DataKing 800 ad and run it nationally in magazines? There are some great magazines out there and you could really do well. I'll even give you some advertising incentive to do it."

Technology Was Moving Too Fast

The suggestion did not appeal to me. I knew how long it took to get into magazines—often two or three months—and I didn't want to risk being hung out there with an ad that would be quickly knocked off by another product. Technology was still moving too fast. "But Joe," argued Aaron, "this is the technology of the next decade. Nobody is going to knock it off because nobody can sell it at retail."

Aaron was right about it not selling at retail. When somebody walked into my store not having seen the DataKing 800 and I tried to sell them the unit, they didn't respond at all. They wanted something more conventional. On the other hand, those who had seen the DataKing ad wanted only the DataKing when they walked into the store. My ads were proving to be more persuasive than even my personal selling—or anybody's personal selling. There was something about advertising appearing in print that had a major persuasive effect, beyond the mere selling message.

A Quantum Leap into My Future

Aaron continued, "Joe, you have the reputation and the skill. You have the advertisement—the golden egg. All you need to do is run your ad in other magazines and you'll be amazed at the response. You may not see it, but I do. It's clear. Run the ad and you will make a quantum leap into your future. I can see it clearly."

Aaron finally persuaded me to make a commitment to several magazines. He would give me a slightly better price in return for my gamble of running my ad in several of the more scientific, business and high-income type publications. The stage was set for what was to become a major turning point in my career and the future of my company. But what was to follow I would never have anticipated. And it wasn't just the great response. It was the series of events that happened subsequent to my running the campaign. Let me explain.

All the ads were placed in April 1974. There were ads in everything from *Psychology Today* to *Popular Science*, from *Playboy* to *Business Week*. I went well beyond the seven or eight magazines I had promised Aaron and was running in almost anything that made sense. And as the *Journal*'s DataKing ads were nearing their final run, the magazine ads' response kicked in and eventually thousands of calculators were sold. But I'm getting ahead of the story—let's backtrack a bit.

Already Knocked Off

Just as the magazine ads were about to run and the ads in the *Journal* had been run at least seven times, an ad appeared in the *Journal* for the same DataKing 800 calculator from a company in Connecticut using many of the copy lines from my ad.

When I saw this I was really upset. Here I was about to run nationally with a product that was exclusively mine, and Aaron was already selling it to somebody else who was running it in the same publication I had been using. This was rotten. But I should have expected it from Aaron.

"How could you do this to me, Aaron!" I shouted on the phone. "How could you pull this cheap shot on me?"

Aaron tried to explain that the ad was run by some small retail store he had supplied with the product, thinking that it wouldn't interfere with my sales. He apologized and assured me that he wouldn't supply them with any more product. I accepted his explanation, but in my mind I questioned Aaron's motives.

Our magazine ads started to break. Our company grew so fast that we outgrew our small office space within a few weeks and I was soon looking to buy our very first office building. We had to hire dozens of temporaries to take the orders and our small 1,000-square-foot office became packed with humanity. We even had to use my home basement again for storage. Shipping was being done by an outside fulfillment house, but we were still jammed with returns and customer service calls as well.

We Reached a Major Breakthrough

Toward the end of our promotion, I realized that I had indeed reached a major breakthrough for our company. We had discovered that when an ad worked in *The Wall Street Journal*, it worked elsewhere. And by multiplying the number of publications that carried my ads, I would be able to multiply my persuasive selling technique in print, and indeed by many times. I now had the means and the experience to expand on this knowledge, using this format.

But I wasn't finished with Aaron. Despite all the product we moved for him and the completion of my commitment to him, he wasn't satisfied. He wanted me to continue. I explained that the response rates were starting to fall off and that new calculators were appearing at lower prices and I couldn't really justify risking all that money on an ad campaign that I didn't have confidence would work again. Aaron had an answer.

"Joe, I really believed that you would continue selling my calculator. I've got about 5,000 that I want you to sell in one big promotion to get rid of them for me. Otherwise, I'm going to run my own mail order ad at $39.95."

This sounded like blackmail. The thought of Aaron running the same product for $20 less after I had done all the work establishing the price of $59.95 was rather frightening. What would my customers think? And how would this affect my credibility and reputation? I simply couldn't let Aaron do this to me. Then I remembered it was his persuasion that had allowed my company to really expand. I therefore decided to give it a try and see if I could find some clever way to move Aaron's final inventory. And that's when I came up with an ad that was to become quite a surprise, as you will discover in my next marketing story.

But first, it's time for another direct marketing lesson. And in this next lesson, we're going to take a close look at the effect of price on sales—a subject that we will examine from a few different angles.

Marketing Lesson 11

Price vs. Sales

There may come a time when you must determine the price of a product. Should you price it high and make more profit with fewer sales or should you price it low and make less profit with more sales?

Many times we have no choice about the price—because of competition, the requirements of a supplier or our own requirements in order to earn a profit.

If you do have a choice, then there is only one real answer. Test. That's right, test. Run an ad with one price point and another with a different price point. Measure the response to both ads and then determine the bottom line. If you end up with more profit with one price point than another, then you've got one answer. But there may be other factors to look at too.

Price Point Affects Copy—An Example

What if you are trying to build a mailing list or establish a membership? You might choose a less profitable price point if it brings you more names for your mailing list or more members for your club.

How does the price point affect the copywriter? Do you change your copy based on the price point of the product you are selling? There was a point in my seminar where I took the participants on an emotional roller coaster of decision-making during which they learned a very important lesson about how copy is affected by price point.

It was during our creative session. I was showing them how to get their creative juices flowing with the de Bono Think Tank. This is a spherical device that holds 14,000 words printed on small pieces of plastic with a window through which some of the words are visible. First I'd mix up all the words and then select somebody from the group to read out loud the first three words that he or she saw through the window of the Think Tank.

The Think Tank held 14,000 words on small plastic strips.

The rest of the class would then shout out ideas on a possible concept using those three words. For example, if the product was a treasure detector and the words were 'uncle', 'caterpillar' and 'deceive', then the story line might be about this uncle who hid a treasure in a toy Caterpillar tractor and deceives everybody about its true whereabouts.

As you can see, by using unrelated words, the thinker or writer has to get away from the traditional way of telling about just the features of a product and focus on some concept. The Think Tank gives you a tool to break away from the traditional way of thinking and reach out to different combinations, relationships and permutations from your vast mental network.

Demonstration of Price vs. Sales

After I'd present the exercise to the class and they'd see the magic and fun of the Think Tank, the device really sold itself. I always waited for somebody in the class to raise his or her hand and ask, "Where can I buy one of those things?"

I would then go into a demonstration to prove several points about the topics I had been teaching during the day. It usually went like this:

"The Think Tank costs only $19.95 wholesale, so if there's anybody here who wants one, just raise your hand." At that moment, all the participants raise their hands. And why not? The item looks well worth a lot more than $19.95 and for an aid to creativity and the help that it provides, it makes a great purchase as well as a conversation piece. Then too, $19.95 is certainly an "impulse buy" price point. But then I come back with my first surprise.

"Well, I'd like to buy them for $19.95 too. Actually the price is $99.95. I was kidding about the $19.95 price. I mean, what do you expect? How many want it now?" About one-fourth of the participants raise their hands. The rest are straining to decide . . . maybe a few more hands go up after some contemplation.

I then continue: "Now listen, $99.95 isn't really a lot. First, because there are 14,000 words on little pieces of plastic all in this beautiful plastic sphere and mounted on this three-point tri-pod. Look at it this way—if you get just one idea from this Think Tank and you make just $1,000 more from your ad, isn't it worth it? *Now* how many people want to buy this at $99.95?"

A show of hands go up and now two-thirds of the partici-pants want the Think Tank. Certainly not as many as wanted it at $19.95, but quite a few. Then I come in with the final part of the exercise. "OK, I'm really happy to see the enthusiasm here for the Think Tank, but I've got to confess something to you— I only have three of them left, they aren't made any more and one of these days these things are going to be a collector's item. If there is anybody who would like one of these from my col-lection, I'm not going to part with it unless somebody offers $250." Only four people raise their hands.

The Lessons Learned

At this point I explain to the class, "We have just learned several important marketing lessons. At a very low price, you don't have to say much about the product. Just present the prod-uct and if people understand what the product is and the per-ceived value is low enough, there will be enough people who will buy it whether they need it or not. No need for long copy, no need to explain too much.

"But raise the price without describing the features as I did, and the response drops dramatically. Then still at the higher price point, by describing the product, justifying its purchase and pre-senting it with enthusiasm, you can bring up the demand—but interestingly, not to the same high level as at the $19.95 price point.

"Finally, by limiting the amount of product available and creating exclusivity or rarity, I can now offer it for $250 and justify the price so that four people would want one.

"Notice that as we raised prices, the response rates dropped. The only thing that saved the $99.95 price point from avoiding complete disaster was a good selling job." The lesson learned from this experience can be summed up in a pricing theory.

Pricing Theory: Generally speaking, when the price of a product goes up, the number of units sold goes down and more effort to educate and persuade is required to sell the product.

Since each of the participants was emotionally involved in this marketing lesson and personally saw the effect on them at each price level, the lesson was indelibly etched in their minds.

I've always told my class that you don't need long copy if you have a low enough price point. But with a higher price point, you have to add some salesmanship.

Our next marketing story continues where we left off in the previous marketing story with Aaron and his calculator when I decided to help him dispose of his remaining inventory. Little did I suspect what was about to happen to our company.

A Marketing Story

The Halloween Sale Fiasco

Halloween Sale

All treats and no tricks in America's most spectacular calculator sale.

TEXAS INSTRUMENTS $9.95
BOWMAR $19.95 APF $29.95
KEYSTONE $39.95 DATAKING
KINGSPOINT $99.95

It was meant to be a real treat for the consumer, but turned out to be a really bad trick on us.

I have often come up with my most creative marketing ideas simply from being under pressure to do so. They usually arose as solutions to specific problems. I would have a serious marketing problem and by simply looking at the problem as an opportunity and then acting on that opportunity, I would often succeed. Such was the case with the DataKing 800 and what was to become one of the wildest promotions I have ever run.

Aaron dropped the price on his remaining inventory of calculators so that I could sell them for only $39.95—$20 off the price I had been selling them all over the United States. Since I didn't want to upset my previous customers, who now numbered over 50,000, I had to come up with a way to mask the new price point and, at the same time, blow them all out in one spectacular sale and with one spectacular ad in *The Wall Street Journal*.

At the time there were some pretty hot-selling calculators. For example, the Texas Instruments 2550 was one of the most coveted of all the new calculators and was selling for $69.95. Dealers couldn't get enough of them. In fact, they were being sold for a premium as they were in short supply.

Although there was talk of a potential $9.95 calculator, there were none yet being offered, either by design or through discounting. They didn't yet exist in October 1974.

I Felt Pressure to Act

Feeling both the pressure from Aaron and the need to protect my reputation with those customers who had bought the DataKing for $59.95, I put together a promotion that was to become a model for several future promotions. It also became

219

such a success that it disrupted our company for over a month and actually resulted in a loss because of the overwhelming response. Here's what happened.

I wanted to use the occasion of Halloween to liquidate the DataKing calculators by running my first annual "Halloween Sale." As the ad's subheadline indicated, "All treats and no tricks in America's most spectacular calculator sale."

I was offering the nation's first $9.95 pocket calculator—a major price breakthrough. But the model I was selling for $9.95 was the Texas Instruments model that was in great demand for $69.95. I bought 24 of them at the full retail price, yet I was offering them to my customers for only $9.95 as part of the promotion.

I then listed several other models. The more the perceived value, the more I discounted the price. I gradually built up to the DataKing 800 price of $39.95. It too was a major bargain, but couched among the other bargains, the DataKing 800 discount was not as obvious as it would have been otherwise.

There were eight models that I listed in all. Each was a bargain and we had all of them in stock for the promotion.

The Unique Concept or Big Idea

The concept was simple. I would offer the opportunity to buy these products to anybody who sent in an order prior to the deadline of November 12, 1974. I clearly stated that the more spectacular the price, the more limited the quantity we had. I explained that we had only 5,000 calculators to offer and that we would simply have our accounting firm retrieve all the orders from a lockbox, spread them on a table, number them sequentially and then open the envelopes in a random order generated by our computer until all the calculators were sold.

I advised participants to indicate their first choice and list a second and then a third choice. They were to put into the envelope a check for the amount of their highest-priced of the three choices. If they got their first choice and the price was less than the amount enclosed, they would get a refund. If we didn't have their first choice, we would send them their second choice or perhaps their third choice.

We had our big-eight accounting firm of Deloitte, Touche and Ross assure us that the selection process was aboveboard and in keeping with proper standards. Using a public accounting firm also assured the public as well. And even though I had to pay full retail for the 24 Texas Instruments calculators I used in the promotion, I was keeping my pledge to have all the calculators in stock.

I'm sure you've figured out the purpose of the promotion by now. I was hoping that I would generate enough traffic in the form of orders that I could move sufficient inventory of my DataKing 800 as second and third choices. The value was there for the DataKing and I certainly had made a name for the product through our national advertising.

I Run the Ad

Instead of running the ad first in the Southwestern edition of *The Wall Street Journal* as I had done with all my ads, I felt I couldn't go too wrong if I ran it nationally. Time was of the essence. It made no sense to check the response at the post office because I wouldn't have access to those orders. It was the responsibility of the accounting firm to pick up the orders at the end of the promotion. So I placed the ad and coordinated the promotion with the accountants, who were planning to be at the post office on the morning of November 12th.

The post office was advised of the promotion by the accounting firm and we were assigned the lucky box number of 777. I also called Aaron. "You're going to be pleased with what I am doing," I boasted. "Just watch *The Wall Street Journal* for our ad. I hope to move most of your remaining inventory in one major promotion. You'll be quite pleased, I assure you."

Aaron thanked me and said that he would look for the ad. I felt relieved in a sense. Now I would not be embarrassed by a $39.95 price point run by somebody else—especially my supplier. And I might even have a successful promotion as a result.

Just prior to running the ad we had moved into our new office building purchased from the profits earned from previous sales of the DataKing 800 calculator. It was a beautiful one-story contemporary building around 5,000 square feet and we had plenty of room for all our staff and even more room to expand. My own business and my own office building—it was indeed a magic moment, not only for me but for my assistant Mary

Stanke. Mary had now been with me for almost three years and had seen the company grow and prosper. It was as much an accomplishment for her as it was for me.

"Grand Opening" Party Organized

We organized a party for the evening of the November 12th opening of the mail. We invited all our business associates, suppliers, lawyers, friends and our accounting firm to attend what we called our "Official Grand Opening." It was to be a small grand opening for the office building as well as a grand opening for some of the mail we were expecting from the Halloween Sale.

In short, the evening of November 12 was the date we chose for two proud grand openings and it was a date that will live in our minds for a long time.

As the days passed after Halloween, we got word that we were getting a pretty good response at the post office. We had arranged our offices for the grand opening with our new furniture and typewriters, and we decorated everything with flowers and installed a few tables to hold the trays of mail we were expecting.

We were all set. The office building looked beautiful. The decorations were in place and our employees were all dressed up and talking about the party they were going to be part of in the evening. I took great joy in the festive feeling that was filling our offices.

The Day Arrives

In the morning, around 10 AM, two employees from the accounting firm showed up to prepare to pick up the mail from the post office and place it in trays for the selection process. The rubber stamps they were going to use were all laid out and the processing techniques were discussed with the office personnel to make sure everyone understood the procedures.

Then around noon with everything in place and the procedures understood by everyone, the accountants left for the post office in their small Dodge car. About fifteen minutes later we received an emergency phone call.

"I think we need some help here," said one of the accountants.

"What do you mean?" I asked.

Millions of dollars were in those envelopes.

"There are at least 14 huge bags of mail and it won't all fit in our car," sighed the accountant. "You better send somebody with a station wagon."

It took a station wagon and their car to bring all the mail bags to our office and when I saw what we had generated, I almost panicked. First of all, there were thousands of dollars in checks in all those envelopes. We couldn't possibly open all the envelopes, remove the checks and keep them in a safe place. We needed armed guards to protect the money. And second, we couldn't possibly spread all the envelopes out on the few tables we had. We needed several more tables. And finally, with our party coming up in the evening, we had to get this all accomplished by the time the party started at 6 PM.

The mail response overwhelmed us. We had to number and sort each envelope.

Guards were hired, more tables were brought in and the accounting firm was trying to figure out a way to protect the mail so none of our staff could possibly touch the envelopes overnight. The armed guards therefore played two roles. They made sure that nobody would touch the envelopes until the accountants returned the next day and that nobody would break into our offices and steal the envelopes.

The evening of the party we laid out all the envelopes in dozens of trays on tables. The area was all roped off, and the guards made sure that nobody touched the envelopes. I gave a small speech at the start of the party. I talked about what the envelopes represented and with the help of the accounting firm opened the first of the envelopes.

It was a great night—a night to celebrate a response unmatched in our history. Our friends were all there to celebrate with us and we really enjoyed the evening. But the next morning we felt the hangover—thousands of calls on our toll-free lines asking for the results of the promotion. We had to hire dozens of temporaries to handle the stamping and opening of the mail.

It Cost Us a Fortune

The extra expense of the temporaries and the armed guards and the fact that the accountants had to stay for almost a week to complete their function in the promotion—all of this cost us a fortune. In addition, I increased my purchase of those Texas Instruments calculators from 24 to 96. In all fairness, I wanted to match the size of the promotion's response and give our customers the opportunity to buy the TI calculators at the $9.95 price, even though I was losing my shirt on each one I bought.

Not only was the telephone response blocking our regular business, but it was expensive to handle. I needed to do something immediately to stop the phone response and at the same time inform my customers. So I prepared another ad for *The Wall Street Journal,* planning to run it as quickly as possible.

A Disturbing Call Came

Before I had a chance to complete the ad, I got a very disturbing phone call. It was an angry customer. "How could you dare charge us $39.95 for the DataKing 800 calculator and sell it to us as a bargain when I see it here in *The Wall Street Journal* for $34.95?"

"What?" I said. "How can that be?" But I checked the *Journal,* and indeed the DataKing 800 was being offered in a large ad for $34.95 along with a free bonus of a carrying case—something I had not been offering. And by whom? Aaron's company. He had gone behind my back and had run his first mail order ad, undercutting my major promotion to help him liquidate his inventory.

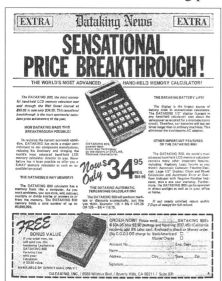

Their ad took us totally by surprise.

Now the phone calls were really coming in. If our lines were jammed earlier with people trying to find out the results of the promotion, it was even worse now with them calling and demanding to know why we were ripping them off.

I Totally Blew Up

I tried to call Aaron. He repeatedly refused to take my calls. When I finally spoke to him I was calm at first. Maybe I was missing something, and just maybe Aaron had a very valid reason

The Results

Here's the story behind America's most spectacular calculator sale and an exciting new digital watch offer.

The pressure was on us to announce the results of our promotion and explain DataKing's action.

for running the ad. But he had none. He had seen how successful I had been and just wanted to see if he could make a mail order ad work too. At that point I became outraged and told him what I thought. I don't remember exactly what I said, but I rarely lose my temper like I did during that call. In fact, Mary Stanke had to rush to my office and close the door; people across the street must have been complaining.

Aaron finally agreed to provide a lower price point for me so I could match his price. Then I immediately got my next ad going. I took out another ad in the national edition of *The Wall Street Journal* entitled: "The Results—Here's the story behind America's most spectacular calculator sale and an exciting new digital watch offer." In short, I was going to announce nationally the results of the sale and at the same time explain the price discrepancy for the DataKing 800, paying for the cost of the ad with another offer. The ad copy tells it best. Here's an excerpt, after I explained the premise of the sale:

On November 12th, the final day of the sale, the public accounting firm drove to the post office and picked up the mail which was later protected by two armed guards. When the 12,000 responses were stacked, they extended 57 feet, turning our office into a sea of mail.

We sequentially numbered each of the 12,000 envelopes and then produced a computer printout of all the 12,000 numbers randomly listed. The public accounting firm then supervised the random selection to insure that each lucky customer was fairly chosen. With over 12,000 letters, it wasn't until late Thursday that the lucky participants eligible for the 5,000 calculators were selected and the remaining steps of our order processing and typing began.

A total of over one half million dollars was enclosed in the envelopes. Consequently, a contingent of armed guards kept constant watch until all the checks were either processed or returned. Checks ranged from $13.45 for the Texas Instruments calculator to over $1,200 for 12 of the KingsPoint units. With 11 others in his office a man bought 12 Texas Instruments Calculators at

$9.95 each and regretted not ordering all twelve for himself. Entire engineering departments were pleasantly surprised when they were notified that their scientific calculators were going to cost them up to 40% less than what they'd have to pay at any retail outlet.

But we did have one surprise. DataKing made a quantity of their units available to us to sell at $39.95 as part of the Halloween Sale. Worried that JS&A would be unable to liquidate DataKing's entire inventory, DataKing overreacted by offering the unit for $34.95 directly to readers of *The Wall Street Journal*. They later apologized and credited our account so that we could offer the same unit with carrying case at $34.95. All those who ordered the DataKing 800 will be receiving a refund and a new carrying case.

In addition to the overwhelming responsibility of processing the orders, we now had to send a refund to all those customers who bought the DataKing 800 unit and then pay the extra costs to ship the carrying case.

The ad did break even. The sale of the digital watch did well, so it really didn't cost us anything to announce the results. But this promotion taught me a great deal.

The Lessons I Learned

I learned how even the best promotions can be so successful that they end up costing you a lot more than you expected. I learned that had I followed my intuition completely at the very beginning and never dealt with somebody like Aaron, I might never have achieved the success that I did. Maybe my intuition was simply telling me that I had to be very careful when dealing with him. Whatever. So, in a sense, everything worked out in the long run.

But even with the success or failure of the Halloween Sale, I had figured out a way to start a business from scratch, as you will soon see in the next two marketing stories.

A month passed and the Halloween Sale promotion was behind us and we had acquired a pretty good mailing list of its participants. Although the promotion itself was not profitable, it was a real learning experience. And finally, I realized that even though I would never do business with Aaron again, he was the individual who had convinced me to launch my first national ad campaign using a toll-free number and my first major random-selection promotion, which would be followed by several more in the future.

Although I started to use the toll-free number to take orders in 1973, the DataKing promotion was the first to use a toll-free number in a major national campaign for credit card order-taking. And this was before anybody recognized the significance of the toll-free number and its impact on others. New industries were created and it maybe even helped expand the catalog industry.

It was the DataKing 800 that initiated me into the mass market national advertising arena and established JS&A as a major contender in the direct response field. Indeed, the DataKing 800 promotion was a turning point in my career.

In our next marketing lesson, I talk about a very important aspect of any direct marketing program—namely, the product that people return when they are not satisfied with their purchase, or what is called the "return rate."

Marketing Lesson 12

The Return Rate

At my seminar, I was showing slides of ads created by previous seminar participants and we came to an advertisement of an audio system run in several magazines by a California mail order company. The president of the company happened to be in my class. I asked him how the product did.

You want to achieve a good balance when it comes to returns.

"We sold thousands of them and we had an incredibly low 3% return rate," beamed the president. The rest of the class was impressed.

The return rate he was referring to is the percentage of customers who purchase an item, receive it and then, for some reason, return it. At the time, a typical return rate was anywhere from 10 to 15%. Some customers might change their mind about an item, find it cheaper elsewhere, or just plain try it and not like it. If you had a return rate over 20%, there was usually some latent defect in the product, or the product wasn't described properly and therefore didn't fulfill the customer's expectations.

But a 3% return rate was really unusual. I looked at the class and asked them, "Would you say that a 3% return rate is good? And if so, why?"

Is a Low Return Rate Good?

The class responded with several comments. They felt that 3% was indeed very good. Obviously, the president had satisfied his customers and they were pleased with their purchase. Some in the class mentioned that the price must have been quite reasonable and others said that when the customer received their purchase, it must have been a lot better than what they expected.

After everybody had finished, I looked at the class and said, "I think a 3% return rate is totally unacceptable."

The class looked rather puzzled. I explained, "A 3% return rate tells me that he didn't sell hard enough. He didn't get across all the terrific features of the product. One of the symptoms of not doing a good marketing job is when most people feel they got a better product and value than they thought they would."

I turned toward the president of the company and said, "Think how many more sales you could have gotten with a 12% return rate, which is normal in this type of product category!"

The Return Rate Examined

Let's talk about return rate in general for a moment to understand my comments more completely.

The one thing I learned very early in my advertising career was that you can't please all of the people all of the time. Remember my first pocket calculator ad for the Craig 4501 that I told you about in an earlier marketing story?

I was personally very excited about this new pocket calculator back in 1971—one of the first in the world. It was selling for $240 and it could actually fit in your pocket. At the time it was truly a revolutionary product.

When we received our first response to a mailing I made, we got a 10% return rate. Some of the people who returned it thought it was the biggest rip-off they had ever seen. One letter said, "You guys should be put in jail for trying to foist something like this on the consumer."

But we also received some very complimentary letters. One said, "I must congratulate you on this wonderful and exciting product and your excellent service."

Had I examined just the return letters without looking at the complimentary letters, I would have been worried. But I still wondered, how could a small percentage think a product is terrible while another group thinks the product is terrific? I soon realized that you cannot please all of the people all of the time and that a return rate of about 10% was a normal day-to-day average, for a variety of reasons.

But whenever my return rate dropped well below that 10%, I always reread my copy to see if perhaps I was not selling hard enough. And if the return rate was very high, I took a close look at my copy to see if the product lived up to my promises.

Look at it another way. I satisfied 90% of my customers. Not bad. When does a political candidate satisfy that large a percentage?

Factors That Affect Return Rates

Return rates reflect more than the way you've written your copy, of course. The performance of your product is also important, and there are other subtle factors that also affect return rates. One of the most important is speed of delivery. If you ship a product right away, your customers who receive it are still in a state of anticipation. They still desire the product and this desire is fresh in their mind.

But ship a product late, and often the customer may even forget he or she ordered it. Customers may change their minds, financial circumstances may take a turn for the worse, or buyer's remorse may surface—and all of these factors grow in direct proportion to the time it takes you to ship your product.

Another factor is the presentation itself, the impression the customer gets when he or she receives a package. Is the box substantial enough so it arrives in good shape? Is the merchandise wrapped properly? In short, what is the impression your customer gets upon receiving the product?

Returns as an Opportunity

Finally, you should look at a customer return not as a problem but more as an opportunity—an opportunity to show what a terrific company you really are. Unfortunately, the simple act of fulfilling orders does not make customers enthusiastic. But how you resolve their problems does. And supplying the customer with simple instructions and a simple procedure for returning their purchase will ensure you of an enthusiastic customer when it comes time to order again. Or, as my friend Murray Raphel says, "Turning an occasional customer into a full-time advocate is your primary goal."

If you understand the meaning of the return rate associated with the products you ship in response to your advertising and know that an average return rate (neither too high nor too low) means that you can get the greatest response and still satisfy the largest segment of your customers, you'll hold the secret to maximizing your profits.

And if you realize that a returned package from a dissatisfied customer is not a problem but an opportunity, then you've got one of the real secrets of growing a mail order business.

Return Theory: The product return rate is a gauge to determine the successful presentation of a product and its acceptance and an opportunity to turn a regular customer into a loyal and enthusiastic advocate.

Now it's story time again. And the next story is a good one. It's about a company that I started from scratch with just one ad and a strategy. It's all in the following marketing story on Consumers Hero.

A Marketing Story

Consumers Hero

The ad created a membership program and the membership bulletins sold product. A new business was created out of this one ad.

One day, in the fall of 1976, I was approached by a local businessman in the industrial park where our offices were located in Northbrook. John had an unusual business. He bought defective merchandise from major manufacturers for a few cents on the dollar and then repaired and sold these products. Large companies such as General Electric used John's company as an outlet for their rejects and for products that were returned by retailers. These products couldn't be sold as new, so instead of just throwing them out, they would allow companies like John's to bid for them. John used former federal prisoners to repair the products—a program that was funded by the U.S. government. The funding from Uncle Sam underwrote the labor and John was able to sell products at really good prices.

John knew of my success with electronic products and wondered if I could set up a program to sell his refurbished stuff. "I think that there is a great opportunity here," he said. "I know you can write a great ad, and once you tested it, I could take over and make the rest of the business flow."

John was a serious businessman who had a tremendous amount of respect for what I did. We'd play racquetball together, go to lunch and discuss marketing or the problems he was having in his business. Since he was down the street from our offices, it was easy to get together with him. I'd give him a call, "John, what are you doing for lunch?" And we'd end up having a round of racquetball in which he would beat me silly.

I Surprised John with Ad

One day, I decided to surprise John with an ad that I wrote

233

to sell his merchandise. The ad, called "HOT," is shown at the start of this marketing story.

My strategy was to use the name of a different company—Consumers Hero—to sell the concept. Too many people associated JS&A with innovative space-age electronics and for us to sell remanufactured merchandise was not in keeping with our image. Our products were all at the forefront of the electronics revolution, whereas John's products were at the back end.

I realized that the big advantage in selling John's products was the price. In selling my other products, advertising costs made up a very large percentage of the price I charged for the product. In order to keep his prices low, it was very important to keep advertising costs low.

I figured that if I could cull bargain hunters out of the mass market, qualify them by charging them a membership fee and have them join an exclusive membership club comprised of other bargain hunters, then I could use direct mail—a more targeted medium than print ads—to present these bargains to my membership.

Dealing with Bargain Hunters

Since I was dealing with bargain hunters, I had to relate to them not only in my copy, but also in the price I was offering for membership. And that is where testing came in.

First I tested the graphic look of the ad and then the headline and then the price of our membership program. In each of the tests, we always discovered one new version that did better than our control ad. In our last ad, I discovered the powerful effect of some slight changes to the ad near the end of the copy. For example, in one ad I guaranteed satisfaction or my customer would get a refund for the unused portion of their membership subscription. In the second ad, I changed the guarantee to include getting a refund for everything they paid for their subscription including interest. That simple guarantee doubled response. We also found out that we attracted twice the number of buyers with a $5 offer as with our original $10 membership price.

The ad worked wherever we ran it. It was simply a matter of finding just the right combination of elements through testing that would make the ad even more successful.

I wrote the direct mail package and membership materials in the same style that the ad was written in. The letters we sent with the mailings had that same homespun sound—like letters written from a dedicated small company designed to serve the average consumer.

Glitch Quickly Discovered

We discovered one glitch right away—some magazines would not run our ads because of the controversial headline and subheadline or even because of the little box in the middle of the ad. The second glitch was actually pretty funny.

I had created a form letter, the first bulletin and the membership card which introduced members to the club. I wanted the letter signed by somebody other than myself, so I decided to invent a name that was rather bland and non-ethnic. I sat and thought. . . . "Hmm, bland . . . 'Alan' sounds bland. How about 'Alan Glans'? That really sounds bland." Yes, I had my name for the president of this new club—Alan Glans.

Fictitious or assumed names used in place of the actual name were very common in mail order solicitations at that time. They still are today.

One of my acquaintances and good friends was, and still is, Bernard Gittelson—one of the great public relations persons in New York and author of the book *Biorhythm, a Personal Science*. His book sold over 3 million copies and his abilities in public relations are legendary. I met him when I was selling a biorhythm calculator and one day he called me to congratulate me on my sales efforts. Soon we became good friends and I would see him in New York whenever I came into town.

I Received an Emergency Call

Bernie always enjoyed my copy, so it was not unusual for me to send him samples of whatever I did. Consumers Hero was no exception. I sent him a copy of my Consumers Hero mailing along with a copy of the ad and asked for his comments.

Bernie responded with an emergency call. "Joe, I just received your mailing. Very clever and I enjoyed reading everything, but who is this guy Alan Glans?"

"Bernie," I responded, "that's just a fictitious name. I wanted a very bland name to head the company, so I came up with 'Alan Glans'. That's a pretty bland-sounding name, isn't it?"

"Holy cow, Joe," shouted Bernie. "You don't want Alan Glans running your company!"

There was a short silence on the phone as I was trying to sort out what he meant. Bernie continued, "Joe, when I got your letter and saw the name 'Glans' at the bottom of the letter, I thought I had seen that word somewhere before. So I looked it up in the dictionary and it means the tip of the male penis. Is that the type of person you want running your company?"

My stomach sank. I had sent the same letter to the printer and they were supposed to duplicate it for our mailing. Were the 20,000 letters already printed? Even though I had never seen the word nor knew what it meant, many of my customers might know it. I now found myself with a potentially embarrassing situation. I thanked Bernie, quickly hung up and raced to the outer office where Mary Stanke was talking to a few employees. "Mary, please, this is very urgent. I must talk to you privately."

Mary excused herself and asked what was wrong. "I can't explain it right now," I said, "but you've got to call the printer and make sure that he doesn't print the Consumers Hero letter with Alan Glans's name on it. Don't ask me why. Just stop the presses and let me know if it is too late."

Imagine what would have happened if we had mailed his letter?

Mary indeed caught the job in time and we changed the name. When she later asked me, all I told her was to look up the word 'glans' in the dictionary, which she did. And when she next walked into my office, with a smile on her face she said, "That's the last person we want running our company."

Company Did Well

The company did quite well the first year and we accumulated a very nice mailing list. Our customers loved our communications and even wrote and told us. It wasn't just the bargains, but the really off-the-wall way we were selling them.

But eventually I dissolved the company. We couldn't get

enough products to satisfy our 25,000-name mailing list. Some of the criminals hired by John took off with a trailer-load of merchandise, and the program, although profitable, wasn't nearly as profitable as JS&A. I gave the list to a small start-up company in Minneapolis and they had great success with the names. The company's name was COMBS and they soon became a multi-million-dollar entity selling closeout merchandise. They credited a lot of their early success to our list, and I was proud that we helped them get a good start. COMBS was eventually sold to a major public company.

The lesson to be learned from this case history is one of understanding what the actual objective of the enterprise was from the very beginning. It was not just to sell the products (although this was obviously one of our goals), but to develop a mailing list as an efficient and low-cost means of selling products to a prospect.

It's now time for another marketing lesson. And this one is about what not to do when you're running your advertising. You'll find it helpful and interesting and my advice may save you a lot of time and money.

Marketing Lesson 13

Things to Avoid

In my years of marketing I have learned that there are a few things to avoid in advertising. Some of them I learned the hard way and some of them I knew by instinct.

The following are my recommendations about those things you should totally avoid when writing or publishing your advertisement.

The Use of Your Own Photo

Putting your own photo in an advertisement can be a mistake. Why? It may draw an emotional response that can hurt sales.

For example, let's say I have a beard (which I did for over 27 years before I shaved it off in 1996), and Aunt Martha in Portland, Oregon, is browsing through a magazine and sees a picture of me in one of our ads. Here's how the conversation might go between Aunt Martha and her husband at the breakfast table.

"Look at this ad, dear, for this wonderful blender I was going to get. But you know, Herman, how I feel about men who wear beards. I just don't trust them. I mean, especially this guy. Look at him."

A Negative Emotional Response

Aunt Martha was developing an emotional reaction to my picture. The product was fine, but somewhere in her life she may have met somebody, under bad circumstances, that I reminded her of, and when she saw my picture, she reacted to this past remembrance. She might not even remember why, but in her subconscious mind lies this negative emotional reaction.

The point is simple. For every company owner who appears in an advertisement, there is always somebody who might get a negative emotional reaction and not buy the product. And that only limits your response rate. So if your market was originally 100 orders, you might end up with 95 or even 90.

There are times, however, when you should put your picture in your advertisement, usually in times of crisis. It was appropriate for Lee Iacocca to step right up front, even at the risk of turning off some of his public, and say, "I am president of Chrysler and we will survive and here's what I'm going to do about it." That's leadership, that's confidence building and it probably turned off very few people and indeed inspired a generation of car buyers to purchase Chryslers back in the '80s.

This was an example of using my picture in an ad to back up my stand.

I ran my picture in an ad when I was fighting the FTC. The public always wants to see who is asking for their support in any political or social cause because in essence you are selling yourself. And just as products are shown in an ad, your prospect expects to see you. That's why politicians run their pictures. But if you're selling a product rather than yourself, you should never run your picture. The only other time I ran my picture was when I was offering my personal copywriting services to raise money for the American Cancer Society as I related in the second marketing story in this book.

Another exception to this recommendation of not using your own photo is in catalogs. I believe it is important to put your picture in your catalog along with a personal message. Remember, when people open your catalog, they are "walking into your store" and you want to be there to welcome them. You set the tone for the entire catalog, and like any shopper in a store, the buyer would find it a privilege to meet the shopkeeper. The picture makes it a more personal shopping experience. A good example of this is Richard Thalheimer and his Sharper Image catalog. Richard can always be found in the front of his catalog welcoming his customers into his "store" with his picture and a personal message.

Although I encourage you to have a picture of yourself in your catalog, it can easily be omitted if you have a personal letter to your customers. You must relate personally with your customers, not only welcoming them to your store, but actually taking them by the hand and showing them some of your products. A good example of a personal letter that I used in the front of one of my catalogs can be found in Appendix A. Although I did not use my picture at the time, if I were doing it today, I would.

Photos of Models

Models, on the other hand, are fine to show in an ad if they look good or make the product look good or if they are appropriate for the product or concept. But the people you use to represent your product in your advertisement should be professionals and either pretty, beautiful or handsome—not your next-door neighbor who did some modeling at one time or your kids who are a lot cheaper than hiring professional child models. People want to identify with beautiful people. Where they feel good about beautiful people they are more likely to respond.

I mentioned a good example of this previously in Marketing Lesson 5, describing the time I ran an ad featuring an average-looking man cringing and holding a vitamin pill and tested it against another ad showing a beautiful lady and handsome guy holding the same pill. Everything else in the advertisement was identical except for the picture. The ad with the beautiful couple pulled 30% more response than the ad with the average-looking guy. It really meant that the beautiful couple drew more prospects into reading the ad copy, which then sold 30% more of them.

The Use of Humor

Humor rarely sells. Avoid it entirely. Trying to get people to exchange their hard-earned money for your product is serious stuff and nobody makes fun of the process and wins.

If the humor is used to entertain or call attention, then it's possible to get away with it, but only with the idea that it gets you into the sales message rather quickly.

Humor can be used to make somebody appear more human or to put the product in a lighter environment. But I've never seen humor sell a product effectively unless the humor was used to humanize the message. Humor used in spot TV commercials might draw a lot of attention, but it often doesn't work to sell the product as proven in many marketing failures. Again, selling is serious stuff and is not to be taken lightly.

I used to write humor for my college newspaper and on occasion I've written humor since. It's not easy. It requires an incredible sense of timing, a tremendous sense of the emotion in each word and a great command of writing ability to pull it off. Very few people can do it and even fewer have a background of direct response copywriting to make it really work. I love to read humor. All of us, I'm sure, enjoy going to a movie to see a really funny film. But the use of humor to get me to exchange my hard-earned dollars for a product or service just won't work, and it rarely works for others.

Some of my ads are lighthearted or considered tongue-in-cheek and even flip by some. But the message is not humorous for the sake of being funny. I'm usually portraying myself as being human.

To Summarize

In general, avoid using humor in advertising copy and avoid using your picture in a print ad. There could be a whole list of other things I could tell you to avoid, like:

1. Avoid not testing an ad before you spend much money to run it in other publications. (I've done it with disastrous results.)

2. Avoid bad customer service. (It will kill your business.)

3. Avoid putting your creative department right next to your accounting department. (I've done it and learned to separate the creative types from everybody else in the company.)

The two most important theories for this lesson are:

Avoid Theory 1: The sale of a product or service is a very serious experience and should be treated as such.

Avoid Theory 2: Use your picture in your ad only if you're running for office or trying to save your company.

Now it's time for me to tell you about a single ad in a single publication that created a company overnight. It's all explained in the next marketing story about the Battram Galleries.

A Marketing Story

Battram Galleries

We weren't going to make a dime, had too few to sell and barely broke even. But profit wasn't our goal.

As you may remember from the previous marketing story, the objective in starting the Consumers Hero company was not just to sell low-priced refurbished merchandise, but to create a mailing list of potential buyers of low-priced refurbished merchandise. There is a big difference.

In one case, you are selling product while trying to build your mailing list, whereas in the other, you focus on building your mailing list and let the sales take care of themselves. The same principle that was used with Consumers Hero was also the basis of the next business I started.

Imagine running a mail order ad where you not only didn't expect to make any money, but didn't have enough product to supply all your customers. That's exactly the premise of the marketing case history that follows.

When Pablo Picasso died in 1973, he was one of the most renowned artists in the world and remains so even today. After Picasso's death, a friend of mine, Jack Childers, represented the Picasso estate as its American licensing agent. With his very hot licensing property, Jack decided to call me with a new idea of his.

"Why don't you offer your customers a different product—a collectible—something that has never been offered before, such as Picasso tiles?"

Jack had previously approached me with the idea of offering collector plates with Picasso images. And we had done a single ad in *The Wall Street Journal* with relatively good success under the name of JS&A Collector's Guild. But it seemed that many companies were offering collector plates and Jack was interested in coming up with something entirely different to really showcase the Picasso art.

Jack's Idea Was Quite Sound

Jack had met a man who silk-screened 6-inch square tiles with colorful images. The tiles could then be displayed on small wooden holders similar to the way collector plates are displayed.

Jack's idea was to take a series of six images selected by a major Picasso art authority and silk-screen them onto the tiles. The seal of the Picasso estate embossed on the reverse side would authenticate them as limited-edition Picasso tiles. I would have the opportunity to craft the entire promotion. I could select every-thing—from how many tiles should be offered to their retail price—and simply pay the Picasso estate a royalty or fee for the privilege of doing this.

Idea Seemed Different

I liked the idea, first because it was different. That has always been a driving force in my life. Second, it had tremendous credibility with the name of Picasso, the endorsement by his estate and the selection of the images by a Picasso expert.

But once again, this was a promotion that did not fit the image of JS&A. Even though we had a loyal customer base—one that knew and trusted us—they were not the type of customer who would be interested in Picasso tiles. By this time, we had a solid reputation in electronics and the name JS&A Collector's Guild no longer made sense.

Realizing that I had to attract a new type of customer meant that I needed a new type of business and a new name as well. So I named it "Battram Galleries" after my wife's maiden name. She was born and raised in England and Battram was not a common name either in England or the United States. I didn't want to make up a name off the top of my head and end up with some pri-vate part of the human anatomy as I did in my Consumers Hero story.

As a side note, Rod MacArthur, the son of the late billion-aire John D. MacArthur and a successful entrepreneur in his own right, was also a friend of mine and owned a direct marketing company called Bradford Galleries that sold collector plates. His company was located in my hometown of Northbrook.

Rod MacArthur was a really neat guy. Spurned by his father, he had to make it on his own and finally hit it big with Bradford

Galleries. He became the dominant force in the collector plate market and we often talked about his company and the strategy he used before he passed away from cancer in 1984. I remember once visiting him and hearing him talk to his wife in French. "Oh, your wife doesn't speak English?" I asked.

Rod smiled. "No, she speaks very good English, but my wife is from France and we have always spoken French at home to hone my skills with the language."

"What a coincidence," I replied. "My wife is from England and we have the same philosophy."

Strategy Formulated

But I'm getting ahead of myself. Several months earlier I formed the company and then started to formulate the strategy. Once again, as with my Consumers Hero start-up, I realized that my first priority and my immediate goal was not to sell the product, Picasso tiles, but rather to create a mailing list. The tiles would indirectly sell themselves if my premise was correct. But what did I have to do to create the demand? The answer was to develop a very large mailing list by offering something that many people would want and that only few could get, much like the Texas Instruments calculators offered in my Halloween Sale.

My concept was to oversubscribe the sale of the tiles. I didn't need to make a penny on the promotion if I could create such demand for the tiles that more people would subscribe than I had tiles to fill the orders. I could then take the names of those who were denied the opportunity to obtain the tile series and offer them a second series—in a larger quantity by the less costly method of direct mail—and expect to earn my profit from the sale of that second series.

Needed Different Writing Style

I also knew that I needed to write the copy in a style different from my typical JS&A ads and definitely different from my recent Consumers Hero approach. I loved the challenge. Too often people typecast your copywriting style. This gave me the opportunity to prove to those who had been following my advertising that I could write effective copy in a completely different tone while still following many of my distinctive copywriting principles. And that is what I did.

The headline was not the three- or four-word headline typical of the JS&A style but rather a long one—20 words. There was no subheadline either, just a caption at the top of the page that I was counting on my prospects reading after they read the headline.

The copy had longer sentence structure and fancier words than I would normally use even in a JS&A ad. In short, I was communicating in a way that harmonized with the prospective buyer—somebody at a higher income and educational level who would be interested in a limited-edition piece of art from the famed Pablo Picasso.

Profit Not Necessary in First Ad

Since I didn't need to make a profit on the first ad, I could not only state this fact, but also disclose all my costs to add credibility to the statement that we wouldn't be making any profit.

I also didn't need to receive any payment, as I could ask for the money later when those selected were notified. This made it easy for my prospects to respond. We didn't allow toll-free calls—our prospects had to mail in their entry.

I explained why this limited edition was different: "The Picasso les Artistes series, however, is the world's first Random Selection Collectors Series—a series whose quantities will not meet the demand created for them and will thus necessitate a form of objective random selection to choose participants."

We had the promotion take full advantage of *The Wall Street Journal*'s reputation by using their name in the headline and then revealing their advertising costs. We used the statement, "To insure that little or no profit was made on the initial offering, the licensing group accepted the proposal of Battram Galleries to market the collectors tiles through a *Wall Street Journal* advertisement."

I proudly announced the fact that "the chances of acquiring the series from this advertisement are very remote," which created a high level of exclusivity—something very important in the sale of any product but particularly for limited editions. Deny something to somebody and they will demand it even more. That is exactly what I was doing.

Ad Already Had Credibility

I didn't need a famous celebrity to add credibility to the promotion. It already had credibility with Picasso's name and his art. Nevertheless, I hired Franz Schulze, a renowned art critic and Picasso art authority, to select the images and describe them—and I indicated this in the ad copy.

The entire premise of the promotion was really different—something readers of the *Journal* or any magazine would find unusual. No payment was required, there wasn't enough product to sell, no profit was made on the sale and, finally, a random selection process was used to pick the lucky customers.

Once again, the strategy emerged only because I was not interested in selling tiles but rather in building a mailing list. And it wouldn't have worked for anything other than a famous artist whose art had a very high perceived value. Like the Bears Super Bowl promotion (described in the very first marketing story in this book), there was a lot of serendipity involved.

What I haven't told you about yet was all the deliberations I went through to bring this ad to completion.

I Fine-Tune the Ad

After I created the ad in November of 1975, I had our platemaker make the plate and send it to all the editions of the *Journal.* I had to run the ad in the national edition to assure the profitability of the promotion, and that meant I couldn't cut the promotion short if it turned out to be a loss. It was all or nothing.

But something bothered me. I had offered only 750 sets of tiles. The ad was at the *Journal* ready to run when I realized that I needed more sales and a slightly higher price to break even. I decided to change a few of the lines and recalled the ad from all the printing plants at the *Journal.*

As we were approaching the holiday season, I delayed running the ad and made all the corrections I wanted. I tightened up on the graphics by putting a bolder box around the center statements that neatly summarized the offer. I raised the price from $6 to $7 per tile and raised the quantity from 750 sets to 1,250. I wanted to improve it. This was a very important ad and I took great pride in making sure that it not only read well but accomplished exactly what I wanted it to accomplish.

Then I sent the ad to the platemaker again. It was January of 1976. Once again, the platemaker made plates and sent them to *The Wall Street Journal* printing offices and I waited for it to run. But again, there was something in the ad I didn't like and I had it recalled. I added a few minor lines, made sure the *Journal* had returned the plates from the previous ads (Murphy's Law applies especially to the advertising business) and sent the third and final version to the *Journal*.

Incredible Response

The ad ran in February of 1976. We were swamped with over 8,000 responses. Overnight, from one single newspaper, I had created enough of a customer base to build and run this new company for years to come. We had enough customers to buy every available tile and a list of eager buyers waiting for the next release.

The reaction from my friends who read the ad really surprised me. They thought that I indeed was privileged to have been chosen by the Picasso estate to offer the tiles in a well-controlled special promotion. They had no idea that this was a plan created by me, orchestrated and executed by me and only approved by the Picasso estate. I guess if Picasso had been an advertising man instead of an artist, he might have really appreciated what I had accomplished.

When we wrote the winners of the random selection process offering them the les Artistes tiles, 97% of those selected bought the series and sent in their checks. And when we sent letters to the remaining prospects to advise them they were not eligible, we did not offer them another set of tiles. I just gave them the bad news and thanked them. I waited before contacting them again, as otherwise it might have appeared like a deliberate plan—which indeed it was.

Finally, about a month later, I offered the remaining list a new set of full-color Picasso tiles in a very impressive mailing and received a response rate of over 66%. It was one of the most responsive mailings I've ever conducted. A few more mailings followed and each one was quite profitable.

Second Ad—Low Response, Good Example

Around this time, I had hired a marketing manager and he tried to convince me that the tiles were absolutely beautiful by themselves and that all I had to do to sell the tiles was to run print ads describing their beauty.

Even though I knew that you never sell the product, but always the concept, I was getting tired of hearing about the business I was "missing" by not selling just the product and I decided to write a product-oriented ad and test it in the *Journal*. The response was quite poor and I never rolled out with it. I had proven to my marketing manager that despite the beauty of the product and all the other benefits, setting up an environment and positioning the product were essential to selling it successfully.

I used the second ad in my seminar as a good example of the importance of selling the concept and not the product.

Classic Approach Could Work Again

Battram Galleries, after a very successful first year, lost the rights to the Picasso images. It seems that there was a great deal of confusion with the Picasso estate, and they stopped licensing any further reproductions. Jack was proud of what I had done and instead of looking to other art to expand our little business, I simply let it die a natural death. We did exchange some tiles between buyers and sellers and the tiles did increase in value through the years, but it was a business that I decided not to pursue.

I had proven that I could write an entirely different style of ad, create a completely new business from scratch and earn a profit in the process. If it had been my only business, I would have gladly continued and found a way to make it prosper. But JS&A was growing very rapidly and I needed the time to devote to it. It is difficult to hire entrepreneurial talent to run a second start-up business and I didn't have the time to do it myself. Finally, about five years later, I closed the business down for good.

The Battram Galleries ad, however, was a classic approach. It could work in a number of situations, but I haven't seen anybody use it since. When the Pope visited New York City in 1995, I was called by an old acquaintance who was given the rights by the Archdiocese of New York to market the carpet on which the Pope was to walk and drive during his visit. The plan was to cut the carpet into hundreds of thousands of pieces, mount each one on a plaque and sell them as a limited edition. I advised him to use my Battram Galleries approach and sell complete rugs in a limited quantity to cull all the names of serious collectors interested in the Pope's memorabilia. Once again, the name of a very famous individual adding credibility to the product would create the demand and generate the subsequent mailing list required to make this promotion a success.

But the deal fell through. And in the long run, nobody was willing to invest in the carpet and the promotion to make it a success. Too bad. It might have worked, created a nice business and earned a substantial income for the church.

One day as I told the story of Battram Galleries to my seminar group, one of my students was sitting there shaking his head. When I asked him why, he said, "I spent six years building my mailing list to 10,000 names and you built one with one ad to 8,000 names in one day. You created a business with a single ad. Amazing."

In the next marketing lesson, I discuss some of the factors that cause a poor response. Some of them can be easily avoided and others can't even be anticipated. Simply knowing what these factors are and being aware of them, however, will help you as a direct marketer to avoid many of the mistakes that I have made. A lot of the following information can't be found anywhere else.

Marketing Lesson 14

Poor Response Factors

We may create a great ad for a great product with a great price but we may run it at the wrong time and have a total flop. Ironically, had we waited a few months or sometimes just a few days, the ad could have done much better.

After running mail order advertisements with such intensity for so long a period of time and being sensitive to the response figures, I became keenly aware of the factors which cause response rates to drop. Some of those factors involve the time of year, economic cycles, fallout from a major event and the effect of presidential actions. Let's start with the yearly factors.

The Worst Months

I have found that direct response rates are the lowest in the months of April, September and December—in that order, with April having the lowest rate.

Al Eicoff, in his excellent book on TV marketing, mentioned very similar times of the year. But he didn't quite understand why those months experienced such a drop. I don't profess to know for sure either, but I do have a theory.

Look at those months carefully. What big activity usually takes place during those months? If you guessed income tax time in April, back to school in September and the holidays in December, those are very valid reasons. And they may be factors. But what activity takes place very heavily in each of those months that really ties all the months together?

Tying Them Together

They are all very big retail months—months when people go to their retail stores to buy. In April, retailers sell items for Easter, summer, vacation, the garden. The weather is turning warm and people are getting out of their homes and visiting the stores to buy the items they need for the next several months. They're not sitting home searching through catalogs or glued to their TV sets.

They're out taking a nice drive to their local shopping center and buying for summer.

In September, the activities of going back to school, coming back from vacation and preparing for work, and buying winter clothing all involve going to the store. You generally don't buy your school supplies from a mail order catalog. Stores are running specials, selling school supplies so cheaply that not only are you compelled to buy school supplies there but you end up being sucked into the store to buy something else too.

The more money spent at retail, the less money available for mail order and direct mail offers. The more time spent at the store, the less time spent watching TV or reading catalogs. This away-from-home activity greatly affects mail order response rates.

December is the biggest retail shopping period of the year, but mail order marketers who deliver quickly still see reasonable sales in December.

I realize that some direct marketers might have higher response rates in the three months listed above or see no difference from other times of the year, but they are not in the majority and they may be dealing in goods and services that parallel the needs of consumers during those months. I've heard about these response rate drops from enough other direct marketers to realize that my experiences during these three months are not unique.

The Economic Factors

Some other factors which I feel greatly affect response rates are on an economic level. Just before a recession, consumer confidence wanes and consumers become less likely to make impulse purchases. This sudden drop is really felt in mail order, where many of the purchases are made on impulse. It is an economic early-warning indicator, but for some strange reason, retail sales do not suffer until later when a recession is very obvious. Another early-warning indicator is the car rental business. It is the first element in the travel industry that feels the effects of an oncoming recession. In fact, the Dow Jones Transportation Average is among the first of the measured indices that start to tank at the beginning of a recession.

Then comes the recession. Direct response still suffers and now retail sales take a plunge. And for good reason. People are retrenching. They are worried about their future, their finances, their job and their ability to weather the storm. But then an amazing thing happens.

Suddenly, right in the middle of a severe recession, catalog sales rebound. Direct marketers are noticing that their response rates are surprisingly better than expected. Is it that new copywriter or that new catalog layout? Or maybe it's a harbinger of a pending boom. I say it's none of these. The real reason that mail order sales start to boom in the middle of a recession while retail sales continue in a slump is really quite simple.

People Are Staying at Home

During a recession people know it is not a good idea to go shopping unless they have to. They make their shopping list and go to the store and get what they set out to get. Their trips are shorter because they've cut back on the dollars they are willing to spend. People are now at home. They receive a catalog. They have more time at home now that they aren't shopping, so they read the catalog. They "traffic" the catalog just as they would shop in a store, and eventually they buy from the catalog.

In short, during a recession when the consumer isn't going to the store, the catalogers bring the store to the consumer.

Fallout from Major Events

There are other times when sales can take an unexpected plunge for no apparent reason and everybody starts scratching their heads wondering why. Or, if they're not scratching their heads, they're coming up with some of the most creative guesses you can imagine.

If you were alive when President John F. Kennedy was assassinated, you might still remember that day. I was in the Army in Frankfurt, Germany, and can remember every moment surrounding that event for the next several days. It was during that time that direct response took its biggest nosedive. Nothing worked and it doesn't take much of a marketing genius to guess why. The public was so grieved, shocked and scared that all they could think of was survival. Some of the worst direct response horror stories took place during that week.

But there are other, more subtle events that take place in our society that also directly involve the president of the United States and the response rates from our advertising. It is my theory that:

Poor Response Theory: The president of the United States has a tremendous impact on the emotional state of our subconscious minds and as such directly affects the world marketplace as no other single individual or factor.

I have come to this conclusion over a long period of time and through many observations in marketing and history. Let me cite some examples.

The *Mayaguez* Incident

It was May 1975. Gerald Ford had taken over the presidency from Richard Nixon the year before and a U.S. merchant ship, the *Mayaguez*, was attacked and captured by Cambodian communist forces in the Gulf of Siam.

At the time, President Ford, as a true leader in a time of crisis, took immediate action and sent U.S. Marines to rescue the *Mayaguez* from the Cambodians. The American maneuver was successful and Ford's leadership was widely admired. America was proud of him. Imagine Ford as your father. Wouldn't you be proud of him too?

JS&A was right in the middle of a major advertising campaign when the action took place and we experienced a 30% increase in sales over our projections. There was no explanation. Sales just shot up. All of our previous testing and all of our experience running various campaigns told me that it was definitely caused by that American victory. But I just filed the thought in the back of my mind and continued to enjoy the afterglow of this unexpected bonus. Now skip to 1976.

Jimmy Carter's Nomination

Jimmy Carter was at the Democratic Convention in New York about to be nominated. His was truly an American Horatio Alger success story. The former governor of Georgia started as an unknown candidate nationally, but by the time he reached the convention, his reputation and his momentum were enormous.

At the time, it was his religious background (he was a former Sunday school teacher) and his honesty that captured the hope of the American public. We had just come from the Nixon era with the Watergate incident and a complete breakdown of honesty and ethics in the highest echelons of the United States government. Even Ford's pardoning of Nixon strained government credibility.

In Carter, Americans finally had somebody who represented all the values that we wanted America to represent: honesty, integrity, good moral judgment and the guts and verve to engage the political process and make it to the top. The spirit at the Democratic Convention was so contagious that watching it for a few days on television gave us a tremendous lift. The Democrats had nominated a new, honest leader—just what America hungered for after the Nixon years.

And it was during that nominating process that our sales, for no valid reason, jumped over 40%. America once again saw leadership. Americans saw in Jimmy Carter the father image we all so desperately needed in America. But it was short-lived.

The Lance Resignation

Bert Lance, the president's advisor, was accused of wrongdoing within one year of Carter's taking office. Lance denied any wrongdoing and Carter backed his advisor. Later, as the truth emerged, it became known that indeed Lance did not have the highest integrity and he resigned, but the entire affair cast serious doubt on Carter's leadership and the very ethics which had gotten Carter elected president.

Sales plummeted 40% during that time. We had a steady flow of advertising but our results were not jibing with our projections. Once again, an event so closely linked with the leadership of the president seemed to have caused a change in response. Was it coincidence? Was there indeed a relationship?

Jimmy Carter's Credit Card Speech

In the spring of 1980, President Carter went before national television to make a very important announcement. It was April, consumers were in a pretty good mood and both mail order and retail sales seemed to be holding steady. His announcement that spring did more, in my judgment, to hurt the American people and the country than any other single event that led up to the recession of the early '80s.

In his speech, he announced that the American consumer was spending too much—that we were going into such high debt that there would surely be a problem and that we should tear up or put away our plastic credit cards until we got some balance in our personal finances.

And boy, did Americans put away their credit cards. They put away their money, they stopped buying and they brought us into a recession. Our sales dropped 80%. You read it right. If we had expected to sell 20,000 of something, we ended up selling only 4,000. Never before had we experienced such a collapse in response in our history. And I wasn't the only one.

Later I found out from other direct marketers that entire mail order companies went under. Response rates on some items dropped as much as ours. An action by the president of the United States caused a major change in Americans' thinking and the nation took several years to recover. Our sales for many years never recovered fully to the pre-Carter-speech era. And the irony was that it wasn't the consumer who was overspending; it was our own government. In my opinion, it was the instructions from Jimmy Carter and the lack of confidence in Carter's leadership that combined to cause consumers to retrench and eventually, as a direct consequence, cause the recession and the spiraling inflation rate of the early '80s.

The President as Our Parent

As citizens of the United States, we often subconsciously view our president as a parent. And many comparisons can be made between our parents and the president. For example, while I was growing up, I may have had some disagreements with my parents, but whenever we as a family were threatened by outside circumstances, it seemed we got closer. And so it is with the president.

In time of war or major crisis, our political differences with the president seem to vanish and we generally tend to support his efforts. And the stronger the leader he is, the more we rally to his support.

When children do not find parental leadership in their family during a crisis in their lives, they tend to look elsewhere for that leadership. They join cults or gangs where there is strong leadership.

While Carter was president, he was viewed as weak—somebody having difficulty being decisive. During this time, dozens of new cults were created and Americans were flocking in great numbers to those stronger leaders, gurus and even criminals. The 1978 Jonestown Massacre in Guyana, the gurus and communes from India—there was a tremendous increase in cult activity taking place during his weak presidency.

When Reagan took over as president, the cults seemed to disappear. It seemed that we had a strong leader and there was no need to find somebody else. Not all of Reagan's policies were agreeable to the public, but his approval ratings many times during his tenure were among the highest of any president in recent history. But right or wrong, he was a strong leader. He made a decision and stuck to it.

Remember, Hitler was a very strong leader. And history has shown us that a strong leader can totally infect the mind and spirit of his followers to such a degree that they, en masse, can even perform crimes against humanity. So it is with any American president. He can so influence the mind and subconscious of the electorate as a symbol of authority that our entire psyche responds. And this response is felt very solidly on the economic level of this nation and in particular in the marketplace.

The Stock Market Crash

On October 19, 1987, America experienced one of the largest one-day drops in stock exchange history. The New York Stock Exchange Dow Jones Industrial Average dropped over 500 points in a stunning decline that sent shock waves through Wall Street and the world. The next day stock prices throughout the world collapsed. The exchange in Hong Kong was closed. The entire world reacted and it suddenly became very clear that our economy was now a world economy with massive worldwide implications.

And of course, everybody had opinions as to why the market crashed. There were those who cited technical characteristics of stocks, some talked about the federal budget deficit and how action had to be taken to stop its rapid growth and still others talked about program trading and how it affected the volatility of stocks.

I was watching one of the stock market shows on television, and sure enough, everybody interviewed gave one or a combination of the above explanations except for one of the panelists. He was Milton Friedman, a Nobel Prize-winning economist and free market supporter and one of my personal heroes.

Lack of Confidence in President

After the other panelists finished with their comments and it was Dr. Friedman's turn, he simply said that the real reason for the stock market collapse was the lack of confidence in the leadership of the president of the United States. In my judgment, he hit it right on the head.

Reagan had shown a lack of leadership during the Iran/Contra affair. There was some doubt as to his honesty. And with just a little over a year left of his presidency and with the drop in public confidence in his leadership, the bottom simply fell out.

If you recall, I said earlier that the president of the United States affects the entire world. If you agree with my theory, the stock market collapse of '87 is the perfect example of how he indeed affects the world.

If you are lucky and happen to catch an economic boom due to a positive action by the president, congratulations. But he can also surprise you too.

As marketers, we can plan which month to mail a promotional piece or run a TV commercial or publish one of our print ads, but there are factors affecting our response rates—and indeed the entire world—that we are helpless to anticipate or control.

It is therefore important that whenever we test, we always test cautiously. And whenever a test is successful and we decide to increase our expenditure for advertising, we should always expand conservatively with the thought in mind that we don't want to spend more than we can afford to lose. Remember, a total collapse of our marketing effort is always possible due to an unexpected event that is beyond our control. There are no sure things in marketing, as in life.

Now it's time for a very successful product that taught me many lessons. In the next marketing story, I show you how offering a product in the middle of a fad can accelerate success beyond your wildest expectations. But the big success can also be elusive, as you will soon discover.

A Marketing Story

The Pocket CB

It tied into a fad and sales exploded.

This is the story of one of my biggest successes, a story that will give you great insights into many of my principles including the importance of timing.

The story starts out in Chicago in June of 1975. I was at the Consumer Electronics Show reviewing many new products being unveiled for the first time.

Our company was doing quite well. We were starting to emerge as a major factor in the electronics industry by virtue of our introduction of many innovations. Companies were starting to come to us asking us to introduce their products before they were sold to the public through retail stores. Some products were sold to me on an exclusive basis.

Idea for a New Product

The Consumer Electronics Show (CES) was a very busy time for me. It seemed everybody wanted to meet with me and there was only so much time I could spend with my current and prospective suppliers. After booking appointments in advance for almost the entire show, I received a call from Michael Weschler, who was referred to me by a friend. "Joe, I have a product that I want to show you at the CES and I was wondering if you could make some time."

"What is the product?" was my first question. Even though I was busy, it made sense for me always to be open to something that might be an interesting and innovative product idea.

"It's a small walkie-talkie that uses an integrated circuit in its electronics, making it one of the smallest communication devices on the market," said Mike. "It's a great new idea."

I checked my schedule. It was booked solid. "I can't see you formally at the show but I can meet you for a few minutes in the lobby. How about 10:50 AM before my 11 o'clock meeting?" Mike agreed and I penciled in the time.

Citizens Band Boom

Radio communication was a hot topic at the 1975 CES. The citizens band boom was in full swing and it was already becoming a major fad. We were still recovering from the 1973 oil crisis and in 1974 President Nixon had placed a nationwide speed limit of 55 miles per hour to ease the consumption of gasoline.

But the nation's truckers were upset. Their livelihood depended on their ability to move freight quickly. Our highways were built to accommodate a speed much higher than 55 miles per hour. So to ease their frustration and as a defensive move, the truckers bought citizens band (CB) radios, installed them in their trucks and then communicated with each other to warn of state and local police who were more than willing to enforce the reduced speed limit. In fact, the police were obligated to enforce these laws. If they didn't, the government would restrict highway funding.

Truckers Formed Convoys

The truckers also formed convoys—groups of trucks traveling together—all communicating and on the lookout for the "Smokeys," the term they gave the police.

A whole new culture and language developed when the new radio buffs incorporated the standard list of police radio abbreviations like, "That's a ten-four, buddy," meaning that the talker "copied" the information transmitted.

Truckers were also using "handles" or fictitious names instead of their own. Happy Jack, Tall Dark and Lonesome, Long Tall Sally—the variety of names really stretched the imagination. It was fun just to monitor the conversations, which usually took place on the truckers' channel 19. When two people made contact on channel 19, to alleviate congestion and make it easier to hear each other, they would switch to another channel to communicate. The emergency channel, monitored by the police, was channel 9.

The use of citizens band radios became widespread and very popular. The fad continued to grow. Books on the subject, T-shirts, songs—the variety of products that typically surround any fad—soon appeared. And everything was selling briskly. In fact, one of the newest and biggest crimes in America was the stealing of CB radios from cars. A good CB radio was easy to pawn off and got top value because stores were constantly sold out of the devices.

Dramatic Increase in Radio Interest

There was also a dramatic increase in amateur radio licenses issued to radio hobbyists (called hams) who had access to many channels and frequencies and took their hobby seriously. Each was assigned a call letter, just like a radio station, and was responsible for his or her own mobile or permanent station. It was a logical next step up for those who had played with CB and really enjoyed the thrill of radio communication.

Hams needed a license to operate on the broad range of frequencies available to them. And as a ham, you had to pass a number of tests to gain access to more frequencies—each level challenging you to acquire more knowledge and achieve a faster Morse code speed. At the time, "general class" was the goal that most hams aspired to reach. To be a general-class ham, you had to learn the Morse code at 13 words per minute and pass a written test with many technical questions about electronics, frequencies and radio protocol.

I was a general-class ham radio operator and still am today. My call sign was K4TDL in 1958 when it was first assigned and then W9IQO four years later when I moved back home to Illinois. With all my radio experience in 1975, I had a sense of what was happening in the communication industry, an emotional grasp of the thrill of communication and a comprehensive understanding of the technology.

Discovered Product Fits Fad

The walkie-talkie that Mike described seemed to fit into the communication fad of the time. And consumer products using integrated circuits were the main marketing thrust of my company. Any product that used an integrated circuit, was a new or miniaturized version of an old product, appealed to a broad market and was priced right would make a very good product. But what I discovered during our meeting made the miniature walkie-talkie more than just that. I discovered a product that would tie nicely into a fad.

I met Mike in the lobby of the McCormick Place Exposition Center in Chicago at the time we agreed to meet. We introduced ourselves. Mike was from Canada and with him was a scientist-type assistant who was there to answer any technical questions.

Mike was a typical salesman—a gregarious sort of guy who didn't know too much about the technical features of the product but sure knew how to sell. "Amazing product, isn't it, Joe?"

I didn't respond, feeling defensive against the typical sales chatter. I looked over the small product and held it in my hand. It was light, looked very attractive and had a frequency switch on the front. You could choose between one of two frequencies. It had one large push-to-talk button and was a very simple device.

I began to ask questions. I asked about the integrated circuit; I asked about the batteries required; I asked about the range of the unit and then I asked about the exact frequency.

"The unit operates on 27 megahertz, which is the permanent frequency and the same one that all walkie-talkies operate on, and the second frequency is open for the consumer to select. There are crystals for as many as ten more frequencies."

"Hmm," I said. And then from my ham radio background, I remembered that 27 megahertz sounded awfully familiar. "Isn't 27 megahertz the same frequency as the CB frequencies?"

"Yes, it's channel 12 on the CB band," was the scientist's answer.

A lightbulb lit in my head. We were right in the middle of the CB boom. Stores couldn't get enough CB radios to sell and there was a tremendous shortage as companies throughout the world were gearing up to produce them. Here in my hand I was holding the world's first pocket CB—the perfect device to satisfy the broad market waiting to gobble up everything CB that was out there. Even if you owned a CB radio, the pocket CB could be a great additional device to keep with you when you were away from your car or truck.

I tried to hold back my enthusiasm. "I'm interested in the product. What do I need to do to get an exclusive on this item?" I asked.

"No problem," was Mike's response. "We'll need an order for 20,000 pairs and I can fly to my factory in Hong Kong and arrange the manufacturing."

We worked out the terms of the deal. My cost was going to be around $12 per pair complete with batteries and carrying case. The product would take about two months to produce and I had to allow about four weeks for shipment—or a three-month lead time. But the CB fad was just starting to take off and the timing couldn't have been better. As a matter of fact, the more people who bought into the CB boom and had a unit in their car, the more popular my new product could be.

I named the unit "PocketCom" and registered the name with the U.S. Patent Office. I also registered the name "Mega" as the name of a new company we would set up to import the product and eventually sell it to the retail trade, after we had milked the product through the mail order channels. It was going to be the first product that we actually manufactured ourselves and the first branded product that JS&A would offer.

Ad Tested in Advance

Mike left for Hong Kong. I went back to my office with the prototype and I created the advertising copy. I wanted to make sure that I had a winner, so I decided to test my ad. I ran it in the Southwestern edition of *The Wall Street Journal* clearly stating in the ad to call for product availability.

To run an ad in many magazines would typically take about two months from the time the material was sent to the publications until the time the ad would run and the orders would be taken. In the *Journal*, I could get my ads to run usually within a week and then get my response within a few days. Then, if the ad was successful, I would order the product and run the ad campaign nationally.

Since this was the first product we were actually manufacturing and importing, I needed to allocate more time for the product to arrive, and more importantly, I had to know if I had a winner as I would be making a major commitment for product. In addition, I had to pay for this product in advance as opposed to the way I had been operating, which was to pay one month after delivery. Importing presented a new set of challenges.

I tested the ad in the *Journal,* offering the PocketCom for $39.95, and the response was overwhelming. Despite the fact that we told callers they would have to wait a few months, we received a response that was one of the strongest in our history. And no wonder. The PocketCom appealed to a very broad market, it fit right in with the CB fad, it was inexpensive compared to the $150 CB radios available and it was an altogether new and exciting product.

Typically, if a product produced a response that gave me a profit of four times what my ad costs were, then I had a really good winner and I would typically sell about 20,000 of the gadget I was offering. This response was 26 times the cost of the ad. I had no benchmark for comparing it to any other promotion we ran except to assume that the product would draw at least five times the response I'd normally expect from a product that sold 20,000 units. So 100,000 units was not an unreasonable expectation. This was obviously a major product.

For the picture, we shook hands, culminating the signing of a multi-million-dollar contract.

I Fly to Hong Kong

After my test, realizing I needed to increase the order and firmly secure the exclusive rights to it, I decided to fly to Hong Kong, meet with Mike, see firsthand Mike's office and staff and establish immediately a line of communication with him and the factory.

When I arrived, Mike invited me into his small office. There was nobody else there except for his secretary. "Joe, I hope you won't mind, but I've got a photographer coming over here from the local paper to take a picture of both of us signing the documents announcing the purchase by you of several million dollars of this product. I need this to satisfy my bankers and promote a little PR here in Hong Kong."

I didn't mind at all. Anything I could do to help my new partner I would do. Of course, the order wasn't anywhere near several million dollars, but it could eventually be. And besides, I figured that Mike knew what he was doing. Little did I know what he was really doing.

He Had No Financing Available

Mike had absolutely no financing when he presented the product to me in Chicago and no idea where he was going to get any money to make it. He had no factory willing to manufacture it and he wasn't prepared to produce the first order. He had no experience in making the product and the prototype he showed me didn't work.

But I was very innocent at the time. I believed Mike, and when Mike's bank saw all the publicity in the Hong Kong paper, they agreed to finance the project. Mike also took me to a factory where a willing factory owner convinced me that he would have product to me within a few months.

Mike and I agreed to an exclusive contract if I sold at least 100,000 units a year. And indeed, I didn't see this as a problem.

We Gear Up

I returned to the States ready to gear up my entire company to handle the product and the projected response. I revised the ad slightly and decided to place it in magazines throughout the country. Remember, it took two months before the ads would break and I was expecting the product to arrive at about that time.

We prepared the boxes and the materials and placed ads in hundreds of the magazines in which we normally advertised and several others that were new to us. We were in *Time*, *Newsweek*, all the airline in-flight magazines, all the science and technology magazines—in short, we completely saturated the entire U.S. market with our advertising. You couldn't pick up a magazine in the fall of 1975 without seeing our advertising.

Heaviest Response in Our History

And the response was heavy—among the heaviest in our history. Close to 250,000 units were sold between September of 1975 and the spring of 1976. We had the orders and kept getting assurances from Hong Kong that the product was in production and would arrive shortly. But it didn't.

Once Mike had convinced the bank and had gotten the financing, he then had to arrange for the production of the product with all its inherent delays. One of the delays was for the integrated circuit, which they had claimed was already developed but which in reality was still on the drawing board when I first arrived in Hong Kong.

During this horrible backorder situation, I contacted our customers every three weeks by mail. I gave them an update on the progress of the product and urged them that if they wanted to cancel, they could and I would promptly refund their money or simply cancel their credit card order. Very few canceled, although my letters specifically encouraged people to cancel until we had the product in stock. With each mailing I would get more cancellations, but in comparison to the total number of orders, they were relatively few. I also noticed that I received no complaints about the delay. Simply keeping my customers informed precluded any complaints.

Finally, after four months, the product was delivered and we were able to ship. We supplied the second-frequency crystals as an accessory so customers could have the truckers' channel 19 as an optional channel and the built-in channel 12 as their standard one.

Received Celebrity Calls

I received calls from some of the top entertainers in the country who wanted the product during the early days when it was in short supply. I got a call from Marlon Brando, who was visiting his sister in Libertyville, Illinois, just a few miles from our offices. He wanted a pair to communicate on his island in Fiji and talked knowledgeably to me about the technology. I invited him to the offices to meet our staff and even told him that I'd give him a few sets free of charge, but he declined. I got orders from Frank Sinatra and dozens of other well-known personalities.

Many orders came in for two pairs, making the average order around $80, and we had very few returns. Our buying price was no longer $12 for the product. Mike increased our cost once he got into production, claiming the costs he was encountering were higher than he anticipated. I was now paying $15 a unit, but this still allowed me to make a good profit due to the order volume.

MARKETING S ,E C R E T S

Fad Begins to Fade

Then in late 1976, the CB fad started to wane. First, in response to overcrowding on the existing channels, the Federal Communications Commission (FCC) increased the channels available for CB usage from 24 to 40. That made every CB unit obsolete. People stopped buying them, waiting for the new expanded models to arrive. Then, as with any fad, interest started to wane. Dealers were overstocked with the old 24-channel models, and when the new 40-channel units arrived, they were overpriced. Dealers started to drop prices in an effort to liquidate their inventories, and pretty soon, as the fad died, it was rough selling CB units at any price.

The PocketCom sold well during this time although I could see sales starting to drop. So, before our Pocket CB became a statistic too, I dropped the price in February of 1977 from $39.95 to $29.95. And then, to liquidate the product completely, I sold the last remaining inventory for only $19.95 in September of 1977—exactly two years after I nationally introduced the item.

Ironically, dropping the price changed the public's perception of the product. At $39.95, the PocketCom was a serious radio instrument to be used along with a car CB. At $29.95 it became something for the hobbyist—another walkie-talkie. At $19.95 it became a toy. And all these perceptions came from the same ad. Only the price had changed.

The fad was indeed dead, my opportunity to sell the PocketCom through retail was dead and my first attempt to create a major brand name had died with the fad.

Lessons Learned

The lessons learned from this experience were many. I learned that when dealing with a new company, caution is the key word. I should have made absolutely sure that the PocketComs were in production before I rolled out my ad campaign. I learned very clearly the power of a fad in the successful marketing of a product and how quickly a fad can die. I also realized the role government played in killing the fad. In an effort to accommodate hobbyists by expanding channel capacity, the FCC was the catalyst for a major obsolescence problem and unintentionally may have accelerated the demise of the fad.

I saw how cancellations increased each time we sent out a delay notice. And even though it did result in cancellations, I felt an obligation not only to inform my customers of the delays on a regular basis but to be truthful and explain the reason behind those delays. It was costly in postage, printing costs and lost orders, but to this day, many of my customers remember our concern and the communications we provided during this long, drawn-out period of time.

I also established a new benchmark in response and saw how much could be generated in sales during a fad when an ad is rolled out nationally. And I discovered other responsive magazines I could use in future advertising campaigns.

I saw how well my ham radio experience helped me discover the one salient feature about this product that allowed it to take advantage of the CB fad—its 27 megahertz frequency that matched the CB channel 12.

It was the first time I had imported a product with my own brand name and there were many new responsibilities associated with this activity. I had to consider such things as customs, product quality, lead time, packaging, instructions, warranties and service.

And finally, it was interesting to see how the perceived nature of the product changed each time I lowered the price. So I learned this important lesson: Pricing often will establish, in the mind of the consumer, the kind of product he or she is buying even though the product and the ad are the same.

Not only was the PocketCom a profitable and successful product, it also laid the foundation for my eventual experience with marketing a product through stores using mass distribution. More on this in a later marketing story.

But now it is time for another marketing lesson. And this one is on the painful subject of complaints. The complaints you're about to read are not your typical unhappy-customer complaints, but rather reactions to some of the advertising concepts I ran in magazines and my own catalog. Some were valid and some were not. You be the judge.

Marketing Lesson 15

Ad Complaints

Complaints can give you really good insights into what is on the minds of your customers and how they view your company and your products as well as your advertising message. And any good marketer takes complaints seriously.

If one person takes the time to write you and complain, there are dozens more who feel the same way but don't want to take the time to write.

On the other hand, you've got to be discerning. One complaint does not constitute a reason for a major change in policy or the dropping of a product. You can't please all of the people all of the time and you've got to expect to receive complaints. It's part of the mail order process.

In any case, it's important that you acknowledge the complaint, answer it as quickly as possible and notify your customer of the action that you've taken to correct the situation. Often that's all it takes, and the good customer service and goodwill you generate will lead to a much better customer in the future.

I do not want to discuss here the complaints about products or service. That's all a part of running a business. What I'd like to discuss are the complaints I've received about ads I've run in either my catalog or the many publications in which we regularly advertised. From these complaints you'll see some interesting dynamics that have never failed to amaze me.

I've always been very bold and daring in my advertising copy. If I have an idea that I think will sell a product but might offend a few people, I still take a stab at it. That's what often makes my copy interesting. I push the envelope on ways to market products; I try new ways of selling; I experiment with new advertising approaches. In my experience, it is through this freedom to express myself that I discover breakthrough concepts. And it is the breakthrough concepts that have the potential to really explode into successful promotions.

Was I that insensitive to women's issues? I had to seriously think about it.

But when the complaints come in about my advertising, it is time for me to look at them and decide if the complaint is fair or if somebody is only venting frustration after having a bad day at the office.

Gold Space Chains

In 1978 I ran an ad in my catalog selling gold chains. It was in the form of a story about a salesman named Bob Ross who tried to convince me to sell gold chains in my catalog. I resisted until he showed me a picture of his cousin who offered to model the chains in the ad. I quickly changed my mind after seeing her picture—that of a well-endowed young lady. The ad copy was considered by many to be a creative approach to selling a product that had nothing to do with the core products we had been selling—electronic gadgets. However, I did get a few letters as a result. One of them, from a woman in Egg Harbor City, New Jersey, said:

> Dear Sir: Your friend, Mr. Bob Ross, may regard himself as a successful salesman, but unfortunately he comes across in your ad as a consummate asshole. And quite possibly the ad you apparently ran at his urging could cost you a great many sales of your other products to intelligent and educated women.

The letter then went on to point out the achievements of women in many technical fields, the military, air traffic control, sports and leisure, racing and several other professions in which women now play a very active role. Then she described her own family and told how her daughter uses calculators and some of the products we sold. She described how she herself and many women own credit cards and how insulted she was by my ad copy. She finally concluded:

> Perhaps a long, hard look at the person or department responsible for the ad on page 37 is in order. Apparently he has to "come a long way, baby" to catch up to the Twentieth Century. Cordially wishing you immediate bankruptcy, I remain,

And with that she signed her name. It was a two-page single-spaced letter which included a copy of our mailing label.

Was I really insensitive to women? Did I demean them in my ad copy? It caused me to take a second look at the ad copy, count the number of complaints and note where I could make just a few changes to correct the complaint—that is, if I didn't go into immediate bankruptcy. Some people can really be mean.

The Juki Typewriter

Then there was the time I was introduced to a new typewriter with the name of Juki. It was a good typewriter. It was one of the most advanced on the market and even had a computer interface. But the name Juki really bothered me. How could I possibly sell a typewriter in my catalog with the name Juki?

Like many of my previous ads, I took the most obvious fault and covered it right at the beginning of the ad. The copy read as follows:

The copy hit too close to home for one of my customers.

Headline: Juki Ooki

Subheadline: From the same company that stitched your jeans and put buttonholes in your relatives.

Copy: When the salesman called and told me that he had a revolutionary typewriter to show me, I asked for its name.

"Juki," replied Bob.

"Juki?" I asked.

"Yes, Juki," answered Bob.

"Are you kidding me, Bob? Is it really called Juki?"

"Really, Joe. That's what it's called, Juki."

Now, I realize that a product can be a good product regardless of the name. But who would want to name a typewriter Juki?

So when Bob called, I asked him to bring background information on Juki along with a sample typewriter.

It seems that Juki is a Japanese company that started in business in 1938 making automatic machine guns. The company prospered. During World War II, if you or any of your relatives were shot with a machine gun, it was probably a high-quality Juki.

"How pleasant, Bob," I sighed. "I'm sure my readers would be delighted to hear all this."

"But wait, Joe," Bob responded. "That was the war. Juki went on to prosper after the war by making commercial sewing machines

273

which dominated the world market. In fact, if you own a pair of Levi's jeans, chances are they were sewn on a high-quality Juki."

The ad went on to explain about all the awards that Juki has received for their quality and the fact that they decided to go after the typewriter business by building one of the best typewriters on the market. I then explained the outstanding features and in a tongue-in-check approach offered a free pen so that the people who bought the typewriter could write over the old label and change the name.

It didn't take too long before I got a letter from a gentleman in the Office of Consumer Advocacy in Harrisburg, Pennsylvania, telling me:

> My best friend was killed with a machine gun but my arm was blown off with a mortar shell. Did they make mortars, too? I hope your sense of humor makes you a lot of money! Would you have my name removed from receiving any more of your material.

The tongue-in-cheek humor obviously was taken very seriously and I changed the ad the next time I ran it. The product did marginally well but was not a big seller for us. The one complaint above turned out to be the only one I received about that ad before I changed it.

The customer didn't appreciate being called an ass.

The Mouse Buster

I then wrote a very flip ad for my catalog about a computer keyboard. I got into a silly mood one day and wrote what I thought was outrageously good copy that really sold the product I was offering. The following was the start of the ad:

Headline: Mouse Buster

Subheadline: The mouse is not as smart as you thought. Here's a very intelligent replacement for an idea whose time has passed.

Copy: Wico is not stupid. They know a good thing when they see it. So when video games were the rage, Wico saw an opportunity to make and market quality replacement joy sticks and track ball attachments. They prospered.

When the roof fell in on video games, Wico realized that there was another market waiting to be tapped with a quality accessory—the home computer market. So they developed something that was missing from the home computer—namely a really intelligent keyboard called the SmartBoard.

Now before you mutter to yourself, "What a stupid thing to replace" and turn the page to some other great JS&A product, let me get your attention for just a few more paragraphs.

I then went on to describe what a clever keyboard they had developed with all its features and advantages. Then around two-thirds into the copy I wrote the following:

If you're concerned that the Wico SmartBoard is too much too late—stop being an ass. First, it is so easy to operate that anybody who owns a computer will marvel at how much easier it is to learn programs and use hardware than those plain keyboards that just lie there and make you do all the work.

And the ad continued in my typical style. Somebody, however, objected to my use of the phrase "stop being an ass" and wrote the following letter:

To Every Employee of JS&A:

Joseph Sugarman must be a real obnoxious arrogant jerk. He thinks that he can enter the sanctity of our homes and insultingly call us asses. I invite you to read the advertisement titled "Mouse Buster" and would like others to express their feelings of insult and outrage as I am sure you will feel. I have chosen not to initiate legal action against the Jerk or his company at this time, but I want no more of his rude and abusive garbage sent to my family. Immediately remove my name from JS&A's mailing list now.

The letter was signed by a gentleman from Thousand Oaks, California, and came with a copy of the ad. It was the only complaint about the ad and although I respected his opinion, I had the strong feeling that he didn't have much of a sense of humor. Some of the letters you get from customers are real gems.

The Nuclear Mail Box

Another ad that drew some response was the one for the Nuclear Mail Box. Again, this was a tongue-in-cheek approach to selling a product during the cold war when there was still a nuclear threat and children were beating up mail boxes with baseball bats. The original copy read as follows:

Headline: Nuclear Mail Box

Subheadline: We'll guarantee that this mail box will survive a nuclear explosion or we'll refund double its cost.

Copy: If you own a rural mail box and your home was nuked, it is highly unlikely that your mail box would survive. Who'd care anyway, right?

But, let us say you owned a typical rural mail box and your home wasn't nuked. Chances are that your mail box would rust within a year, corrode something horrible within two and have to be replaced within three. That's a three-year life if the neighborhood kids didn't smash it with their bats, explode firecrackers inside or blast it with a 22mm rifle.

The ad from our catalog was shown on national television.

The ad went on to describe the features of the product and how it could benefit the consumer. You could pretty well guess how the ad copy flowed.

The ad copy was so unusual that it came to the attention of *The Tonight Show* and Johnny Carson featured it on national television. So far so good. But then I got a letter from a disgruntled consumer who read the publicity we got in the *Chicago Sun-Times* newspaper. His letter read:

> I was offended by an article that I read in the Suburban *Sun-Times* (Nov. 30) regarding the sale of nuclear mailboxes. Are you people joking (and I quote) "Double your money-back guarantee in the event of a nuclear explosion." I don't know about anyone else, but mail delivery is the last thing I'd worry about during or after a nuclear war. I can't believe your company and the inventor is making nuclear war into a lucrative business. The sale of such an item is in poor taste.

We also got a letter from the advertising manager of a publishing company in Ridgefield, Connecticut, pointing out that a 22mm rifle was bigger than many of the cannons in fighter planes and that I had mistakenly used millimeters instead of the correct term, 'caliber'. It should therefore have read, ".22 caliber rifle." We corrected the ad in our next issue.

Complaints as Guideposts

Complaints have always been somewhat of a guidepost for me in determining whether I was pushing the envelope a little too far. In the case of the Juki, I might have been. In the case of calling my readers asses, well, you be the judge. In the case of the Nuclear Mail Box, I was simply exercising my creativity to conceptualize a very novel approach. It was simply a way of emphasizing the strength of the mail box, and practically everybody else realized it was a tongue-in-cheek approach. It also showed that with publicity, you run the risk of not having your complete ad copy run, as was the case in the *Chicago Sun-Times*. Apparently a subscriber, not having read the entire ad, responded to the publicity he read in the paper. (I discussed publicity in Marketing Lesson 10.)

And of course in the mail order business you get some pretty sick letters as well. The letter examples I've used here were actual letters signed by the individual authors. The really sick letters usually come unsigned with the most obscene and hateful commentary you can imagine.

I had always wanted to catch a person who sent this unsigned hate mail. Often we would get this type of mail after we had sent out our postage-free envelopes along with a mailing. So one day I decided to send out a mailing where each customer was assigned a unique code printed on his or her return envelope. It worked. We found a few of these people and immediately removed them from our mailing list. And I personally called a few of them and asked them their motivation for sending the letter. They were usually so shocked that they hung up on me.

Complaints about advertising are rarely talked about in marketing books, but they are an interesting and challenging part of direct marketing and give you valuable insights into the way your customers think. It's a really novel way for any student of marketing to look at what goes on inside a mail order company.

In 1982, after having published several catalogs during the previous five years, I started reproducing some of the letters I received in a column called "Letters." It was similar to a "Letters to the Editor" column you'd find in many magazines. I printed both positive and negative letters on this very controversial page.

This single page was soon copied. "Letters" columns

started to appear in other catalogs and a new trend of open candor with the consumer began. The letters we got gave us a pretty good idea of how our customers were responding to our catalogs and the items that we offered in it. One customer would love a product and praise it and then be followed by somebody who hated it. One customer would complain bitterly about the beautiful models we used in our catalog and another customer complimented us. One customer complained about our use of grammar but misspelled two words in his letter. Our "Letters" column provided entertainment, but at the same time, it reassured my customers that they were dealing with an open and honest company who took great care of their customers. We did just that and I'm proud of the job that we did do as reflected in those letters.

To give you the flavor of many of the comments, I've reproduced several of the letters from pages in our catalog in Appendix A. You'll have as much fun reading them as many of my good customers have had throughout the years.

I've talked about successful companies I started from scratch and even from a single ad, demonstrating the potentially great power of your pen. The following story is about a company I started from scratch that was not successful. The company might have been successful had it not been for the development of a new product that was to become a major consumer electronic product from Sony called the "Soundabout." But you might know it by another name.

A Marketing Story

The Bone Fone

We thought we had a major breakthrough. We did. But only for a few weeks.

This is the story of a marketing project that had great promise but went sour due to bad timing, bad people and bad judgment.

I received a call from somebody (let's call him Eric although that wasn't his real name) who lived in Northbrook. Eric was a tall blond Scandinavian in his early 30s who had an invention that he wanted me to manufacture and sell.

The device was a thick scarf that you wore around your neck which contained a radio at one end, volume controls at the other end and speakers near the center. When you put the scarf around your neck with the speakers just below your ears, you heard an incredible sound coming out of the built-in radio. Your bones even vibrated and despite the full sound you were hearing, those around you didn't hear much at all.

When I met with Eric I saw a real potential with the product, but all he had was a prototype. I needed to name it and get it manufactured. I also saw it as one of the first products around for which I could create a brand name using JS&A's advertising exposure and then eventually sell it through retail.

I worked out a royalty agreement with Eric giving him an incentive as well as a position. I named the product "Bone Fone" and in 1978 set up Bone Fone Corporation with offices located at our JS&A facility.

Eric's first responsibility was to go to Hong Kong and find a manufacturer, source the components and get the product into production. My role was to create the ad concept that would best sell the product and, of course, JS&A would fund the project.

I Create the Ad

I had a series of photographs taken of a very attractive model wearing the Bone Fone and wrote the ad copy. Eric managed to get an early shipment of Bone Fones so we could test the product in the Southwestern edition of *The Wall Street Journal*.

I realized that I was taking a risk by manufacturing a product myself that I had never market-tested, but by this time my sense of what would succeed and what wouldn't was quite keen. In fact, I was now having many more winners than losers as I was first testing everything in my catalog and seeing the results before I even tested the product in a mail order format. When I discovered a hot product in my catalog, I ran it as a mail order ad nationally.

The ad ran in the *Journal* and the results were good—strong enough to justify a national rollout at around $250,000. I had thousands invested in making the product and prepared to commit hundreds of thousands more to advertise it. It was very exciting for me. We finally had our own product and we were about to make a national name for it. Then disaster struck.

Little did I realize that Sony was about to pull the rug out from under me.

Sony Corporation announced their Soundabout—a small portable radio with headphones designed for personal listening. They changed the name shortly thereafter to the name you might recognize—the Sony Walkman—and the product took off. Sales were so brisk you had a difficult time finding one even though they were selling for more than $100. The writing was on the wall for Bone Fone.

The Bone Fone was a nice product but it was bulkier than the Sony Walkman and wasn't as personal. But I was stuck with the Bone Fone and tried through our advertising to make a niche for the product.

Major customers like Radio Shack and several other national retailers purchased our product and did very well in the very early stages, selling it at $69.95. But soon the Walkman's price started to drop and we had a price-competitive situation.

We then went on TV, producing an expensive spot and advertising nationally. It was costly and our new ad agency was very aggressive in convincing us that the more retail advertising we would do the faster the product would sell. It didn't and we were caught with the problems of heavy inventory, big advertising bills and a product that wasn't selling.

Sony Destroyed Our Market

Around this time, I was fighting the FTC as I mentioned in an earlier marketing story and not spending the time necessary to really spearhead the venture. I had hired a marketing person to work with Eric, but it wasn't the same as having a hands-on entrepreneur at the formative stages of your company when you need one the most. With the loss of control over costs and expenditures, with Sony slowly destroying our market and with the tremendous expenses of my battle with the government, I was struggling to support the company.

Then one day I discovered that Eric had been taking the checks we were receiving from our customers (which were to go toward paying past-due bills), depositing them in the Bone Fone account and then immediately issuing himself a check. He didn't feel it was embezzlement as he was a principal of Bone Fone Corporation, was authorized to sign checks and was simply paying himself money that he felt he deserved to cover his royalties even though he was drawing a good salary.

That was the last straw. With the money being siphoned out of the company without my knowledge, with the tremendous pressure from the ad agency trying to collect their money and not being willing to wait and with the mounting costs of maintaining the company and the inventory, I finally threw in the towel. Bone Fone Corporation declared Chapter 11 bankruptcy.

We eventually settled with our creditors, but by that time the product was dead and my willingness to continue the company was not there anymore. We managed to liquidate all our Bone Fones through closeout ads from JS&A (which was still solvent) and in an orderly fashion closed Bone Fone Corporation for good.

Bad timing with Sony's introduction of the Walkman and my lack of personal attention to running the company were the primary reasons Bone Fone Corporation did not succeed. I learned that you can't delegate hands-on entrepreneurship.

But with the lessons learned from both the Pocket CB and the Bone Fone and the desire we had to find our very own product and create a brand name, we were getting close to the time when we would indeed hit it right with our very own product.

In our next marketing lesson we cover a very important aspect of any business—running your business. I discuss it from a point of view that is not so much procedural as profit-oriented—how running your business can affect your sales and profits. It's really a lot of common sense but something many people do not realize when they start a company. The next lesson will open your eyes, stimulate your thinking and make you aware of issues you may not have previously thought about but which greatly affect your bottom line.

Marketing Lesson 16

Mail Order Operations

The focus of this book is, of course, marketing. But it would be foolish to dismiss the importance of the operations end of your business and the effect that it has on your marketing.

First, let me explain what I mean by "operations." It is all of the things your company does in the course of filling your customers' orders. Since this is a marketing book, I will not go into too much detail on how to set up the operations end of your business, but I will give you plenty of information on how your operations may affect your sales.

If you are serious about being in business and remaining there, you'll want your customers to be repeat customers. You've spent a lot of time and money to attract them in the first place and a satisfied customer is extremely valuable to the future of your business. It often costs 10 times more to obtain a new customer than to keep an old one happy, so in this last marketing lesson, I am going to cover some of the things you'll want to do to enhance your operations now and in the future.

Ways to Take Orders

Two main types of telephone methods are used by direct marketers—inbound telemarketing (receiving calls and taking orders) and outbound telemarketing (making calls to sell a customer). You can take inbound telemarketing orders in three ways:

1. You Take Them

The first way is to take the orders yourself. That's right, yourself. If you're just starting out and your offer is going to a small enough audience, it's a good idea to experience your customers firsthand. Some of the greatest marketing lessons I've learned were from my customers when I was taking orders on the phone. Even when we were really busy, I would go to the back of our offices where the telephone operators were located and I would personally talk to our customers and take orders like just another telephone order taker.

2. Outside Service Bureau

The second way is to use an outside toll-free answering service. They charge per call or inquiry and provide 24-hour live operators to answer your customers' calls and take their orders. They can even input the order information directly into their computers and then the orders can be automatically transferred to your computer by modem. The advantages of this system are low overhead, 24-hour service and fewer employees to deal with. But because these operators must become familiar with many products, you often do not get a well-trained telephone salesperson who can make a strong pitch to enhance the sale of the product or sell another product to the same customer.

3. Separate Telemarketing Department

The third way is to set up your own separate telemarketing department and train your own operators. The advantages are that well-trained operators can result in an increase in sales that will more than justify the overhead. The disadvantage is the major investment in time and money required to set up this type of department.

Today, many of the very successful marketers have their own inbound and outbound telemarketing operations. In the early days of order taking, telemarketing was only for taking incoming orders. But now many companies are doing both, with outbound telemarketing becoming a major new profit center.

If you are selling in print, either through a catalog or through mail order advertising, you want to use the mail to offer your next product and not the telephone. But if you are selling on TV, you want to use outbound telemarketing to offer your next product. The TV buyer is a lot different from the print buyer, and the sooner you realize this the more effective your after-the-sale marketing campaign can be. This doesn't mean, however, that you shouldn't use outbound telemarketing for your print customers nor mail offers for your TV customers. You can use any method, but the most efficient use of your time, money and customer list is to address the TV and the print customers differently. These suggestions are based on extensive testing done not only by me but by several other marketers who sell both in print and on TV.

Rapid Fulfillment

One of the most important steps you can take to turn good customers into solid customers—so motivated to buy from you that they can't wait to see your next offer—is to provide such fast delivery that they are amazed at how quickly they get their purchases. Remember, the disadvantage of mail order compared to retail is lack of instant gratification, and if you can overcome that disadvantage by providing overnight or within-a-few-days delivery, then you are turning that retail advantage into your own.

The key to mail order is fast service.

The longer the customer has to wait for your package to arrive, the greater the chances are for your product to be returned because the buyer has developed what is called "buyer's remorse" or has lost his or her desire for the product.

Simple Return Policy

If a customer doesn't like your product and wants to return it, consider it a blessing. It is here that you can show how good a company you really are. First, make a return policy that is easy and simple to execute. The forms should be clear and easy to fill out. And if you can provide one extra degree of service such as free pickup at your customer's door, you'll ensure yourself of a customer for life.

The important point here is to look at those customers who are unhappy with their purchase as an opportunity for you to really show what an understanding and good company you are. And then after customers return their product, make sure you credit their account with a refund immediately. Then send them a letter acknowledging the return and telling them that you appreciated the fact that they tried the product. It's this type of response that customers remember. Even if a customer returns something and doesn't follow your instructions exactly, that's OK. You might get taken advantage of a few times, but for those legitimate customers who may have been confused when they returned a product, you'll be appreciated.

If you are dealing with a single product—whether on a TV promotion or a major ad campaign—it is easy to set up instructions on how to treat each customer who returns the product. You can be extremely liberal in the case of products that have a big margin and a little less liberal in the case of products that have much less margin. If you want to encourage good customer loyalty and you are building your company, the key word here is "liberal."

Good Customer Service

A really efficient way to operate is to have your order takers (if you have an in-house order-taking department) also act as customer service representatives. If your customers have a problem, one call, one operator and they've got their answer. If the operator can't handle the problem, it is always good to have somebody in your organization who can tackle the really tough problems. Again, remember that your customers are always right. It's nice to have this as the basis of your customer service policy even though sometimes a few customers may not be totally honest. Unfortunately, with today's credit card scams, market morality and attitude toward business, it is sometimes difficult to know which customer is honest and which one is trying to rip you off. That's why having a bright and intelligent decision maker head your customer service department can make a big difference.

Good Products

I know this may seem rather obvious, but it is still worth mentioning. If you don't sell good products that are well presented and fulfill the expectations of your customers, you are hurting your credibility the next time you make an offer to those customers. Make sure that you present the product properly and that you only sell products you are proud to offer. Your return rate (discussed earlier in Marketing Lesson 12) will tell you how effective you are in your presentation, and the customer comments that accompany the return can also give you a really good clue as to what might be lacking in the product.

Congratulations. You've finished the toughest part of my seminar course. You've got enough information to take that great product you've selected, buy media for your ad and test your product or service to see if it will sell. You've also gotten some valuable insights—concepts that I doubt you'll read anywhere else.

And you've gotten a pretty good idea of what it was actually like to run a mail order company from a good dose of my storytelling relating some of the strategies and lessons I've learned in the mail order business. But now it's time for the best story of all—the BluBlocker story.

A Marketing Story

BluBlocker Sunglasses

The ad that started a major new corporation that eventually sold 20 million pairs of sunglasses.

There comes a time in life when one is shown an opportunity for which one is totally prepared. The discovery of BluBlocker sunglasses was just such a time in my life.

I had spent 15 years writing ads, experiencing failure and success and making a lot of money only to lose it fighting for principle. I was an experienced copywriter and my mail order copy appeared everywhere. I was able to recognize successful products, create unique selling concepts and know which magazines to advertise in to get the greatest return.

Our company was well set up to buy advertising space and we had a good reputation with all the magazine representatives. Our operations ran quite smoothly thanks to the guidance of Mary Stanke, who was now in charge of practically everything except the creative end of our business.

And my experiences in mail order were extensive. I had started several businesses through the power of my pen. I had gone through the Bone Fone experience (which I related in the previous marketing story) and had gotten a good taste of manufacturing my own product and selling it to retailers. We had our own store where I saw firsthand many of the issues of running a retail operation.

I had perfected my skills as a professional photographer by taking many of the pictures for my catalog. I knew typesetting and graphic arts and did all the layouts and paste-ups for my catalogs and all my mail order ads. I selected the products, dealt with the suppliers during the initial stages of a product presentation and often dealt with them during the explosive stages of a product's sales.

I Had Climbed the Mountain

I had shared my knowledge through many speeches and through my intensive seminars on which this book is based. I had run 16 seminars in all—one in Switzerland, three in Maui, Hawaii, and 12 in northern Wisconsin. I was a published author with a book, *Success Forces,* that shared many of my experiences and provided motivation to my readers.

I had climbed the mountain, been knocked off and climbed it again. From all these experiences—from all the pain and joy, the failures and successes—I was now fully prepared for what I was about to encounter.

A Call from Sunny California

Len was a manufacturer's representative who had sold me products when he was based in the Chicago area. He saw how I took something that nobody else wanted and turned it into a hot-selling product by virtue of the way I positioned the product and wrote the copy that sold it. He knew that if I accepted one of his products, he had a good chance to make a good living. But when he moved to California, we lost touch.

One day in the summer of 1986, I got a call from Len. He had heard I was going to California the following week to look at some products there and conduct a few meetings, and Len asked if he could show me a few products he had discovered. "It will only take a few minutes of your time and it would be nice getting together with you and catching up on how things are going," said Len.

Len wanted to show me a new portable fax machine that one of his clients imported. Fax machines were just starting to become popular in 1986 and this machine was designed to be used in a car and transported between office and home. It provided a lot of flexibility for an executive on the go.

It didn't sound like a great product to me—not even to this day when fax machines are everywhere. Oh sure, it had certain applications, but fax machines back then were a rarity and this line extension—a portable version of a device that was perceived as being a nonportable product—was a little too impractical to be accepted in the mass business market.

As a courtesy, I accepted Len's invitation and he picked me up at the Los Angeles airport. We exchanged pleasantries and started our drive to the location of the company importing the fax machine.

As we were driving, I was squinting. The bright California sun during the noon hour was reflecting off the other cars and off the road. Len saw this and said, "Why not try these sunglasses on. They're really different."

I Was Actually Amazed

I put on the pair and noticed that not only was the glare gone and not only did I stop squinting, but everything appeared brighter and clearer. "What are these?" I asked.

"They're called Perception sunglasses. I'm in the process of selling these. It's one of my new accounts," said Len.

I kept putting them on and taking them off. "Len, this would be a great mail order item. I think I could do well with them. What do they sell for and what would they cost me?"

Len smiled, shook his head side to side as if to say no and then said, "You don't want to sell them. First, sunglasses are rarely successful in mail order. I can't even get a catalog to carry this pair. Second, sunglasses are typically sold at retail and you need several different styles—some for men and some for women. And I'm not sure about the stability of my supplier. He's a guy here in Los Angeles who, quite frankly, I don't like and I'm not even sure I'll be representing much longer. Joe, do me a favor and drop the idea."

But I was still curious. "Why are they so different?"

Len explained that they blocked all of the ultraviolet light. Many people didn't realize that ultraviolet light is bad for your eyes and causes cataracts—a white milky substance that forms in the lens of your eyes and clouds your vision. He also pointed out that the lenses also blocked blue light. He explained that blue light isn't good for your vision either, as it can cause gradual blindness as you age. In fact, it causes what is called age-related macular degeneration—a form of progressive blindness.

At this time in history, the public did not know that sunlight causes cataracts or that blue light is not good for your eyes. Very little was said about it.

Len continued, "Another good reason for blocking blue

light is the fact that blue light doesn't focus on the retina—the focusing screen in your eyes—like most of the other rays. Blue light focuses in front of the retina. So by eliminating blue light, objects will appear sharper, clearer and more defined."

Len Discourages My Involvement

"The sunglasses sell for $60 and they would cost you around $22—a pretty good margin. But again, I would forget about this product. Seriously, I'm not playing games with you. It just is not worth your effort. And besides, the product is not new. It was used during World War II by our fighter pilots, and there was even a 1974 German patent issued on the idea. It's been around for ages."

I thanked Len for the explanation and didn't pursue the subject any further. I felt strongly that the product was a perfect mail order item but, sensing Len's reluctance for me to get involved with the manufacturer, I decided not to push the issue for now. With a cost of $22 and a retail of $60, it seemed to me to be a great opportunity. Most of the electronic products I had been selling had margins of only 40%, so a product with more than a 60% margin seemed a really good mail order opportunity to me. And the fact that the sunglass concept had been around for years was not a deterrent to me at all. Many times I've taken products that others had given up on and I made them big hits. The DataKing 800 calculator was a dead product when I took it over and I sold thousands.

I went to see the portable fax machine, didn't like it and expressed this to Len and then thanked him for his hospitality. I also asked him if I could have a pair of the Perception sunglasses for my own use. Len did not have an extra pair and advised me, "I'll see if I can send you a pair when I get another sample from the manufacturer."

Missing Product Presents Opportunity

I finished my business in Los Angeles and flew back to Chicago only to discover a disaster waiting for me. I had been working on an eight-page insert for the United Airlines merchandise catalog. JS&A and several other mail order merchants were given from two to eight pages to advertise our best-selling products. The catalog organizers and United Airlines would make a commission from the sale of our products. It gave us exposure, tying in with our mail order advertising in the regular in-flight magazines.

But on my return I discovered that one of our suppliers, a manufacturer of water filters, had gone bankrupt and was no longer in business. And we had prepared a full-page full-color ad for the product for the United catalog, which had a deadline in a few days. What should I do? Put in another product that was marginal at best or take a chance?

I called Len. "Len, remember that pair of sunglasses I saw during our little visit? I have an opportunity to advertise them in the United Airlines catalog and I need a few pairs right away. Please send them to me via Federal Express along with a formal price and delivery quotation. I'll place a big order right away and then subsequent orders as we determine the response."

Len sent the sunglasses. I sat down and wrote the ad in two hours, using as the concept my experience with Len in Los Angeles and describing how I discovered this exciting new product.

I then put the ad together within a few more hours and got the sunglasses photographed at a local photo studio. The ad was ready and completed in time to meet United's deadline.

Couldn't Believe the Sales

It was now September 1986 and I had to take a flight to Detroit to give a speech. I had not checked into how the United catalog was doing, as it was really too early to make any decisive conclusions. But on this trip, I decided to take along a computer printout of all of the catalog's products just to scan the sales results.

I was sitting on the airplane with the printout and my calculator, noting the profitability of each product listed when I realized that the Perception sunglasses results might be exaggerated. I examined my computation again and thought that maybe I had made a mistake. The profitability of the product was at least 10 times greater than any other product in the catalog. I thought there must be a mistake. Maybe a misplaced decimal point—maybe a mistake in the printout. Maybe I was missing something.

On my arrival in Detroit, I walked to the nearest phone booth and called Mary Stanke. "Have we sold 2,000 of these sunglasses?" I asked. "Is this correct and am I correct that it is the best-selling product in the catalog by a factor of ten?"

I got my confirmation. Not only were my hunches right, but the product was one of the most responsive of anything I had done in the catalog before this time.

When I returned to Chicago, I studied the sales results to determine how much confidence I should have in making a major commitment for advertising. I decided to risk $500,000 to run the sunglasses in a national print campaign, this time not under the name of Perception sunglasses but under my brand name— BluBlocker. I saw this as an opportunity to develop my own brand of sunglasses.

But there were problems. The manufacturer, as Len had warned, was not very stable. The supply of sunglasses was erratic. And I knew that I had to develop an outside source of sunglasses to support any major advertising commitment.

Len suggested a manufacturer in Korea and we started to manufacture a small backup supply to complement the product we were getting from our original supplier. Since Len would not be getting a commission from the original supplier, I paid him a commission on each pair of sunglasses made in Korea.

Success Strikes Again

The ad campaign broke and it was a huge success. We increased the advertising budget to $1 million since the first results were so positive. We had made a nice profit in over 50 major publications. We advertised in *Time*, *Newsweek*, *The Wall Street Journal*, all the in-flight magazines and even magazines that we had never advertised in before. They all did exceptionally well.

It was about this time that I realized the opportunity that was presenting itself. Here was my chance to create brand name recognition for my own product. So I established BluBlocker Corporation as a separate entity for the sole purpose of marketing the BluBlocker brand of sunglasses.

We started to also become a supplier to the oil and credit card company syndicators. These are the people who send offers enclosed with your oil company or credit card bill. Our representative to these accounts was Len and he was earning a nice commission from that activity as well.

Then we found out something that was a big disappointment for me personally. Len was manufacturing sunglasses on his own, putting the BluBlocker brand name on each pair and then selling them directly to an account that he represented for us. There were approximately 50,000 pairs involved.

My relationship with Len ended immediately. And the sad part of this story is that he was earning a very nice living selling to me and could have been very wealthy today had greed not gotten the better of him.

I then went to Taiwan where we were to make our sunglasses and lined up several manufacturers. We continued to do well when I was approached later in the fall of 1986 by Pat Riley, the president of the company that made our MDR vitamins. She was pleased with the success we had with her vitamin products and wanted us to expand our efforts.

I Discover the Infomercial

She informed me that there was a new format in television advertising called the "infomercial" and she knew a producer in California who could help me make a commercial for MDR vitamins. I contacted the producer and agreed to make a commercial for the vitamin product and the sunglasses as well. Why not do two of them?

Infomercials were a lot more expensive to do than print ads. You often had hundreds of thousands of dollars at risk before you knew if your product would sell. But with the success that I was already having with the vitamin program in print and with the success I was experiencing with the sunglasses, I felt it was worth doing both products at the same time.

There was another good reason why I wanted to do them at the same time. The vitamins sold very well in print but we barely made money. That was OK as we had set up a "continuity program" with our vitamin sales. After we acquired a new customer, with their permission we sent them a fresh supply of vitamins every two months. There were no additional advertising costs and the customers even paid the postage and handling charge. So when we computed the cost of the advertising, even though we only broke even on the initial sale, we knew that each customer on average was worth many months of additional sales.

The sunglass program was different, however. We made a good profit on each sale, but after the sale was made there weren't many residual sales. So to be successful on TV and to have the funds to support a major campaign, I needed both products to run concurrently—the sunglasses would make the immediate profits and the vitamins would be subsidized in the initial stages by the working capital generated through the sunglass profits.

In print there was no problem as the vitamins produced enough of a profit to support the advertising, but I wasn't sure about TV.

Our New Program: *Consumer Challenge*

I wrote out the script for some of the elements in the show, and the program, called *Consumer Challenge*, was created. I appeared in the show playing the part of the president of the company and talked briefly about the product and our commitment to the BluBlocker sunglasses. And I suggested to the producer that he walk up to people, let them try the sunglasses on for the first time and ask them to comment on the experience. The MDR vitamin show was a little different and was conducted mostly by interviewing our previous customers, who talked about their experience with the vitamins and how good they felt from taking them.

Both shows ran and both were successful. In fact, it was costing us $14 for the sunglasses, plus $3 per pair in advertising costs, and the sunglasses were selling for $39.95 on the show. We had reduced the price to $39.95 from $60 to make BluBlocker sunglasses more of a mass market product. And we were buying the product directly from the Far East, thus bringing down our costs.

The vitamin sales, on the other hand, were quite surprising. They actually broke even during the running of the infomercial and we soon established an incredible vitamin continuity program to coincide with our sunglass effort.

We were now firmly entrenched in the new area of infomercials, doing quite well with these two shows on the air.

Back to the Future II

Then in 1989, an advertising agency that was interested in working with me, Rosenfield & Lane, informed me that Steven

Spielberg was about to start production on his new film, *Back to the Future II,* and there was to be a scene in the film that could use some futuristic sunglasses. It was a great opportunity for BluBlocker Corporation to participate, supply those sunglasses and have our name featured in the movie.

We designed several futuristic styles specifically for the movie and presented them. Dan Rosenfield, president of Rosenfield & Lane, approached me with a great idea. Pizza Hut was also appearing in the film in the future segment and maybe, just maybe, they would be interested in a tie-in with our sunglasses. We would supply them with replicas of the sunglasses used in the film and they would sell them in their restaurants as part of a promotion.

We met with Pizza Hut and they loved the idea. We then took our movie designs, modified them for Pizza Hut and they approved the program. We were to produce four sunglass styles for a total of 10 million pairs for this program and they had to be shipped not only all over the United States but to Canada, Australia, New Zealand and England. This was going to be one of their biggest promotions ever and they had selected our company and our styles to be part of their program.

But there was a catch. By the time all the details were worked out and the agreement was signed by all the attorneys, we had only a few months to produce these 10 million pairs. If we missed our deadlines and did not ship on time, we would be penalized and could literally lose our shirt. This meant that we were at the mercy of our suppliers. Finally, this was a product that was going to be sold in an environment where food would be served. The sunglasses therefore had to be packaged in a clean-room environment and they had to meet certain quality standards determined by an outside independent inspection team that would conduct daily quality and sanitation checks.

Major Production Project

I flew to Taiwan along with my team from BluBlocker Corporation, met with all my suppliers and worked for a month to set up the factories and manufacture the molds required for the immense production effort that we had to implement. I met with the inspection team hired by Pizza Hut to set up the parameters and then briefed our 10 supplier factories.

Dan Iannotti joined me in Taipei. Dan was a friend from Las Vegas for whom I had worked 20 years earlier as his advertising agent. He was semi-retired, but worked with me and with each factory representative as my assistant while the production was taking place. We had a command center in one of the hotels in Taipei and a computer and fax machine to communicate with all of the factories.

An armada of ships was organized by Mary Stanke to ship the product to all five destination countries and she eventually stayed on in Taiwan for almost a month to supervise some of the factories.

To Ensure Delivery on Time

To ensure delivery on time, I did what probably was the best thing I could have done. I gave each factory two of the four designs we were making, with instructions to focus on one design but to make a small quantity of the other design. They also knew that if they committed to making a certain quantity by a certain time and did not meet those commitments, we would immediately go to one of the other factories and have them make up the difference. In short, I created factory competition.

One of the other incentives I gave the factories was that if they met our deadlines, I would supply a free round-trip to Los Angeles from Taiwan for the owner of each factory and his wife and I would treat them to an all-expense-paid vacation to include the world premiere of *Back to the Future II*. The world premiere was to be a charity party with all the stars from the movie and a buffet dinner. It was to be a major Hollywood event.

Whether it was a matter of pride or the profit they were making or the prospect of a trip to Hollywood, I don't know. But each factory produced on time and within the quality standards that we required.

Production Completed

With production now completed, the sunglasses were shipped and Pizza Hut's advertising was about ready to hit the papers. Screaming loud and clear on the posters and point-of-purchase advertising next to the sunglasses (selling for $2) were the words, "As seen in *Back to the Future II*."

The Chinese businessmen arrived in Los Angeles with their wives and, I will admit, we did show them a good time. They took a VIP tour of Universal City, had a wonderful dinner and assembled for the movie.

Drums rolled and the movie started. What a thrill. What a crowning achievement and moment to have reached. All our months of work, all the effort made by the manufacturers. Here we all were—ready for the final product of our efforts—a Hollywood movie of incredible proportions and a great promotion to tie into it.

The Big Surprise

But we were all in for a surprise. It was a great movie, but our name and Pizza Hut's sunglasses were not in it. The parts of the movie that originally contained them were on the cutting room floor. The name BluBlocker did not appear in any of the signs nor in the future scene.

I was disappointed. My suppliers walked around bewildered and I had to explain to them what had happened. But could you imagine what Pizza Hut must have felt? They had all their advertising to run and sunglasses to sell but the sunglasses were not in the movie as their advertising claimed.

Pizza Hut did manage to sell practically all of the sunglasses in a promotion that increased unit sales for them and was regarded as a success. They often commented that we were one of their best suppliers and that we certainly performed as we had promised we would.

The Taiwan suppliers were happy with the experience and to commemorate the accomplishment, I supplied each of the factories with a large plaque honoring them for participating in the largest sunglass order in the history of Taiwan and the United States. To this day they have these plaques proudly displayed in their offices.

From Infomercials to QVC and Retail

For six years—from 1987 through 1992—we ran our BluBlocker infomercials on national television. During that time we also had other infomercial products, but our primary focus was to create a brand name for BluBlocker. In 1991, I appeared for the first time on QVC, the home shopping channel, and did exceptionally well. I've appeared on QVC for over six years and now my daughter April appears there occasionally for me.

BluBlocker sunglasses then made it to the retail market in 1992, when we became the hottest-selling promotional product in the history of the Walgreens drug chain. They cautiously ordered 30,000 pairs to tie in with the Christmas shopping season and sold out within a few days. We ended up shipping hundreds of thousands of pairs to them to fill the pipelines.

Today we are in retail stores throughout the United States and our infomercial has appeared throughout the world, selling BluBlocker sunglasses to a global audience. I appear on QVC in the Philadelphia area and on their sister companies in England and in Germany. I appear on television and sell in German—a language I was taught while I was in military intelligence in Germany in the 1960s.

Today, BluBlocker Corporation is our primary focus. Our retail program flourishes as well as my home shopping TV appearances. The name BluBlocker is a respected name in both the sunglass industry and throughout the world. And finally, our trademark—which we've defended vigorously for the past several years—is the third most recognized sunglass brand behind Ray-Ban and Oakley sunglasses, according to a recent Sunglass Association of America survey.

Preparation Meets Opportunity

I define luck as "that point in time and space where preparation meets opportunity," and it certainly was luck in this case. Had I not agreed to visit a supplier as a favor to Len, had it not been a sunny day and had Len not shown me the pair of sunglasses as we drove to our meeting, I would never have had the success I've had with this single product. Finally, had the company whose water filter product I was considering for the United Airlines catalog not gone out of business, all the success that I achieved with BluBlocker sunglasses might never have taken place. Sometimes your worst problems turn into the most wonderful opportunities.

It is only fitting that I end this marketing book on a very

positive note. I had finally accomplished my goal of starting a company from scratch, establishing a brand name and securing a presence in retail. Finally all of the pieces fit together in a wonderful adventure that to date has lasted over 12 years and continues.

Epilogue

The Power to Start a Business

You have the power to start a major business right now. Mail order marketing gives you the ability to start small and, through determination and effort, build a large business from scratch.

In this book I've described several companies I've indeed created from scratch—all from a basic idea and often from a single advertisement. And I've shown how I developed the strategy to make an advertisement succeed.

Even if you're with a very large corporation, direct marketing can dramatically help your company grow and prosper reaching more prospects in an efficient and cost-effective way.

I wasn't perfect, as you are aware. I failed many times along the way. But it didn't matter if I won or lost—I still played the game. And somewhere along the line, if you play the game long enough, you'll win—and often win big. You must always remember never to give up.

There are opportunities that develop every day. If you've read my first book in this series, *Advertising Secrets of the Written Word*, you've learned how to create a powerful advertising message—a goose that lays golden eggs—as you discover the power of the written word to persuade, motivate and sell. And you've learned how to use that powerful message in a mail order business by reading this book, *Marketing Secrets of a Mail Order Maverick*.

Once you've succeeded in becoming successful in marketing through the format of print, you may want to explore the power of television: infomercials, direct response TV spots and even TV home shopping. These too are powerful vehicles to achieve tremendous success in mail order.

My next book in this series, *Television Secrets for Marketing Success*, takes you through my infomercial and TV direct response experience. You'll see how print advertising can easily translate into effective TV advertising. You'll learn from my mistakes as you have in the two previous books, and you'll gain valuable insights into television that you won't find anywhere else.

I hope you've enjoyed this book and learned from it. I hope you can also experience the thrill of success that comes from having a winning product or a winning ad and having your prospects, en masse, reach into their pockets and exchange their hard-earned money for your product or service. For in the final analysis that's what marketing is all about—a fair exchange.

Appendix A

Letters to the Editor

One of the innovations introduced to the catalog industry was JS&A's "Letters" page, which published both the good and bad comments from readers. The more controversial the letters, the more interesting, so it wasn't unusual for us to print the negative comments as well.

You can get a pretty good idea of some of the public's reaction to our catalog from the many letters we received. You'll get a sense of the spirit, style, copy, product selection and marketing approach we used in our catalog just from reading these letters: first, the "Dear Reader" letter I wrote for the introduction of the JS&A *Products That Think* catalog in 1982 that requested these letters, and second, many of the actual letters that we received.

Notice the copy in the "Dear Reader" letter. It is a good example of the image we wanted to convey to all our customers— warm, friendly, serious, trustworthy and honest. And you can see how important that letter was in establishing our image. What is your impression?

Dear Reader

Let me share a few secrets that guide me in the presentation of products in our catalog.

I have discovered that all products have their own personality. Some are serious like our Sage emergency telephone dialer, others are entertaining like the Sanyo Super Woofer and still others are just plain fun like our Mafia Auto Gadget. By recognizing each product's personality, we can communicate both the product facts and the emotional appeal as well.

What makes our style of advertising different? First, we don't try to insult your intelligence. If a product is lacking something, we tell you. If it's expensive, we admit it. And we try hard not to exaggerate, but if our enthusiasm gets the better of us occasionally—well, we're only human. (Incidentally, our description of the sound you'll hear from the Digital Watch Radio on page 3 is very conservative. You will be amazed by the powerful sound when you first hear it.)

We also insist on value and your complete satisfaction. We don't just mention that you can return a product within 30 days if you're not happy—we insist on it, and point this out continually in our advertising. And if you do return a product, we refund your postage and handling charge too.

And finally, if our products are sold for less by anyone else, you may show us proof that they are currently being sold for less within 60 days of your purchase and we will issue you the difference in the form of a credit towards future JS&A purchases. These are not advertising promises but commitments that JS&A has consistently made and lived by during the past eleven years.

When my staff selects a product, I must personally use it or be thoroughly acquainted with it and its manufacturer before I'll accept it for inclusion in my publication. And because companies prefer having JS&A introduce their products, they usually come to us first. If we're not carrying something, chances are there's a good reason.

There are a few products that I personally want to highlight in this letter. The first is in the advertisement shown to the left. The Fresh Air Bubble has been our best selling item for the past several months and its reorder rate indicates its enthusiastic acceptance.

The second product is the Scanset Data Bank Dialer which is one of the greatest new products ever offered in a JS&A catalog. The article on page 18 will explain why. We also use the Scanset to introduce what we predict will be the Data Bank explosion—a new era in consumer electronics. Spearheading this explosion is the small, portable IXO telecomputing terminal that brings enormous data retrieval powers into the hands of anyone who can use a telephone. The descriptions of the products and our predictions start on page 16.

And last of all, please read the Secret Spark Plug story on page 39. I personally have experienced the tremendous difference the Super Igniters have made in my car and in the cars of our staff. They're expensive but they'll more than pay for themselves in the future.

A few of the products we describe in this issue, we don't expect to sell in great numbers—certainly not in sufficient quantities to justify presenting them in a sales catalog. But once again, that's why we're different. If a product represents a major technological breakthrough then we want to give it the recognition it deserves. The Sansui unit shown on our cover and again on page 22 is a good example. Another is the new Kodak camera described on page 30. We have devoted almost five pages to these two items alone.

In future issues of our catalog JS&A will introduce a telephone you can bring with you on an airplane to make phone calls while flying. We'll also introduce a complete word processing system that fits in your briefcase, and we'll point out our choice for the best home computer. By remaining an active JS&A customer, you can be assured of receiving future catalog issues.

JS&A customers are well above average—an alert group sincerely interested in the excitement of consumer electronics. I want to assure you that I will do my best to bring you the most exciting new electronic products first, describe them as thoroughly, objectively and as honestly as possible, point out new trends, provide good service, timely delivery, and personally make sure you are enjoying the benefits of remaining our customer. Put us to the test and order an exciting product from JS&A at no obligation, of course.

Sincerely,

JS&A Group, Inc.

Joseph Sugarman
President

PS: In our next issue, we're going to reprint some of your letters in reaction to our catalog, to this letter, or to our products. Just address your comments to "Letters to the Editor." If we use them, we'll list your name, city and state and mail you a $25 check. Comments need not be complimentary as we will try to be objective.

LETTERS

Here are some of your comments from Catalog 7. Some are good, some are bad.

In our last catalog we asked for letters which we could reproduce in our Letters column. You may submit your comments on Catalog 8 to "Letters to the Editor," One JS&A Plaza, Northbrook, Illinois 60062. If your letter, or a portion of your letter, is used, we will send you a $25.00 check. We reserve the right to accept or reject all letters for publication and the right to edit letters for brevity purposes. No responses will be made to the letters. However, all letters will be read by our management.

In our next catalog, we wish to mention the full name of the individual submitting a letter, so please state the following at the end of your letter: "You have permission to reproduce my letter using my full name, city and state in your catalog." Then sign your name under that statement. This will assure us that we indeed do have your permission. The writers of all letters reproduced here have received a $25 check.

This catalog was about to get thrown away since I don't have much interest in electronic gadgets, but when I realized it was yours, I read it almost entirely. Mostly, it is an attractive, well-done catalog, but I find the female photos on pages 15 and 36 too sexy for my taste. My husband likes them, and since most of your buyers are probably men, I suspect it sells the products. I realize that the goal is to sell the products, but I think it detracts from the overall dignity of the catalog.
M.A.G., Bensenville, Illinois

Why spoil your beautiful catalog with this kind of advertising? Your products speak for themselves. We see enough of this nudity on TV.
I.N.S., Miami Beach, Florida

Your "Products That Think" catalog arrived on my desk, and as I looked through it I found it somewhat interesting and rather tastefully done—that is, until I ran across the metal detector displayed on Page 15. To use a scantily-clad woman to draw attention to a product is not only in bad taste, but is also very personally insulting to a large number of your readers, male and female alike, I am sure. As you point out in your editorial, "If a product represents a major technological breakthrough then we want to give it the recognition it deserves." However, using such ploys to bring attention to a product hardly constitutes giving it "the recognition it deserves."
D.N., Harrisville, New Hampshire

Your witty, straightforward approach to advertising makes your catalog more fun to read than most magazines. So much so that I have ordered J.S.'s book. However, I hear the FTC is coming out with a new rule that is sure to change all this. Whenever an ad pictures a fabulously sexy female, she must either come with the product, or at least come out and install it.
R.L.S., Friendswood, Texas

Please remove my name from your mailing list! I'm out almost $200 because I bought a Sinclair TV from you for my wife. It lasted less than 10 hours! Now I find that Sinclair is "out of the TV business" and into the personal computer scam. I hope Uncle Sam ties you up in so much litigation that you're too busy to find new 'suckers' for your slick approach.
F.X.B., Westfield, New Jersey

The JS&A catalog is the best designed and written catalog in the mail order business. I actually read every word. I've been in advertising, publicity and marketing for seventeen years and wish some company would give me the opportunity to put out such a fine publication. I admire your work and your company.
R. N., W. Hollywood, California

As a salesman, I appreciate the objectivity in the advertising of your products. You emphasize the good points of the products—but not overly so—and you aren't afraid to point out their limitations.
R.J.B., W. Allis, Wisconsin

I receive many catalogs in the mail, and yours is the most creative and captivating I've ever seen! Your style of advertising not only grabs my attention, but holds it throughout your publication. The honesty and personable way you present a product is appreciated. I feel I can trust your company. I like that.
J.B., Bettendorf, Iowa

Your catalog gets a larger circulation in our Engineering Department than my latest copy of Playboy. As an original customer of JS&A (you still maintain my Sensor watch in perfect order) I can verify that not only do you have "products that think" you have even more importantly "Managers that Care"—an ingredient certainly lacking in many organizations today! If I don't get your latest catalog back from the Engineering Department soon, I may request you to send my next catalog in a brown wrapper.
B.S., Pomona, New York

Even if I was mad at you (which I'm not) and even if your products didn't perform and do what you claim they do (which they usually do better than you claim), I wouldn't miss reading your complete catalog from cover to cover. I love your copy man's (or woman's) unusual method of describing your products.
P.W., Kane, Pennsylvania

I have just been reading through your last catalog and I find it very unusual and very interesting. I obtained this copy from a friend. What I want to ask you is, may I receive your catalog on a regular basis? If there is a subscription rate, I will be pleased to pay it. May I hear from you?
D.L.S., Golden, Colorado
Note: Our customers remain on our mailing list as long as they buy something from us within 18 months.

Your catalog is marvelous. You are the source of supply to the connoisseur of consumer electronics. I don't know how I got on your mailing list but please make sure I stay there as I plan to do a lot of business with you. PS: If you have the Technidyne "Toll Guard" telephone attachment I am ready to buy it.
D.D., Olympic Valley, California
Note: We occasionally rent mailing lists but usually only mail once to those lists.

Yesterday's mail with its usual bundle of "round file" circulars also had a very impressive catalog with an eye-catching title of "Products that Think." My curiosity was aroused with the beautiful audio set pictured on the front cover, and I began thumbing through the wonderful pages. Immediately I was transported mentally into a fantastic world of colorful and ultra-futuristic items illustrated in the catalog. This mental fantasizing endured for the next thirty minutes beginning with the Digital Watch Radio to the Nuclear Submarine Rocket Launcher. Bravo JS&A!! You have done it again! I have become "hooked" on your irresistible and truly magnificent new futuristic electronics catalog!
D.G., Duluth, Minnesota

I love the headlines on your advertisements "Zap Your Mom," "Stereo System for Monsters," "Eliminate Blood Pressure," etc. Your catalogs are more fun to read than any I've come across. I realize it takes good products and good service to be successful, but it's those intriguing ads that sell me.
J.F., Niles, Illinois

Your latest catalog has left me rolling over with laughter, impressed, stunned at what man can invent, and amazed that anyone could come up with as creative a publication as you have. Sure, most Atlanta area law offices have (hopefully) no need for Mafia Auto Gadgets, Pickle Power, and Mickey Mouse Computers, but, nevertheless, I enjoy reading about them. I enjoy even more your detailed advertising of new technology such as printing calculators, Data Bank Phone Dialers, and other such gadgets that will benefit even we non-gangsters. Most of all, I am impressed that you would run an ad for the Kodak disc camera (even though you in effect told us to buy it elsewhere), using valuable space to tell us about a new innovation that may profit your competition more than you.
G.E.A., East Point, Georgia

I recently had occasion to view Products That Think for the first time. Never before have I been so mesmerized by a collection of advertisements! I find your catalog refreshingly clever, creative and exciting. Accolades to your writers who present new product pros and cons in a manner that allows the reader to make an informed rather than pre-formed judgment.
J.K., Champaign, Illinois

I received your unsolicited catalog bearing the attached mailing label, and my first impulse was to send the label to you with a request that you delete my name from your mail-
(Continued on Order Form)

(Continued from front of issue)

ing list. That was before I happened to look through the catalog. Instead, I would like you to identify your list supplier and ask them to remove my name and stop supplying it to others. I don't need or want any other catalogs for this type of mechandise. But I certainly do want to stay on your mailing list. Your catalog is definitely unique, both in the advanced kind of high-technology items you offer, and in the tone of your presentation and apparent way of doing business. I assume those comments are actually written by Mr. Sugarman. My only task now is to figure out what I ought to order.

J.D.M., Wallingford, Connecticut

Kudo's on your beautiful new catalog which makes me want everything listed which is a tribute to your photographer, copywriter and layout artist.

R.H.S., Calabasas, California

I truly do enjoy your conversational and friendly advertising, and I do appreciate that you make the effort to fully describe a product with the assumption that your reader has an IQ in excess of that of a tomato plant.

H.E., Santa Rosa, California

I truly enjoyed every page of your recent catalog. Grade A advertising!! Your unique way of introducing your most unusual products was refreshing to say the least. The emotional appeal of each product shines, and the major technological breakthroughs speak for themselves (in a loud roar, I might add!). Your catalog ended up in my "in basket" by an enjoyable human error. Please direct the next issue to my undoubted attention at the address listed below. Thanks again for opening my eyes to this rapidly expanding market of electronic miracles.

H.W., Parsippany, New Jersey

Finally, a catalog with a "no-holds barred" explanation of each item – mixed with some humor. I'll swear, you've really got something here! I was intrigued with your catalog and its in-depth explanation of the various items. You can bet that I'll be ordering one or two. Mostly though, I'm looking forward to your next catalog and its thought-provoking products. To say you are unique would be the understatement of the year. Keep up the good work.

R.B.W., Port Orange, Florida

I must admit that your catalogs are very witty and enticing – especially for an electronics buff such as myself. As a physician I laughed at your campaign to "stamp out blood pressure."

S.J.V., San Antonio, Texas

Firstly, let me take this opportunity to thank you for sending me your recent "Products That Think" catalog. I can't remember when I've received a catalog that I've so thoroughly enjoyed.

B.C., Forest Hills, New York

Recently I returned a product for a refund. I accidentally had placed my car keys in the package I was returning. I was searching for them over a week. I was happy to have them sent back to me by one of your employees, Ed Henry at the warehouse. I would like to express my gratitude for having my keys returned to me. It is another example of JS&A's fine customer relationship.

L.A., Las Vegas, Nevada

I've enjoyed the past 6 catalogs – they keep getting better – and number 7 was no different. Even if I absolutely don't need them, I'm tempted to try all of your products. Occasionally I do, and even if I'm not entirely satisfied with the product (Bone Fone), the service is always super! Keep it up.

P.M.G., Davers, Massachusetts

As it happened, on the same day that I received the current issue of Science Digest, your new catalog came. This made it necessary that I determine priority of reading; your catalog came first. No theoretical possibility, developmental stage, time lag to production, and the like. Your products are in existence, on hand, now, fully developed and being marketed with a guarantee of satisfaction equalled by none.

P.L.W., New Orleans, Louisianna

I am regularly deluged by a mountain of mail, so much so that I hardly have time to read my "Time," but I thoroughly enjoyed taking the time out to read your catalog (though that seems to be an inadequate word). I'm amazed that you actually do point out defects or drawbacks in the merchandise you sell. I've ordered the Canon printer in spite of your hon-

esty. Truly a unique sales approach. Your humor is a welcome relief from "dry" jargonese catalogs or hard sellers that praise their products to the moon. Though I laughed out loud when I saw your "Mafia Auto Gadget," as an Italian American I was slightly ruffled. May I suggest "anti-terrorist device" as an alternative? Thank you for putting together an electric and interesting collection of items. I'm sure you'll hear from me again.

R.J.D.E., Ridgewood, New York

This is a fun magazine to look through, but also educational. I work full-time as a word processor, and I am looking forward to your future issue introducing the word processing system that fits in a briefcase.

D.T.R., Torrance, California

I bought one of your products but I have yet to use it as you intended. It is the LocLoc digital lock. Your ad says it is to be worn on a belt loop. I don't wear it there. I use the watch and enjoy it very much. You see, I was looking for an inexpensive, small digital pocket watch that I could use as a key ring. (I don't like to wear conventional watches. They are uncomfortable on my wrist.) I could find no such object until I saw your ad. There it was. The watch key ring I had been looking for. Even though your ad says nothing about using the watch as a key ring. I saw no reason why I couldn't use it as such. Many people have commented on my neat pocket watch. Thank you for your product that I seem to be using incorrectly.

J.W., Dallas, Texas

Without saying anything to my wife, I installed a set of your Cibie quartz halogen headlights on my Lynx. After seeing what good night vision they provide, she asked "Do you have your bright lights on?" "No," I replied and we were both surprised that no one flashed the 'you've got your bright lights on, Dummy' sign. Must be those precision optics. Joe, thank you for making these better, brighter and safer headlights available to the American driving public.

C.C.A., Northbrook, Illinois

LETTERS

Here are some of your comments about Catalog 8.

Dear Editor:

For sometime I have been experiencing headaches, cold sweats, nervous tics, and an uncontrollable urge to play chess constantly. Now I know what has happened to me. The answer is in your latest catalog. I have been "robotized"–like the character in the movie "Tron." I have been captured and imprisoned in a computer. Gladstone's Revenge indeed! You think you've had legal problems before? You ain't seen nothing yet. I am filing suit against you and your manufacturer for false imprisonment and mental rape.

Judge Arthur A. Gladstone (Ret.)
Alexandria, Virginia

Almost all of today's advertising is fakey, disgusting, boring, and many times nauseating. Yours is fresh, innovative, sincere, informative and entertaining. I love it. Thanks JS&A.

Mr. John S. May
Linton, Indiana

All of the mail that comes into our office is gone through by me. As my boss is fond of saying, "Don't put any junk mail on my desk." So it is my job to sort out the mail and pitch out the junk mail and advertisements. Not so with your catalog. I have shown it to everyone, including my boss. (I'm even considering purchasing my husband's Christmas present from you.) To say the least, your catalog will not be thrown away.

Mrs. Judith Scott
Indianapolis, Indiana

I don't like your catalogs–they are too full of good sales psychology; but I am fascinated by them. I've just received number 8 and it certainly is on a par or even better than previous catalogs. But as I read through this one, I was plagued by the same strong, almost irresistible, urge to purchase several of the items shown. I still proudly wear my Sensor wrist watch, even though digital watches have come down drastically in price. I ordered a Bone Fone, but found it impractical for my use during the trial period. Now I am ordering the really advanced Brother EP-20 typewriter because it will suit my needs perfectly. I'm really pleased that I received your catalog before I purchased another model not so advanced. Congratulations.

Mr. Richard Anderson
Rogers, Arizona

I began reading the letters section and noticed that most praised your wit, style, copywriters, photography, etc., but said little of their experience with purchases from you. As a true "gadget freak," I have on several occasions indulged myself with your offerings. My first purchase, a Sensor watch, was repaired once at no charge. I did have to check out 4 or 5 Bone Fones before finding 2 that worked, but replacements were swift and my postage was refunded. All this is great, but to me the most impressive thing is the fact that you are always able to recognize the truly important features of an item. *Consumer Reports* can do a detailed 5 page article on a product area and totally miss those features that set one product apart–you never seem to miss it.

John Kuhn
Ballwin, Missouri

I just received your #8 catalog and set aside the newspaper, *National Geographic,* and read the catalog. Needless to say, dinner was a little bit late that evening. Being a chess player, I was very interested in Gladstone's Revenge. I had finished reading the article, and was looking at the picture where the arm is holding a pawn. I was curious as to where the pawn had come from on the board, and noticed that Gladstone had captured his own pawn. Are you sure Gladstone has recovered from his "breakdown?" And furthermore, since when is the chessboard set up with the bishops and knights switched around? Aside from all that, it is a terrific catalog, my Sensor watch still works, and I still use the metal detector each summer when I am out hiking.

Mr. Glen M. Nichols
Seattle, Washington

In your letter to readers in your latest Products That Think catalog, you state that the issue may become a collector's item. You're behind the times. As a collector of old books and other unusual material, I've been saving past issues of your catalog for some time now. Your catalog and marketing approach are so unique that I assumed they would become collectible.

R.P.C.
Tiburon, California

I am glad to see that someone is giving IBM some real competition. It will force them to come up with something better yet, and at the same time reduce their prices. I read the "Letters to the Editor" about your catalog #7. They were very interesting and you are to be complimented for your honesty in publishing those containing derogatory remarks as well as those who praised you. I did not receive a copy of the #7 catalog, but after reading these interesting comments, I would like to receive one if that is possible. I have enclosed my check for $1.25 to cover the cost of sending it to me.

Mr. Elmer M. Click
Kent, Washington

Thoroughly enjoyed Catalog 8 as I have previous ones. As a commercial artist I am aware of what goes into the production of a magazine catalog similar to yours. You spare no expense to produce one of the finest. The copy, layout and photography are par excellent. The icing on the cake is the type of product you advertise. There are electronic items for everyone, all age groups, all economic levels. Last but not least, your promise of satisfaction guaranteed. If every business went out of their way to satisfy customers the way you do, Better Business Bureaus throughout the country would shut down. I feel privileged to receive your catalog.

Mr. Leonard R. Adams
Evansville, Indiana 47710

From a woman's point of view, your ads are terrific. Not only do they entertain, but believe it or not, I feel I'm getting an education in electronics. Some of your products are simply awe-inspiring. Trouble is, I'm tempted to order everything in the book–like the spark plugs in your last catalog when I don't even have a car. I'd be very grateful if you'd keep my name on your mailing list even though I don't order very often.

Ms. Mildred Fodor
Los Angeles, California

As you have chosen not to reply to the letter from F.X.B. in Westfield, New Jersey (catalog #8), allow me to do it for you.
Open letter to F.X.B.

"Concerning the Sinclair TV you bought and lasted only 10 hours. If you feel you are "out almost $200," this my friend is your fault not JS&A's. All products are "try for 30 days, if not satisfied return for prompt and courteous refund." Last year I returned a good, as advertised product because "I didn't like it" and got a prompt, courteous refund plus postage and handling. This guarantee is on the bottom of the order blank in bold letters. Next you state "Sinclair is out of the TV business and into the personal computer scam," and continue with some statements that don't need repeating. If you had purchased the TV direct from Sinclair, then you would have a problem, but you didn't. Sinclair being out of the TV business is a problem for JS&A, not you. JS&A guaranteed the product and had you wanted another one in place of the defective one, they would have had to replace it at an equal or higher value or refund your money." Back to JS&A, you have a class company, built on honesty, a rarity today.

Mr. Bob Cross
Visalia, California

You may submit your comments on Catalog 9 to "Letters to the Editor," One JS&A Plaza, Northbrook, Illinois 60062. If your letter, or a portion of your letter, is used, we will send you a $25.00 check. We reserve the right to accept or reject all letters for publication and the right to edit letters for brevity purposes. No responses will be made to the letters, however, all letters will be read by our management.

Please state the following at the end of your letter: "You have permission to reproduce my letter using my full name, city and state in your catalog." Then sign your name under that statement. This will assure us that we indeed do have your permission. The writers of all letters reproduced here have received a $25 check.

309

LETTERS

Here are some of your comments about Catalog 9.

Dear Editor:
I am a thief. I stole your catalog from a friend's apartment because I knew he wouldn't give it up, and I couldn't put it down. I am an overseas civilian worker and here, somewhat isolated from the world, catalogs are worth their weight in gold. Yours, with its great products, terrific presentation, readable and enjoyable format from front to back is Fort Knox.

M. G. Risher
Johnston Atoll, South Pacific

Your products are, as you say, space age and innovative, and your advertising methods are creative and dare to break traditional roles. So, why, why, why do you resort to the antiquated use of a picture of a buxom, flirtatious, scantly clad woman (p.2) in your catalog? (The "Barbie Doll" nurse on p.33 wasn't much better.)

Mary Pat Stadtherr
Minneapolis, Minnesota

As the unchallenged "catalog queen" of Frankfort, I must admit to a growing feeling of burnout as I receive more and more catalogs from more and more companies. Increasingly, the merchandise all begins to look the same and the extravagant descriptions and claims lose meaning. Your catalog is refreshingly different. I look forward to each issue to see what new gadget your copy will convince me I can't live without.

L. W. Bledge
Frankfort, Kentucky

The unusual format of your catalogs is undoubtedly getting exposure by people talking about it. As a pastor I have found an unusual use for them. As every public speaker knows, rapport between people can be accelerated with humor, so I have read some of your ads within sermon introductions. Because of the unique approach you've had, several people have borrowed your catalog to completely read. Your style is making friends fast here. Now if you had a gadget for getting borrowed catalogs back?

Paul Slocum
Fallbrook, California

An advertiser once told me that the worst part of his job was that after many years it left him doubting his capacity to recognize the truth about anything. After reading your catalog, I found it encouraging to learn that exaggeration and lying are not necessarily inherent in advertising. May others in the field be driven by shame and starvation to follow your example.

Stanley R. Rudcki
Chicago, Illinois

Catalog 9 arrived a few days after I returned from the hospital following my heart attack. The hospital gave us several classes about the heart while we were there. After reading "New Heart Discovery" we understood much better what they had been trying to tell us.

David Prudden
Cedar Rapids, Iowa

I receive a lot of merchandise catalogs each week in the mail. Some end up in the trash after I've read a few pages. When I get your catalog, it gets read cover to cover even before *Time* magazine. From my past experience with your company I know I can't lose. Why? For example, several years ago I ordered a chess computer from you, but after playing it for a few weeks it developed a defect. I sent it back requesting a replacement. A replacement was sent promptly and the unit has worked perfectly ever since. Also, your guarantee is ironclad and I know that if I am not satisfied with a product of yours, I may send it back for a refund. I have never felt more confidence in any other company than JS&A.

Daniel P. Czerwonka
Minneapolis, Minnesota

Your catalog just fell into my hands by mistake. It was addressed to an engineer who had been visiting and working from time to time at the facility where I am employed. Being a curious and somewhat mechanically inclined female, I decided to thumb through the catalog. Needless to say, it was all that I could do to put your publication down. I have just ordered the Magic-Stat thermostat and can hardly wait to receive it. Being a widow, the simplicity of installing and operating this thermostat is mind boggling. Everyone that picks this catalog up off my desk has nothing but praise for the format, contents, refreshing approach to selling and all-around interest to both male and female. Please put my name on your mailing list, and that is a first for me (asking to be put on a mailing list).

Faye Thomas
Lancaster, California

I have just received your Catalog 9 today and at the same time received the "Love/Hate" thermostat. I was so intrigued by the thermostat that I set the catalog aside until the thermostat was installed. This was one of the easiest home installation projects I have ever done. The installation took a total of ten minutes, six of which were involved with removing the old thermostat. The unit is functioning as you said it would. I have already noticed that the furnace is not running as often as with the old thermostat, which means money is already being saved. I'll let you know in the spring how much I saved over the winter. Catalog 9 is just super. If all mail order catalogs depicted their products as well as JS&A does, you would have some serious competition. A couple of others have tried to copy JS&A's technique, but they just don't compare.

David M. Horvath
Mentor, Ohio

Hmm, very interesting. I noticed the "different" catalog on my employer's desk among many other media items but yours caught my attention because of the front cover. Personally I feel it was a little too much (too busy) but anyhow it caught my attention and after I had picked it up to look through it, well, the layout and photographs are excellent. Now I'll keep

looking forward to locating your catalog by looking for the "different" cover. (P.S. Keep it interesting-looking and I'll keep finding it.)

Lucinda L. Landis
Lancaster, Pennsylvania

It's so obvious that you not only turn out the highest quality catalog, you not only offer a genuine 30-day trial (which I have experienced when a product did not really fit my needs), but you are also helping speed the integration of "hi-tech" products into a society that is sometimes even fearful of the change promised by new developments.

Hugo P. Buehring
Honolulu, Hawaii

I wish to write that I remain continually interested in the products you offer and the unique style of the catalog—particularly the informative style of prose. I am left with the feeling that I am being treated as a respected consumer who is being informed and educated about a product rather than being sold a product. I deeply appreciate the service you provide in this regard. The excitement of the writing style is contagious.

Henry A. Mumm
Sacramento, California

Like most, perhaps all, those who receive your catalogs I enjoy reading them, am impresses by their quality and style and find their even-handed approach refreshing. That is why I was surprised (and a bit disappointed) to find the following on page 37 of catalog No. 9 "...can store this data..." Data is the plural of datum. So, it must be either "this datum" or "these data" (just like "this medium" and "these media"). You use the English langauge well and therefore you should also use it correctly.

Professor Joseph Arditti
University of California
Irvine, California
Note: Thank you professor but while reading your letter, we noticed that you misspelled the word "language" and the word "impressed."

You are smart to include two order blanks. Few people, I will wager, throw your catalogs away. They make too interesting reading. And when the next in line reads it, and perhaps orders from it, there is still an order blank to be used by the one to whom he hands the catalog.

Herman Herst, Jr.
Boca Raton, Florida

You may submit your comments on Catalog 10 to "Letters to the Editor," One JS&A Plaza, Northbrook, Illinois 60062. We reserve the right to accept or reject all letters for publication and the right to edit letters for brevity purposes. No responses will be made to the letters, however, all letters will be read by our management.

Please state the following at the end of your letter: "You have permission to reproduce my letter using my full name, city and state in your catalog." Then sign your name under that statement. This will assure us that we indeed do have your permission.

LETTERS

Here are some of your comments about catalog 10.

Dear Editor:

I was furious when I opened your catalog and saw the picture of a lady sitting by a typewriter in an office environment wearing a sexy evening dress. I am a secretary and belong to Professional Secretaries International. Our association is striving to change the stereotype of secretaries that you portray in your catalog to our true image—that of a professional. We dress and act as professionals and to see advertisements such as yours is very demeaning. It destroys what our association has worked so hard to change.

> Debbra Backlund
> Fargo, North Dakota

I just received your catalog and read the comment made by Mary P. Stadtherr. Please don't listen to her. There are some of us that like the old antiquated use of pictures of buxom, flirtatious, and scantly clad women in your catalog. The "Barbie Doll" nurse on p. 33 was terrific.

> Dick Barlow
> Salt Lake City, Utah

Of all your products, I can't imagine who would buy the Record Muncher. Is this a joke? I have shown this product to several friends and no one would even think of buying it. How many have you stocked in your warehouse? In your next catalog would you publish a report as to how many you have sold? I really am curious as to why people would buy this and would like to hear their comments.

> Jack Stevenson, Jr.
> Winston-Salem, North Carolina

I have never done this before (no reference to virginity) but I am so pleased with the mini record player (Record Muncher) that I just had to drop you a line. I've known, and had, Audio Technica equipment so my expectations were high. The unit surpassed all my expectations.

> P.D.
> Des Moines, Iowa

I second all the good remarks about your catalog and writing, having just read your Catalog 10. What made my day for entertainment

was the professor who wanted you to use English correctly, and to write "these data" or "This datum" and in his letter he misspells the words 'impressed' and 'language,' which you point out to him. That's why I ordered the dot matrix pre-editing little typewriter for notes and quick letters. The professor should have one.

> Robert H. Koenig
> Huntington Hills, New York

I plead guilty to being sloppy in not proof reading my letter carefully before sending it. "Impresses" and "langauge" were clearly misspelled. But, these were typographical errors. This is not the same as the incorrect use of "data" which is widespread. Like the previous letter you have permission to reproduce this letter using my full name, city and state in your catalog including, if you wish, any and all words I may have misspelled. I am simply a bad typist. PS: I still like your catalog.

> Professor Joseph Arditti
> University of California
> Irvine, California

I have just spent 2 delightful hours reading your #10 catalog and find myself overwhelmed by the power of the written word. Your product descriptions have convinced me that I want to purchase at least 6 of the items described, if not more. How I wish all publications, broadcasters and public speakers would use language to communicate as effectively as does JS&A. Bravo. My order is on its way to you.

> Ann V. Cousins
> El Segundo, California

Bravo. Encore. Keep up the good work JS&A, because I love your catalog. Even after reading it a dozen times, I still find it interesting. The catalog is laid out so well, and I wish I had enough money to buy one of every item in it. (Buying a 'Pickle Power' shot my savings, for I am 14 years old.) I sincerely hope that you continue to produce such a fine service for the people in this world who love 'firsts.'

> Jeff Loiter
> Columbia, Maryland

I am a twelve (12) year old boy with a few interests. One of my interests happens to be electronics and how they can affect us. Your issues of "Products That Think" are very fascinating to me. They tell and offer me products that deal with our rising technology and capability. We have already received our Magic Stat thermostat which we will install sometime during this week. From reading your article about it in issue #10, I can hardly wait to see how well it works. Your other products are just as fascinating to me. (Record Muncher, Word Processor, etc.) I hope we receive more of your fantastic issues. Keep 'em comin,' I'll just keep readin.'

> Erik Dubovik
> White Plains, New York

Two weeks ago I ordered a Canon TP-8 printing calculator and received it by mail a few days ago. Your service is really as good as everyone says it is.

> G. Juris Zommers
> Bainbridge Island, Washington

You may submit your comments on Catalog 11 to "Letters to the Editor," One JS&A Plaza, Northbrook, Illinois 60062. We reserve the right to accept or reject all letters for publication and the right to edit letters for brevity purposes. No responses will be made to the letters, however, all letters will be read by our management.

Please state the following at the end of your letter: "You have permission to reproduce my letter using my full name, city and state in your catalog." Then sign your name under that statement. This will assure us that we indeed do have your permission.

Free Gifts

Earn one or more of these products free when you order $40 or more. See details on order form.

TimeBall Clock

First a quiz. What is round, looks like a billiard ball and goes beep? Sorry, it's not the JS&A Electronic Billiard Ball. The answer, of course, is the JS&A TimeBall digital clock. Not only does this sharp-looking alarm clock go beep, but it has a drowse alarm and backlight. It makes a great gift or travel alarm.
TimeBall (2083SB) . . . . .Free With Purchase*
TimeBall (2080CZ 3.00) **$19.95**

Super Watch

It's a multi-function digital chronograph alarm watch. You get an LCD display of time (hours, minutes, running seconds), month, date and day of week, plus an alarm function and backlight. There's also a full-function 8-digit calculator with memory. And with all these features you won't believe how thin it is.
Super Watch (2046SB) .Free With Purchase*
Super Watch (2045CZ 3.00 per order) **$19.95**

*See instructions on other side.

LocLoc

The LocLoc is a full 5-function digital watch with night-light—all housed in a solid brass water resistant case. Just twist the clasp on the lock and it opens. Then slip it over your belt loop. You'll enjoy the freedom of having nothing on your wrist and the correct time at a glance.
LocLoc (2015SB) . . . . . .Free With Purchase*
LocLoc (2020CZ 2.50) **$19.95**

Appendix B

Ways to Protect Your Product

The following are some additional ways you can protect your product:

Disclosure Document

In this form of preliminary protection you protect your idea for the initial two years. This allows you to generate revenue for a patent-pending application, patent search and patent or trademark. To file a disclosure document, send copies of any blueprints, photos, illustrations and supporting documentation with a $10 fee and self-addressed, stamped envelope to: The Commissioner of Patents and Trademarks, Washington, DC 20231.

Free Consultation

This service provides you with a free 30-minute consultation with a patent attorney. Simply contact the American Intellectual Property Law Association, 2001 Jefferson Davis Highway, Suite 203, Arlington, VA 22202.

Non-Disclosure Agreement

The following is a form that you can have prospective manufacturers or marketing partners sign before you present a product or an idea to them for consideration. The form is very basic and simple, but it will afford you some protection and certainly a piece of evidence if litigation is later involved. Remember that many companies will not sign a non-disclosure agreement and will, in fact, want you to sign a form releasing all rights to your idea or product before they'll even look at it. The problem is that our society is so litigious that nobody trusts anybody today, and unfortunately this holds back progress. Being an inventor is not an easy profession.

Non-Disclosure Agreement

Whereas, [*your name as the inventor or representative*] has developed a novel [*type of product*] and related technical and commercial information (collectively, Proprietary Information); and

Whereas, the undersigned and the firm of which he or she is an authorized representative (individually and collectively, the Undersigned) are interested in examining the Proprietary Information with a view to entering into a business arrangement in connection therewith; and

Whereas, [*your name*] considers the Proprietary Information to be highly confidential; and

Whereas, [*your name*] is willing to allow the Undersigned to examine the Proprietary Information pursuant to the conditions set forth herein;

Now therefore, in consideration of [*your name*] supplying the Undersigned with the aforesaid Proprietary Information, the Undersigned agree that for a period of two years from the date hereof such Proprietary Information shall be utilized only for the aforesaid purposes and that no other use or disclosure or copying thereof will be made without explicit prior written authorization from [*your name*].

Notwithstanding the above, the obligations of the Undersigned hereunder will be limited in regard to any specific portion of the Proprietary Information which (a) was in the public domain prior to the date of this agreement, or subsequently comes into the public domain other than as a result of actions of the Undersigned, or (b) is subsequently received by the Undersigned from a third party who did not acquire it directly or indirectly from [*your name*], or (c) the Undersigned can show was in their possession prior to the receipt thereof hereunder.

Dated: _____

By: (Signature) _____

Printed Name: _____

Title: _____

Company: _____

Sample Order for Advertising Space

Insertion Order

To the Publisher of: (Name of magazine)

Address: (Address of publisher)

Ad Title: (Name of ad)

Space: Full page, 1 color

Frequency: (Usually expressed as 1x, 2x, 3x, etc.)

Issue Date(s): (Month or exact date(s) ad will run)

Position: Far forward in publication, right-hand side

Key: Order number WSJ-103

Gross Amount: (Ad cost)

Minus Agency Commission: (15% of ad cost)

Net Due Publication: (Ad cost minus 15%)

Special Instructions: (Any instructions required)

> Send tear sheet to agency (two tear sheets).
>
> Send publication to agency (six copies).

Special Notice: The word "ADVERTISEMENT" is not to appear on this or any other of our advertisements in your publication. If this request is not adhered to, it is understood that the undersigned will refuse payment of this order and will not be under any obligation to pay for this advertisement.

_____

Authorized Signature

_____

Publication Representative

_____

Date

Appendix D

Direct Marketing Principles and Theories

Product Principles

Product Principle 1: The product must appeal to everybody in a category. (page 16)

Product Principle 2: The product must be priced to appeal to the largest segment of a category. (page 16)

Product Principle 3: Unless you dominate your category, the demand you create is quickly filled by others. (page 17)

Product Principle 4: Successfully offer your first product in a category and others will offer you similar products in that category. (page 20)

Product Principle 5: When a new product that is of benefit to society is discovered, it will, by the dynamics of a free marketplace, grow to fill the greater need of that society. (page 27)

Product Principle 6: Your product must harmonize with your prospect. If it doesn't, make sure that you change it so it does. (page 43)

Reading Theories

Reading Theory 1: Any layout design which forces the reader to work against reading gravity or fails to return the reader to a logical axis of orientation tends to destroy reading rhythm and should be avoided. (page 69)

Reading Theory 2: Certain typographic elements impede readability by throwing unnecessary distractions into the reader's path, thereby interrupting the reading rhythm. (page 69)

Reading Theory 3: Typography fails if it allows the reader's interest to decline; it fails absolutely if it contributes to the destruction of the reader's interest. (page 70)

Photo Theories

Photo Theory 1: Photography offers you the opportunity to complete the story, express the visual drama in your product and enhance the likelihood of prospects reading your copy. (page 88)

Photo Theory 2: The difference between a good photographer and a bad photographer is that a good photographer doesn't show his or her bad pictures. (page 90)

Media and Testing Theories

Media Theory: The single most important factor in earning a profit from any mail order campaign in print or on TV is how cheaply you buy your media. (page 105)

Testing Theory 1: Each and every ad you run is a test. (page 165)

Testing Theory 2: Testing each element of an ad and the entire ad provides a valuable tool in 1) determining what really works in an advertisement and 2) avoiding the magnification of a costly mistake. (page 169)

Testing Theory 3: A successful test should accomplish three things: 1) Tell you if your ad is profitable, 2) Give you a level of confidence to determine what your next media expenditure should be, 3) Earn a profit. (page 169)

Observation Theories

Comparison Theory: In print advertising, the place you make your money is often in the media savings. In direct mail, the place you make your money is in the responsiveness of the mailing list that you rent. (page 190)

Publicity Theory 1: Publicity will not tell you if you have a winning product. It can, in fact, be a sign that your product will not sell well. (page 205)

Publicity Theory 2: Publicity often means that your product or service is not yet in the public mainstream and therefore will not appeal to your prospect. (page 205)

Pricing Theory: Generally speaking, when the price of a product goes up, the number of units sold goes down and more effort to educate and persuade is required to sell the product. (page 217)

Return Theory: The product return rate is a gauge to determine the successful presentation of a product and its acceptance and an opportunity to turn a regular customer into a loyal and enthusiastic advocate. (page 232)

Avoid Theory 1: The sale of a product or service is a very serious experience and should be treated as such. (page 242)

Avoid Theory 2: Use your picture in your ad only if you're running for office or trying to save your company. (page 242)

Poor Response Theory: The president of the United States has a tremendous impact on the emotional state of our subconscious minds and as such directly affects the world marketplace as no other single individual or factor. (page 254)

Appendix E

Recommended Reading

Reading a number of books on a variety of subjects prepares you to become a good direct marketer and helps you avoid many of the mistakes others have made. That's one of the benefits you have realized from reading *Marketing Secrets of a Mail Order Maverick*. Many other people in the direct marketing industry have also written books that might be helpful to you. By reading other perspectives on advertising and copywriting, you can further your education and avoid costly errors that many before you have made. I wish I had read many of them earlier in my career.

How to Sell Anything to Anybody, Joe Girard. The world's greatest salesman shares his secrets on how he made a fortune selling cars in Detroit. The book details how he eventually was listed in the *Guinness Book of World Records* for having sold the most cars in one year. An interesting read and some valuable insights from a friend and powerful salesman. ISBN 0-446-38532-8. Warner Books. 192 pages.

Sales Magic, Steve Bryant. Bryant is one of QVC's top show hosts and a master at selling. Here he talks about his proven techniques for selling that will give you new insights on what works and why. Here's your chance to increase your sales dramatically through many of the techniques this popular and effective salesman shares with you. I've personally seen him use many of these techniques on QVC in the sale of BluBlocker sunglasses. ISBN 0-936262-24-9. Amherst Media. 152 pages.

My First 65 Years in Advertising, Maxwell Sackheim. One of the former deans of direct mail advertising shows you how to attract attention, create interest, carry conviction, and get action. Sackheim shows you how to write a good ad and a selling headline and then gives you many firsthand experiences. One of the true pioneers in the business, he is often quoted by others. ISBN 0-8306-5816-5. Tab Books. 200 pages.

Tough Selling for Tough Times, Murray Raphel and Neil Raphel. How to overcome tough times in your business is the basic message of this book, but it goes beyond just that. How would you handle a key employee of your mail order company getting sick, a bank refusing to loan you money for your next mailing or a flood destroying all your inventory? This book tells you the eight success characteristics of entrepreneurs who faced different "tough times" such as the ones I've just listed, and how they overcame them. Case histories and exclusive interviews. ISBN 0-9623808-19. Available from Raphel Marketing, 12 S. Virginia Avenue, Atlantic City, NJ 08401. 197 pages.

Up the Loyalty Ladder, Murray Raphel and Neil Raphel. The authors give you an efficient way for even the smallest business to compete with the big guys in building a loyal customer base. When someone first comes into a store initially as a prospect they give you many clues as to what you need to do to bring them the rest of the way up the loyalty ladder: from a prospect to a shopper, to a customer, then to a client and finally to becoming an advocate. This is good information, as many of the case histories will teach you excellent principles for direct marketing. Also available from Raphel Marketing (see above). ISBN 0-88730-725-6. HarperCollins. 289 pages.

Ice to the Eskimos, Jon Spoelstra. This is one of my favorite marketing books of all times. And not because Jon was one of my former seminar participants. When Jon gave me the draft of his book to read, I took it with me thinking, "Oh well, just another marketing book," but I was totally wrong. It is one of the most interesting, witty and well-written marketing books I've ever read and there's a wealth of great ideas in its pages. Jon's premise is how to market products nobody wants because if you can do that, you can market anything. After several successful years with the Portland Trail Blazers basketball team as their general manager, Jon left to become the president of the New Jersey Nets basketball team—one of the worst franchises in the league. He had his work cut out for him. As the NBA's top marketer, Jon shares his battle-tested secrets he used with the Nets—secrets that can help you jump-start your sales, excite your customers and improve your bottom line. An absolute must to read. You won't regret it. ISBN 0-88730-851-1. Harper-Collins. 280 pages.

✓ **Commonsense Direct Marketing**, Drayton Bird. Hailed as "the authoritative textbook" on direct marketing, this book is packed with global case histories of how companies using Bird's ideas have managed to grow and prosper. His writing is witty and practical but never boring. A great book to read and reread and one that I wish I had read a lot earlier in my career. ISBN 0-7494-0996-7. Kogan Page, London. 375 pages.

Elephants in Your Mailbox, Roger Horchow. A classic book on the experiences of one of the nation's top catalog entrepreneurs and the 25 mistakes he made in building his company. Filled with insights on what really goes on in an upscale catalog house, this very honest and disarming book is a must-read for any catalog entrepreneur. ISBN 0-8129-0891-0. Times Books. 250 pages.

To Catch a Mouse, Lewis Kornfeld. Take somebody who was responsible for spending in excess of $600 million in advertising over his career at Radio Shack and add his 65 rules of marketing, and you've got the mix that makes this book a great read. Kornfeld is intimate, witty and tells you how to do it better, cheaper, quicker, with less hocus and more focus, with or without an ad agency. ISBN 0-13-922930-2. Prentice-Hall. 360 pages.

✓ **Selling the Invisible**, Harry Beckwith. This is a field guide to modern marketing with many of the principles applying to direct marketing. A really down-to-earth, practical guide on how markets work and how prospects think. Beckwith presents hundreds of quick, practical and easy-to-read strategies with most no more than a page long. An eye-opener to new ideas in the critical area of marketing. ISBN 0-446-52094-2. Warner Books. 252 pages.

Selling by Mail, John W. Graham and Susan K. Jones. This is an entrepreneurial guide to direct marketing at the serious level. Not for mail order professionals or for the small start-up but for the person ready to invest $20,000 to $50,000 in a venture. ISBN 0-684-18215-7. Charles Scribner's Sons. 310 pages.

Mail Order Moonlighting, Cecil C. Hoge, Sr. A very complete book on how to start your own mail order business in weeks, from home in your spare time and at your own pace. Lots of common sense in this book too. You will read how you can greatly lower your risks, create capital, increase your income and gradually change careers in the process. This is the perfect book for the beginning entrepreneur. ISBN 0-89815-222-4. Ten Speed Press. 360 pages.

Breakthrough Advertising, Eugene M. Schwartz. One of the really creative marketing and copywriting geniuses of his time has written this compendium of his philosophies. He shows how to develop an entirely new market for a new or old product in a number of clearly defined steps. Schwartz takes you through those steps and shows you how to write effective copy in the process. ISBN 0-932648-54-1. Boardroom Books. 240 pages.

MaxiMarketing, Stan Rapp and Tom Collins. Rapp and Collins take you in a new and exciting direction in promotion, advertising and marketing strategy. Reading almost like a novel, this wonderful book challenges you to seek your own applications of its principles and ideas—to get your juices flowing and to open your eyes to what advertising and, in particular, direct marketing will be like in the future. Many of their predictions have already come true. ISBN 0-07-051191-8. McGraw-Hill. 280 pages.

Direct Marketing, Edward L. Nash. One of the most complete books on direct marketing available. This step-by-step tells you everything you need to succeed in every aspect of direct marketing—from writing a basic marketing plan to writing direct mail copy. Nash guides you through planning an offer to planning a layout and even designing the product. You'll discover the analytical methods for forecasting and you'll get a good dose of list selection. Even infomercials are discussed. A great reference book you'll refer to often. ISBN 0-07-046032-9. McGraw-Hill. 480 pages.

Tested Advertising Methods, John Caples. One of the true bibles of the direct marketing industry, this commonsense book on direct marketing talks about everything from writing effective copy and the power of words to testing and the effectiveness of the right concept. Caples was also famous for many of his successful ad campaigns, among which was the classic "They laughed when I sat down at the piano." If you had to read just one book on direct marketing, this is the one to be read cover to cover. ISBN 0-13-244609-X. Prentice-Hall. 300 pages.

✓ **My Life in Advertising/Scientific Advertising**, Claude C. Hopkins. He was the founding father of modern advertising and these two reprinted classics together in one paperback book are a must-read for any advertising practitioner. Hopkins covers all of the scientific approaches he utilized in the 1920s when he wrote these books—approaches that are still used today in direct marketing. This book will be an essential and vital guidepost for present and future generations of advertising professionals. ISBN 0-8442-3101-0. NTC Business Books. 320 pages.

✓ **The Lazy Man's Way to Riches**, Richard Gilly Nixon. One of the classic books originally written by Joe Karbo, the mail order legend, whose ad we feature in Chapter 24 of this book. This completely revised edition covers the spiritual and motivational aspects involved in making a success of yourself and starting a successful business. Using a commonsense approach, this book combines motivational exercises to build self-esteem with worksheets to define your goals. Then it gives you a moneymaking guide to success in mail order. Very well done and a help to any beginner in the direct marketing business, or any business for that matter. ISBN 0-14-024936-2. Penguin Books. 385 pages.

✓ **Influence: The Psychology of Persuasion**, Robert B. Cialdini, Ph.D. A great book for understanding the tools of influence at work in today's marketplace. Cialdini takes us through a journey exploring some of the very subtle ways to influence a customer, a loved one or even the mass market with many of the techniques he's tested and personally used. As a consultant to many of the Fortune 500 companies, Cialdini's wisdom and insights will help amplify your marketing knowledge. ISBN 0-688-12816-5. Quill. 325 pages.

Confessions of an Advertising Man, David Ogilvy. I read this classic when I first started my career in advertising in the '60s and it has been an influence ever since. Ogilvy strongly believed in the disciplines direct marketers utilized to ply their craft. Much of his knowledge and wisdom was acquired from being a student of direct marketing. As a brilliant adman he created great advertising for such clients as Rolls-Royce, Sears, Campbell's Soup and IBM. He was also responsible for creating campaigns for the governments of Britain, France and the United States. ISBN 0-8442-3711-6. NTC/Contemporary. 170 pages.

Positioning: The Battle for Your Mind, Al Ries and Jack Trout. The concept sparked a revolution in advertising and it is also very important in direct marketing. You've got to find that unique selling proposition—that big idea that will position your product or service to outclass and outsmart the competition. Ries and Trout show you how with many lessons that relate to direct marketing. ISBN 0-446-34794-9. Warner Books. 220 pages.

The 22 Immutable Laws of Marketing, Al Ries and Jack Trout. A very interesting and easy-to-read book on the 22 laws that every marketing person should learn. Each of the laws presents a conclusion based on both disasters and successes observed by the authors. Many of the biggest disasters were the results of flawed advice put forth by some of the most brilliant minds in marketing. So before you decide to market your next product, make this excellent book one of the first you read. ISBN 0-88730-666-7. Harper Business. 150 pages.

A Trademark Guide for Entrepreneurs, Robert E. Lee. You already know the importance of trademarks. This is a handy reference book that provides information you'll need to know about protecting trade names, trademarks and service marks. It's written in easy-to-understand language by an author with over 35 years experience in this field. He'll show you how to register trademarks with both state and federal offices, and teach you how to police the marketplace for possible infringers. He also explains the best ways to exploit the marks through assignments, licenses, and joint ventures. This is a very valuable book with lots of ideas and good guidance. ISBN 1-888206-05-5. Kent Press. 250 pages.

Being Direct, Lester Wunderman. An advertising legend, Wunderman was one of the pioneering fathers of direct marketing. The American Express Card, the creation of the Columbia Record Club and the high profile of L.L. Bean are just a few of the things he's been known for. But it was the visionary marketing techniques that he conceived and perfected over his long and brilliant career that transformed the advertising industry and will shape the interactive marketplace of the future. This is Wunderman's own story and the insights he shares so openly are well worth your reading. The book includes 19 principles used by all successful direct marketing companies. ISBN 0-394-54063-8. Random House. 315 pages.

✓ **How to Make Millions with Your Ideas**, Dan S. Kennedy. A very comprehensive book with many references. Worth the purchase for just the references, but there's a lot more. As a direct marketing consultant, Dan has been called upon for such a variety of tasks that he's become well versed in almost every phase of direct marketing. His book is packed with true stories and proven advice about ordinary people who began with just an idea, a simple product, or a fledgling business and wound up with millions. It talks about the methods and principles of dozens of successful entrepreneurs and some of the strategies they employed. It's a great current reference book to have in your library. ISBN 0-452-27316-1. Plume/Penguin. 270 pages.

Building a Mail Order Business, William A. Cohen. This excellent direct marketing book covers many aspects of legalities, product selection, copy and graphics, list selection and marketing on TV, radio and in print. Cohen calls it a complete manual for success and it indeed is very comprehensive, covering just about any topic you'll need to know to succeed in this business. It is well illustrated with examples shown throughout. Cohen covers many of the industry's entrepreneurs and their strategies, lots of history and plenty of examples. A very good basic book for the beginner or the advanced practitioner. ISBN 0-471-08803-X. John Wiley & Sons. 450 pages.

Reality in Advertising, Rosser Reeves. I have several copies of this book. It seems that whenever I would hold my seminar, somebody from the class would present me with a copy as a gift. I bought this book when it originally came out in 1961 and it is now considered one of advertising's greatest classics. In this excellent book, Reeves distills thirty years of experience in a very candid and incisive way. The book formulates certain theories of advertising, many quite new, and all based on 30 years of intensive research. His central concept throughout is that success in selling a product is the key criterion of advertising effectiveness. Lots of good stuff in this book. No ISBN number listed. Alfred A. Knopf. 160 pages.

Million Dollar Marketing Secrets, David L. Deutsch. Plenty of good ideas are found in this well-written book authored by a marketing consultant and excellent direct response copywriter. Any successful direct marketing copywriter has a lot of valuable information to share and Deutsch shares a lot in his self-published book. He reveals 20 powerful techniques which he guarantees will turbocharge your marketing abilities. At the end of each chapter he also lists resources where you can get more information to further your knowledge. This 200-page book can be purchased directly from Deutsch at (804) 379-6855.

Advertising Secrets of the Written Word, Joseph Sugarman. A comprehensive textbook that teaches you the step-by-step approach to writing advertising copy. The well-illustrated book provides insights into the skills it takes to be a great copywriter and what you can do to develop them. It then takes you into the thought process of ad creation, providing a very disciplined procedure that anybody can follow. A major chapter discusses the "psychological triggers" and how they can be used effectively to "cause prospects to exchange their hard-earned money for your product or service." The book also gives many personal stories, advertising examples and many of my own ads along with the reasons for their success or failure. ISBN 1-891686-00-3. DelStar Books. 350 pages.

Television Secrets for Marketing Success. Joseph Sugarman. A comprehensive review of selling your product or service through a home shopping channel, an infomercial or spot TV advertising. I talk openly about how I launched one of QVC's most successful promotions, how I created and built BluBlocker sunglasses into a nationally recognized brand name, and how I effectively used the TV medium to influence over 10 million customers to buy my products. Learn how to determine if your product is suited for TV, what margins you'll need, the importance of various elements in a commercial and helpful tips for breaking into TV—the most rewarding of the direct marketing disciplines. ISBN 1-891686-09-7. DelStar Books. 300 pages.

Success Forces, Joseph Sugarman. A book I wrote in 1980 about those forces that drive you closer to success and those that draw you towards failure. Knowing the forces and controlling them is the goal of any successful person and this book describes how to do it. The first part of the book is autobiographical and the last half contains the basis of the Success Forces concept. No longer available from bookstores but may be found at some libraries. Soon to be updated and reprinted. ISBN 0-8092-7061-7. Contemporary Books. 215 pages.

Other Book Resources

Out of Print: Some of the books listed here might be out of print and no longer available. If you can't obtain a copy and all else fails, try reaching Carl Galletti and his Hard To Get Books and Tapes club. He can be reached at (609) 896-0245 or fax him for his latest catalog at (609) 896-2653. You might even check him out on the web at: www.magic7/htg.

Hoke Communications: This is another resource for a number of good direct marketing books. Contact them for their catalog at (800) 229-6700.

Newsletter

The Gary Halbert Letter, Gary Halbert. This monthly newsletter on copywriting and marketing is a must read for anybody actively engaged in marketing and copywriting. Halbert is one of the nation's top copywriters and entrepreneurs and his newsletter is one of the most helpful around. Each issue contains a new concept or copywriting technique which can be easily implemented. Halbert's copy is both entertaining and fun and I personally look forward to my copy each month. Study and collect them as I do. To subscribe, call: (305) 294-8425.

Appendix F

Classic JS&A Ads

In this appendix you will find the ads that were especially significant in my marketing career for any of several reasons. They either were very successful, created a new business, started a new trend, were the first to introduce a new concept or technique or were important in learning a very valuable marketing lesson. The title of each ad is listed below followed by the date when it was first published and then a brief description of the ad and its significance.

During my seminars I would present these ads and explain how sometimes even the most minor change could affect response. I talked about everything from how the graphic elements of an ad can affect response to how an overall concept can be implemented effectively to break the rules of marketing and produce outstanding results.

There were many more ads presented in my seminars. Hundreds more. But the most significant ones are shown here. In addition, I have presented 16 other classic JS&A ads in my first book, *Advertising Secrets of the Written Word*. Those ads basically illustrated my writing style and are not repeated here.

You'll notice a big gap in the number of print ads I show here from November of 1979 until 1985. Although I wrote many ads during this period, most of them were placed in my catalog. There are a few reasons for this. Shortly after I ran my ad on the FTC I lost a lot of interest in running my business and stopped placing mail order ads in magazines. My time was being consumed by my fight. When I did have time, I focused on writing and producing catalogs and mailing to my mailing list and loyal customer base. It was a more efficient way of marketing my products without risking too much on running mail order ads.

Finally, after my disastrous appearance at the congressional oversight hearing (which I explained earlier in my marketing story starting on page 137 of this book), I realized I needed to really get my company jump-started as I was practically broke.

I used the catalog as a way to rebuild my business, and then seeing that I now had some pretty strong competition I decided to diversify into other types of products—specifically health-related items.

Finally, in 1985 I was running a successful MDR vitamin program and in 1986 I started running the ad that was going to launch JS&A to a new level—BluBlocker sunglasses. In 1987 I started advertising BluBlockers and MDR vitamins on infomercials—moves that took me right out of print and into television. Since that time, my focus has been primarily TV although I have had the opportunity to write a few print ads for products that I wanted to either introduce on QVC or run on an infomercial.

The ads are reproduced on the following pages in as large a format as possible for the size of this book. All of the ads shown here, along with many others, are reprinted in a workbook which will be available in late 1998. The workbook is considerably larger and allows for easier reading. If you are on our mailing list, we will advise you of the workbook's availability or simply call DelStar Books at (800) 323-6400 to place your name on a reservation list for the workbook announcement.

1. Announcing the Portable Calculator (February 1972) This was the introduction of the first pocket calculator and my first mail order ad. It sold very well and launched me firmly in the mail order business while creating strong demand at the retail level.

2. America's First Liquid Crystal Digital Watch (January 1973) This was the first nationally advertised digital watch which helped launch the revolution for these products. Interestingly, after the introduction of this watch, the light-emitting diode (LED) display became the hottest-selling watch product as the liquid crystal was more expensive, not as reliable and harder to read than the LED versions. Later the trend was reversed as the liquid crystal displays (LCDs) were refined.

3. The Truth About Pocket Calculators (January 1973) This was one of the biggest and most successful calculator ads in our history. When this ad was combined with a smaller ad inside *The Wall Street Journal*, the response almost buried us. It was the first of many all-text ads that I would run in the years ahead.

4. Up-date (October 1973) This was the first ad that carried

a toll-free number for credit card order taking. We used the toll-free number for a year before noticing any other company copying us. This ad and the use of the toll-free number started a major trend in direct response.

5. The Future of the Pocket Calculator (November 1973) This ad contained no pictures, no order vehicle—just text—and was one of our most successful calculator ads. People trusted us and bought in large numbers.

6. The End (March 1974) A turning point for our company and a major success. This ad sold a calculator that couldn't sell at retail but sold exceptionally well for us in mail order. It was the first ad we rolled out nationally in hundreds of publications.

7. Shaver Breakthrough (August 1974) A departure from our regular electronic products, this Remington shaver was a huge success and totally took us by surprise. And I didn't even shave.

8. Human Calculator (October 1974) This was a moderately successful ad that presented a very good product in a very clean and effective way. It was one of my favorite calculator ads and I adopted this clean format for many ads at the time.

9. Printer Breakthrough (October 1974) This was extremely successful and a major price break for printing calculators. The company was stuck with them and looked to us to close them out. We did the job in a few short months.

10. Halloween Sale (October 1974) This was the ad that was the subject of a marketing story in Section Two of this book and that produced one of the biggest responses in our history. It was the germ of a new idea on how to market products using a "random selection" process that was further developed in my later advertising.

11. Checkbook with a Brain (March 1975) Our biggest failure up to this date. Response to the product was marginal but took a nosedive as we headed into one of the worst economic recessions in a long time. We lost $250,000 but the casual observer thought we were making a fortune.

12. Digital Watch Breakthrough (May 1975) Digital watches were developing the reputation of being unreliable. We presented our Sensor watch as rugged and reliable and we even

offered a loaner watch if the Sensor failed for any reason. The ad was a huge success and firmly established us as a major supplier of both calculators and digital watches during this time period.

13. Pocket CB (September 1975) The citizens band radio fad was in full swing when we introduced this pocket-sized version of a CB radio. The fad allowed JS&A's PocketCom to become an incredible success selling over $10 million over a few years while the fad lasted.

14. Laser Beam Digital Watch (January 1976) A major success as we introduced the continuously backlit display which was made possible by the laser beam. This watch sold for over a year generating millions of dollars in sales.

15. The Picasso Tiles (February 1976) After several false starts, this ad ran only in *The Wall Street Journal* using a technique I pioneered in my Halloween Sale ad and not only generated a large mailing list but launched a new company. The ad broke even but the next mailing generated a 66% response rate and lots of profit.

16. New TV Game (February 1976) Pong was the first of a new generation of TV games from Atari Corporation. The ad was only moderately successful for me because the product was becoming available at retail, but it did introduce the concept of computerized games to my customers and was the first in a long chain of products that started a major new consumer electronics industry.

17. Hot (January 1977) Sounding like we were selling stolen merchandise, this ad ran in dozens of magazines and launched a new company that sold refurbished products from major brand-name companies. Called Consumers Hero, the new company had a membership club that sent out bulletins in monthly mailings. The ad was one of the best examples of the "slippery slide" concept that distinguished many of our JS&A ads at the time.

18. Telephone Answering Breakthrough (April 1977) Before the breakup of Ma Bell, Ford Industries sold their equipment only to the phone company. The phone answering unit I was offering was their first venture outside their normal channels of distribution. They failed to sell their product at retail, but we did an excellent job for them via mail order. I wrote the ad while

visiting relatives in France and it became a big success for JS&A during a three-year run.

19. Burglar Alarm Breakthrough (June 1977) This ad sold burglar alarms for almost four years and we were soon protecting more homes than many of the major burglar alarm companies. A very big success that provided steady sales and income and represented a much more low-key approach to selling these devices.

20-21. Home Library Computer (September 1977) This two-page ad offered one of the first home computers. Bally Corporation had designed their new computer and had given JS&A an exclusive to market it, but they failed to manufacture it on time. We lost sales, and Bally's failure to deliver resulted in JS&A filing a lawsuit against them, which we did not win. Later the judge in the case was sent to prison for taking bribes in several other cases, but nothing could be proved against him in my case. I often suspected during the trial that the judge was not treating us fairly, but authorities could not prove he took a bribe from Bally.

22. Home Blood Pressure Computer (November 1977) This was our first ad for a blood pressure monitor and it was a very big success. It was the first of a series of ads selling computerized health monitoring devices and created a new category for JS&A and other consumer electronic companies as well.

23. The Nose (November 1977) This moderately successful ad was offering a smoke detector during a period of time when smoke detectors were a commodity and available everywhere. The ad basically offered the same product that was available at retail, but by explaining the integrated circuitry and how it functioned, we added value to the unit and were able to sell it for $10 more than the retail price. This is a good example of mail order copy educating the consumer and thereby adding value to a product.

24. Jogging Computer (January 1978) This product created a fad in Japan but did not relate to the American market. We imported and sold it exclusively in the U.S., but it never really took off.

25. Printer Breakthrough (January 1978) Canon was stuck with 20,000 P10-D calculators that weren't selling at retail.

They approached me with it and presented what I felt was an outstanding product. Our ad not only sold out their inventory but created national demand for the calculator, forcing Canon back into production. It became a standard in calculator design and was sold for many years afterwards.

26. Miracle Fuzz (August 1978) This was the first mass-marketed ion generator and it sold exceptionally well over several years. It created a new ion generator category and was the first of several different units offered by JS&A. The ugliest part of the unit was the fuzz at the top, so we made it the highlight of the ad.

27. Dial Free (September 1978) The first mass-marketed telephone launched right after the Supreme Court allowed consumers to buy and plug in their own telephones. The Flip-Phone from GTE became a success and was one of the very first consumer phones offered by any company.

28. Micro TV Breakthrough (January 1979) Even when we weren't introducing the latest in technology, we could take an existing product, justify either a higher or lower price and then sell it quite successfully to the mass market. In the ad for a Sinclair TV, I took what was basically a closeout, justified its lower price and sold thousands of them at a $150 savings. It was quite a successful ad.

29. Cordless Wonder (August 1979) One of the first of the cordless telephones ever mass-marketed. Following the Supreme Court's decision to deregulate phone ownership, the cordless phone was the next major consumer product to hit the stores. This unit, one of the very first low-priced units, was crude by today's standards. We did very well but experienced a higher-than-normal return rate due to the high expectations of the consumer and the state of the technology at the time.

30. Ding Dong Digital (September 1979) My five-year-old daughter Jill was the hero of this ad for a Texas Instruments digital watch. To drive home the concept of a new product that was slowly becoming a commodity, very often what did the job was a simple story with a human twist. This ad ran successfully, further establishing our reputation as a major watch supplier.

31. FTC Revolt (November 1979) This was the opening blast against the FTC and their threats of imposing a fine against my company for failing to deliver products in accordance with

their mail order rule. The ad appeared in dozens of newspapers and magazines and resulted in over 10,000 letters of support and eventually an oversight hearing in Congress.

32. Bone Fone (November 1979) It was an exclusive radio product that we manufactured in Hong Kong and that did well when we started offering it. But then Sony introduced the Walkman and sales took a dive. So did the company we created to sell it. A painful experience that resulted in a major loss for me.

33. Magic Baloney (October 1983) This long-running ad was a great example of copy that grabs you and holds your attention until you finish the entire ad. We sold thousands of these and were responsible for establishing the brand name and building the manufacturer's business so that he was able to sell his company to Honeywell for $20 million.

34. Stop Taking Vitamins (October 1985) The approach was to first attract the attention of everybody who takes vitamins and then slowly convince them to try MDR vitamins. The concept worked and JS&A convinced thousands of customers to switch from the brand they were taking. We also developed a very nice continuity program and eventually produced an infomercial on the product.

35. Vision Breakthrough (October 1986) This ad was written very quickly and placed in a United Airlines catalog to test. The rest is history. This ad sold 100,000 pairs of BluBlocker sunglasses during a six-month ad campaign and was the catalyst for an infomercial which then started me on a direct marketing career in television.

36. Gasoline Breakthrough (June 1993) This ad offered The Pill—a new type of fuel conditioner that we introduced on QVC. We decided that a print campaign was a good way to supplement our exposure on TV and did well with the ad, although many of the automotive magazines refused to run it as they didn't believe the product worked—and if it did, they felt that their readers wouldn't believe it. We had scientific tests and plenty of evidence to prove that it did, but to no avail. The product continued to do quite well on QVC.

37. German Graphite Laser Blades (August 1993) This was another very good product that we first presented on QVC and wanted to test in print. The ad did well, but the complexities

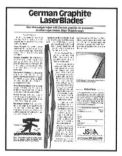

of having to stock dozens of different sizes and mounting brackets discouraged us from running this ad too often. Although the product was manufactured in Taiwan, the graphite used on the blades was German graphite and thereby gave us a good quality hook for the product.

38. America's Oldest Sunglasses (June 1995) This ad never ran. I sat down and wrote three ads for BluBlocker sunglasses and four new ads for The Pill—all in two days. After not having written an ad for a number of years, my creative production amazed even me. It was as if I had been incubating for a number of years and the power to write great ads had been growing even during my absence. All of the ads were unique, had good concepts and were very persuasive. But the auto magazines wouldn't take any of The Pill ads and the three BluBlocker ads were never run for a variety of reasons. I still have all three ads and may run them soon. One is reproduced here as an example of what my most current approach to layout and copy would look like if you saw it in a magazine.

In addition to the ads that I have presented here, there were a few other ads that I wrote during the same period of time for products totally out of the mainstream of my typical products.

One of them was for a sunglass product that helped you lose weight. You read it correctly. But I was cautious and decided to test a full-page ad in a city newspaper to see if it pulled any response. I didn't even want to take the orders, so I had all the fulfillment done by the eye doctor who brought me the idea. He had wonderful testimonials and impressive test results, but something inside me told me that this one was a program that had to be handled from a distance. I was right. After I wrote and ran the ad, the FDA came in and confiscated all of the doctor's glasses and closed him down.

Then there was a three-page ad for my seminars that I ran in 1979 in a few of the direct marketing publications. I ran a number of ads throughout the years for my seminar, but this ad was one of the most comprehensive in that it was a full three pages long.

And there were many other ads that launched companies besides the ads mentioned here or earlier in the text of this book. I started a company called American Adaptogenics to sell ginseng.

I started a company called Keepin' Cool and another one called Keepin' Warm, each offering products that—well, you guessed it—kept you cool in summer and warm in winter. But none of these companies lasted very long and the ads themselves were not that significant.

This appendix was written after the book you have just read was completed. After I finished, I quickly realized that without the other JS&A ads, my readers would be missing much of what my seminar participants had experienced. Hence this last appendix.

I hope you find these ads as fascinating as my seminar participants did. They should give you hours of enjoyable reading. Always remember that anything is possible and the more unusual the approach the greater your chances of a big success. Or even a complete failure. But even if you experience a few failures, you'll soon discover that it will only take one success to cover your losses and make you a small fortune. So always go for that unusual approach.

ANNOUNCING
THE WORLD'S FINEST PORTABLE CALCULATOR
FOR ONLY $179⁹⁵

It's the most exciting new breakthrough in electronics since the transistor radio!

As a result of new solid state circuitry, the Craig Corporation brings you the Mark II—an **American made** calculator that can add, subtract, multiply, and divide and easily fit into your coat pocket or briefcase. Even more exciting are the features that make it **far more advanced than any comparable calculator** selling for much more.

Features such as the weight—only **twelve ounces**. Such as the **16 digit input** with **8 digit display** or the **constant switch** that permits the multiplication or division by the same number without having to re-enter the constant for each calculation. Such as the **automatic cut-off**—a circuit that automatically dissolves the display and cuts off most of the power if you forget to turn off the calculator. In its cut-off position—the re-chargeable battery will last 40 hours between charges or five hours in constant operation. The letter "L" appears on the display to indicate that your battery needs recharging. And the size— only 1½" thin, 3" wide and 5 ⅛" long.

Features include: **a Clear Entry button** which clears a mistake without erasing your previous calculations; **a limiter system**—a microsecond delay that prevents the accidental entering of two digits simultaneously; **custom keys**— larger keys than a touch-tone telephone—and all packaged in a handsome two-tone housing. It's also easy to learn how to operate the Mark II since a clear, easy-to-follow instruction booklet is enclosed with each unit.

Even the numbers are new—easy-to-read digits designed for quick recognition.

At the office, the executive can place the Mark II next to his telephone and silently and quickly have all calculations right at his fingertips. Executives who use the Craig as their only

calculator find that the **savings in desk clutter** alone make it worth the modest investment. The Craig Mark II is a precision solid state instrument that can save you time, money, and yet **costs about the same as a good adding machine**. At home, the executive can prepare his notes for an important meeting, balance his family's checking account, or teach the decimal system to his children.

Slip the Mark II into your coat pocket or into your briefcase for a sales visit. Figure out the exact costs, margins or quantities right before your client's eyes. No need ever to postpone a decision because you didn't have the exact figures at hand.

Many of the uses for the Mark II came to us from people who own the calculator:

1. As the ideal device to carry with you when conducting a parts **inventory**.

2. As the perfect **in-flight calculator**. The undisturbed atmosphere of a plane trip is the best time to do your serious financial planning.

3. As the **ideally priced unit** to give all your salesmen, purchasing agents, or estimators. Think of the hours saved running to the company calculator.

4. As an important tool for **company presidents**—the most important man in your organization—the man whose decisions should be supported by the finest tools available—like a professional Craig Mark II portable calculator.

The executive, the engineer, the CPA, the surveyor, the insurance adjuster, the salesman, the comptroller, the stockbroker, the buyer—almost anybody in business can certainly use one. The benefits are numerous. The Mark II also makes an excellent gift for the man who has everything.

The Craig Mark II is a direct spin-off of the space-age on-board computers used in the recent Apollo flights. It's integrated solid-state circuitry, built by Texas Instruments, is dependable and designed for a service-free lifetime. In fact the **Craig Corporation guarantees the Mark II for a full year**.

Even under heavy usage the battery will last over 3 years without replacement. After the one year warranty period, any local calculator repair center can change your commercially manufactured rechargeable battery and there are two national Craig service locations that provide "Repair-By-Mail" service. When you purchase your unit—you get the assurance of **complete** calculator service even though the Mark II is designed to be service-free.

As part of a total package the Craig Mark II comes complete with soft imitation leather carrying case, recharger/AC power supply, instruction booklet, one year guarantee and shock resistant plastic carrying case for all the components.

The Mark II was originally introduced last year for $239.95. Thousands of units were sold. The same complete unit is now offered by JS&A for sale through the mail **only** for $179.95 complete with ALL components and with the option to charge the Mark II on your **Master Charge, BankAmericard or American Express** credit card account, PLUS there's a ten-day money back guarantee—you must be **completely satisfied** or return your unit for a full refund.

Please act today during the first day of our national introductory offer. Simply fill out and send in the coupon below and we'll rush your calculator to you by return mail immediately.

RUSH ORDER FORM

☐ Please rush me _____ complete Mark II portable electronic calculator(s) @ *$179.95 each with your one year guarantee and 10-day return privilege.

Name _____

Company _____

Address _____

City _____ State _____

Zip _____ Phone _____

☐ Enclosed please find my check for payment in full.

☐ Please charge my Master Charge, BankAmericard or American Express credit card account:

Number _____ Expiration _____
For Master Charge also give four numbers above name.

*Illinois residents subject to 5% sales tax. Add $2.45 for postage and handling. Sorry No C.O.D.'s

Send all orders to:
Order Fulfillment Section
Lock Box 725
Wheeling, Illinois 60090

JS&A

©JS&A, 1972

JS&A *Northbrook, Illinois 60062 ★ (312) 498-6900
*Speed Skating Capitol of the World

ANNOUNCING

Announcing the
Microma™360
the first real change
in telling time since
time began.

AMERICA'S FIRST
LIQUID CRYSTAL DIGITAL
QUARTZ WATCH

The era of the wristwatch computer has arrived! The JS&A National Sales Group proudly introduces the Microma 360—the nation's first liquid crystal digital watch—a solid state computer that electronically displays the exact time in digits, 24 hours a day, 365 days a year.

THE ACCURACY OF QUARTZ

Imagine the accuracy of quartz and the miracle of space-age electronics in one handsome time piece. The quartz crystal is the latest development in conventional watches. Quartz oscillates at a precise 32,768 oscillations per second. In the Microma 360 one micro integrated circuit containing over 1,000 tiny transistors translates the precise quartz crystal oscillations into an equally precise digital readout of time.

NO BUTTON TO PRESS

The Microma 360 has no springs, no hands, no jewels. There are no moving parts to run down, wind up or wear out. There is no button to press since the exact time is constantly shown on a liquid crystal display screen. To adjust the Microma 360 you insert a timing fork into the body of the watch and you advance the time either by the hour or by the minute—ideal for frequent travelers who must only change the hour while passing through time zones.

PROVEN IN 6 MONTHS OF CONSUMER TESTING

Prior to our national introduction approximately 5,000 Microma 360's were sold to consumers over a six month period. Their reaction was enthusiastic. But more important it proved that the Microma 360 liquid crystal digital watch system was accurate, reliable, and indeed a proven and tested instrument worthy of its unprecedented two year guarantee.

WATCH THE REACTION

Many people have heard and read about the liquid crystal digital watch. But few have seen one. Just wait for the questions and reaction when your watch is noticed. The 360 is a handsome time piece that says a great deal about the man who wears one. In addition, its low introductory price makes it the ideal gift for the man who has everything.

BATTERY OPERATED

The power source for the Microma 360 is a tiny commercially available silver oxide battery. The battery lasts approximately one year and can be easily changed by your local jeweler.

THE PRINCIPLE OF LIQUID CRYSTAL

Liquid crystal is a clear chemical substance that turns opaque when charged by currents of electricity. In the Microma display system, small electrodes are systematically arranged to form numbers. When a set of preselected electrodes is charged, numbers appear on the hermetically sealed watch display. The numbers, which change every minute, display the time continuously while a small colon (two dots) oscillates once every second.

TWO YEAR GUARANTEE

The Microma 360 electronic watch system is fully guaranteed for two full years. If your watch does not function properly, mail it to Microma for repair or replacement—free of charge. Although the 360 has proven to be relatively service-free, the ease of mailing a watch and the prompt Microma service-by-mail center provide the right combination to satisfy all your service requirements.

WHO IS MICROMA?

Microma is a subsidiary of Intel Corporation. Intel is recognized world wide as a leader in semi-conductor technology and is a well-rated firm—further assurance that your two year guarantee is backed by a substantial and reliable firm.

WHO IS JS&A?

The JS&A National Sales Group is one of the leading national distributors of space-age consumer and business related products. We were the nation's first company to introduce the electronic pocket calculator and we have since pioneered the introduction of many other widely accepted new products. Despite our size we insist upon complete customer service and satisfaction. Our descriptions must be accurate, our products must represent good value and you must be completely satisfied. You deal with people (not computers) and you receive answers to your letters and prompt refunds if you so request. The names of our customers

are kept confidential and are not sold for mailing lists. Our insistence on the highest standards of customer service is your assurance of complete satisfaction.

IT PAYS TO BUY FROM JS&A

Where can you get the opportunity to be among the first to buy and wear a totally new product yet have the option to return it if you are not absolutely satisfied? JS&A offers you a two week return privilege—if you are not absolutely satisfied with the Microma 360—return it for a prompt refund. It's just that simple. You can charge your Microma 360 on your American Express, Diners Club, Bank-Americard or Master Charge credit card account. Or send your check for $149.95 plus $2.50 for postage and handling. If you've been looking for that special opportunity to own a solid state digital quartz watch—here it is!

MODESTLY
PRICED AT **$149**^{95}

JS&A NATIONAL SALES GROUP
NORTHBROOK, ILLINOIS 60062 (312) 498-6900

January 1973

The truth about pocket calculators.

What you are about to read may surprise, enlighten or possibly help you. But one thing is clear—you'll have a greater understanding of what is really happening in the calculator industry. There is so much competition, price cutting and look-alike models that today even the most knowledgeable person is confused. We hope this article not only stops the confusion but provides you with the basic knowledge to properly evaluate the best calculator for your requirements. Our first step is to explain the most popular pocket calculator features.

FLOATING & FIXED DECIMAL POINTS

A floating decimal point is one that automatically moves to the correct position in your answer. For example if you divide $100 by 3.25 pounds to determine the cost of one pound, your answer would be $30.76923. The decimal would float five places to the left to give you the exact answer. If you set your calculator to a fixed two position decimal two things would happen. First your answer would drop all but the most significant two digits to the right of the decimal and secondly if your unit had automatic round-off, it would round off the third digit possibly raising the number to the left of it. An answer of $30.77 would therefore result.

CONSTANT FUNCTION

A constant function is a device for locking in a number that you plan to use in successive calculations to save you from constantly re-entering that number. To multiply a series of numbers by 2 you would enter two as the constant. Then when you enter 7, press the equal button, your answer is 14. Press 8, press the equal button and your answer is 16. The 2 remains locked in without its re-entry for each calculation. Most constant functions work on both multiplication and division.

THE DISPLAY

The display is the screen on which the numbers are shown. Displays on pocket calculators vary in size and composition. Each figure is generally composed of seven segments. They are arranged to form the number 8 when they are all illuminated. In some calculators each segment is broken down into three or four fine dots—others in solid lines. As a general rule—the larger the display read-out, the more power is consumed. That is why AC powered desk calculators have a considerably larger display than portable units. Manufacturers have used magnifying lenses for increasing the size of displays without requiring more power thus providing considerably larger read-outs for portable units. The displays most commonly used are the LED (light emitting diode) and more recently, the liquid crystal display. The LED display consists of segments that are self-illuminating whereas liquid crystal is a chemical that turns opaque forming numbers when charged by currents of electricity. The opaque formations are then illuminated by an outside light source. Both systems provide excellent service and legibility.

THE POWER SOURCE

There are two types of portable calculator power sources—rechargeable nickel cadmium batteries or throw-away alkaline batteries. Both have advantages and disadvantages. You can recharge nickel cadmium batteries up to 500 full charges without having to worry about battery replacement. However when you do replace batteries, you pay considerably more for them and they must be changed at a factory service center. In addition, frequent travelers must always bring their AC adapter/chargers with them on trips. With units that are not rechargeable you can throw away the old batteries and slip in new ones yourself.

THE KEYBOARDS AND COMPONENTS

If you think most keyboards are alike—you're right. Actually one manufacturer supplies most of the industry's keyboards. The other components are also supplied by only a few suppliers. In fact, many calculators contain practically the same components with the exception of the outer case.

THE CHIP

The chip in calculator terminology is actually the integrated circuitry that transforms what is entered on a keyboard to an answer on a display. The chip does the job of what formerly took thousands of transistors and is no larger than a dime.

THE COST OF BUILDING A CALCULATOR

The labor cost to assemble the average American made electronic pocket calculator is less than $2. Automation, and American know-how have practically eliminated the labor advantage Japanese manufacturers held for years.

THE TOTAL COST

The most expensive part of a calculator are the components whose costs have remained fairly stable. Components in a rechargeable pocket calculator cost a manufacturer between $60 and $80. He in turn must add his overhead, profit and then sell to a distributor. Based on the above you can see that calculator prices have pretty well bottomed out.

HOW PRICES VARY

Even if prices appear to go lower, look carefully at the features. A Japanese pocket calculator presently being offered for $59.95 has just six digits, no decimal and few other features. That same unit with all the features of a good pocket calculator would cost well over $100. But if all you need are six digits the unit is more than adequate. Another point of confusion is the look-alike unit whose price varies considerably. As an example, North American Rockwell manufactures desk calculators for both Sears and Lloyd's Electronics. Both calculators are very similar. Sears list price is $99.95 with occasional special sales at $89.95. But the Lloyd's unit sells for $69.95. Another example is a popular pocket calculator that sells for $119.95. The UDM-300 manufactured by Universal Data Machine sells for $95. Both have practically the same features with UDM providing a larger display yet there is a $25 price difference. Probably the most spectacular value is the JCE Mark II. With the exception of rechargeable batteries, the calculator has all the features of the popular units, plus an additional two and three position fixed and floating decimal and sells for $75—a full $45 less than current prices.

THE BRAND NAME MAGIC

Of course the magic of a brand name such as Sears might be worth an extra $20 to $40. Appearance also plays an important role. The manufacturer who spends thousands of dollars designing a handsome case can usually demand more for it. Always be careful of calculator close-outs. These units have either been discontinued or didn't sell well in the first place. In the fierce calculator price competition the real winner though has been the consumer . . . if he knows what to look for.

SERVICE

All pocket calculators must be serviced by their respective manufacturers. We know of no manufacturer that operates differently. No matter where you buy, your nearest service depot is generally your mail box. It is therefore important to know that the manufacturer is service conscious and will return your calculator as quickly as possible.

HOW TO DECIDE ON A GOOD CALCULATOR

To intelligently buy a calculator you should first analyze your requirements. It is both foolish and unnecessary to buy a $400 special purpose unit when a $75 calculator would be easier to operate and more practical. There are several ways to determine the type of pocket calculator best suited for your particular needs. Our first suggestion, however, is to forget completely about price. We'll tell you more about that later.

START WITH YOUR EYES

Your most important consideration should be your eyesight. If your eyesight is not perfect or if you use your pocket calculator a great deal, consider first a magnified display. Eye fatigue is not worth the few dollars you'd save by buying a calculator with a tiny display. Your next consideration should be the features. First, do you need a floating decimal? Do you need a constant? If all you do is add dollars and cents—you need neither.

THE POWER CHOICE

Next in importance is your power source. If you use your calculator a great deal in its portable mode consider rechargeable batteries. They generally add to the cost of the calculator but are a practical investment for the really heavy user. If your use is moderate to occasional, throw-away batteries are your best bet. Their ease of replacement makes them quite practical.

THOSE OTHER OPTIONS

Most calculators have a clear entry feature which permits removing a mistaken entry without removing the entire calculation. A battery saving feature causes the display to fade out if the calculator is left undisturbed for ten or more seconds. This help saves the battery power. The sign change feature permits you to change your answer from positive to negative or back to positive at the touch of a button. This is a great convenience if you wish to add or subtract an answer from a chain calculation. Incidentally, a chain calculation is the process of using one or more of the four functions in a series. For example: $2 \times 3 = 6 \div 3 = 2 + 3 = 5$. All pocket calculators do chain calculations yet practically every ad you see mentions this fact.

CHOOSING A SIZE

Most pocket calculators were not designed for your pocket. The most successful units fit into briefcases and measure 1½" x 3" x 5". They are also used frequently as desk units. There is a calculator manufactured by Summit International that actually fits in your pocket. It measures 1¼" x 2¾" x 4" (about the size of a pack of cigarettes). A truly pocket-sized calculator requires more engineering and assembly and generally costs more than the conventional "pocket" calculator. If you really need a unit that takes up the least amount of space or you use your pocket calculator constantly in its portable mode, the extra few dollars are well worth the convenience.

HOW MUCH TO PAY

Now that you understand the different features choose the calculator that best fills your requirements. The price should be your last consideration. It is silly to get less than you require for the sake of saving a few dollars. Don't forget, too, that a pocket calculator is tax deductible if purchased for the purpose of figuring out your income tax.

WHERE AND HOW TO BUY

There are three ways to buy. The first is through a calculator dealer or department store. You have the advantage of personally seeing, touching and making your decision on the spot. There are probably many reputable department stores in your area.

THE DISCOUNTER

The second is the big discounter. In the days when pocket calculators were selling for over $200, this was a good way to buy. Savings were evident. Nowadays with margins so low and the difference between the retail price and the discount price quite small, there is little to gain in buying from a discounter. After all, the discounter who makes just a few dollars on a sale has less of an incentive to issue a refund or provide extra customer service.

THE MAIL ORDER DEALER

The third way to buy is through the mail. A mail order company generally allows you two weeks to decide if you wish to keep a unit. This gives you the opportunity to thoroughly acquaint yourself with your calculator yet have the piece of mind in knowing that you can return it if you are not absolutely satisfied. Mail order companies keep their prices competitive and offer convenient credit card charge options. If you buy a calculator from a company in another state you'll also save on sales tax. Be careful though. Make sure the mail order company is reputable. A check with Dun & Bradstreet or the firm's local Chamber of Commerce can usually get you the information. A good mail order company should be financially strong for prompt refunds, they should answer their mail, and not exploit their customers by selling their names to others for mailing lists.

A NEW WAY TO BUY

The calculator market is confused. Price drops and look alike models have only added to the confusion. JS&A has tried to clear up many of your questions and help you understand what is really happening in the calculator industry. We also hope you consider buying your next calculator from us. We were the nation's first company to introduce the pocket calculator in 1971 and have pioneered the introduction of many widely accepted space-age products. We promise to provide honest descriptions, good value, prompt delivery and the option to return your calculator within two weeks for a prompt refund if you are not absolutely satisfied. In fact we go one step further. To practically eliminate any inconvenience to our customers we have made arrangements with United Parcel Service in practically all but the Western states to pick up your unit at our expense right at your door. JS&A customers are the most pampered in the nation. They have come to expect good service, honest value and the opportunity to be the first to purchase the really exciting new products of our decade. Isn't it time you joined us? **See our calculator ad in today's issue**

JS&A NATIONAL SALES GROUP
628 Michelline, Northbrook, Ill. 60062 (312) 498-6900

January 1973

342

You own a portable calculator.
It has become part of your right arm.
It's time to....

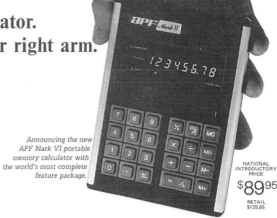

Announcing the new APF Mark VI portable memory calculator with the world's most complete feature package.

NATIONAL INTRODUCTORY PRICE
$89⁹⁵
RETAIL $129.95

Only the man who owns a calculator can fully appreciate all the features and value of the totally new APF Mark VI. And for the man thinking of buying his first unit—your timing is perfect.

APF built the Mark VI to accommodate every important calculator feature in the most practical size. The results combine the newest memory technology and every desired feature in one classic calculator value.

CHAIN MEMORY SAVES TIME

Store the answers from any calculation in a memory bank and automatically obtain the total of those answers. Chain memory then permits you to recall the total stored in the memory and use it in further chain calculations or as a constant . . . all without disturbing your original memory total. It's the ultimate achievement in memory logic.

CHAIN MEMORY OPENS NEW POSSIBILITIES

You can now figure out invoice extensions and add or subtract percentage discounts from your total in a few easy steps. You can compute compound interest, cost analysis, expense reports, stock and bond investments—easily and quickly. You'll be amazed at the savings in time. There are no numbers to write down and later re-enter and you enter the minimum amount of data thus avoiding the chance of error. It's like working with two calculators.

NEW PERCENTAGE SYSTEM

The new Mark VI percentage system lets you automatically add or subtract a percentage while still reviewing the percentage amount. For example, to add 5% sales tax to a $50 purchase, enter 50 then the plus key, the number 5 and press the percent key. $2.50 is displayed. Now press the equal key, $52.50 is displayed. In short, you are able to automatically review the percentage amount and by pressing one button, add it to your total. On a conventional calculator it would have taken eleven entries to obtain the same answers.

SUPER LARGE DISPLAY

The large 8 digit green display with zero suppression also has a negative balance sign, an overflow sign, a low battery indicator plus a memory indicator to let you know when you've got something stored in memory. The display also has a 25 second battery saving fade-out. If you forget to turn your unit off, it will automatically conserve 95% of its power.

FOUR FUNCTION CONSTANT

There's a separate four function automatic constant for addition, subtraction, multiplication and division. The constant is automatic. There is no constant switch to turn on and later forget to turn off.

MULTI-PURPOSE KEYS

Three keys serve dual purposes. The MR key (Memory Recall) not only recalls the total in memory but when you press the MR key and then the clear button, your constant appears on the display. The Clear button also acts as a clear entry key and the equals key automatically locks in the constant.

MANY MORE FEATURES

The APF Mark VI also has algebraic logic (you enter the negative sign before the number you wish to subtract as you normally think), a full floating decimal and a limited sign change feature (you can change the sign of numbers entered before you press the equal button).

DESIGNED FOR YOUR DESK OR YOUR BRIEFCASE

The Mark VI complete with batteries weighs only 12½ ounces and measures 1½'' x 4½'' x 6''—just perfect for your briefcase and large enough to make a great all-purpose desk unit. Or give this unique unit as a gift. Its value, features and appearance make it one of today's great product discoveries.

COMPLETE AND SOLIDLY BACKED

Each unit comes complete with 4 AA penlight batteries, an AC power supply, a black soft imitation leather carrying case, and detailed instructions on how to obtain the maximum use from your unit. There's also a one year warranty backed by JS&A. If anything goes wrong with your unit during the first year JS&A will replace it with a brand new unit. After the warranty period APF will repair your unit at any one of their national service-by-mail facilities. Although the Mark VI is built to last, it's still good to know that the manufacturer is service conscience—a very important consideration when you purchase any calculator.

EXPERIENCED MANUFACTURER

APF may have even built your unit. APF is one of the nation's largest manufacturers of private label calculators—calculators labelled with other company's names. They have recently decided to establish their own brand name identity similar to the Bowmar and Texas Instrument trend. So, if you've never heard of them, you will soon. APF is a financially strong public company eager to establish a reputation as America's value and service leader.

A NEW WAY TO BUY

The best way to buy a calculator is to first use it. JS&A's concept of a two week trial period gives you the opportunity to use the APF Mark VI in your home or office under your everyday conditions—not showroom conditions. After two weeks of actual use, you decide whether or not you want to keep it. If you decide to keep your unit, you have the first-hand knowledge that the Mark VI fits your requirements and the peace of mind in knowing that you've made the right choice. If you decide to return it, there's no obligation and you'll receive a prompt and courteous refund. In fact, we go one step further. To practically eliminate any inconvenience to our customers we will pick up your unit in practically all but the Western States, at our expense, right at your door. JS&A customers are the most pampered in the nation. They have come to expect good service, honest value and the opportunity to be the first to purchase the really exciting new products of our decade. Order your Mark VI at no obligation today.

Credit Card Buyers—Call (800) 323-5886 if you wish to phone in your order.
Illinois residents call collect.

UP-DATE
(TO A MEMORY UNIT)

HANDSOME STYLING

The handsome Mark VI is slightly angled to accommodate desk-top viewing. Its full-thrust keyboard and well-spaced keys make blind entry a breeze.

ORDER FORM

Please rush me _____ APF Mark VI calculator(s) at $89.95 each complete with batteries, AC adapter, carrying case, instructions and one year warranty. I understand that if I am not completely satisfied, I may return my purchase within two weeks for a prompt refund.

Enclosed please find my check for $_____ which includes $2.50 postage & handling.

*Illinois residents add 5% sales tax.

Mail all orders to: JS&A National Sales Group
628 Michelline, Northbrook, Illinois 60062

☐ Please charge my Master Charge, (also include four numbers above name) Bank Americard, Diners Club, or American Express (be sure there are 13 digits) credit card account:

NO. _____ EXP _____

SIGNATURE _____

NAME _____

COMPANY _____

ADDRESS _____

CITY _____ STATE _____

ZIP _____ PHONE _____

The JS&A National Sales Group is one of the leading national distributors of electronic calculators and other consumer and business related electronic products. Despite our size we insist upon complete customer service and satisfaction. Our descriptions must be accurate, our products must represent good value and you must be completely satisfied. You deal with people (not computers) and you receive answers to your letters and prompt refunds if you so request. The names of our customers are kept confidential and not sold for mailing lists. Our insistence on the highest standards of customer service is your assurance of complete satisfaction.

JS&A
NATIONAL SALES GROUP
628 Michelline, Northbrook, Ill. 60062 (312) 498-6900

October 1973

The future of the pocket calculator.

Facts, comments, predictions and an exciting offer from America's leading calculator marketing organization.

Exciting changes are taking place in the calculator industry. JS&A will discuss some of these changes and what to expect in the future. We will also make the most spectacular offer we've ever made . . . but first a few words about current calculator pricing.

LOOK OUT BELOW

Prices may appear to be dropping at a frantic pace with no bottom in sight. This is not entirely true. During the first quarter of this year prices stood at $99.95 for a good rechargeable pocket calculator with constant and floating decimal—a drop of $140 from the year before. That same calculator has dropped only $30 since then.

Prices may appear to be lower because some calculator companies with financial difficulties have been dumping product at distressed prices. Such a company offered us an 8 digit pocket calculator with a constant, floating decimal, carrying case and power supply for $26. We declined the offer. It is now more important than ever to make sure that the manufacturer is financially responsible and can back the purchase with service. Most calculators selling at retail now for $39 and $49 are also missing many of the important features such as constant and floating decimal.

APPLES, ORANGES AND THE $19.95 CALCULATOR

We predict that by this time next year a calculator will sell for $19.95. It will be blister packaged to sell on racks in supermarkets. It will have six digits with no decimal point and provide only the basic four functions. It will have a 90 day warranty and when the warranty expires the owner sends $10 to a service center with his old unit and gets a new one by return mail. In short, the era of the disposable calculator may soon be here.

THOSE GOOD OLD DAYS AT HEWLETT PACKARD

Hats off to Hewlett Packard. This remarkable company managed to hold its very own market position for almost two years selling its $300 to $400 technical calculators directly to the consumer. But watch for two changes. The first—competition. JS&A will shortly introduce an electronic slide rule that compares to the Hewlett Packard HP-35 for under $200. Secondly, we predict Hewlett Packard will market their units very shortly through normal retail channels.

MEMORY—THE MOST IMPORTANT NEW FEATURE INNOVATION

Memory has become such an important new feature that calculators without it are practically outdated. Not only is it a great time-saving feature but memory provides a new degree of flexibility that practically doubles a calculator's utility. Memory performs two basic functions: 1) as a means of storing a specific number that can be recalled for future use, 2) as a storage area for the total of answers to chain calculations. In both cases, the number in memory can be recalled yet the memory will retain that same number until you erase it.

TO STORE A NUMBER

Take for example the standard advertising agency mark up of 15%. The actual mark up percentage is 1.1764705 times the actual cost. Using memory you can store that complicated number and use your calculator for other computations always knowing that you can recall your mark up percentage whenever you need it—and even use it as a constant. Once you get accustomed to using memory your present calculator will appear antiquated.

AND LEADING THE PLUNGE

We must congratulate Texas Instruments. They have always led the way introducing the retail price drops first and usually taking their competition by surprise. They were also responsible for pioneering the development of miniature integrated circuitry that actually started the pocket calculator boom. Although they do not sell a basic pocket memory unit (other than their technical units) we predict that by next year they will and we hope they call on us to introduce it.

AMERICAN MADE WITH A SPANISH ACCENT

Thanks to automation, it costs only two dollars in labor to assemble a calculator in America. Intense competition however, has driven U.S. manufacturers to Mexico to do some of their assembly. America's three largest are there now. Although most components will continue to be manufactured in the U.S., the phrase "Assembled in Mexico primarily of American components" may be appearing on cases for the majority of "U.S. Made" calculators. We also predict that calculator assembly will eventually be simplified into five snap together components—the display, keyboard, integrated circuitry, power source, and case so that in two years the calculator owner can repair his own unit.

AND NOW ONE THOUSAND WORDS FROM OUR SPONSOR

In October of 1971 JS&A introduced the nation's first pocket calculator—the Craig 4501, manufactured by Bowmar Instruments. Since then we have been instrumental in introducing every major calculator price and feature breakthrough and have accurately predicted both future trends and product directions. We are also committed to providing the nation's finest value and service.

TO NOBODY'S EMBARRASSMENT

We have purchased a quantity of calculators with chain memory at a very low price. The unit retails for $129.95 and is selling at a rock bottom price of $89.95 at a few discount stores. We have copies of recent ads to prove it. Our price to you is only $69.95 plus $3.50 (postage, handling and profit). To avoid embarrassing the manufacturer (who is aware of this ad), we are not mentioning his name for if we did, his present distribution would obviously be adversely affected.

THE MYSTERY CALCULATOR

Our mystery calculator has a large 8 digit florescent green display with a floating decimal, automatic add-on percentage system, four function constant plus all the best features of the other memory units. The most spectacular aspect of this unique product is its outstanding good looks and compact size. It outstyles every other product—even those near its retail price class.

GUARANTEED BEST BUY

If you purchase our unit and feel it is not the best looking most versatile feature-packed chain memory unit available—then return it and we'll promptly refund your money. And you have until December 31, 1973 to make that decision. An unparalleled trial period and a great opportunity to buy a chain memory unit with assurance in time for Christmas. Each unit comes complete with batteries, AC adapter/charger, carrying case, and an unconditional one year warranty backed by a financially responsible and service oriented firm. For the price of a basic four function calculator, you can now get a fully automatic five function unit with chain memory.

THE GROUND RULES

We are keeping our profit margins extremely low for this offer so we cannot accept phone orders, COD's, purchase orders or credit card charges even from our current customers. If you send us a self-addressed stamped envelope or postcard we will gladly mail you a descriptive flyer on the product. If you wish to purchase the unit now on our assurance of your complete satisfaction simply send a check for $69.95 plus $3.50 or $73.45 for each unit ordered to "Special Offer," in care of the address shown below.

There are no quantity discounts. At this price even dealers can easily sell this unit at $129.95 and realize a handsome profit. We cannot reveal the name of the manufacturer on the phone, the unit is not available for sale in any of our showrooms and it is a brand name we have not sold before. We of course reserve the right to withdraw this offer and return your check should we run out of product. Time is therefore of the essence.

WHY THIS UNUSUAL OFFER

JS&A feels an obligation to its customers to supply them with calculators at the lowest possible prices without upsetting normal channels of distribution. To advertise our memory unit at $69.95 we had to combine the most unusual calculator mail order offer ever made with the hope that you the reader would respond with trust and confidence in our integrity and selection. We won't let you down. If you presently own a basic four-function calculator and you're thinking of updating, or if you're looking for a gift—we urge you to buy our mystery unit. You'll have today's current technology at next year's prices. Order one at no obligation today.

JS&A NATIONAL SALES GROUP
628 Michelline, Northbrook, Ill. 60062 (312) 498-6900

November 1973

the End

A new memory calculator breakthrough means the end of the AC adapter, rechargeable battery and small display and the introduction of a new memory system.

$59⁹⁵
NATIONAL
INTRODUCTORY
PRICE
Sug. Retail $79.95

The world's first ambient light liquid crystal memory pocket calculator—the DataKing 800 manufactured by Rockwell International, can operate for one year on the same set of disposable batteries.

If you've been waiting for the world's most advanced memory calculator—your timing is perfect.

Powered by two inexpensive 9 volt batteries, the 800 will last almost one year on the same set of batteries or ten times longer than even the lowest drain pocket calculators. But there are several other very exciting new feature breakthroughs.

RECHARGEABLE VS DISPOSABLE BATTERIES

It all boils down to convenience vs savings. Rechargeable batteries cost roughly $3.00 per year to power the average pocket calculator. That isn't very expensive. But the calculator owner who wishes to recharge his batteries is always at the mercy of his AC adapter/charger. And the adapter 1) is always subject to malfunction, 2) is often heavier than the calculator and 3) requires AC power to drive it.

If you've ever been on an airplane when your calculator pooped out or if you have been unable to use your calculator because your AC adapter didn't work, you can appreciate the convenience of the disposable battery. But disposable batteries are more expensive—an average of about $4 to $7 to operate the average calculator per year.

The DataKing 800 costs roughly $1.00 per year to operate using readily available 9 volt batteries. Therefore no AC adapter is required nor is one provided.

BIG DISPLAYS VS SMALL DISPLAYS

The display is the biggest consumer of battery power in a calculator. The bigger the display, the more power required to light it. Sunlight can easily overpower the display's light-emitting elements making legibility impossible.

The DataKing 800 has a large easy-to-read liquid crystal display. When small electrodes, arranged to form digits, are charged by microcurrents of electricity, the liquid crystal turns opaque. The resulting numbers must then be illuminated by a light source to provide the contrast needed to read the display. The 800 employs a light-gathering prism that eliminates any need for an internal lighting system and consequently uses a mere fraction of the power required by other conventional calculators. And the brighter the room light, the easier it is to read—even in sunlight.

NEW CLICK-THRUST KEYBOARD

The DataKing 800 has taken the full-thrust keyboard feel and added a click to provide the world's first "click-thrust" keyboard. Not only do you get a very positive data entry feel, but your chance of false entry is greatly minimized by the unique widely-spaced keys.

NEW ACCESS MEMORY SYSTEM

Memory on a calculator is such an important feature that units without it are practically outdated. Memory permits you to store individual numbers or answers to calculations

in a memory bank and then recall the total of those numbers directly onto your display without erasing the total in your memory.

The DataKing 800 has the new access memory. You can now take any number on your display and divide or multiply your memory total by that number—all while retaining that same number on your display. No other calculator has this feature. For example, to add a number to memory, press "M" and the plus key. To divide a number into memory, press "M" and the divide key.

MANY OTHER FEATURES

Now that we've told you all about those revolutionary features, here are some additional qualities that make the DataKing the nation's unquestioned memory leader.

1) Easiest to use Even if the 800 is your first pocket calculator, you'll find it a snap to learn. The algebraic logic (you perform the functions as you think) makes it easy to perform chain calculations. The automatic constants on all six functions require no separate switch to turn on, and there's a separate memory-plus and memory-minus entry system.

```
COMPARED TO
TEXAS INSTRUMENTS
```

America's leading brand-name calculator is Texas Instruments. TI recently announced their new TI 2550 memory unit for $99.95. That same calculator is now outdated by the introduction of the 800. The TI 2550 uses rechargeable batteries and has a small display and the older chain memory system. Compare price, features, performance and dependability, and you can easily see why the DataKing is America's greatest memory calculator value.

2) The best percentage system To add 5% to a $50 purchase, simply enter $50, then press the plus key, the 5 key and then the percent key. The percentage amount of $2.50 is displayed. Then press the equal key—$52.50 is displayed. In short, you perform percentage problems exactly as you think for both addition, subtraction, multiplication and division.

3) The finest display The large 8-digit liquid crystal display with floating decimal has negative balance and overflow indicators. You can also clear any overflow condition and continue your calculations.

4) Shock resistant The calculator enclosure also eliminates the need for a carrying case and provides a high degree of shock resistance. The display and prism are recessed and thus protected by its rugged high impact resistant case even when accidentally dropped.

5) Handsome styling Rarely do you find so many outstanding features in a highly-styled calculator. The DataKing 800 measures only 1½" x 3½" x 6" and weighs only 10½ ounces. Other features include a clear entry system for memory or mistaken entries, zero suppression, and a full floating decimal.

You are no doubt familiar with Rockwell International and their approach to quality. The DataKing 800 is no exception. Although the 800 was designed to be service-free, your unit is backed by a one year warranty and DataKing's national service-by-mail facility. DataKing, Inc. is a well financed and established company and a leading consumer electronics firm—further assurance that your modest investment is fully protected.

JS&A is so convinced that the 800 is the best memory unit you can buy that we are making the following offer: try the DataKing 800 for a full month. Compare it with every other calculator on the market for features, value, keyboard—whatever. If you are not absolutely convinced that it is the finest calculator value ever offered, return it anytime within that month for a prompt and courteous refund. Truly an unprecedented offer.

EXCHANGE YOUR PRESENT UNIT

Want to exchange your old, outdated calculator for the DataKing 800 without losing too much money? We've got a way. After you are absolutely satisfied with your DataKing 800, send us your outdated unit. JS&A will then send it to a deserving school, nonprofit organization, or charitable institution who in turn will send you a letter of appreciation and a certificate acknowledging your contribution. Then use that contribution as a legitimate deduction on your income tax return. You'll be helping somebody in need, while justifying the purchase of the latest calculator technology.

TO ORDER BY MAIL

Each unit is supplied with batteries, warranty card and a thorough instruction booklet. To order the 800 simply send your check for $62.45 ($59.95 plus $2.50 postage and handling Illinois residents add $3.00 sales tax) with your name, address, city, state, and zip code to the address shown below. If you wish to charge the 800 to your Master Charge, BankAmericard, Diners Club, or American Express credit card account, call our toll-free number or send us a brief note listing all numbers on your credit card, expiration date, signature and telephone number. Pick up the phone and order your DataKing 800 at no obligation today.

CREDIT CARD BUYERS CALL:

(800) 323-5880
IN ILLINOIS CALL (312) 498-6900
Lines open until 11pm (C.S.T.)

JS&A
NATIONAL SALES GROUP
4200 Dundee Rd.
Northbrook, Illinois 60062

March 1974

Shaver Break-through

Remington's revolutionary new miniaturized shaving system has produced America's first space-age electronic shaving instrument.

The 7 ounce shaving miracle—the Remington F-10 electronic shaver. All chrome with soft leatherette side panels, the F-10 measures only 1" x 2 5/16" x 3 1/8"—smaller than a pack of cigarettes.

Space-age science invades the shaving industry

The exciting new Remington F-10 electronic shaver is so small it will fit in your pocket, so rugged it will shave the toughest beards and so portable it doesn't even come with a cord or recharger.

Using space-age shaving technology, Remington has produced a portable razor that actually fits in your pocket.

PRECISION QUALITY CONSTRUCTION

The F-10 is no toy. Its precision super-thin head contains over 1,800 tiny perforations. Through a new electro-forming process, each miniature perforation is funnel-shaped to give a slick, smooth and speedy shave. Remington's new powerful micro motor and power source combine to produce one of the outstanding product breakthroughs of the year.

THE HIDDEN RECHARGING SYSTEM

To charge the new power system, you simply slide out the hidden plug and insert your razor into any available receptacle. There is no recharger, charging cord or transformer to fuss with. And since one good overnight charge is all you need for a full week of shaves, you can use it practically anywhere.

FREE CARRYING CASE

You'll also be amazed at the quality construction and features of the high-impact carrying case that you get free with each unit. There's a built-in mirror, a self-contained cleaning brush and a snap-lock lid to fully protect your razor during transport.

The entire recharging system is built into the electronic shaver. To recharge, simply slide out the built-in plug and insert in any 110 volt electrical outlet. There are no cords, AC adapters, transformers or rechargers to fuss over.

A GREAT NEW IDEA

The Remington F-10 is a great way to spruce up on an airplane or in your car before an important meeting. Even if you own another shaving instrument the Remington F-10 makes the perfect alternate system for home or for travel.

WHAT A GREAT GIFT FOR THE MAN WHO HAS EVERYTHING

Imagine the surprise when you give the Remington F-10. One thing's for sure—he won't have anything like it because there is nothing like it available anywhere.

$**29**^{95}$ NATIONAL INTRODUCTORY PRICE
Future Retail $49.95

ONLY 4,000 UNITS WILL BE SOLD

JS&A has been selected as the company to introduce and sell the Remington F-10 until Christmas at its special introductory price. Only 4,000 shavers per month will be available for sale. So act quickly. Each unit comes with a 90 day warranty and a two week trial period. If you're not absolutely satisfied, return your F-10 within two weeks for a prompt and courteous refund.

The Remington F-10 will be one of the surprise purchases of your life. Order one during our limited offer at no obligation today.

TO ORDER BY MAIL

Each Remington F-10 comes complete with shaving head protector, cleaning brush, protective case and instructions. To order your unit simply send your check for $32.45 ($29.95 plus $2.50 postage and handling—Illinois residents add 5% sales tax) with your name, address, city, state, and zip code to the address shown below. If you wish to charge the F-10 to your Master Charge, Bank Americard, Diners Club or American Express credit card account, call our toll-free number or send us a brief note listing all numbers on your credit card, expiration date, signature and telephone number. Pick up the phone and order your Remington F-10 electronic shaver at no obligation today.

CREDIT CARD BUYERS CALL:
(800) 323-5880
IN ILLINOIS CALL (312) 498-6900

JS&A
NATIONAL SALES GROUP
4200 Dundee Rd.
Northbrook, Illinois 60062

© 1973, JS&A

August 1974

Presenting America's First
Human

Three major design breakthroughs and a one year insurance policy humanizes the answer to the four most common calculator errors.

CALCULATOR

You're human! You make mistakes. And finally a company has come up with a calculator that realizes this.

ERROR 1: Oops, I forgot to shut it off!

Ever forget to turn off your calculator? Chances are, even if you're careful, you've made that mistake. The Litronix 2220 actually turns itself off. After one minute of unattended use, a small integrated timing circuit causes the display to blink on for one second and shut off for three seconds, thus conserving power without affecting the data. Then after 15 minutes, it shuts itself off completely.

ERROR 2: Oops, I entered the wrong digit!

You're working a problem and you've entered 1.2356 when you wanted to enter 1.2345. With most calculators, you'd clear the entire last entry and start again. And you can do that with the Litronix. But the Litronix also has a backspace key which means you can backspace the number, digit by digit, and then enter the correct digits. In the example above, press the backspace key twice eliminating the 5 & 6 so you end up with 1.23 on the display. Then add the 4 and 5 to make 1.2345.

ERROR 3: Oops, I read the decimal wrong!

Look at where your decimal point is on your present calculator. It's probably nothing more than a pinpoint of light adjacent to one of the digits. Litronix has developed an eight digit display with a "digit-position" floating decimal. This means that the correct position of the decimal is in the center of a digit position and automatically separates the whole numbers from the decimals by the widest margin of any display. So there's no guesswork when it comes to reading your display.

LITRONIX L.E.D. DISPLAY

`1 2 3 · 4 5 6 7 8`

CONVENTIONAL L.E.D. DISPLAY

`1 2 3 . 4 5 6 7 8`

The Litronix "digit-position" floating decimal provides a clear distinction between the whole number and the decimal on the display.

ERROR 4: Oops, I dropped it!

You're stepping out of your car, your briefcase flies open and out falls your calculator onto the solid cement walk. No problem with the Litronix. Just pick up the pieces, mail it to Litronix and they'll send you a brand new one anytime during the one year warranty period. It's the first pocket calculator actually insured against accidents during its year warranty.

BUT THERE'S SO MUCH MORE

Now that we've told you about how we've humanized the electronic calculator, let's show you the other exciting Litronix features:

Easy-to-use The Litronix features algebraic logic which means that you perform the functions exactly as you think.

Four key memory The memory system has four separate keys for data entry. You can now do calculations on your display and store the answers in a memory bank recalling their total

The keyboard on the Litronix was patterned after the expensive Hewlett Packard unit and has a four button, color-coded memory system. Instead of the conventional on/off switch the Litronix has on/off keys.

without erasing what was previously stored in the memory.

Fast percentage system You perform percentage problems exactly as you think. For example, to subtract 5% from $50, enter $50, press the minus key and then the five and percent key. An answer of $47.50 is on your display. In short, only four sets of entries were required to get your final answer.

Floating negative sign The Litronix not only has a full floating decimal, but it has a full floating negative sign. This means that when the display shows a negative number, the negative sign floats directly to the left of the first digit. There is also a key that permits you to change the sign of your answer from a positive to a negative number or from a negative to a positive.

More hidden features The separate "on-key" replaces the standard "on-switch" thus eliminating a calculator's only moving part (a major cause of calculator problems). The decimal point always remains in the two position unless the entry or answer is greater than six digits. This makes the Litronix especially useful when computing dollars and cents.

The Litronix has a true automatic constant on all five functions and can do reciprocals, raise numbers to whole powers, and show overflow conditions. You can do invoice extensions, compound interest problems and it has many other business and scientific applications.

The new Litronix memory calculator has no moving parts, shuts itself off, backspaces, and floats a decimal like no other pocket calculator. It weighs 6 ounces and measures only 3/4" x 3 1/8" x 6 1/2".

$49.95
NATIONAL INTRODUCTORY PRICE
RECHARGEABLE: $59.95

Litronix is the world's largest display manufacturer, supplying over 40% of the world's calculator displays. Every component in your Litronix memory calculator is manufactured by Litronix—from the integrated circuit to the unique keyboard. And their advanced calculator display and circuit technology means that you'll be getting one of the most advanced memory calculators in the nation.

AVAILABLE IN RECHARGEABLE OR DISPOSABLE BATTERY OPTIONS

The Litronix 2220's introductory price is only $49.95 complete with carrying case and three disposable AA cell batteries. The battery-saving features and the low-drain circuit will give many hours of carefree use. Also available is an optional AC adapter at only $4.95.

The Litronix 2220R (the exact same unit) is only $59.95 and comes complete with carrying case, rechargeable batteries, and AC adapter/charger. If you use your calculator daily in its portable mode, the rechargeable version is the better option. Both units are backed by a solid one year Litronix warranty and a prompt Litronix service-by-mail facility.

JS&A IS AMERICA'S LARGEST SINGLE SOURCE OF ELECTRONIC CALCULATORS

If you own a Master Charge, BankAmericard, Diners Club or American Express credit card, simply call our toll-free number below or send us your check or money order including $2.50 for postage and handling (Illinois residents add 5% sales tax). Please specify the option you wish and we'll rush your unit out by return mail. If you're not absolutely satisfied, you may return your Litronix within ten days for a prompt and courteous refund.

IT'S ONLY HUMAN

Finally, one of the very best calculators you can buy is also easy-to-operate and totally worry-free. What a refreshing change! Why not pick up your phone and order one at no obligation today.

NATIONAL SALES GROUP
DEPT. 000   4200 DUNDEE ROAD
NORTHBROOK, ILLINOIS 60062
CREDIT CARD BUYERS CALL:
(800) 323-5880
IN ILLINOIS CALL (312) 498-6900 ©JS&A Group, Inc., 1974

October 1974

Printer Break-through

The revolutionary new Casio AS-P electronic printing calculator uses no ribbons or special paper and represents a major new printing calculator breakthrough.

The new Casio printing calculator with a new printing head and cartridge inking system spells the end of the mechanical adding machine.

$99.95
NATIONAL INTRODUCTORY SALE PRICE
Sug. Retail: $149.95

It no longer pays to buy an adding machine. The new Casio AS-P now makes owning a fully electronic printing calculator a very positive and practical idea.

Let's face it. The only drawback in those exciting pocket calculators is the lack of a tape to check your calculations. And because printing calculators were either too expensive, too cheaply built or behind technologically, it made sense to stick it out with a hand-held unit. But that's all changed with the AS-P.

The large full-thrust keyboard responds nicely to your touch making the AS-P one of the easiest electronic printing calculators to use.

Forget about ribbons. The AS-P employs a new cartridge inking system that permits you to use up to 100 rolls or thousands of feet of paper tape without worrying about changing ribbons. Simply slip in a new cartridge once a year or every 100 rolls.

Forget about special paper. The AS-P uses any standard adding machine tape. There's no special thermal paper required.

Forget about noise. The Casio is one of the best built and solidly designed printers. The sound-deadening system and mounting shocks reduce noise levels to a minimum. And the Casio doesn't annoyingly shut off as do many of the time delay units.

Forget about the poor printout. The digits on Casio's new Matrix printing head register in a solid large number with no dots or disjointed elements. You get truly the most legible printout in the industry.

Forget about the price. For $99.95 you can own a fully-functional, quality, breakthrough product for the cost of an adding machine.

BUT YOU'LL REMEMBER THE GREAT FEATURES

The Casio AS-P is a four function printing calculator that you can operate as easily as an adding machine. It can subtotal, show negative balance, give grand totals, clear errors and produce a clear sharp printout.

The AS-P has a decimal selector, permitting the selection of either a full-floating, zero, two or four position decimal. In the fixed decimal positions, you can either round off the digit beyond the displayed number or simply cut the last numbers off. There's also dollar mode—a switch that always keeps the decimal in the two position so you don't have to continually enter the decimal point when you're adding dollars and cents.

If you enter more than the eight digit capacity of the printer, the unit prints E on the tape and the unit will not operate until you press the clear key to clear the error. Even

The tape on the AS-P registers large solid figures actually easier to read than most conventional adding machines.

the paper roll position is unique. By placing the paper roll inside the basic unit, there is no conventional overhang—a great space-saving design feature.

The Casio's compact size, only 4 3/8'' x 9 7/8'' x 9 7/8'' and light 10 lb weight make it the ideal desk unit for both home and office. Now everybody in your office can own their own printing calculator thanks to the revolutionary features and price of the Casio.

JS&A is America's largest single source of electronic calculators and Casio is a major calculator manufacturer known for their quality products and dependable service. Although the AS-P was designed to be service-free, Casio's national service network stands behind every machine—further assurance that your modest investment is well protected.

ORDER BY PHONE OR MAIL

If you own a Master Charge, BankAmericard, Diners Club or American Express credit card account, you may call our toll-free number and order by phone, or mail your check for $103.45 ($99.95 plus $3.50 for postage and handling). Ill residents add 5% sales tax.

THE MAGIC OF THAT TAPE

It no longer makes sense to own an adding machine or desk calculator when you can own a fully electronic printing calculator with major feature breakthroughs at an unbelievable low price. Pick up your phone and order your Casio AS-P today.

**15 DAY FREE TRIAL
ONE YEAR WARRANTY**

JS&A NATIONAL SALES GROUP

DEPT. 000   4200 DUNDEE ROAD
NORTHBROOK, ILLINOIS 60062
CREDIT CARD BUYERS CALL
(800) 323-5880
In Illinois (312) 498-6900 ©JS&A Group, Inc., 1974

"Now everybody can afford their own printer."

October 1974

348

Halloween Sale

All treats and no tricks in America's most spectacular calculator sale.

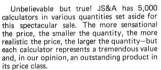

TEXAS INSTRUMENTS $9⁹⁵
BOWMAR $19⁹⁵ APF $29⁹⁵
KEYSTONE $39⁹⁵ DATAKING
KINGSPOINT $99⁹⁵

Unbelievable but true! JS&A has 5,000 calculators in various quantities set aside for this spectacular sale. The more sensational the price, the smaller the quantity, the more realistic the price, the larger the quantity—but each calculator represents a tremendous value and, in our opinion, an outstanding product in its price class.

JS&A is America's largest single source of electronic calculators. Our company introduced the nation's first pocket calculator three years ago and has since been the first company to break every price barrier, often months ahead of any other company. But prices have practically bottomed out, and with inflation and shortages, there may be no more major price drops. Even those $19.95 calculators are turning out to be more like toys than computers.

So in one unprecedented crowning sale spectacular, JS&A will reduce its inventory by breaking every conceivable price barrier and offering the greatest selection of the finest calculator products ever manufactured.

HERE'S HOW WE'VE ARRANGED THE SALE

We have commissioned a nationally recognized public accounting firm to objectively administer every aspect of this sale. Although their professional ethics prohibit us from mentioning their name, they are one of the nation's largest accounting firms and their name will be sent to those who request it.

All orders will be sent to a post office lock box and retrieved by the accounting firm on November 12, 1974. This firm will then supervise the opening of the mail to objectively insure that the rules of this sale will be strictly adhered to.

All envelopes will be placed on a table and selected and opened one by one until all calculators are sold. If your envelope is chosen and your first selection is sold out, you can have your second choice if it is still available. Envelopes will be chosen at random so everyone has an equal opportunity to get their first selection.

HOW TO ORDER

1. On a sheet of paper, write down the calculator of your choice. Make sure you indicate your first, second, and third choice if you wish to select alternates. You may order no more than 12 of each calculator model.

2. Include your check for the amount of your highest-priced selection. If your first choice was the $9.95 Texas Instruments unit and you listed a DataKing 800 @ $39.95 as your alternate selection, include enough money to cover the DataKing unit. In this manner you will have a greater chance of getting something from this sale.

3. Add a total of $3.50 to your check per entry (not per unit) to cover postage, handling and profit. The $3.50 will actually go towards paying the cost of this ad and the mailing of your selection if we fill your order. Illinois residents pay 5% sales tax on your purchase only.

If your envelope is chosen after we run out of all your selections, we will immediately mail back your check. If you obtain the lowest priced item of your selections, we will refund the difference to you.

SOME HELPFUL HINTS

1. Don't assume that because a price is so low, you'll have no chance of getting your selection. We have enough stock of even the lowest-priced merchandise to surprise quite a few people and remember, every entrant has an equal opportunity to receive the desired purchase.

2. Follow the rules carefully and choose alternate selections. You'll have a greater opportunity to obtain a bargain-priced calculator. There will not be a second chance, and this may possibly be the last sale of its type.

3. Christmas shopping? Order the maximum of twelve units. If you're lucky, you'll get all twelve.

4. Make sure you address the envelope properly. The correct address is:

**JS&A Halloween Sale
Lock Box 777
Northbrook, Illinois 60062**

5. Make all checks payable to the "JS&A National Sales Group, Inc." and endorse the check properly.

Remember: JS&A will not make any sale decision. All sales will be determined by an independent public accounting firm in a fair and objective manner.

This is not a contest, sweepstakes, or gimmick, but a truly unique consumer buying opportunity. Dealers may also order. Many of the products offered are well below factory costs and a great profit opportunity for any wholesale calculator dealer. All orders must be accompanied by a check for the full amount. No credit card charges, C.O.D.'s or purchase orders can be accepted.

If you feel that the calculator you receive is not the spectacular value we say it is, return it within a week for a prompt refund. There is no way you can lose.

JS&A has introduced practically every major new calculator price and feature breakthrough. It is with great pride, therefore, that we present the most spectacular calculator sale in our nation's history. Join us in this tremendous buying opportunity.

TEXAS INSTRUMENTS 2550 memory and percentage calculator. The TI 2550 is really our most spectacular value and our first $9.95 calculator. Each unit comes complete with carrying case, one year warranty, rechargeable batteries and AC charger. A $69.95 retail value, only $9.95

BOWMAR MX75 memory calculator. This automatic accumulating memory and percentage calculator currently retails for $69.95. This unit comes complete with AC charger, rechargeable batteries, carrying case and one year warranty. Only $19.95

APF Mark 14 This four-button memory and percentage calculator has a bright LED display, five function constant, and sign change feature. Truly one of the easiest and best memory calculators to operate. Priced to sell retail at $59.95, only $29.95

DATAKING 800 pocket memory calculator has an exclusive, large liquid crystal display, true access memory and an easy-to-operate percentage system. The DataKing 800 has the longest battery life of any calculator sold today and comes complete with batteries and a one year warranty. Considered a superior calculator at $59.95, only $39.95

KEYSTONE Exponent 1 Scientific memory and square root calculator is rechargeable. It comes complete with charger, carrying case and one year warranty. A great bargain for school or science. Only $39.95

APF Mark VII 4-function 8 digit desk calculator comes with built-in digital clock, floating decimal, constant, and a large display. A great gift idea only $39.95

KINGSPOINT SC40 10 digit scientific calculator has scientific notation, bracket memory system, square root, pi, exponential functions, trigonometric functions, rechargeable batteries and a one year warranty. Comes complete with charger and carrying case only . . $99.95

SCIENTIFIC 8-digit calculator features fully addressable memory, trigonometric functions, pi, square root and exponents. The unit comes with a one year warranty, rechargeable batteries, carrying case only $69.95

SPECIAL BONUS We've obtained thousands of a brand name electric shaver rated highest in a leading consumer testing publication along with a handsome travel case. The shaver is a heavy duty 110/220 volt unit with several unique features. Your cost for either the man's or lady's version is only $19.95

4200 DUNDEE ROAD
NORTHBROOK, ILLINOIS 60062
(312) 498-6900   © JS&A Group, Inc., 1974

March 1975

Digital Watch Breakthrough!

The new CDR display dramatically increases legibility and battery life and opens a new era of watch technology.

AT NIGHT   **IN SUNLIGHT**

Would you do this with your solid-state watch? Of course not. Practically all solid-state watches require care and pampering. Not the Sensor 770. You can dunk it, drop it and abuse it without fear during its unprecedented five year parts and labor warranty.

At night or during the day, the Sensor's large, constantly "alive" CDR display is clear and easy to read.

A glance at your solid-state watch won't give you the time. Sound incredible? If it's an LED (light-emitting diode) watch, you've got to press the button first. If it's an LCD (liquid crystal display) watch, you must have plenty of light at just the right angle.

Now there's a new solid-state display technology called CDR (crystal diffusion reflection) incorporating the best features of the LED and the LCD displays. You can easily and constantly read your watch under any light conditions without strain or inconvenience.

The new CDR display takes the properties of the field-effect liquid crystal display, puts a strong reflective substance behind two closely-alligned polarization lenses, and the resulting large digits can be read clearly from practically any angle. When engaged, an integrated light source illuminates the display at night. The Sensor's constantly "alive" high-contrast display makes legibility outstanding under **all** light conditions.

Press the button on the Sensor 770 and the date and seconds appear in large black numerals—easy to read in any light.

A WORRY-FREE WATCH

Solid-state watches pose their own problems. They're fragile, they must be pampered, and they require frequent service. Not Sensor! Here are just five common solid-state watch problems you can forget about with this advanced space-age timepiece:

1. Forget about batteries Sensor is powered by a single EverReady battery that will actually last years without replacement. In fact, if your battery fails during the first five years, we will replace it free of charge. A low-power indicator tells you when to change the battery one month in advance and you simply open the hatch at the back of your watch and replace the battery yourself.

2. Forget about water Take a shower or go swimming. The Sensor is so water-resistant that it withstands depths of up to 100 feet.

3. Forget about shocks A three foot drop onto a solid hardwood floor or a sudden jar. Sensor's solid case construction, dual strata

crystal, and cushioned quartz timing circuit make it the most rugged solid-state quartz watch ever produced.

4. Forget about service The Sensor 770 has an unprecedented five-year parts and labor unconditional warranty. Each watch goes through weeks of aging, testing and quality control before assembly and final inspection. Service should never be required, but if it should anytime during the five year warranty period, we will pick up your Sensor at your door and send you a loaner watch while yours is repaired—all at our expense.

5. Forget about changing technology The Sensor is literally years ahead of every other watch in durability and technology. But should Sensor's technology improve anytime during the next five years, you may trade in your watch for Sensor's newer model under JS&A's liberal trade-in policy.

COMPARED TO EVERY OTHER

The $275 Pulsar uses the LED technology which requires pressing a button each time you want to review the time. Even the $500 solar-powered Synchronar watch, in our opinion, can't compare with the Sensor and its 5-year warranty. And no solid-state watch can compare to Sensor's quality, accuracy, ruggedness and exceptional value.

PLENTY OF ADVANCED FUNCTIONS

Sensor's five functions give you everything you really need in a solid-state watch. Your watch displays the hours and minutes constantly. Depress a button and your watch displays the seconds and date constantly. There's also an AM/PM indicator. To adjust the time, insert a ball-point pen into the four-channel time-control switch. Each channel independently controls one time function. In short, you can change the hours without affecting the date, and the minutes without affecting the hours.

A pin points to the new decoder/driver integrated circuit which takes the input from the oscillator countdown integrated circuit and computes the time while driving the display. This single space-age device replaces thousands of solid-state circuits and provides the utmost reliability—all unique to Sensor.

Sensor's accuracy is unparalleled. All solid-state digitals incorporate a quartz crystal. So does the Sensor. But crystals change frequency from aging and shock. And to reset them, the watch case must be opened and an air-tight seal broken which may affect the performance. In the Sensor, crystal is first aged before it is installed, and secondly, it is actually cushioned in the case to absorb tremendous shock. The quartz crystal can also be adjusted through the battery compartment without opening the case. In short, your watch should be accurate to within 5 seconds per month and maintain that accuracy for years without adjustment and without ever opening the watch case.

STANDING BEHIND A PRODUCT

JS&A is America's largest single source of electronic calculators, digital watches and other space-age products. We have selected the Sensor as the most advanced American-made, solid-state timepiece ever produced. And we put our company and its full resources behind that selection. JS&A will unconditionally guarantee the Sensor—even the battery—for five years. We'll even send you a loaner watch to use while your watch is being repaired should it ever require repair. And our liberal trade-in policy guarantees that new watch technology will never leave you behind.

Wear the Sensor for one full month. If you are not convinced that the Sensor is the most rugged, precise, dependable and the finest quality solid-state watch in the world, return it for a prompt and courteous refund.

To order your Sensor, credit card buyers may simply call our toll-free number below or mail us a check in the amount indicated below plus $2.50 for postage, insurance and handling. (Illinois residents add 5% sales tax) We urge you, however, to act promptly and reserve your Sensor 770 today.

Stainless steel w/leather strap $99.95
Stainless steel w/metal band $109.95
Gold plated w/leather strap. $119.95
Gold plated w/metal band. $129.95

JS&A NATIONAL SALES GROUP

DEPT. BA   4200 DUNDEE ROAD
NORTHBROOK, ILLINOIS 60062
CALL TOLL-FREE. . . . (800) 323-6400
In Illinois call . . . . (312) 498-6900
© JS&A Group, Inc., 1975

Pocket CB

New integrated circuit technology and a major electronic breakthrough brings you the world's smallest citizens band transceiver.

SMALL ENOUGH FOR YOUR POCKET

Scientists have produced a personal communications system so small that it can easily fit in your pocket. It's called the PocketCom and it replaces larger units that cost considerably more.

MANY PERSONAL USES

An executive can now talk anywhere with anybody in his office, his factory or job site. The housewife can find her children at a busy shopping center. The motorist can signal for help in an emergency. The salesman, the construction foreman, the traveler, the sportsman, the hobbyist—everybody can use the PocketCom—as a pager, an intercom, a telephone or even a security device.

LONG RANGE COMMUNICATIONS

The PocketCom's range is limited only by its 100 milliwatt power and the number of metal objects between units or from a few blocks in the city to several miles on a lake. Its receiver is so sensitive, that signals several miles away can be picked up from stronger citizens band base or mobile stations.

VERY SIMPLE OPERATION

To use the PocketCom simply turn it on, extend the antenna, press a button to transmit, and release it to listen. And no FCC license is required to operate it. The PocketCom has two Channels—channel 14 and an optional second channel. To use the second channel, plug in one of the 22 other citizens band crystals and slide the channel selector to the second position. Crystals for the second channel cost $7.95 and can only be ordered after receipt of your unit.

The PocketCom components are equivalent to 112 transistors whereas most comparable units contain only twelve.

A MAJOR BREAKTHROUGH

The PocketCom's small size results from a breakthrough in the solid state device that made the pocket calculator a reality. Mega scientists took 112 transistors, integrated them on a micro silicon wafer and produced the world's first transceiver linear integrated circuit. This major breakthrough not only reduced the size of radio components but improved their dependability and performance. A large and expensive walkie talkie costing several hundred dollars might have only 12 transistors compared to 112 in the Mega PocketCom.

BEEP-TONE PAGING SYSTEM

You can page another PocketCom user, within close range, by simply pressing the PocketCom's call button which produces a beep tone on the other unit if it has been left in the standby mode. In the standby mode the unit is silent and can be kept on for weeks without draining the batteries.

SUPERIOR FEATURES

Just check the advanced PocketCom features now possible through this new circuit breakthrough: 1) Incoming signals are amplified several million times compared to only 100,000 times on comparable conventional systems. 2) Even with a 60 decibel difference in signal strength, the unit's automatic gain control will bring up each incoming signal to a maximum uniform level. 3) A high squelch sensitivity (0.7 microvolts) permits noiseless operation without squelching weak signals. 4) Harmonic distortion is so low that it far exceeds EIA (Electronic Industries Association) standards whereas most comparable systems don't even meet EIA specification. 5) The receiver has better than one microvolt sensitivity.

EXTRA LONG BATTERY LIFE

The PocketCom has a light-emitting diode low-battery indicator that tells you when your 'N' cell batteries require replacement. The integrated circuit requires such low power that the two batteries, with average use, will last weeks without running down.

EXECUTIVES · POLICE · MOTORISTS
SHOPPERS · HIKERS · FOREMEN

The PocketCom can be used as a pager, an intercom, a telephone or even a security device.

MULTIPLEX INTERCOM

Many businesses can use the PocketCom as a multiplex intercom. Each employee carries a unit tuned to a different channel. A stronger citizens band base station with 23 channels is used to page each PocketCom. The results: an inexpensive and flexible multiplex intercom system for large construction sites, factories, offices, or farms.

NATIONAL SERVICE

The PocketCom is manufactured exclusively for JS&A by Mega Corporation. JS&A is America's largest supplier of space-age products and Mega Corporation is a leading manufacturer of innovative personal communication systems—further assurance that your modest investment is well protected. The

The PocketCom measures approximately ¾" x 1½" x 5½" and easily fits into your shirt pocket. The unit can be used as a personal communications link for business or pleasure.

PocketCom should give you years of trouble-free service, however, should service ever be required, simply slip your 5 ounce PocketCom into its handy mailer and send it to Mega's prompt national service-by-mail center. It is just that easy.

GIVE IT A REAL WORKOUT

Remember the first time you saw a pocket calculator? It probably seemed unbelieveable. The PocketCom may also seem unbelieveable so we give you the opportunity to personally examine one without obligation. Order only two units on a trial basis. Then really test them. Test the range, the sensitivity, the convenience. Test them under your everyday conditions and compare the PocketCom with larger units that sell for several hundred dollars.

After you are absolutely convinced that the PocketCom is indeed that advanced product breakthrough, order your additional units, crystals or accessories on a priority basis as one of our established customers. If, however, the PocketCom does not suit your particular requirements perfectly, then return your units within ten days after receipt for a prompt and courteous refund. You cannot lose. Here is your opportunity to test an advanced space-age product at absolutely no risk.

A COMPLETE PACKAGE

Each PocketCom comes complete with mercury batteries, high performance Channel 14 crystals for one channel, complete instructions, and a 90 day parts and labor warranty. To order by mail, simply mail your check for $39.95 per unit (or $79.90 for two) plus $2.50 per order for postage, insurance and handling to the address shown below. (Illinois residents add 5% sales tax). But don't delay.

Personal communications is the future of communications. Join the revolution. Order your PocketComs at no obligation today.

$39⁹⁵ NATIONAL INTRODUCTORY PRICE

AT NIGHT

SUNLIGHT

Laser Beam Digital Watch

Never press another button, day or night, with America's first digital watch that glows in the dark.

Announcing Sensor's new Laser 220— the first really new innovation in digital watch technology.

It's ingenious, it's simple and it makes every other digital watch obsolete. Scientists have perfected a digital watch with a self-contained automatic light source—a major scientific breakthrough.

SELF-CONTAINED LIGHT SOURCE

The Laser 220 uses laser beams and advanced display technology in its manufacture. A glass ampoule charged with tritium and phosphor is hermetically sealed by a laser beam. The ampoule is then placed behind the new Sensor CDR (crystal diffusion reflection) display.

The high-contrast CDR display shows the time constantly—in sunlight or normal room light. But, when the room lights dim, the self-contained tritium light source automatically compensates for the absence of light, glows brightly, and illuminates the display.

No matter when you wear your watch—day or night—just a glance will give you the correct time. There's no button to press, no special viewing angle required, and most important, you don't need two hands to read the time.

Replace the battery yourself by just opening the battery compartment with a penny. Free batteries are provided whenever you need them during the five-year warranty.

A WORRY-FREE WATCH

Solid-state watches pose their own problems. They're fragile, they must be pampered, and they require frequent service. Not the Laser 220. Here are just five common solid-state watch problems you can forget about with this advanced space-age timepiece:

1. Forget about batteries The Laser 220 is powered by a single EverReady battery that will actually last years without replacement—even if you keep the 220 in complete darkness. In fact, JS&A will supply you with the few batteries you need, free of charge, during the next five years. To change the battery, you simply unscrew the battery compartment at the back with a penny and replace the battery yourself.

2. Forget about water Take a shower or go swimming. The Laser 220 is so water-resistant that it withstands depths of up to 100 feet.

3. Forget about shocks A three-foot drop onto a solid hardwood floor or a sudden jar. Sensor's solid case construction, dual-strata crystal, and cushioned quartz timing circuit make it one of the most rugged solid-state quartz watches ever produced.

4. Forget about service The Laser 220 has an unprecedented five-year parts and labor

warranty. Each watch goes through weeks of aging, testing and quality control before assembly and final inspection. Service should never be required. Even the laser-sealed light source should last more than 25 years with normal use. But if it should require service anytime during the five year warranty period, we will pick up your Sensor, at your door, and send you a loaner watch while yours is repaired—all at our expense.

5. Forget about changing technology The Sensor Laser 220 is so far ahead of every other watch in durability and technology that the watch you buy today, will still be years ahead of all others.

THE ULTIMATE ACHIEVEMENT

Other manufacturers have devised unique ways to produce a watch you can read at a glance. The new $300 LED Pulsar requires a snap of the wrist to turn on the display, but the Pulsar cannot be read in sunlight. The new $400 Longine's Gemini combines both an LED and liquid crystal display. (Press a button at night for the LED display, and view it easily in sunlight with the liquid crystal display.) But you must still press a button to read the time. All these applications of existing technology still fail to produce the ultimate digital watch: one you can read under all light conditions without using two hands. Until the introduction of the Sensor.

PLENTY OF ADVANCED FUNCTIONS

Sensor's five time functions give you everything you really need in a solid-state watch. Your watch displays the hours and minutes constantly, with no button to press. But depress the function button and the month and the date appear. Depress the button again and the seconds appear. To quickly set the time, insert a ball-point pen into the recessed time-control switch on the side. It's just that easy.

Sensor's accuracy is unparalleled. All solid-state digitals use a quartz crystal. So does the Sensor. But crystals change frequency from aging and shock. And to reset them, the watch case must be opened and an airtight seal broken which may affect the performance. In the Sensor, the crystal is first aged before it is installed, and secondly, it is actually cushioned in the case to absorb tremendous shock. The quartz crystal can also be adjusted through the battery compart-

The new exclusive laser-sealed tritium and phosphor light source is a thin solid-state tube that automatically illuminates the display when the lights dim.

Would you do this with your solid-state watch? Of course not. Most solid-state watches require care and pampering but not the Sensor. You can dunk it, drop it and abuse it without fear during its unprecedented five-year parts and labor warranty.

ment without opening the case. In short, your watch should be accurate to within 5 seconds per month and maintain that accuracy for years without adjustment and without ever opening the watch case.

STANDING BEHIND A PRODUCT

JS&A is America's largest single source of digital watches and other space-age products. We have selected the Sensor Laser 220 as the most advanced American-made, solid-state timepiece ever produced. And we put our company and its full resources behind that selection. JS&A will warranty the Sensor (even the batteries) for five full years. We'll even send you a loaner watch to use while your watch is being repaired should it ever require repair. And Sensor's advanced technology guarantees that your digital watch will be years ahead of any other watch at any price.

Wear the Laser 220 for one full month. If you are not convinced that it is the most rugged, precise, dependable and the finest quality solid-state digital watch in the world, return it for a prompt and courteous refund. We're just that proud of it.

To order your Sensor, credit card buyers may simply call our toll-free number below or mail us a check in the amount indicated below plus $2.50 for postage, insurance and handling. (Illinois residents add 5% sales tax.) We urge you, however, to act promptly and reserve your Laser 220 today.

Stainless steel w/leather strap $129.95
(Add $10 for matching metal band)

Gold plated w/leather strap $149.95
(Add $10 for matching metal band)

DEPT. WJ   JS&A Plaza
Northbrook, Illinois 60062
CALL TOLL-FREE .. 800 323-6400
In Illinois call . . . . **(312) 498-6900**
©JS&A Group, Inc., 1976

January 1976

Only 1250 sets of four special Picasso *les Artistes* tiles will be offered to a select group of collectors.

This advertisement in the Wall Street Journal will be the only one you will ever see on this special release.

This advertisement is being run for what may well be the most unusual limited edition offer ever made. And for good reason. First, your chances of purchasing it, even if you have the funds, are very remote. Secondly, the concept behind its issuance gives even art collectors, with meager means, the same opportunity to purchase the series, at its initial offering, as wealthy collectors. Finally, it is a ceramic tile series—an innovative new art form with reproductions by one of the world's most admired names in art—Pablo Picasso.

There have been no licensed coins or collectors plates issued with reproductions by Picasso since his death. In an historic decision, approval was granted for a special release of tiles, but under the strict supervision of the official Picasso licensing group. The price of seven dollars per tile was established or twenty eight dollars for the complete series.

Each ceramic tile in the four-part series was processed initially in England using the highest quality clay. The exact Picasso drawing is then silk-screened on the tile and then baked at 1862 degrees Farenheit until the image is firmly in the ceramic.

Several authentification steps are then taken. Each tile 1) is sandblasted on the reverse side; 2) has a 14 karat gold spot glazed in the tile itself; 3) is numbered and the thumb print of an agent of the official licensing group is imprinted and ceramitized on the reverse side. All tiles are registered, a certificate is issued, and the owner's name is kept on file in a registry. Any sale or transfer of the tile can also be registered.

UNLIKE ANY OTHER LIMITED EDITION

A limited edition is simply the production of a specific quantity of an item. Usually the molds or dies are destroyed after production to preserve the value and uniqueness of the specific art form. Franklin Mint, for example, normally limits the quantity by the number of participants who apply for the series before the registration date closes. The Picasso *les Artistes* series, however, is the world's first *Random Selection Collectors Series*—a series whose quantities will not meet the demand created for them necessitating a form of objective random selection to select participants.

To acquire the series you must fill out the coupon below and mail it to Battram Galleries. All applications will be entered into a computer and numbered consecutively. A public accounting firm will then generate a random number list equal to the number of participants. The first 1250 participants whose numbers correspond to the first 1250 numbers on the random list will be eligible to purchase the series. All applicants will be notified of the results. No money is required with your application and duplicate applications will be disqualified.

The first tile will be issued in April, 1976 and the remaining three tiles at three month intervals. If you are selected to receive the series, you will receive a reservation form insuring your participation in this exclusive offering.

When the licensing group licensed the Picasso *les Artistes* tile series, it did so with two provisos: that the offering company be prohibited from purchasing the series itself and not greatly profit from the initial offering.

To insure that little or no profit was made on the initial offering, the licensing group accepted the proposal of Battram Galleries to market the collectors tiles through a *Wall Street Journal* advertisement.

OFFERING DISCLOSURE

Gross Sales
Offering price of $7.00 per
tile x 4 tiles per set x 1250 sets $35,000
Costs
5 col. x 16'' advertisement
(1120 lines x $15.75 per line) . . $17,640
1250 sets x 4 tiles per set
x cost of tiles ($2.88 each) $14,400
Minus Costs $32,040
Gross Profit $2,960
NOTE: The gold embedded in each tile was contributed, at no charge, by the licensing group and is not included in the cost of the tiles.

The profit to Battram Galleries will probably be absorbed by the handling costs but the prestige of being associated with this new Picasso art form and the ancillary benefits are well worth our association.

> **THIS LIMITED EDITION IS DIFFERENT
> HERE ARE FOUR REASONS WHY:**
> - Your chances of acquiring the series from this advertisement are very remote.
> - We'll guarantee to buy back your entire collection anytime within five years.
> - Little profit, if any, will be realized from the sale of these tiles.
> - No money is required to participate.

For its participation in the initial offering, Battram Galleries will also be designated the official registry and transfer agent for the tile series. When title to the series transfers from one collector to another, if the collection is registered, a $5 registration fee is paid. Battram Galleries will also act as broker for the re-sale of the series and will receive a 20% brokerage fee for this service.

ABOUT THE SERIES

Picasso went through at least a half dozen identifiable periods in his prolific artistic career. In one of the phases, called the Classical period, he specialized in figures and narratives reminiscent of the art of ancient Greece and Rome. The four scenes portrayed on the *les Artistes* tiles are from that period. Each set of four tiles comes with a complete background explanation of the sketches written by nationally renown art critic and art authority Franz Schulze. In his contribution, Mr. Schulze describes the exceptional ease with which Picasso's line traces a common theme: The relationship of artist, model and art work.

The Picasso *les Artistes* tile series consists of four 6'' x 6'' square ceramic tiles with a green felt easel backing. The series can either be displayed in its own handsome presentation case on a counter with attached easel or hung on a wall. The square format, the fine craftsmanship, the exclusive nature and the limited distribution all add to its value but the name Picasso adds a dimension not available on any other similar art form.

FIVE YEAR BUY-BACK GUARANTEE

Battram Galleries will also buy back the collection from the original collector anytime within the first five years after issuance at the full original purchase price including the postage and insurance expenses incurred by the collector for the return of the collection.

HOW TO OBTAIN THE SERIES

All applicants may either send a post card or fill out the application form below and mail it to the address indicated. Remember, any applicant sending in duplicate applications will be disqualified. **Please do not send any money.** All applicants, including those selected, will be notified by March 10, 1976 and applications will not qualify if postmarked after February 29, 1976. No offer of any kind, whether it be for substantially more than the offering price or for special favors will be accepted. The Board of Governors of Battram Galleries, and suppliers and employees of the other JS&A Group companies will not be allowed to participate and will be disqualified if selected. If any buy-back request is made to Battram Galleries anytime within five years, we agree to advise the collector of the then current value of the *les Artistes* tile series and any other orders pending, as brokers for that series, before arrangements are completed for the return of the collection.

Battram Galleries further states that it will not substantially profit from the initial sale or offering of the tile series in accordance with the requirements of the Picasso licensing group and that any subsequent sale by Battram Galleries will be within the licensing provisions.

AN INVITATION TO PARTICIPATE

Battram Galleries extends an invitation to all of America's serious collectors to participate in this offering. If you have the honor of being selected, you will join an extremely small group of collectors who have distinguished themselves by both the process with which they were selected and the artistic value and achievement of owning a very limited Picasso reproduction. Your participation is invited.

INVITATION TO PARTICIPATE

I wish to be entered, at no cost or obligation, in the random selection process to determine those eligible for the Picasso *les Artistes* tile series.

Name _____

Address _____

City _____ State _____ Zip _____

Country _____ Phone _____

Signature _____

Battram Galleries, Ltd.
235 Anthony Trail
Northbrook, Illinois 60062   ◀ Mail
                                         Coupon

Battram Galleries is a **JS&A** company.

© JS&A Group, Inc., 1976

February 1976

ELECTRONIC BREAKTHROUGH!

New TV Game

Turn your TV into an electronic playground with a new computerized remote control TV game with a psychological twist.

Atari's new remote control, pre-programmed computer ping-pong game can be used with any size TV set—black and white or color.

How many fun things can your entire family enjoy? TV is certainly one of them.

Now through solid-state technology and remote control electronics, you can convert your TV into a ping-pong game so authentic, it even sounds like ping-pong.

This new electronic breakthrough, called Pong, automatically keeps score with its own scoreboard, automatically increases speed, and is psychologically designed to be quick, exciting, and a challenge for all age levels. In fact, with a little practice, it's even possible for an eight year old to beat her father.

FUN AND EASY TO PLAY

A ball is projected from the middle of the screen to one side of the playing field. The paddle is a narrow line on the screen which you move up and down by twisting a knob on the remote control panel. To hit the ball, you position the paddle to collide with the ball.

A speaker in the unit generates a different ping-pong sound when the ball is either served, hits the paddle, or is missed. And each hit of the ball at different angles can propel it in any one of seven different directions, thereby adding the element of "english" to each paddle stroke.

"I beat ya dad!" The screen displays an array of squares signalling the end of the match as one of the players reaches fifteen points.

To start the game, you just turn on your TV to channel three or four, switch on Pong, and press the start button. Your screen is suddenly covered by a playing field (in color on a color TV), and the ball is projected from the middle of the screen. Two can play or you can play by yourself. And, since Pong is on the TV, the whole family can watch and enjoy the action too.

DESIGNED WITH A CHALLENGE

The game is programmed to slowly serve the ball at a variety of different angles to the player who lost the last point and then speed up after four strokes. The ball will then speed up again after four more strokes. The double speed-up feature keeps Pong a constant challenge as you improve your skill.

A typical game goes quickly—normally between 2½ to 4 minutes. After each point is scored, the new score is flashed on the screen and then disappears as the ball is served again. The first player to reach 15 points wins, and a pattern of squares fills the screen to signal the end of the game. To play again, just press the start button.

NO SPECIAL INSTALLATION REQUIRED

Is Pong hard to install? Not at all. A special receiver/switch clips onto the antenna connection of any TV and you're ready to play. It's just that simple. You can also leave the switch permanently clipped onto your TV while you watch your favorite TV shows.

PONG WAS NO ACCIDENT

Pong was invented and built in America by Atari, an American company (with a Japanese name) that manufactures 65% of the nation's coin-operated electronic games—games that sell for thousands of dollars and must produce a profit for their owners.

Atari knew from experience what the public enjoyed in a game. It was their business to know. So Pong was designed with all the proven fun, psychological twists and appeal of the expensive coin-operated models.

DON'T CONFUSE PONG

There are other TV games on the market that appear to be the same as Pong. Don't be confused. Pong is the only game that uses a single, large-scale integrated and pre-programmed circuit. There's nothing to put over your TV screen to make it work, and it's completely portable. You can play it from as far away as fifteen feet and use it on other TV sets.

AND TALK ABOUT ABUSE

You can really abuse Pong. Its solid-state circuitry and high impact case mean that you can drop it, kick it, and abuse it, without fear. Pong should never require service, but if it does during or after the unit's 90 day warranty, mail it in its handy mailer carton to Atari's prompt national service-by-mail center.

Pong comes complete with four "D" cell flashlight batteries that give over 50 hours of fun. With its low voltage and the unit's fully-sealed, tamper-proof enclosure, there is absolutely no danger to you or your children. Even the FCC (Federal Communications Commission) has personally inspected and approved the game's amazing electronics. Pong will not cause interference to other TV sets on your block or in your house.

The automatic scoreboard displays the score in large numerals after a point is won and then disappears when the next ball is served.

AN INVESTMENT IN YOUR FAMILY

Pong will bring your entire family closer together with a game all of you can play whether you're five or ninety-five. Your children will spend less time watching TV shows and more time playing with their friends. Pong will teach coordination, speed and dexterity. The young, the elderly, the sick or the bed-ridden—all will find Pong fun. Pong is also the perfect gift, an unexpected executive toy, or an exciting way to entertain at parties.

The large-scale integrated circuit with 2,487 active transistors is the new computer component that makes Pong the nation's most advanced and easiest-to-operate TV game.

We feel so strongly about Pong, that we'll make this offer. Order Pong. When it arrives, give it a real workout. Play it with your family and friends. If you do not thoroughly enjoy it or if you do not think that it is a great investment in your family's entertainment, return it within two weeks after receipt for a prompt and courteous refund. There is no risk. No other company offers you the opportunity to personally try this product in your own home with no obligation. JS&A is America's largest single source of space-age products for business and pleasure.

To order Pong, credit card buyers may call our toll-free number below or send a check for $102.95 ($99.95 plus $3.00 for postage, insurance and handling) to the address shown below, (Illinois residents add 5% sales tax). You'll receive by return mail, one complete remote control unit, clip-on receiver/switch, batteries and instructions. An optional AC adapter for $9.95 is available. Additional receiver/switches for other TVs in your house are also available for $9.95. But don't delay. Start enjoying the fun of computer electronics at home on your own TV screen, today.

JS&A NATIONAL SALES GROUP
DEPT. WJ   JS&A Plaza
Northbrook, Illinois 60062
CALL TOLL-FREE . . 800 323-6400
In Illinois call 800 648-4990
©JS&A Group, Inc., 1976

February 1976

HOT

A new consumer concept lets you buy stolen merchandise if you're willing to take a risk.

We developed an exciting new consumer marketing concept. It's called "stealing." That's right, stealing!

Now if that sounds bad, look at the facts. Consumers are being robbed. Inflation is stealing our purchasing power. Our dollars are shrinking in value. The poor average consumer is plundered, robbed and stepped on.

So the poor consumer tries to strike back. First, he forms consumer groups. He lobbies in Washington. He fights price increases. He looks for value.

So we developed our new concept around value. Our idea was to steal from the rich companies and give to the poor consumer, save our environment and maybe, if we're lucky, make a buck.

A MODERN DAY ROBIN HOOD

To explain our concept, let's take a typical clock radio retailing for $39.95 at a major retailer whose name we better not mention or we'll be sued. It costs the manufacturer $9.72 to make. The manufacturer sells the unit to the retailer for $16.

THE UNCLE HENRY PROBLEM

Let's say that retailer sells the clock radio to your Uncle Henry. Uncle Henry brings it home, turns it on and it doesn't work. So Uncle Henry trudges back to the store to exchange his "lousy rotten" clock radio for a new one that works ("lousy" and "rotten" are Uncle Henry's words).

Now, the defective one goes right back to the manufacturer along with all the other clock radios that didn't work. And if this major retail chain sells 40,000 clock radios with a 5% defective rate, that's 2,000 "lousy rotten" clock radios.

CONSUMERS PROTECTED ALREADY

Consumers are protected against ever seeing these products again because even if the manufacturer repairs them, he can't recycle them as new units. He's got to put a label on the product clearly stating that it is repaired, not new, and if Uncle Henry had his way the label would also say that the product was "lousy" and "rotten."

It's hard enough selling a new clock radio, let alone one that is used. So the manufacturer looks for somebody willing to buy his bad product for a super fantastic price. Like $10. But who wants a clock radio that doesn't work at any price!

ENTER CONSUMERS HERO

We approach the manufacturer and offer to steal that $39.95 radio for $3 per unit. Now think of it. The manufacturer has already spent $9.72 to make it, would have to spend another $5 in labor to fix and repackage it, and still would have to mark the unit as having been previously used. So he would be better off selling it to us for $3, taking a small loss and getting rid of his defective merchandise.

Consumers Hero is now sitting with 2,000 "lousy rotten" clock radios in its warehouse.

Here comes the good part. We take that clock radio, test it, check it and repair it. Then we life test it, clean it up, replace anything that makes the unit look used, put a new label on it and presto—a $39.95 clock radio and it only cost us $3 plus maybe $7 to repair it.

Impossible-to-trace ★ ★ Guarantee ★ ★

We guarantee that our stolen products will look like brand new merchandise without any trace of previous brand identification or ownership.

We take more care in bringing that clock radio to life than the original manufacturer took to make it. We put it through more tests, more fine tuning than any repair service could afford. We get more out of that $10 heap of parts and labor than even the most quality-conscious manufacturer. And we did our bit for ecology by not wasting good raw materials.

NOW THE BEST PART

We offer that product to the consumer for $20—the same product that costs us $3 to steal and $7 to make work. And we make $10 clear profit. But the poor consumer is glad we made our profit because:

1) We provide a better product than the original version.
2) The better product costs one half the retail price.
3) We are nice people.

BUT THERE'S MORE

Because we are so proud of the merchandise we refurbish, we offer a longer warranty. Instead of 90 days (the original warranty), we offer a five year warranty.

So that's our concept. We recycle "lousy rotten" garbage into super new products with five year warranties. We steal from the rich manufacturers and give to the poor consumer. We work hard and make a glorious profit.

To make our concept work, we've organized a private membership of quality and price-conscious consumers and we send bulletins to this membership about the products available in our program.

Items range from micro-wave ovens and TV sets to clock radios, digital watches, and stereo sets. There are home appliances from toasters to electric can openers. Discounts generally range between 40 and 70 percent off the retail price. Each product has a considerably longer warranty than the original one and a two week money-back trial period. If you are not absolutely satisfied, for any reason, return your purchase within two weeks after receipt for a prompt refund.

Many items are in great abundance but when we only have a few of something, we select, at random, a very small number of members for the mailing. A good example was our $39.95 TV set (we had 62 of them) or a $1 AM radio (we had 1257). In short, we try to make it fair for everybody without disappointing a member and returning a check.

EASY TO JOIN

To join our small membership group, simply write your name, address and phone number on a slip of paper and enclose a check or money order for five dollars. Mail it to Consumers Hero, Three JS&A Plaza, Northbrook, Illinois 60062, %Dept. A I.

You'll receive a two year membership, regular bulletins on the products we offer and some surprises we would rather not mention in this advertisement. But what if you never buy from us and your two year membership expires. Fine. Send us just your membership card and we'll fully refund your five dollars plus send you interest on your money.

If the consumer ever had a chance to strike back, it's now. But act quickly. With all this hot merchandise there's sure to be something for you. Join our group and start saving today.

January 1977

Telephone Answering Breakthro

Let a new remote control answering computer free you from your next telephone call.

The new
Ford Code-A-Phone
1400 answering computer.

It's a telephone answering computer. The Ford Code-A-Phone 1400 has the first large-scale integration of solid-state componentry —a major change in telephone answering systems since the first mass consumer models appeared five years ago. This means more features, lower cost and greater dependability. Here are some of its exciting features:

Forget about tapes There are no tapes to buy. The Ford unit has a special polymer-based magnetic tape that will record over 25,000 phone calls without replacement. That's over five solid years of use. There are no cassette tapes to buy, wear out or replace.

Forget about microphones When you want to change or record your message, just press a red button, record your message and let go. The message (any length up to 20 seconds) will record and be immediately ready to play-back since the message tape does not have to recycle. There are no separate microphones or level controls since the built-in microphone automatically adjusts to your voice.

Forget about touching it You can adjust your unit to answer on either one or four rings. When the unit is set on four rings and you reach the phone before the 1400 answers, you will not activate the unit. But let us say you're outside or indisposed. No problem. Code-A-Phone will automatically answer after four rings. This means that your unit can always be "alive" in the four-ring position so you never have to remember to set it whenever you leave your home or office.

Forget about going home Just bring your optional remote control pager with you. If you want your messages while you're on vacation or away, call your number and the coded pager will remotely signal your unit to play back all your messages.

Forget about service If you've owned a telephone answering device for more than a year, there's a good chance that it's been in for service at least once. The Code-A-Phone, however, is solid state and built with the same heavy duty components used in commercial units. It should dependably stand up to years of heavy usage. (Ford Industries is the world's largest supplier of telephone answering equipment for the Bell system.) If service is ever required, there are over 200 authorized service centers plus a service-by-mail center. There's also a toll-free "Help-Line" number to call 24 hours a day for advice or suggestions, and your unit has a limited ninety day parts and labor warranty.

The entire printed circuit-board with its integrated circuits is easily replaceable and contains the "Brains" required to control the audio amplifier and tape transport system.

PLENTY MORE FEATURES

Code-A-Phone has a monitor feature—you can listen to the caller leave his message and pick up the phone to intercept the call. If you want to skip over a message on the tape, just tap a button and it fast-advances to the start of the next call. It has a selectable erase feature that lets you erase a specific message or the entire tape if you wish.

KNOW HOW MANY CALLS

With other answering machines, you never know how many calls you receive until you play them back. With Code-A-Phone you have a call counter—a device that displays the exact number of calls you've received when you arrive home. If you now own another answering machine, you can really appreciate this convenient and exclusive feature.

Hold the small pocket-sized remote-control pager up to any telephone in the world and you can playback all your messages.

Code-A-Phone is the first really versatile answerer that works equally well at home or in the office. It's perfect for the busy or working housewife who spends little time at home. And, if she's home and just plain busy when the phone rings, she can always call back later without offending the caller.

The executive can now leave his office, call from the field and get all his messages. An inefficient operator at a telephone answering service may offend your customers by putting them on hold. Code-A-Phone, however, takes your message quickly—without delay.

There are very few people who haven't left a message on a telephone answering machine, and callers really appreciate the convenience.

NO PHONE COMPANY TARIFFS

Code-A-Phone is equipped with an FCC-registered interconnect device so your unit is actually welcome on your phone line. The 1400 comes with a four-pronged plug so you just plug it into your phone jack. If you don't have a phone jack, just call your phone company and tell them you are purchasing an approved Code-A-Phone and that you want a four-pronged jack for your phone. They'll know exactly what you want and charge you around $12 for the installation, depending on where you live. If you have a multi-line phone, they can install a jack to tie into any or all of the lines you wish. There are no additional monthly charges.

STANDING BEHIND A PRODUCT

JS&A lets you use the 1400 in your home or office for one full month. Use it to screen your calls, take messages while you're gone or as a back up system when you're busy. Use the remote pager and retrieve calls while you're out. See how easy it is to change the message in seconds, and see how much it uncomplicates your life. Use it under your everyday conditions at home or at your office and then decide after one month whether or not you want to keep it. If you decide to keep it, you'll own the best. If not, return your unit for a full and prompt refund. There is no risk. Even if you already own a phone answerer, it would pay for you to see how much better the Code-A-Phone performs.

JS&A is America's largest single source of space-age products and a substantial company —assurance that your purchase is protected.

The Code-A-Phone comes in two models: the Remote Control unit for $259.95 called the 1400 and the same unit without the pager but with all the other features for $179.95 called the 1200. Simply select the unit you want and send your check for the correct amount to the address shown below. Credit card buyers may phone in their orders by calling our toll-free number below. (Illinois residents add 5% sales tax.) **There are no postage and handling charges.**

By return mail, you'll receive a Code-A-Phone complete with all connections and instructions (extra pagers are available for remote unit) plus your ninety day limited parts and labor warranty. The unit measures 3¼"x 8½"x 12" and weighs six pounds.

Code-A-Phone compares to units that sell for much more but do not have the simplicity and the advanced electronics. Don't be confused. Code-A-Phone is the finest telephone answerer you can buy at any price and is years ahead of all other conventional systems.

JS&A gives you everything you could possibly expect from a telephone answering system: 1) A unit years ahead of every other unit at a very reasonable price. 2) A service network that covers the United States with repair centers and free telephone assistance. 3) The chance to buy a unit in complete confidence, knowing that you may return it without being penalized with a postage and handling charge if it's not exactly what you want. You can't lose.

Computer technology has even touched the telephone answerer. Now is the best time to get the finest system available. Order your Code-A-Phone without obligation, today.

Dept. C-1 One JS&A Plaza
Northbrook, Ill. 60062 (312) 564-9000
CALL TOLL-FREE.... 800 323-6400
In Illinois call .... (312) 498-6900
©JS&A Group, Inc., 1977

Burglar Alarm Breakthrough

A new computerized burglar alarm requires no installation and protects your home or business like a thousand dollar professional system.

The Midex security computer looks like a handsome stereo system component and measures only 4"x 10½"x 7."

It's a security system computer. You can now protect everything–windows, doors, walls, ceilings and floors with a near fail-safe system so advanced that it doesn't require installation.

The Midex 55 is a new motion-sensing computer. Switch it on and you place a harmless invisible energy beam through more than 5,000 cubic feet in your home. Whenever this beam detects motion, it sends a signal to the computer which interprets the cause of the motion and triggers an extremely loud alarm.

The system's alarm is so loud that it can cause pain–loud enough to drive an intruder out of your home before anything is stolen or destroyed and loud enough to alert neighbors to call the police.

The powerful optional blast horns can also be placed outside your home or office to warn your neighbors.

Unlike the complex and expensive commercial alarms that require sensors wired into every door or window, the Midex requires no sensors nor any other additional equipment other than your stereo speakers or an optional pair of blast horns. Its beam actually penetrates walls to set up an electronic barrier against intrusion.

NO MORE FALSE ALARMS

The Midex is not triggered by noise, sound, temperature or humidity–just motion–and since a computer interprets the nature of the motion, the chances of a false alarm are very remote.

An experienced burglar can disarm an expensive security system or break into a home or office through a wall. Using a Midex system there is no way a burglar can penetrate the protection beam without triggering the loud alarm. Even if the burglar cuts off your power, the four-hour rechargeable battery pack will keep your unit triggered, ready to sense motion and sound an alarm.

ARRIVE HOME SAFE

There's personal danger in arriving home and finding a burglary in progress. And, if you surprise the burglar, you risk the chance of serious injury. With the Midex 55 protecting your home, you can open your front door with the confidence of knowing that no burglar lurks inside.

When the Midex senses an intruder, it remains silent for 20 seconds. It then sounds the alarm until the burglar leaves. One minute after the burglar leaves, the alarm shuts off and resets, once again ready to do its job. This shut-off feature, not found on many expensive systems, means that your alarm won't go wailing all night long while you're away. When your neighbors hear it, they'll know positively that there's trouble.

PROFESSIONAL SYSTEM

Midex is portable so it can be placed anywhere in your home. You simply connect it to your stereo speakers or attach the two optional blast horns.

Operating the Midex is as easy as its installation. To arm the unit, you remove a specially coded key. You now have 30 seconds to leave your premises. When you return, you enter and insert your key to disarm the unit. You have 20 seconds to do that. Each key is registered with Midex, and that number is kept in their vault should you ever need a duplicate. Three keys are supplied with each unit.

As an extra security measure, you can leave your unit on at night and place an optional panic button by your bed. But with all its optional features, the Midex system is complete, designed to protect you, your home and property just as it arrives in its well-protected carton.

The Midex 55 system is the latest electronic breakthrough by Solfan Systems, Inc.–a company that specializes in sophisticated professional security systems for banks and high security areas. JS&A first became acquainted with Midex after we were burglarized. At the time we owned an excellent security system, but the burglars went through a wall that could not have been protected by sensors. We then installed over $5,000 worth of the Midex commercial equipment in our warehouse. When Solfan Systems announced their intentions to market their units to consumers, we immediately offered our services.

COMPARED AGAINST OTHERS

In a recent issue of a leading consumer publication, there was a complete article written on the tests given security devices which were purchased in New York. The Midex 55 is not available in New York stores, but had it been compared, it would have been rated tops in space protection and protection against false alarms–two of the top criteria used to evaluate these systems. Don't be confused. There is no system under $1,000 that provides you with the same protection.

YOU JUDGE THE QUALITY

Will the Midex system ever fail? No product is perfect, but judge for yourself. All components used in the Midex system are of aerospace quality and of such high reliability that they pass the military standard 883 for thermal shock and burn-in. In short, they go through the same rugged tests and controls used on components in manned spaceships.

Each component is first tested at extreme tolerances and then retested after assembly. The entire system is then put under full electrical loads at 150 degrees Fahrenheit for an entire week. If there is a defect, these tests will cause it to surface.

PEOPLE LIKE THE SYSTEM

Wally Schirra, a scientist and former astronaut, says this about the Midex 55. "I know of no system that is as easy to use and provides such solid protection to the homeowner as the Midex. I would strongly recommend it to anyone. I am more than pleased with my unit."

Many more people can attest to the quality of this system, but the true test is how it performs in your home or office. That is why we provide a one month trial period. We give you the opportunity to see how fail-safe and easy to operate the Midex system is and how thoroughly it protects you and your loved ones.

Use the Midex for protection while you sleep and to protect your home while you're away or on vacation. Then after 30 days, if you're not convinced that the Midex is nearly fail-safe, easy to use, and can provide you with a security system that you can trust, return your unit and we'll be happy to send you a prompt and courteous refund. There is absolutely no obligation. JS&A has been serving the consumer for over a decade–further assurance that your investment is well protected.

To order your system, simply send your check in the amount of **$199.95** (Illinois residents add 5% sales tax) to the address shown below. Credit card buyers may call our toll-free number below. There are no postage and handling charges. By return mail you will receive your system complete with all connections, easy to understand instructions and a one year limited warranty. If you do not have stereo speakers, you may order the optional blast horns at **$39.95** each, and we recommend the purchase of two.

With the Midex 55, JS&A brings you: 1) A system built with such high quality that it complies with the same strict government standards used in the space program, 2) A system so advanced that it uses a computer to determine unauthorized entry, and 3) A way to buy the system, in complete confidence, without even being penalized for postage and handling charges if it's not exactly what you want. We couldn't provide you with a better opportunity to own a security system than right now.

Space-age technology has produced the ultimate personal security computer. Order your Midex 55 at no obligation, today.

JS&A PRODUCTS THAT THINK ®

Dept.   One JS&A Plaza
Northbrook, Ill. 60062   (312) 564-7000
Call TOLL-FREE 800 323-6400
In Illinois Call .... (312) 564-7000
ⒸJS&A Group, Inc.,1979

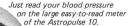

Just read your blood pressure on the large easy-to-read meter of the Astropulse 10.

Home Blood Pressure Computer

A new space-age measuring system lets you easily check your blood pressure quickly and accurately without a stethoscope.

The new Astropulse 10 lets you quickly read your blood pressure without a stethoscope and without even rolling up your sleeve.

The system is based on three micro-electronic circuits and a microphone transducer. The microphone picks up pulses in your artery, and the integrated circuits measure the pulses and relay this information to a meter which visually displays your two blood pressure readings. There is no expensive stethoscope required, no guesswork or complicated steps to follow.

EASY TO USE

Taking your own blood pressure is quite simple. Just stick your hand through a self-tightening velcro cuff, slide the cuff up your arm, pull the tab and attach the tab to the velcro material. The tab will stick automatically without loosening. Then squeeze the rubber bulb to inflate the cuff, and take your blood pressure readings.

When a doctor reads your blood pressure, he uses his skill and a stethoscope to recognize your systolic and diastolic readings. Now a computer can do this in the convenience of your home and on a regular basis.

The Astropulse 10 also flashes an LED signal and an audible tone at the two blood pressure readings to assist the hard-of-hearing or those with poor eyesight.

DOCTORS ENCOURAGE USE

Knowing your correct blood pressure is very important. Statistics show that as many as 25 million Americans suffer from hypertension, yet only half know about it. Hypertension results in high blood pressure, and high blood pressure usually goes unnoticed until other symptoms of hypertension occur—often too late to correct.

The Astropulse 10 is so easy to use that it encourages regular blood pressure monitoring —exactly what doctors recommend. Even if your health has been perfect, hypertension and blood pressure can occur at anytime.

SOLIDLY BACKED

The Astropulse is powered by a readily-available 9-volt battery supplied with each unit. The Astropulse uses solid-state electronics so service should never be required. But if service is ever required, JS&A's prompt

The Astropulse 10 was designed to take your own blood pressure in the privacy of your home. The cuff is easily tightened with the self-tightening bar and the velcro material. Just pull the flap and attach it to the cuff.

The entire blood pressure kit fits nicely in the carrying case supplied free with each unit. The carrying case measures 3½"x 4"x 7" and the entire system weighs only 20 ounces.

service-by-mail center is as close as your mailbox. JS&A is a substantial company selling advanced space-age products directly to consumers for over a decade—further assurance that your modest investment is well protected.

To order your Astropulse 10, simply send your check for $69.95 plus $2.50 for postage and handling (Illinois residents add 5% sales tax) to the address shown below, or credit card buyers may call our toll-free number below. By return mail, you'll receive your Astropulse 10 complete with a 90-day limited warranty, carrying case and blood pressure record book.

TEST IT YOURSELF

When you receive your monitor, see how easy it is to slip the cuff on your arm, tighten and inflate. See how easy it is to read. If for any reason you are not absolutely pleased with your unit, return it within 30 days for a full refund, including your $2.50 postage and handling. There is no risk.

Space-age technology has made it easy to know your own blood pressure. Order an Astropulse 10 at no obligation today.

Dept. WJ   One JS&A Plaza
Northbrook, Ill. 60062   (312) 564-9000
CALL TOLL-FREE.... 800 323-6400
In Illinois call . . . . (312) 498-6900
©JS&A Group, Inc.,1977

November 1977

TEACHING DEVICE · ARCADE GAME · MUSICAL INSTRUMENT · HOME COMPUTER

Home Library Computer

The handsome and highly styled Bally Library Computer is made of high impact clear plastic and imitation walnut with gold trim. It measures 5" x 11" x 15" and weighs five pounds.

The new Bally Library Computer provides more entertainment and services than man has ever dreamed possible from a single consumer product.

This is the story of an incredible product. So incredible that we know of no future consumer product that will have such a far-reaching technological impact on society.

The Bally Library Computer is a small console unit manufactured exclusively for JS&A that resembles a programmable TV game but whose computing capabilities resemble that of a mini-computer. This calculating power and its present and future programs will provide more convenience and benefits than any recent electronic product.

ELECTRONIC PRINTING CALCULATOR

Imagine the computer as a printing calculator with ten separate memories. You enter the data on the unit's keyboard, but instead of a paper tape, you use your TV screen to scroll out the answers similar to the credits on a movie screen. You can balance your checkbook and then double check your calculations by scrolling back to your first entry. By comparison, an electronic calculator with ten memories alone would cost what this entire computer costs—but there's much more.

A CHALLENGING TEACHING TOOL

Your child inserts a cartridge in the Bally console. Three random math table problems are then flashed on your TV screen. Depending on the speed and accuracy with which those problems are answered, the Bally automatically programs the computer with your child's math level. Problems in addition, subtraction, multiplication and division are then flashed on the screen for the next three minutes, and the computer continually adjusts to a level slightly better than the math level indicated by the previous three answers. The math tables, therefore, remain a challenge no matter how good your child becomes. Psychologists, who were consulted by Bally, helped design the cassette. They stated that the cassette should stimulate math learning and improve grades.

On the same math cartridge is a two player game called Math Bingo. It adjusts to each player's ability so a parent can play against a child or two children can compete against each other at their own math levels—both with an equal opportunity to win. You first answer a math table problem similar to the first exercise, and with a pistol-grip pointer you move a square on your TV screen to the correct answer position on your TV bingo card. The game involves both math skill and dexterity. Each game is totally different since the bingo cards have a million different possibilities. Scoring is constantly displayed, and a typical game lasts approximately three minutes. You can play as many consecutive games as you wish. However, to start the score over, you press the reset button.

FUN AND ACTION ARCADE GAMES

Picture nine baseball players running out on your TV screen to the sounds of "Take Me Out to the Ball Game" as you step up to bat. That's the scene with Baseball, the arcade cartridge that plays two teams against each other with play so real that you hear all the music, sound effects and see all the action. There are walks, balls, and such realism that the pitcher covers first base when a ball is hit to right field—just like the real game. There are double plays, walks and errors—all part of nine innings of Baseball. On the same cartridge are several paddle ball games but with a new twist. Players can move the paddle, not only up or down like most TV games, but sideways and diagonally.

The Bally circuit board contains 34 integrated circuits including a Z80 microprocessor. This package represents more computing power in the hands of the consumer than was thought possible this early in the history of micro electronics. The mass production of these components and circuit board has made possible a quantum leap in lowering the cost of what normally would be a very expensive system.

Other popular arcade games include, Sea Wolf, Red Barron, Panzer Attack (similar to Tank) and dozens of games only previously available at arcades. These same games cost arcade owners up to $2,000 each.

MORE VALUE PER FEATURE

Let's quickly review the features—an electronic printing calculator with ten memories, a teaching machine that adjusts to your child's math level and an arcade center that replaces about $10,000 worth of electronic arcade games with just a few cartridges. Use any one of these features and you could justify buying this unit—but there's plenty more.

With all its sophistication, the Bally Library Computer was designed to keep current with advancing computer technology no matter how sophisticated the development. Bally has provisions in its present system for expansion modules. These devices will permit you to: 1) draw directly on your TV screen with an electronic wand in 32 different colors and eight shades of each color, 2) compose, record and playback music on an electronic synthe-

sizer, 3) record your personal belongings and their value for security purposes and add or delete items while keeping the list in tact, 4) record all your phone numbers and then use the system to dial those numbers on your telephone, 5) play chess on the phone with another player and be able to see all the moves on your TV screen.

EXCELLENT BUSINESS TOOL

With these expansion modules, businessmen will be able to do all their bookkeeping functions, payroll, inventory control and billing. There will be printers, telephone modems and a variety of peripheral computer equipment that will turn your Bally Library Computer into a significant business tool. And, when used in your business, your Bally unit is depreciable like all your other capital equipment. Even large corporations can use the Bally for specific applications to avoid tying up their larger computer systems.

The Bally Library Computer will turn these incredible add-on features into reality in a planned program starting now. Each month, a new cartridge or accessory expanding the unit's capability will be announced. If you purchase your system from JS&A, you will be alerted to these new accessories by mail on a regular basis in advance of their availability and before any national announcement. You may then order the accessories directly.

Each new cartridge or accessory will offer you a new way to use your system—a way that would justify, by itself, the purchase of the entire system.

NOT JUST A TV GAME

Don't confuse the Bally Library Computer with the many inexpensive programmable TV games. The Bally computer is a powerful system using the Z80 microprocessor whose cost per byte (the measure of computer memory power) is even lower than a home computer. Yet it has 12,000 bytes of computer power in its most basic system and you are not just limited to teaching, music, entertainment or business applications. The Bally computer can be programmed to do anything any mini-computer can do. A programmable TV game at any price is (and will always be) just a programmable TV game. It cannot be expanded. The Bally Library Computer is actually a computer with a variety of expansion capabilities.

A COMPUTER IN EVERY HOME

This is the first time a full-scale computer has been offered to the consumer. The home hobbyist with his home computer started the revolution a few years ago. With the specific programs, software and accessories available from Bally, the age of affordable consumer computer ownership is here now.

INTERNAL TASK LIBRARY

The computer you buy now has within its 34 integrated circuits an internal library of over forty tasks that it performs. With such an extensive internal library, your computing power is already in the unit you buy. This also means that the Bally unit is a smart computer. (There are such things as dumb computers.) A smart computer can complete a function faster and more efficiently because it depends less on the data it gets and more on what it can already do.

SAFE FOR YOUR TV

The task library includes a built-in electronic timer which determines the end of a game or program by either score or elapsed time. It also times the arcade games and automatically turns off your unit and blanks out your screen if it is left on too long. Most TV set manufacturers have excluded sets that use TV games from warranty coverage because of the possible lines that appear on the screen from sets left on too long with the same picture. This is impossible with the Bally.

If you get a phone call in the middle of a game, you press the pause control which lets you freeze the action right in the middle of a play and blanks out the screen so you won't damage your picture tube.

The library has sound effects so that each arcade game is complete—from the sound of a baseball bat to that of a torpedo hitting a submarine. It has a math program capable of turning your unit into a scientific, statistical or engineering calculator with the addition of the appropriate cartridge. The library contains the capability of creating patterns on your TV screen, playing music, and accepting typewriter entries. It even has an index that displays everything in your library.

The cassette cartridges add between eight to thirty-two thousand additional bytes of computer power to the basic 12,000 byte system. The pistol grip arcade accessory can be used to play all the arcade games.

THE MAJOR BREAKTHROUGH IN BALLY'S COMPUTER

Its extensive internal library and the tremendous power in the computer are the big breakthroughs in the Bally unit. The internal computer has over 12,000 bytes with a minimum of 8,000 bytes in its cartridges. This puts more computer power in the hands of the consumer than six typical programmable TV games or an average hobbyist home computer. It actually has the computational capabilities of a mini-computer, and each time you add a cassette cartridge you increase that capability.

Good resolution on your TV screen is one of the end effects of so much computer power. By comparison, the best programmable TV game image is projected on a screen composed of 64 dots wide by 64 dots deep or 4,096 total dots. The Bally unit is 160 by 100 or 16,000 dots—four times more—so the Bally image is sharper and has finer detail, better resolution, smoother motion, and clearer letters for math or text applications.

SIGNIFICANT EXPANSION MODULES

The most significant expansion accessory will be the dual magnetic tape decks with an alpha numeric (typewriter) keyboard. With this accessory package, which will cost under $500 and be introduced by JS&A next year, you can record data and software programs and do everything you can do on any mainframe computer system within the data storage capacity of the Bally unit.

The Bally console keyboard is used to select specific programs from each cassette.

The implications of this add-on module are mind-boggling. First, it adds an additional 16,000 bytes of memory to the powerful 12,000 already in the basic system. Secondly, it provides not only more power and features than are presently available in any home computer, but it contains peripherals that would normally cost thousands of dollars extra and are considered accessories on all other mini-computer systems. Thirdly, it uses the BASIC language which is easy to understand. And finally, each cassette tape in the system will contain an additional one quarter million bytes of storage capability. With the tape decks and keyboard, the consumer will now own the equivalent of an entire computer system complete with peripherals, storage and memory.

HIGH SPEED PRINTER

A quality high-speed printer will be available soon. This will give you written records from your storage tapes. Store your most frequently called phone numbers, your income tax figures, your savings account deposits, the value of your stocks and bonds or a net worth statement. Then, when you need the information, press a button for a printed record.

DIAL-A-BARGAIN® ORDERING SYSTEM

Our technicians have programmed JS&A's main computer so you can use the Bally to access our computer directly when Bally's dual tape decks become available. With a special module and cassette, you will be able to 1) call our computer on our toll-free number, 2) place an order, and 3) find out when it will be shipped. Since you communicate directly with our computer, your order is processed immediately and can be shipped within a few hours after receipt. To do this, JS&A engineers developed a $100 hardware ordering package that will be sent free to those customers who order the basic unit this year.

THE BIG DIFFERENCE

When you order the Bally computer today, you are making an investment in the future. The basic unit you receive, without a single accessory, will provide more benefits than any other product of its kind in history.

When you buy an expensive product, you must be absolutely satisfied that you get the service and a solid company standing behind your purchase for many years to come. The Bally Library Computer is backed by a substantial company, Bally—in business since 1931 and now the world's largest manufacturer of coin-operated amusement games. JS&A is America's largest single source of space-age consumer products and also a

substantial company—further assurance that your investment is well protected.

A FRANK DISCUSSION OF SERVICE

The Bally unit is a solid-state computer with its electronics condensed on 34 integrated circuits—all hermetically sealed and all pre-tested for a lifetime of service. The Bally Computer is also self-diagnostic. We have developed a cartridge that lets the unit itself check every integrated circuit and every solid-state component and which displays any malfunction on your TV screen. Then all you do is send the circuit board or your entire unit to JS&A's service-by-mail center for prompt replacement. The cartridge will be sent free-of-charge to JS&A customers after you receive your unit.

Please don't think service requirements are common. They're not. But we wanted to assure you that service was such an important consideration in the Bally design that the unit practically repairs itself.

COMPLETE AS IT ARRIVES

Each unit comes complete with four pistol grips for use with the arcade and teaching games, an AC adapter (batteries are not required), three free arcade games, the calculator program, its internal library of tasks, complete easy-to-understand instructions and a one year parts and 90 day labor limited warranty—all for only $299.95.

The arcade games include 1) Gun Fight, in which two cowboys shoot at each other around cactus, covered wagons and other obstacles, 2) Checkmate, a one to four player game in which you build walls around your opponent to win and, 3) Scribbling, a one to four player game that utilizes the pistol grip to doodle different designs on your TV screen (in color with a color set).

A keyboard lets you use your printing memory calculator and a special scroll button lets you scan your entries up or down to review or check your calculations. You may also order with your unit the Baseball and Paddle Games cartridge for $24.95 or the Math Table/Math Bingo cartridge for $19.95. A bulletin will accompany your unit listing all the other cartridges and accessories that are available or will be available in the near future.

We feel so positive about this product that we will 1) not charge you anything for postage and handling and 2) give you a 30 day extended trial period to prove that the Bally is everything you expected after reading this article. When you receive your unit, reconcile your checkbook with the calculator, let your child practice with the math programs or have your entire family play the arcade games. After you have used the system under your own conditions and have personally experienced its fun and benefits, then decide if you want to keep it. If not, return it within our 30 day extended trial period for a prompt and courteous refund. You can't lose.

JS&A is marketing a product that will not only greatly influence the future of the computer industry, but will dramatically add consumer conveniences never before dreamed possible. Order your Bally Library Computer, at no obligation, today.

Unit pending FCC approval—allow 4 weeks delivery. Dial-A-Bargain is a registered trade mark of the JS&A National Sales Group.

JS&A NATIONAL SALES GROUP

Dept. PM One JS&A Plaza
Northbrook, Ill. 60062 (312) 564-9000
CALL TOLL-FREE.... 800 323-6400
In Illinois call .... (312) 498-6900
©JS&A Group, Inc. 1977

SMOKE DETECTOR WITH A BRAIN

The Nose

The JS&A fire and smoke detector acts as a space-age nose in the early detection of a fire.

A new computerized fire and smoke detector continually sniffs the air, measures danger and sounds a new alarm.

It's proven. A fire and smoke detector saves lives, and if you want to own the very best detector with computer circuitry and solid-state alarm, this advertisement is important.

The new JS&A computerized fire and smoke detector is a breakthrough. The unit's integrated circuit takes the dozens of other conventional detector components and reduces them to only a few—a potentiometer, one capacitor and one LED warning light. With fewer components there's less chance of failure. And the integrated circuit also interprets the content of the air and triggers the solid-state alarm.

NEW SOLID-STATE ALARM

The solid-state alarm replaces the electro-mechanical alarms on other fire and smoke detectors. The big advantage here is its reliability, the very low power drain, and the loud sound. Your alarm will sound louder longer, use less battery power, be more efficient, and your single 9-volt battery will last much longer.

The JS&A alarm produces a loud 85db sound at a distance of ten feet with only 12 milliamps of current. With electromechanical alarms, it takes 75 milliamps to produce an 85db sound or six times the power of the JS&A unit to do the same job.

The most dramatic difference is the start-up power required to trigger the alarm. In a standard smoke detector, the alarm requires approximately 300 milliamps during start up. In the JS&A unit only 12 milliamps—or 25 times less power. Even if your batteries are practically expired, the JS&A unit can still operate efficiently.

AUTOMATIC TEST PROGRAM

The unit also has a testing system that does more than just warn you when the battery gets low. The unit will churp every minute every day for one month to indicate that the battery needs changing. Even in an emergency the JS&A will still function perfectly during this churping period. You can then easily remove the cover and replace the 9-volt battery. There is also a test circuit to test the alarm. Just get a broom handle and touch the side of the unit and the alarm will sound—also perfect for simulating fire drills.

SENSITIVE SENSING SYSTEM

The nose or sensing system of the unit has two chambers. The first chamber is sealed and is used as a reference. The second is open and continually samples the air in the room.

Each chamber contains a space-age element called Americium. This element ejects small alpha particles of harmless ionized helium atoms which charge the air in both chambers. If smoke enters the open chamber, the charged particles decrease. The small computer circuit then measures the decrease or change in the charged particles and compares the change with the sealed reference chamber. Even if the charge drops one millionth of a percent, the computer will sense the change and trigger the alarm. The system's computer will, however, differentiate between a real fire and cigarette smoke unless the cigarette smoke is blown directly into the unit.

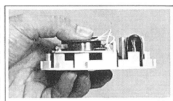

Only 4½ inches in diameter, the new JS&A unit has almost all of its components condensed on one integrated circuit. Shown above is the unit from a side view showing the solid-state alarm and the battery holder.

The encapsulated integrated circuit is shown above. This is the key to the breakthrough that makes the new JS&A detector one of the most reliable products on the market.

HIGH RELIABILITY

The JS&A smoke detector is so reliable that it passes the military performance specification 880. Each unit is so thoroughly tested and "burned in" before it is packaged that the unit also easily passes the most difficult UL217 test for fire and smoke detectors. We designed the JS&A unit for quality. It is not the cheapest unit on the market—but then we felt that reliability and confidence in an early

warning security system was more important than skimping to save a few dollars.

DON'T BE CONFUSED

There are two conventional fire detection systems available—ionization and photo electric. The JS&A detector gives you a new and better choice—the totally solid-state detector. It is the latest development in the computerization of previously conventional systems—a great boost for dependability and efficiency. Don't be confused. You cannot buy a better fire and smoke detector anywhere.

NO INSTALLATION REQUIRED

There is no installation required. Just attach the JS&A detector on your ceiling with pressure sensitive tape supplied with each unit.

The JS&A detector is small due to its few components and small integrated circuit. It measures only 4½" in diameter and 1" deep and weighs only 5½ ounces so it is less obvious than any other detector and it doesn't require the expensive alkaline batteries that other detectors require. An ordinary 9-volt battery will last over a year, whereas an alkaline battery will last almost two years.

JS&A is America's largest single source of space-age products—further assurance that your modest investment is well protected. We have been in business for over a decade providing advanced electronic products directly to consumers. Service should never be a problem. If, however, your tests indicate a defect, JS&A will replace your unit with a brand new one during our one year limited warranty.

To order your JS&A fire and smoke detector, credit card buyers may call our toll-free number below or send a check for $29.95 plus $2.50 for postage and handling (Illinois residents add 5% sales tax) to the address below.

Let the latest space-age computer technology protect your home with confidence. Order your JS&A fire and smoke detector today.

November 1977

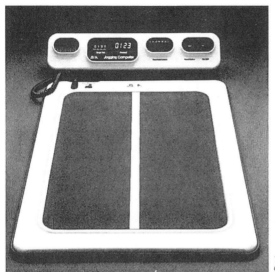

Jogging Computer

Make jogging fun in the privacy of your home with a new space-age indoor exercise system.

The JS&A Jogging Computer is a total system of physical fitness and conditioning.

It's a fact. You reach your physical peak at age 25 and your mental peak at age 40. From then on it's downhill. But it needn't be. A 50 year old who exercises regularly can be healthier and in better physical shape than the average 25 year old.

When you're physically healthy, you are alert and better able to handle stress. You are better motivated and just plain happier. Jogging can keep you in good physical shape.

THE ADVANTAGES OF JOGGING

Jogging as a regular exercise has gained in popularity because it does three things for you. 1) It improves the functioning of the heart, lungs, blood vessels and lymph glands. 2) It helps control your weight without resorting to starvation diets, and 3) It is one of the few safe, strenuous exercises that creates the exertion necessary for good physical conditioning.

A NEW JOGGING COMPUTER

There is now a new, fun way to jog. The new JS&A Computer is a solid-state system that lets you jog in place in the comfort of your own home. It's fun, easy to use and convenient.

You simply set the distance and pace you wish to run and press the start button. An audible beep tone sounds and you jog in place to its rhythm. Each stride is registered on a large LED readout in the control unit so you can see how far you've run.

You jog on a large pad with sensors which register each stride. The pad is designed to feel like grass or soft earth so you can run either barefooted or with gym shoes. The idea is to gradually increase your distance and speed each day to build up your endurance.

Getting yourself to start jogging is often the hardest step. That is why the JS&A Jogging Computer is an ideal system for both the beginner and the experienced jogger.

FOR THE BEGINNER

The first time you step on the Jogging Computer, you run at a pre-selected pace and distance for approximately five minutes. (A chart will show you which speed to select based on your sex and age.) You then take your pulse rate for one minute by touching your wrist. The pulse/rate chart determines the settings and distance you should run the next time you jog.

You could be in poor, average or good shape, and this simple five minute test will accurately tell you. Start the jogger at the distance indicated on the chart, and gradually build up a little each day. In just one week you'll notice the difference, feel great, have greater endurance, and you won't tire as easily. That is what's so nice about the system—how easily and quickly it puts you into better shape.

FOR THE EXPERIENCED

If you jog regularly, you know the many benefits of jogging. But you also know the disadvantages—all overcome by owning a Jogging Computer. For example:

Forget about the ritual You wake up early, drive to your favorite indoor track, change clothes, and you're ready to run. With the Jogging Computer, just step out of bed and start running. The time you save in preparing to jog can be substantial.

Forget about the boredom Running around a track can be quite boring. And if you count laps, how many times have you lost your count? With the Jogging Computer, you can forget about counting, as the unit does it automatically for you. You can concentrate on problems or take flights of fancy—all while you strenuously exercise.

Forget about the weather Even in summer, there are days when you can't jog outdoors. And in a daily exercise program, you must resort to the indoor track. Not so with the Jogging Computer. It's always there when you need it—portable and ready to operate.

Forget about jogger's heel If you've run on indoor tracks, you know the pain of jogger's heel caused by leaning in around those curves. Jogging in place is easier on your whole body and eliminates this common jogging problem.

BRING IT ANYWHERE

The Jogging Computer is powered by four "C" cell batteries and requires no AC power so it goes anywhere—on your patio, in the garage or basement, or at your office. The control unit can be propped up with its built-in easel or placed on a wall using the four foot expansion cord. It's portable, so after you've run a few miles, just turn it off and put it away. There's no large exercise device to take up space.

QUALITY THROUGHOUT

The JS&A Jogging Computer is all solid state, and the 17"x 22" pad was pre-tested to take years of constant, hard pounding under all conditions. Service should never be required, but if anything ever does go wrong, JS&A's service-by-mail center will have it repaired and back to you in a matter of days. Be assured that we stand solidly behind our product's quality, construction and design. JS&A is America's largest single source of space-age products. We've been in business over a decade—further assurance that your modest investment is well protected.

We suggest that you order the JS&A Jogging Computer and use it for 30 days. Jog each day when you get up in the morning or before dinner. Enjoy the thrill of feeling your endurance build. Experience the convenience and fun. See how much better you feel and how much sharper you think. Then after 30 days, measure your progress. If you don't find the JS&A indoor jogger a convenient and fun way to stay trim and healthy, then return your unit for a complete and full refund including the $3.00 charge for postage and handling. You can't lose.

Simply send your check for **$149.95** plus $3.00 postage and handling (Illinois residents add 5% sales tax) to the address below or call our toll-free number. By return mail, we will send you the complete jogging computer system with instructions, charts, personal score card and a one year limited warranty.

Start today on an organized physical fitness program using the latest in solid-state, space-age technology. Order your JS&A Jogging Computer at no obligation today.

January 1978

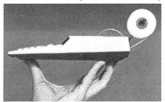

January 1978

August 1978

NEW CONCEPT

Dial Free

The Supreme Court of the United States, GTE, and a major new telephone breakthrough open the door to new consumer savings.

The new pocket-sized Flip-Phone T.M. telephone from GTE will save consumers millions.

The Flip-Phone flips open to reveal the keyboard and the privacy switch.

America's phone system is the world's greatest. No country can compare. But what has made our phone system even greater is the recent Supreme Court decision that permits consumers to plug in their own phones—phones that they can buy themselves.

We are now free to choose which phone we want to plug in. And that creates competition and competition usually results in lower prices, innovative products, and better service.

We now do have lower prices and a very exciting new product which we have selected as the best example of the new telephone ownership decision. The big breakthrough, however, is not the product itself, but an attitude. But more on that later.

THE NEW PHONE

It's called the Flip-Phone and it's manufactured by General Telephone and Electronics (GTE), a supplier of phones to other telephone companies. The Flip-Phone is a major breakthrough described by GTE as "the most advanced new telephone in the last ten years."

Most telephones contain a handset (the thing you talk over) and the base (where the electronics are located). GTE was able to condense the electronics on tiny integrated circuits which have been placed in the handset making the telephone base unnecessary.

THE MISSING MOUTHPIECE

Telephones contain large magnets which add to the handset's weight. The new Flip-Phone uses a very small and lightweight condenser microphone so sensitive that it picks up your voice even better than the conventional phone with its large mouthpiece.

And then there's the dial itself. It's gone. And in its place is a keyboard—a device that lets you tap out numbers without having to dial. This is a major breakthrough for three reasons: 1) It is a very fast way to dial. 2) It works on telephone systems that do not even accept *touch-tone* dialing, and 3) Even if you owned a *touch-tone* phone, you could plug in the Flip-Phone and not be charged for the extra service. You actually are able to push-button dial for free.

We're now going to tell you a few of the other new features, but the really big breakthrough, we'll tell you about later.

Privacy Switch Just flip a switch and you turn off the phone's ringer. It's ideal when you go to sleep, at dinner, or when you want privacy.

New Ring Most telephone ringers sound the same. The Flip-Phone emits an electronic warbling sound—a very pleasant tone.

New Cord Even the cord on the Flip-Phone is different. It's 14 feet long—twice as long as a conventional cord. One end is coiled and the other is straight. You can use either end to connect to your phone while the other end connects to the wall. And if your cord gets twisted, dirty, or plain chewed up, just unplug it and put in a new one. It's just that easy.

Low Cost The Flip-Phone costs only $49.95 which means that it will pay for itself quickly—not only in convenience, but with savings of up to $4 a month in some cities. When you determine the true cost of telephone ownership, you compare costs over a five-year period. In five years even a $2.00 telephone charge per month equals $120 or over twice the cost of the Flip-Phone telephone.

Small Size The Flip-Phone is the size of a large stapler. When you pick it up, a panel flips open revealing the touch-pad dial, and the panel acts as a guide to funnel your voice to the condenser microphone. The Flip-Phone is only 2¼" wide x 1¼" high x 7" long and weighs only seven ounces.

THE BIG BREAKTHROUGH

The really big breakthrough is not the Flip-Phone. GTE did indeed spend several million dollars developing the item, and we feel that it will be the single most important phone in America within a few short years. No, the real breakthrough is the change in attitude of the telephone companies. We can remember when even putting a telephone answering unit on your line almost caused you to lose your phone service.

TIMES HAVE CHANGED

The telephone companies are now so cooperative that they deserve great respect. After all, they lose money every time you plug in your own phone, so their cooperation in light of their loss must be commended.

And they have made connecting your phone easier than ever before. Remember those big four-pronged jacks? Now there's a small connector which the phone company installs for around $15 (depending on your city). Where can you find an electrician or a plumber to come to your home for $15?

If you want to plug in your own phones and don't have the modular receptacles, just call the phone company and see how courteous they are. Tell them that you are ordering a phone with a ringer equivalent of 1.2B, an FCC registration number of AB898Y-62927-TE-R, and that you want them to remove your phones and stop charging you for them. That's all you have to do.

They'll promptly send a repairman to your home to attach the modular connector for the Flip-Phone. If you already have a four-pronged

jack you can use a modular adapter and avoid the service charge completely.

Then order a Flip-Phone from GTE. They'll be in most retail stores sometime this year. Or avoid the wait and order one now directly from us. We were the first major national distributor of the Flip-Phone and have already delivered thousands to homes throughout the country.

Put one in your kitchen, in your study, in your children's room, or even in your office. You'll appreciate the convenience and savings.

If service is ever required, GTE has a prompt service-by-mail center. About the only thing that goes wrong with today's phones is the tangled cord. With the Flip-Phone telephone, you just unplug the old cord and plug in the new one. It's just that simple.

A PERSONAL TEST

We urge you to at least give the Flip-Phone a personal test right in your own home under your everyday conditions. Order one from JS&A under our 30-day trial period. Plug it in. See how easy it is to dial numbers by pressing buttons. See how good it looks and how little space it takes up. Find out how much better you sound at the other end. Then within 30 days decide if you want to keep it. If you are not convinced that the GTE Flip-Phone is a very good investment, return your phone and we'll promptly refund your money—every penny including our $2.50 postage and handling charge. You can't lose.

To order your Flip-Phone, simply send your check for **$49.95** plus $2.50 for postage and handling to the address shown below. (Illinois residents, please add 5% sales tax.) Or credit card buyers may call our toll-free number.

The Flip-Phone comes in four colors: white, yellow, brown and beige. Just specify the color, and we'll send you the phone, cord, 90-day limited warranty, and simple instructions. If you have four-pronged jacks, just order the adapter plugs for $2 each.

Why not act ahead of the crowd and order an exciting new space-age way to cut down on your phone bills? Order your Flip-Phone at no obligation, today.

*Touch-tone is a registered trademark of AT&T.

September 1978

JS&A's new program will save consumers millions.

MISSING ADAPTER

Micro TV Breakthrough

Remember the $400 Sinclair Micro TV? Here's the story on the greatest TV value ever.

That Sinclair TV shown above is small – the smallest TV in the world.

And when it was first introduced last year, it made history. So did its high price – $395.

Our company never sold the unit for two reasons: 1) It was being promoted as a pocket TV and we felt it would not fit in most pockets and 2) We felt $395 was too high a price for the unit regardless of its quality, size and features.

But we were wrong. Thousands of them were sold and it was selected as one of the most exciting new products of the year.

WE BOUGHT ONE

A few months ago we purchased a Sinclair TV and discovered another feature we didn't like. The unit included a 220-volt converter for European operation. This meant that every American who bought the set had to pay extra for the converter even though very few Americans would be taking their TV to Europe.

So we came up with an idea. We went to England and purchased thousands of sets directly from the factory without the converter. We were also able to save money by eliminating the normal mark ups by importers, wholesalers and distributors.

We can now offer you the unit for only $249.95 and if you want the 220-volt converter, your cost is only $19.95 extra.

LESS THAN WHOLESALE

JS&A would be offering the exact same Sinclair TV at a price less than Sinclair's actual wholesale price in the United States and we would still make enough profit to pay for the cost of this advertisement.

There is one feature we liked very much about the set. Its rechargeable batteries are built into the unit. Larger portable TV's offer $60 optional rechargeable battery packs that must be purchased separately. Ours is built in and included in the price.

The Sinclair TV comes complete with an American AC adapter and charger, ear phones, carrying case, rechargeable batteries and a built-in antenna for both VHF and UHF. It also comes with a cigarette lighter power converter, so you can watch all your favorite TV channels from your boat, plane, motor home or car without even using your batteries.

PHOTOGRAPHIC QUALITY

We were well aware of Sinclair's advanced electronics and quality features. But what we found particularly exciting was its picture tube. Even though the 2" (measured diagonally) tube is small, the TV's resolution resembles that of a clear sharp photograph. You can even read small telephone numbers when they're flashed on the screen.

The Sinclair unit is offered in this advertisement with the same accessories available in the $395 system with the exception of the 220-volt power converter.

· The Sinclair is also convenient. You can take it on trips and entertain your children while you fly or drive. You can keep it on your desk at work and monitor the latest news or stock market reports. And you can view the soap operas as you work around the house. We even took ours to the ball game to watch those instant replays.

BIG POCKETS

But don't expect to carry it in your pocket – it won't fit unless you have big pockets. The unit measures 1⅝" x 4" x 6¼" and weighs just 28 ounces which includes the built-in batteries.

The TV is serviced in the United States by Sinclair's service-by-mail facility. If service is ever required during its one-year limited warranty, just slip it in its handy mailer and send it to them for repair. Your solid-state unit should operate for years without a problem, but if it ever needs repair, it's good to know that service is an important part of our program.

For $249.95, the Sinclair Micro TV is worth your test. Order one from JS&A. Take it with you on a trip, bring it to your office, or carry it with you around the house. See how clear and sharp the picture is and how closely it resembles a black and white photograph. Then decide if you want to keep it. If not, no problem. Simply return your TV within 30 days for a prompt and courteous refund. We just want you to prove to yourself, the miracle of space-age electronics before you decide.

AMERICA'S LARGEST

Sinclair Radionics is one of England's largest electronics manufacturers and JS&A is America's largest single source of space-age products – further assurance that your modest investment is well protected even though the unit is offered at such a bargain price.

To order your Sinclair Micro TV, simply send your check for **$249.95** plus $3.00 postage and handling (Illinois residents, please add 5% sales tax) to the address shown below or credit card buyers may call our toll-free number below. But please act quickly.

The Sinclair TV is an outstanding product that was priced too high. If you felt like we did and you waited, your timing is perfect. Order a Sinclair Micro TV at no obligation, today.

Dept.SA   One JS&A Plaza
Northbrook, Ill. 60062   (312) 564-7000
Call TOLL-FREE **800 323-6400**
In Illinois Call . . . . (312) 564-7000

January 1979

Cordless Wonder

For $89.95 the Mura cordless telephone sounds like a bargain. But wait until you hear about its many disadvantages.

The Mura cordless telephone represents a major breakthrough in telephone technology.

It's about time. For years you've seen ads for cordless telephones selling for between three and four hundred dollars.

Now through some very clever planning and a sprinkle of new technology, Mura Corporation has come up with a cordless telephone that sells for $89.95. However, it has major disadvantages that could totally discourage you from buying the system – but more on that later.

ONLY IN AMERICA

The Mura weighs only 12 ounces and measures 1½"x 2¾"x 6½". The system includes a base unit that plugs into your telephone jack. You carry your cordless telephone with you and when your phone rings, you press a button and answer. And you can talk to anyone as long as you remain within 400 feet of the base unit.

But wait. We mentioned that the phone had major disadvantages. And it does. But first, let's outline some of its major advantages. **Convenience** You don't need an extension telephone. With the Pocket Phone you have an extension phone that you can take with you – in the bath, in the den, in the garden, or to your neighbors.

Intercom You can use the base unit to page the person holding the cordless telephone. For example, if you're in your office and someone outside has the unit, you can press a button on the base unit and buzz the portable phone – just like on an intercom. Simply by talking on the phone plugged into your base unit, you can talk with someone on the remote phone. It's ideal for home or factory use.

Price The cost of the Mura remote telephone is only $89.95. Compare this price not only with the cost of other $300 remote telephones but with conventional phones as well, and you can appreciate what a major breakthrough the Mura system represents. But there's more.

You can plug any conventional phone into the base unit and carry on a three-way conversation. You can answer a call at the base unit and signal the remote unit to pick up the line. You can cut out the remote phone from the base unit if you want to keep a conversation private.

TALK OF VALUE

You can carry the cordless telephone with you with its antenna collapsed and the battery on standby. When a call beeps your unit, you simply extend the antenna, turn the power on, and start to talk.

The unit is FCC approved for connection directly into your telephone line. If you don't have a four-pronged jack or a modular connector, simply call your telephone company. They'll promptly install a jack for you and the cost will be around $15 or less depending on your location.

NOW THE CATCH

We mentioned that there was a catch – a few major disadvantages that you, as the consumer, should know about before you consider purchasing this product. Here they are:

Forget About Dialing The new Mura Pocket Phone can't dial out. It only receives calls. To many people, this doesn't matter because 90% of remote phones are used to receive calls and not to place them. By eliminating the dial, Mura has cleverly saved consumers hundreds of dollars.

Forget About Steel Walls The Mura unit won't penetrate them. This means that if you want to use your phone in a factory with metal walls, your unit won't work. But for most factories and practically all homes, the unit is ideal.

Forget About Snooping The unit has only a 400 foot range. At first this might seem awfully short, but nobody can snoop in on your conversations if that person is beyond this range, and 400 feet is more than enough for most applications. Most cordless telephones operate in the 27 megahertz range – the same frequency area used for citizen band radios.

The base unit for the Mura can also be used as a personal paging system or intercom.

The Mura uses the 49 megahertz range. This frequency has clearer reception with practically no interference.

The above are the disadvantages. For 90% of you, they don't mean a thing. For those 10% of you who need a dial, we would recommend the more expensive cordless telephones.

But for those of you who will accept its disadvantages, you'll be in store for the greatest idea in telephone convenience since the cordless telephone was first introduced. In fact, rather than install an extension phone, why not consider the Mura instead?

TRY IT FIRST

We suggest you try the Mura Cordless telephone system in your own home, office or factory. Use it for 30 days. Take the phone to your next door neighbor's house or with you to the bathroom while you take a shower or bath. Take it with you on your patio or balcony, or bring it in your garden as you work. Use it in your factory as an intercom or in your office as a remote telephone.

After you've given it a thorough test, then decide if you want to keep it. If not, no problem. Simply return your system for a prompt and courteous refund including your $3.50 postage and handling. You can't lose.

HERE'S THE WAY

To order your unit for a 30-day test, simply send your check for **$89.95** plus $3.50 postage and handling to JS&A Group, Inc., One JS&A Plaza, Northbrook, Illinois 60062. (Illinois residents please add 5% sales tax.) Credit card buyers, call our toll-free number below. We'll send your base unit, cordless telephone, rechargeable batteries, recharger, complete instructions, our 90-day limited warranty, and the address of the closest Mura Service Center or service-by-mail station.

Your unit is backed by Mura Corporation, a 17-year old company famous for their microphones, headsets, and other audio products. JS&A is America's largest single source of space-age products – further assurance that your modest investment is well-protected.

Very often when a product's disadvantages aren't made clear to the consumer, that product ends up being a disappointment. By explaining the major disadvantages of the Mura cordless telephone, not only are we avoiding a possible disappointment, we're proving just how great a product it really is. Order a Mura cordless telephone at no obligation today.

JS&A PRODUCTS THAT THINK

Dept.RA   One JS&A Plaza
Northbrook, Ill. 60062   (312) 564-7000
Call TOLL-FREE **800 323-6400**
In Illinois Call .... **(312) 564-7000**
© JS&A Group, Inc.,1979

August 1979

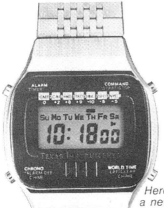

Ding Dong Digital

Here's the story of how we converted a new watch into America's best selling digital by adding a single ding dong.

"Daddy, your watch has a ding dong."

We're in trouble. And we're in trouble with Texas Instruments' engineers.

It seems TI selected JS&A to introduce their most exciting, new, advanced digital watch in a national advertising campaign. But when we wrote our first advertisement and showed it to our customers, they weren't impressed.

CUSTOMERS FALLING ASLEEP

TI engineers however, were delighted with our advertisement. It explained in boring detail how advanced and how technically superior the TI watch really is.

When we tried to figure out why the ad didn't impress our customers, we came to one conclusion. When a customer tried reading all that technical stuff, he probably fell asleep. Sure TI engineers loved it, but the ad wasn't very interesting.

BUILT-IN DING DONG

Our president was home relaxing with his five year old daughter on his lap when suddenly the hourly chime on his TI watch sounded. "Daddy," exclaimed his daughter, "Your watch has a Ding Dong."

When our president returned to the office the next day, he told our creative department of his daughter's description and by the end of the day, TI's watch had a new name: "The Ding Dong Digital."

We tested the name and found that our customers loved it. It drew their attention to the watch and once they read about its many features – especially the hourly chime – they bought it.

ENGINEERS INSULTED

When the engineers heard the name, they were furious. To name their greatest digital watch, 'Ding Dong Digital' was an insult.

But the name caught on. And although this non-technical approach to a most sophisticated product upset TI's engineers, it delighted their marketing people because JS&A started selling large numbers of the watch.

THEY LOVED THE WATCH

The TI watch is thin, looks quite handsome and tells very accurate time. But the other features are really quite appealing. For example:

Laser-Sealed Light Source A luminescent capsule, sealed by a laser beam is hidden behind the display and illuminates it constantly – even at night without having to press a button.

Solar-Power The battery in the Ding Dong Digital is charged by a solar cell. The batteries will stay charged for five full years. It's the first solar powered watch ever offered by Texas Instruments.

Multi-Alarm You can set the alarm quickly by pressing one button and then changing the hours and minutes with a second button that operates at two speeds. We know of no other digital watch that can be set faster than the TI watch.

Chime Function It chirps twice every hour on the hour – a great time organizing reminder. And you can turn off the chime at the touch of a button when you retire at night.

Dual Time Zone A second time zone can be set to display 24-hour time – a perfect way to know AM or PM – and ideal for travelers, pilots or ham radio operators.

Chrono and Timer The TI has both a 24-hour chronograph function with lap and split times and a count-down and count-up timer. But what makes the watch so advanced is that the watch sounds a tone each time a chrono function is entered – a positive feedback device that assures entry of the function. When the timer reaches zero, it sounds another alarm and then starts counting in the opposite direction.

Other Features The TI watch also shows the day of the week on the display and features month and date as well as showing when the chime and alarms are engaged. It's rain resistant and will take more than the normal abuse we all give our watches.

OUR PREVIOUS AD

In our previous ad we discussed the quartz crystal and how technically superior it was. We discussed the new bright display and the advanced integrated circuit. But boy was it dull reading. This easier-to-read ad proved considerably more interesting.

We suggest that you order the new TI digital for a 30-day trial. When you receive it, wear it for a solid month. See how fast you can set the alarm, how the hourly chime organizes your day and how handsome this watch looks. Check its accuracy, its readability and above all, see how easy it is to operate despite its many features and advanced technology.

OUR NEW OFFER

After your 30-day test, decide if you want to keep your new watch. If it does not live up to all of our claims to your total satisfaction, simply return it to us and you'll receive a prompt and courteous refund. There's no risk.

To order your TI Digital watch, simply send us your check for **$150** for the gold tone model or **$130** for the stainless steel version, plus $2.50 for postage and handling (Illinois residents please add 5% sales tax) to JS&A Group, Inc. at the address below. Credit card buyers may call our toll-free number below.

With your watch, you'll receive a one-year limited warranty, handsome gift box and complete and easy-to-understand instructions. Texas Instruments has service centers throughout the United States and a computerized service-by-mail center to insure prompt repair if anything ever goes wrong with your watch. Nothing should, but it's good to know you've got a solid company behind your watch. JS&A is America's largest single source of space-age products – further assurance that your modest investment is well protected.

GREATEST COMPLIMENT

Probably the greatest compliment we can pay the TI watch is that JS&A's president wears one. Although he has the reputation of picking only the finest products, he is extremely careful to select the products he personally uses.

Despite the brilliance of TI engineers and the ability of our president to pick successful products, it took our president's daughter to figure out how to reach the consumer. Why not try the Ding Dong Digital yourself? Order one at no obligation, today.

PRODUCTS THAT THINK

Dept.WJ   One JS&A Plaza
Northbrook, Ill. 60062   (312) 564-7000
Call TOLL-FREE 800 323-6400
In Illinois Call . . . . (312) 564-7000
© JS&A Group, Inc., 1979

September 1979

FTC Revolt

You've heard of the tax revolt. It's about time for an FTC revolt. Here's my story and why we've got to stop federal bureaucratic regulation.

**By Joseph Sugarman,
President, JS&A Group, Inc.**

My story is only one example of how the FTC is harassing small businesses but I'm not going to sit back and take it.

I'm pretty lucky. When I started my business in my basement eight years ago, I had little more than an idea and a product.

The product was the pocket calculator. The idea was to sell it through advertisements in national magazines and newspapers.

Those first years in the basement weren't easy. But, we worked hard and through imaginative advertising and a dedicated staff, JS&A grew rapidly to become well recognized as an innovator in electronics and marketing.

THREE BLIZZARDS

In January of 1979, three major blizzards struck the Chicago area. The heaviest snowfall hit Northbrook, our village – just 20 miles north of Chicago.

Many of our employees were stranded – unable to get to our office where huge drifts made travel impossible. Not only were we unable to reach our office, but our computer totally broke down leaving us in even deeper trouble.

But we fought back. Our staff worked around the clock and on weekends. First, we processed orders manually. We also hired a group of computer specialists, rented outside computer time, employed a computer service bureau, and hired temporary help to feed this new computer network. We never gave up. Our totally dedicated staff and the patience of many of our customers helped us through the worst few months in our history. Although there were many customers who had to wait over 30 days for their parcels, every package was eventually shipped.

WE OPENED OUR DOORS

During this period, some of our customers called the FTC (Federal Trade Commission) to complain. We couldn't blame them. Despite our efforts to manually notify our customers of our delays, our computer was not functioning making the task extremely difficult.

The FTC advised JS&A of these complaints. To assure the FTC that we were a responsible company, we invited them to visit us. During their visit we showed them our computerized microfilm system which we use to back up every transaction. We showed them our new dual computer system (our main system and a backup system in case our main system ever failed again). And, we demonstrated how we were able to locate and trace every order. We were very cooperative, allowing them to look at every document they requested.

The FTC left. About one week later, they called and told us that they wanted us to pay a $100,000 penalty for not shipping our products within their 30-day rule. (The FTC rule states that anyone paying by check is entitled to have their purchase shipped within 30 days or they must be notified and given the option to cancel.)

NOT BY CONGRESS

The FTC rule is not a law nor a statute passed by Congress, but rather a rule created by the FTC to strengthen their enforcement powers. I always felt that the rule was intended to be used against companies that purposely took advantage of the consumer. Instead, it appears that the real violators, who often are too difficult to prosecute, get away while JS&A, a visible and highly respected company that pays taxes and has contributed to our free enterprise system, is singled out. I don't think that was the intent of the rule.

And when the FTC goes to court, they have the full resources of the US Government. Small, legitimate businesses haven't got a chance.

We're not perfect. We do make mistakes. But if we do make a mistake, we admit it, accept the responsibility, and then take whatever measures necessary to correct it. That's how we've built our reputation.

BLOW YOUR KNEE CAPS OFF

Our attorneys advised us to settle. As one attorney said, "It's like a bully pulling out a gun and saying, 'If you don't give me a nickel, I'll blow your knee caps off.'" They advised us that the government will subpoena thousands of documents to harass us and cause us great inconvenience. They warned us that even if we went to court and won, we would end up spending more in legal fees than if we settled.

To settle would mean to negotiate a fine and sign a consent decree. The FTC would then issue a press release publicizing their victory.

At first we tried to settle. We met with two young FTC attorneys and agreed in principle to pay consumers for any damages caused them. But there were practically no damages, just a temporary computer problem, some late shipments, and some bad weather. The FTC then issued a massive subpoena requesting documents that will take us months to gather and which we feel was designed to harass or force us to accept their original $100,000 settlement request.

Remember, the FTC publicizes their actions. And the higher the fine, the more the publicity and the more stature these two attorneys will have at the FTC.

If this all sounds like blackmail – that's just what it appeared to be to us.

We did ship our products late – something we've admitted to them and which we publicly admit here, but we refuse to be blackmailed into paying a huge fine at the expense of our company's reputation – something we've worked hard eight years to build.

We're not a big company and we realize it would be easier to settle now at any cost. But we're not. If this advertisement can attract the attention of Congressmen and Senators who have the power to stop the harassment of Americans by the FTC, then our efforts will be well spent.

ALL AMERICANS AFFECTED

Federal regulation and the whims of a few career-building bureaucrats is costing taxpayers millions, destroying our free enterprise system, affecting our productivity as a nation and as a result is lowering everybody's standard of living.

I urge Congressmen, Senators, businessmen and above all, the consumer to support legislation to take the powers of the FTC from the hands of a few unelected officials and bring them back to Congress and the people.

I will be running this advertisement in hundreds of magazines and newspapers during the coming months. I'm not asking for contributions to support my effort as this is my battle, but I do urge you to send this advertisement to your Congressmen and Senators. That's how you can help.

America was built on the free enterprise system. Today, the FTC is undermining this system. Freedom is not something that can be taken for granted and you often must fight for what you believe. I'm prepared to lead that fight. Please help me.

Note: To find out the complete story and for a guide on what action you can take, write me personally for my free booklet, "Blow your knee caps off."

One JS&A Plaza, Northbrook, Ill. 60062
© JS&A Group, Inc., 1979

November 1979

November 1979

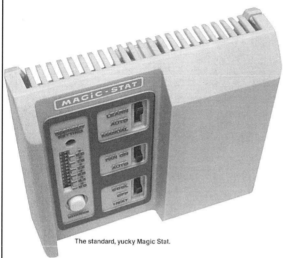

The standard, yucky Magic Stat.

Magic Baloney

It had no digital readout, an ugly case and a stupid name. It almost made us sick.

The new deluxe Super Magic Stat.

You're probably expecting our typical sales pitch, but get ready for a shock. For instead of trying to tell you what a great product the Magic Stat thermostat is, we're going to tear it apart. Unmercifully.

When we first saw the Magic Stat, we took one look at the name and went "Yuck." We took one look at the plastic case and said, "How cheap looking." And when we looked for the digital readout, it had none. So before the salesman even showed us how it worked, we were totally turned off.

Real loser

So there it was—at first blush a real loser. But wait. We did find one good feature—a feature that led us to a discovery. The Magic Stat installs in a few minutes and no serviceman is required. Thermostat wires in your wall follow standard color codes. So when you install Magic Stat, you attach the red wire to the red location and the white to the white. That's play-school stuff. And it's safe. Conventional thermostats installed over the past 20 years are generally only 24 volts, so you can either turn off the power or work with the "live" wires without fear.

OK, let's test it

The Magic Stat installation was so easy that the least we could do was test it. And that's when we made an incredible discovery. We discovered that the Magic Stat was probably the most consumer-oriented, technologically-advanced and most sophisticated thermostat ever developed on the face of this earth and in our galaxy for all times ever. What made us switch from hating the thing to loving it? Read the following.

The Magic Stat has six setback settings per day and a seven-day program. This means that in winter you could set it for 70° when you get up in the morning, drop the temperature to 54° when you go to work, raise it to 68° when you return for dinner, raise it up to 72° after dinner as you watch TV and then drop it down to 62° when you go to sleep. Count them—five settings with one to spare.

In one day the Magic Stat is programmed for the whole week and for weeks to come. If you want a different schedule for weekends,

you can individually program the thermostat for those days, too. "Big deal," you might think. "What's so great about that?" Read on.

You set most electronic setback thermostats to the time you want the furnace to go on in the morning, so when you wake up, your room is once again warm. But what if one morning it's bitter cold outside and the next morning it's much warmer? This means that setting your furnace to go on at the same time may, on one morning, leave you cold and on the next morning cause you to waste energy by warming up your house too soon.

By golly, the Magic Stat has everybody beat on this one, too. Throughout the night it senses and computes the drop in temperature and the time it will take to get your room to your exact wake-up temperature. So if you want to wake up at 7 AM to 70 degrees—that's the temperature you'll wake up to every time. Because it's a patented concept, no other thermostat has this feature. But wait. There is also a patent on the setting feature.

Simple to set

To set the thermostat, you press just one button. A small LED light scans the temperature scale until you reach your desired temperature and then you release the button. You change the temperature naturally, throughout the day, up to six times. The unit responds and remembers that exact living pattern. The present temperature is displayed by a glowing red LED on the scale.

The system also computes the ideal length the furnace should stay on to keep the temperature within a range of plus or minus one and one-half degrees. A battery backup lets you keep your stored program in its memory so power outages as long as eight hours won't let your unit forget. And if something happens and your power is out for a few days, the unit will automatically maintain 68 degrees when the power is restored.

Energy savings are also possible in summer when the Magic Stat controls your air conditioning system.

Quite frankly, we were so impressed with the unit, its ease of installation and setting plus its many energy-saving features, we seriously considered advertising it until we realized that

our customers would probably not want to trust their future comfort to a product called Magic Stat. What if something went wrong with the unit? How substantial was this Magic Stat outfit? Remember, a thermostat is something you live with as long as you live in your home, and they're supposed to last ages. After all, your comfort depends on it.

Well, we did our homework. We found the company to be a sound, well-financed organization. They have been in business for several years, and they back their products with a three-year limited warranty. In addition, the company has a policy of buying back your unit in one year if you haven't saved its full cost in energy savings. We were satisfied with the company, the people, the product, its incredible features, the company's commitment to the product and above all, the energy savings.

We are so impressed now with the Magic Stat that we're going to make buying one irresistible. Buy one from us for only $69. Install it yourself in a few minutes or hire a handyman.

Or order the new Weather Wizard Magic Stat that switches between your furnace and your air conditioning system automatically. You set it once for the whole year and forget about it.

Then enjoy the savings all year long. Not only will you save up to 35% on your utility bills, but you're eligible for the 15% energy tax credit. Then if you're not absolutely in love with this product one year later, return it to JS&A. You'll get all your money back and you can reinstall your old thermostat.

Realize savings

But we're counting on a few things. First, you will realize an energy savings and a comfort that will far surpass what you are currently experiencing. Secondly, you probably will sleep better breathing cooler air yet wake up to just the right temperature.

Beauty is only skin deep and a name doesn't really mean that much. But we sure wish those guys at Magic Stat would have named their unit something more impressive. Maybe something like Twinkle Temp.

Magic Stat (0040B 4.00) $69
Weather Wizard (0044B 4.00) 89
Not available for heat pumps.

October 1983

Stop Taking Vitamins

If you think the vitamins you are now taking are doing you any good, wait until you hear the latest news on why they may not.

Stop taking that innocent looking vitamin pill until you read this report.

By Joseph Sugarman

This may come as a shock. But according to the latest research, those vitamins that you take every day may be doing you absolutely no good. For example.

FACT: Vitamins should be taken after a meal—never before. The body must first have protein, fats, or carbohydrates in the digestive tract to properly break down the vitamins for proper absorption.

FACT: Your body has a need for a natural vitamin balance. Too much of one vitamin may cause another vitamin to be less effective. For example, vitamin A should be taken with Vitamin E but excessive iron should not.

FACT: If you take too much calcium, you may deplete the magnesium in your system. And you need magnesium to convert food into energy.

FACT: Some vitamins are best taken in the morning and others at night. For example, the trace element chromium helps break down the sugar in your food which in turn creates energy—perfect to start the day. But at night you should take Calcium which has a relaxing effect—perfect for the evening.

FACT: Athletes or people who exercise a great deal need vitamins more than people who don't exercise. Vitamins are depleted at a much faster rate during exercise than during any other period of time.

But there was a series of other facts that surprised me too. For example, despite everything I've just mentioned on the care in taking vitamins, there are those people who absolutely need vitamins because of the mental or physical activity that they undergo. People on a diet, under stress, those who smoke, women who take contraceptives and even those who take medication—all rob their bodies of some of the essential vitamins and minerals that they need to help combat the various habits or conditions they are under.

And with proper vitamins in the proper balance and at the proper times, you will have more energy and vitality. Little changes may take place. Your nails may become stronger, your hair may become thicker and your skin may be more elastic which will keep you younger-looking longer.

DOCTORS HAD IDEA

About two years ago a group of doctors had an idea. They realized that many people were taking vitamins and not really noticing any difference in their health. They also realized that, based on the latest nutritional findings, the vitamins people were taking may not have been doing them any good. So they formed a group of advisors consisting of nutritionists, dieticians, dermatologists, biochemists and physicians, and they worked on the development of a vitamin program that incorporated all of the latest information on vitamins, minerals, nutrition, food processing—even stress research. They realized that vitamins were a two-edged sword. They could either help you or hurt you.

They then took all this information and developed the most effective combination of vitamins and minerals, formulated four tablets—one for the morning and one for the evening—and one for men and one for women and then started a test program that lasted over two years. The results speak for themselves.

It was perfect for weight loss programs and it was perfect for people under stress. It helped many increase their energy levels. Smokers benefited. Some under medication benefited. And before long the company that had developed the program became the fastest growing vitamin company in the United States. And no wonder.

SEVERAL BENEFITS

With the proper vitamin and mineral balance, taken in the right quantity in the right combination and at the right time, several obvious benefits occur. First, you may develop a better mental outlook because you've got the energy and the zest to accomplish more. As a result of the trace elements copper, zinc and manganese, your body is helped to make its natural anti-aging enzymes that keep you fit. Improvements in your vitality translate into everything from better job performance to a more fulfilling sex life.

JS&A has been selected by the vitamin company to introduce their medically formulated vitamin program. Every two months we send you a two month's supply of 120 fitness tablets—one to be taken after breakfast and one after dinner.

During the first two months, you will have ample opportunity to notice the difference in your energy level, your mental attitude and your overall stamina. You should notice little things too, like the strength of your fingernails, your thicker hair. Your complexion may even take on a glow. Some of you may notice all of these changes and others may notice just a few.

But you should notice a change.

If for any reason, you do not notice a change, no problem. Just pick up your phone, and tell us not to send you any more vitamins. And if you ask for a refund, you won't even have to send the empty bottle back. It's yours free for just giving us the opportunity to introduce our vitamins. However, if you indeed do notice a difference (which we are confident you will), you'll automatically receive a two-month's supply every eight weeks.

ONE MORE INCENTIVE

I'm also going to give you one more incentive just to let me prove to you how powerful this program really is. I will send you a bonus gift of a fitness bag with your first order. This beautiful bag will hold all your fitness gear and it's great too for short vacation trips. It's a $20 value but it's yours free for just trying the vitamins. Even if you decide not to continue, you keep the fitness bag. I am so convinced that you will feel and see a difference when you take these vitamins that I am willing to gamble on it with this unusual offer.

Vitamins indeed are important. And with today's research and new nutrition technology, you have a greater chance to achieve the fitness and health levels that may have eluded you with the typical store vitamins or the poor advice we may get in health food stores or from friends. Here is a safe, risk-free way to get one of the best vitamin programs in the country, formulated by a physician, with the right combination of vitamins, minerals and trace elements, in a convenient program that assures you of delivery every two months. I personally take and highly recommend them. Order your trial quantity, today.

To order, credit card holders call toll free and ask for product number (shown in parentheses) or send a check and include $2.50 for delivery.

Men's Vitamins (1155BB) $24
Women's Vitamins (1156BB) $24

One JS&A Plaza, Northbrook, Illinois 60062
CALL TOLL FREE 800 228-5000
IL residents add 7% sales tax. ©JS&A Group, Inc.,1986

October 1985

Vision Break- through

When I put on the pair of glasses what I saw I could not believe. Nor will you.

They look like sunglasses.

By Joseph Sugarman

I am about to tell you a true story. If you believe me, you will be well rewarded. If you don't believe me, I will make it worth your while to change your mind. Let me explain.

Len is a friend of mine who has an eye for good products. One day he called excited about a pair of sunglasses he owned. "It's so incredible," he said, "when you first look through a pair, you won't believe it."

"What will I see?" I asked. "What could be so incredible?"

Len continued, "When you put on these glasses, your vision improves. Objects appear sharper, more defined. Everything takes on an enhanced 3-D effect. And it's not my imagination. I just want you to see for yourself."

When I received the sunglasses and put them on I couldn't believe my eyes. I kept taking them off and putting them on to see if indeed what I was seeing through the glasses was indeed actually sharper or if my imagination was playing tricks on me. But my vision improved. It was obvious. I kept putting on my cherished $100 pair of high-tech sunglasses and comparing them. They didn't compare. I was very impressed. Everything appeared sharper, more defined and indeed had a greater three dimensional look to it. But what did this product do that made my vision so much better? I found out.

DEPRESSING COLOR

The sunglasses (called BluBlockers) filter out the ultraviolet and blue spectrum light waves from the sun. You've often heard the color blue used for expressions of bad moods such as "blue Monday" or "I have the blues." Apparently, the color blue, for centuries, has been considered a rather depressing color.

For eyesight, blue is not a good color too. There are several reasons. First, the blue rays have the shortest wavelength in the visible spectrum (red is the longest). As a result, the color blue will focus slightly in front of the retina which is the "focussing screen" onto which light waves fall in your eye. By eliminating the blue from the sunglasses through a special filtration process, and only letting those rays through that indeed focus clearly on the retina, objects appear to be sharper and clearer.

The second reason is even more impressive. It is not good to have ultraviolet rays fall on our eyes. Recognized as bad for skin, uv light is worse for eyes and is believed to play a role in many of today's eye diseases. In addition, people with contact lenses are at greater risk because contacts tend to magnify the light at their edges thus increasing the sun's harmful effects.

Finally, by eliminating the blue and uv light during the day, your night vision improves. The purple pigment in your eye called Rhodopsin is affected by blue light and the eyes take hours to recover from the effects.

SUNGLASS DANGER

But what really surprised me was the danger in conventional sunglasses. Our pupils close in bright light to limit the light entering the eye and open wider at night—just like the aperture in an automatic camera. So when we put on sunglasses, although we reduce the amount of light that enters our eyes, our pupils open wider and we are actually allowing more of the blue and ultraviolet portions of the light spectrum into our eyes.

BluBlockers sunglasses are darker at the top to shield out overhead light. The lens used is the CR-39 which most eye doctors will tell you is one of the finest materials you can use for glasses and is manufactured under license.

The frames are some of the most comfortable I have ever worn. The moulded nose rest will fit any nose. The hinge causes the frames to rest comfortably on your face and can be adjusted for almost any size face.

We also have a clip-on pair that weighs less than one ounce. Both come with a padded carrying case and an anti-scratch coating.

I urge you to order a pair and experience the improved vision. Then take your old sunglasses and compare them to the BluBlockers. See how much clearer and sharper objects appear with BluBlockers. And see if your night vision doesn't improve as a direct result. If you don't see a dramatic difference in your vision—one so noticeable that you can tell immediately, then send them back anytime within 30 days and I will send you a prompt and courteous refund.

DRAMATIC DIFFERENCE

But from what I've personally witnessed, once you use a pair, there will be no way you'll want to return it.

Astronomers from many famous universities wear BluBlockers to improve their night vision. Pilots, golfers, skiers, athletes—anyone who spends a great deal of time in the sun have found the BluBlockers indispensable.

Our eyes are very important to us. Protect them and at the same time improve your vision with the most incredible breakthrough in sun glasses since they were first introduced. Order a pair or two at no obligation, today.

To order, credit card holders call toll free and ask for product by number shown below or send a check plus $4 for delivery.

BluBlockers (0020TN) $59.95
Clip-On Model (0022TN) 34.95
BluBlockers is a trademark of JS&A Group, Inc.

One JS&A Plaza, Northbrook, IL 60062
CALL TOLL FREE 800 228-5000
IL. residents add 7% sales tax. ©JS&A Group, Inc.,1986

October 1986

Gasoline Breakthrough

Here's the story about fuel additives and a new gasoline pill that may revolutionize the auto industry.

By Joseph Sugarman.

Get ready for a shock. For what you are about to read may save you a fortune. Let me explain.

Gasoline has changed. It's not the pure stuff it used to be 20 years ago. Sure, they took out lead to make lead free but I'm talking about gasoline quality and how it's affecting your engine. Listen to the facts:

Fact: Gasoline today is not pure. A barrel of oil contains 18% natural gasoline when refined. Twenty years ago that's what we put into our tanks — natural gasoline. But the refineries are now turning 35% of the barrel into fuel. Unsaturated hydrocarbons are being utilized in the refining process — not to increase energy but to increase volume. This extra matter ends up mainly as gum and carbon deposits on our pistons and in our ignition systems.

Fact: Most people using super unleaded gas are wasting their money. Unless your car absolutely requires the higher octane (as specified in your owners manual), you are throwing money away. There are no other added benefits or performance improvements worth paying for in a car designed to use regular unleaded.

Fact: It costs the oil companies a few pennies per gallon to raise the octane rating in gasoline to the super unleaded status yet the consumer pays up to 20 cents more per gallon. So the oil companies push super for obvious reasons.

Fact: Gasoline will spoil in time because of the newer refining process. Therefore, when left in a car for more than a few months, gasoline will develop sludge and precipitate a range of chemicals which clog up injection and carburetor systems. This is bad news for car collectors and anyone who stores gasoline-powered vehicles.

No mess, no waste and all in a pill.

And if you've fallen for the expensive fuel additive claims, then you're spending money for very little gain. Fuel additives sold in bottles are basically solvents or byproducts of the refining process. They're toxic, flammable and often not formulated specifically for your car but originate from the same solvent-based sources used to make plastics and other petroleum-based products.

For most drivers, placing one simple pill in your gas tank will eliminate the need for fuel additives, save you hundreds of dollars and provide the cleanest driving, most fuel efficient car you can drive.

It's called the Pill™— a new patented breakthrough in fuel enhancement technology that will do a number of important things for your car.

Dissolves in tank.

First, it dissolves completely in your tank

Americans are wasting money and don't even realize it.

and mixes with the fuel. Second, it helps the fuel atomize or vaporize more efficiently, thus promoting more complete combustion of the fuel. Third, the detergent action of the pill cleans out the gums, varnishes and carbon deposits from injectors, intake valves and pistons. But there's much more.

The Pill can save from 4 1/2% to 8% in fuel as proven at independent laboratories using EPA approved procedures.

And the Pill has over ten times the cleaning power and fuel conditioners than those contained in super unleaded gasoline. As one observer put it, "There's nothing on the market quite like this."

Fits in glove box.

The Pill is small, safe and fits in your glove box. It does not melt nor is it flammable. It gives you better gas mileage, cleans out your engine, restores lost performance, saves on fuel costs and eventually even repair costs.

I urge you to give the Pill a no obligation test. If your car pings from carbon deposits, you'll notice the difference quickly. If not, notice how much better your car responds and notice the subtle increases in fuel economy as you experience the latest in fuel enhancement technology.

The Pill costs only $19.95 for a package of ten. Use one every other fill up. That means several months of taking the finest care of your car. And, if you don't notice a difference during the first few fill-ups, or you don't easily cover the cost of your purchase in savings or benefits, simply return the package for a prompt and courteous refund.

The patented Pill is made by ADERCO — one of the leading fuel additive companies in the world. The Pill is made in the USA, is safe for both your car and its catalytic converter and is equally effective with both regular and super unleaded fuel.

Think of the Pill as "Vitamins For Your Car."™ Order them at no obligation, today.

German Graphite LaserBlades™

New three-edged wiper with German graphite, far surpasses all other wiper blades. Major Breakthrough.

By Joseph Sugarman.

It's the latest advance in wiper blade technology. Here in one system are six new advanced features far ahead of any other blade on the market.

Laser Straight: The special blades are molded and then cut laser straight to give you a smooth straight edge. Other multi-edged blades are not as precision made as LaserBlades.

German Graphite: The entire blade is coated with pure German Graphite — the space-age material that causes the blades to glide effortlessly over your windshield. The material, which is absorbed into the blade material itself, gives years of soft, smooth performance.

Gelegenheit™ Rubber: Called the opportunity material, this rubber is a soft but extremely durable synthetic rubber composite that will last for years. It is not as greatly affected by ultraviolet light and weather as are standard wiper blades.

Three Cleaning Edges: A proven concept in wiper blade design, this new variation on the older concept provides better cleaning in all conditions — rain, mud, snow or sleet.

Vented Design: Each unit is vented to allow air to pass through the blade holder. This helps to keep the blade firmly on the windshield even during high speeds.

One Swipe™ Action: Mud, snow, sleet or rain — one swipe of the LaserBlade and your windshield is clear and clean. It's something you'll have to see to believe and you'll be amazed at how seldom you'll use your windshield washer fluid.

Three laser-sharp graphite wiping edges make no squeaks, leave no streaks and cause no smears. And it's guaranteed.

LaserBlades are different. First they should last a lot longer than any other blades on the market — over 500,000 strokes or years of active use. Although few blades will last a lifetime, LaserBlades will make it easy for you to keep them for a lifetime. Here's why.

You can slide LaserBlades in and out of the metal blade holder. This makes changing the blades simple and quick. But here's the best part.

We give you an extra set of replacement blades free with each complete set we send you. Chances are, you'll never need them but if your blades ever get damaged, no problem. Slide out the old, slip in the new. And, in the future, if you ever need more, we'll send you free replacement blades for as long as you own your car. In addition, the windshield wiper holders are rust free and should also last a lifetime. LaserBlades should be the last wiper blade you'll ever have to buy.

I urge you to try LaserBlades on your car for the next few years. LaserBlades come with everything you need to install them quickly and easily — all with easy-to-follow instructions. In addition, a toll-free assistance line is available to answer any questions.

JS&A is one of America's premiere suppliers of quality products by mail for over 20 years — further assurance that your modest investment is well protected.

Experience a set of blades on your car unlike anything you've ever experienced before. LaserBlades will give you the quality, the precision and the safety that no other wiper system can match. And it's guaranteed for the life of your car or your money back. Order a set at no obligation, today.

The One-Swipe™ wiping system cleans your windshield with just one swipe.

America's Oldest Sunglasses.

Discovery at bottom of Missouri River shows pair of sunglasses worn by riverboat gamblers.

By Joseph Sugarman

It was 1856. And the Arabia, one of the finest riverboats of its era, was cruising down the Missouri River. Then disaster struck. It hit a submerged Sycamore tree and the ship sank.

Time passed. Nature slowly rerouted the Missouri river and the ship eventually lay buried under tons of mud below the earth's surface. But many of the artifacts on board were preserved.

Riverboat uncovered.

Finally, in 1988 a group of local citizens decided to unearth the mighty Arabia. Not necessarily to find and sell its booty but to preserve the many artifacts of the era and to display them in a museum.

Greg Hawley from Kansas City, Missouri, and a group of his relatives and supporters worked for a period of three years and with luck and perseverance, unearthed the once great riverboat. It was a long and often perilous fight that took a major commitment of time and thousands of hard earned dollars.

As part of their find, they discovered an unusual pair of sunglasses worn by the earliest settlers of the area. The crude frames were made of leather with green glass lenses held in place by tin wire rims. The frames then wrapped around the face with a cloth-like string.

The BluBlocker Malenium® lens cleaning kit, a $10 value, is yours free with your purchase.

Latest technology.

BluBlocker® Corporation—the same sunglass company you've seen on national TV, found out about the discovery and developed a pair of sunglasses that had the look and feel of the original pair but with all of the latest technology.

For example, instead of leather and tin for the frame construction, they replaced them with nickel silver—a strong but extremely lightweight metal. Instead of glass for the lens material, they used Optic Steel®—a new optical resin that is exceptionally clear and so shatter-resistant that you could hit the lens with a hammer and it wouldn't break.

And finally, instead of a leather material fitting flush to the face, the frame is elevated through the use of soft and flexible silicone nose pads that create a nonslip surface so effective that the frames easily stay on your face.

When BluBlocker Corporation was through, they had created one of the most advanced pair of sunglasses you can buy—for fit, for durability and for eye protection—all inspired by one of the oldest pairs of sunglasses ever discovered.

The new sunglass concept was named Sprokets™—a name that has no relationship to the 1856 design but was more hip for today's sunglass consumer.

Secret to new style.

The secret to this new sunglass style is the lens. The BluBlocker Optic Steel lens blocks all the UV and blue light providing the most protection you can get from any pair of sunglasses. And the blue and UV filtering material is within the lens itself—not a coating that is sprayed on and can later rub off.

Each lens is polarized to eliminate scattered and reflected light rays. This lets you see clearly through your windshield without picking up the reflection off your dash and even lets you see through water.

I urge you to try a pair of Sprokets. Order one under our 60 day money back guarantee. We'll also include a free BluBlocker Malenium lens cleaning kit—a $10 value but it's yours free with your order.

When you receive your pair, look through the lenses and observe the clarity. You'll notice how quickly you stop squinting, how more relaxed your eyes feel and how much lighter the frames are on your temples and your nose.

Examine the space-age frame and how easily it conforms to your face. Adjust the nonslip silicone nose pads so the pair fits your face perfectly. You'll really appreciate the value and the technology in the BluBlocker Sprokets.

It must be your favorite.

If BluBlocker Sprokets don't become your favorite pair of sunglasses, return them anytime within two months for a prompt and courteous refund including our small postage and handling charge. You can't lose. And, just for trying the pair, you may keep the lens cleaning kit as our free gift.

Sunglasses have really advanced since 1856 but in a sense, they've gone full circle. Order a pair of Sprokets, at no obligation, today.

The BluBlocker Sprokets sunglasses were derived from a sunken riverboat in 1856.

To order, credit card buyers call toll-free and ask for product number 0000AB or mail your check or money order for $19.95 plus $4 postage and handling to the address below.

BluBlocker Sprokets polarized sunglasses (0000AB) $49.95
BluBlocker polarized clip-ons (for prescriptions) (0000AB) $49.95

Note: Sunglass lens cleaning kit included free of charge with your order.

JS&A

3350 Palms Centre Drive
Las Vegas, NV 89103
CALL TOLL-FREE 800 862-7777
NV. residents add 7% sales tax. © JS&A Group, Inc. 1995

June 1995

Index

Your Guide to Relevant Topics

P

Your comments are important

I am always interested in your comments, feedback and suggestions on the book you've just read and I may also want to use them for advertising purposes. Please feel free to copy or tear out this form and mail it with your comments to: Joseph Sugarman, JS&A Group, Inc., 3350 Palms Center Drive, Las Vegas, NV 89103. Thank you.

I herewith freely allow and give right and title to Joseph Sugarman and/or DelStar Publishing, or their assigns, to use the following comments, feedback and suggestions either to improve this or any of Mr. Sugarman's books or as a testimonial in the promotion of this book in any advertising medium solely determined by Mr. Sugarman or DelStar Publishing. I also agree to allow the use of part or all of a testimonial as determined by Mr. Sugarman.

_____

Your signature   Date

Would you agree to appear on a TV testimonial? _____

Continue on back of page.

Advertising Secrets of the Written Word

The Ultimate Resource on How to Write Powerful Advertising Copy
From One of America's Top Copywriters and Mail Order Entrepreneurs

A comprehensive textbook that teaches you step-by-step how to write powerful advertising copy that sells. The illustrated book provides insights on what it takes to be a great copywriter and how to develop those skills. The book also takes you into the thought process of ad creation and provides a disciplined procedure that anybody can follow. A major chapter reveals the "psychological triggers" and how they can be used effectively to "cause prospects to exchange their hard-earned money for your product or service." ISBN 1-891686-00-3 (hardcover). 310 pages. $39.95

Television Secrets for Marketing Success

How to Sell Your Product on Infomercials, Home Shopping Channels and Spot
TV Commercials From the Entrepreneur Who Gave You BluBlocker® Sunglasses

The story of Joseph Sugarman's successful experiences with infomercials and the QVC home shopping channel. The book has useful tips on applying the principles of print direct marketing to make TV marketing work more effectively. He talks candidly about his failures as well as his successes, how he launched one of QVC's most successful promotions, how he created and built BluBlocker® sunglasses into a nationally recognized brand name, and how he used TV marketing to influence over 10 million viewers to buy his products. ISBN 1-891686-09-7 (hardcover). 310 pages. $39.95

The Sugarman Seminar Secrets Slipcase

A handsome slipcase designed to hold Joseph Sugarman's three books
based on his exclusive marketing course is **yours free.**

If you've already purchased this book or any one of the hardcover versions of the three Sugarman marketing books, you may receive, free of charge (other than the minimal per order postage and handling charge), a slipcase (a $10 value) designed to hold all three books in the series. Buy all three of the Sugarman marketing books and keep them in this handsome display case. Refer to them often. And start to build your library of Sugarman marketing books. Offer available only in the United States.

The Sugarman Seminar Secrets Boxed Set

Joseph Sugarman's three books based on his exclusive advertising
and marketing course in a special paperback edition, complete with
slipcase and at a special price.

Buy all three of the Sugarman marketing books in paperback and receive, free of charge, a handsome slipcase (a $10 value) as well as a $20 savings off the cost of the hardcover version. Available in paperback only as a complete set. $99.95.

Order Form (See page 393 for details.)

❏ I wish to order the following books:

Advertising Secrets of the Written Word	$39.95	_____
Marketing Secrets of a Mail Order Maverick	39.95	_____
Television Secrets for Marketing Success........	39.95	_____
The Sugarman Seminar Course Slipcase.........	FREE	_____
The Sugarman Seminar Course Boxed Set	99.95	_____

Postage & Handling **Per Order** 5.00

                                                Total: _____

❏ Please put me on the Sugarman mailing list for announcements of books, seminars and marketing courses.

Name_____

Address _____

City, State, Zip _____

Daytime Phone:_____

❏ I wish to charge my credit card:
_____ Exp_____
Visa, MasterCard and American Express Cards accepted.

❏ I am enclosing $ _____

Make checks payable to **JS&A Group, Inc.**, and mail your order to JS&A Group, Inc., 3350 Palms Center Drive, Las Vegas, NV 89103.
Offer available only in the United States. Call for prices in foreign countries.

Phone in your order: (800) 323-6400
Fax in your order: (702) 597-2002

Photocopy or cut out this page to mail or fax in your order.

Advertising Secrets of the Written Word
The Ultimate Resource on How to Write Powerful Advertising Copy
From One of America's Top Copywriters and Mail Order Entrepreneurs

A comprehensive textbook that teaches you step-by-step how to write powerful advertising copy that sells. The illustrated book provides insights on what it takes to be a great copywriter and how to develop those skills. The book also takes you into the thought process of ad creation and provides a disciplined procedure that anybody can follow. A major chapter reveals the "psychological triggers" and how they can be used effectively to "cause prospects to exchange their hard-earned money for your product or service." ISBN 1-891686-00-3 (hardcover). 310 pages. $39.95

Television Secrets for Marketing Success
How to Sell Your Product on Infomercials, Home Shopping Channels and Spot
TV Commercials From the Entrepreneur Who Gave You BluBlocker® Sunglasses

The story of Joseph Sugarman's successful experiences with infomercials and the QVC home shopping channel. The book has useful tips on applying the principles of print direct marketing to make TV marketing work more effectively. He talks candidly about his failures as well as his successes, how he launched one of QVC's most successful promotions, how he created and built BluBlocker® sunglasses into a nationally recognized brand name, and how he used TV marketing to influence over 10 million viewers to buy his products. ISBN 1-891686-09-7 (hardcover). 310 pages. $39.95

The Sugarman Seminar Secrets Slipcase
A handsome slipcase designed to hold Joseph Sugarman's three books
based on his exclusive marketing course is **yours free.**

If you've already purchased this book or any one of the hardcover versions of the three Sugarman marketing books, you may receive, free of charge (other than the minimal per order postage and handling charge), a slipcase (a $10 value) designed to hold all three books in the series. Buy all three of the Sugarman marketing books and keep them in this handsome display case. Refer to them often. And start to build your library of Sugarman marketing books. Offer available only in the United States.

The Sugarman Seminar Secrets Boxed Set
Joseph Sugarman's three books based on his exclusive advertising
and marketing course in a special paperback edition, complete with
slipcase and at a special price.

Buy all three of the Sugarman marketing books in paperback and receive, free of charge, a handsome slipcase (a $10 value) as well as a $20 savings off the cost of the hardcover version. Available in paperback only as a complete set. $99.95

Order Form (See page 395 for details.)

❏ I wish to order the following books:

Advertising Secrets of the Written Word . . . . $39.95 _____
Marketing Secrets of a Mail Order Maverick . . . . . 39.95 _____
Television Secrets for Marketing Success. . . . . 39.95 _____
The Sugarman Seminar Course Slipcase. . . . . FREE _____
The Sugarman Seminar Course Boxed Set . . . . 99.95 _____

Postage & Handling **Per Order** 5.00

Total: _____

❏ Please put me on the Sugarman mailing list for announcements of books, seminars and marketing courses.

Name _____

Address _____

City, State, Zip _____

Daytime Phone: _____

❏ I wish to charge my credit card:
_____ Exp _____
Visa, MasterCard and American Express Cards accepted.

❏ I am enclosing $ _____

Make checks payable to **JS&A Group, Inc.**, and mail your order to
JS&A Group, Inc., 3350 Palms Center Drive, Las Vegas, NV 89103.
Offer available only in the United States. Call for prices in foreign countries.

Phone in your order: (800) 323-6400
Fax in your order: (702) 597-2002

Photocopy or cut out this page to mail or fax in your order.